Comrade Whitman

....
From Russian
to Internationalist Icon
....

Comrade Whitman

From Russian to Internationalist Icon

Delphine Rumeau

BOSTON
2024

Library of Congress Cataloging-in-Publication Data

Names: Rumeau, Delphine, author.
Title: Comrade Whitman : from Russian to internationalist icon / Delphine Rumeau.
Description: Boston : Academic Studies Press, 2024. | Includes bibliographical references and index.
Identifiers: LCCN 2023056267 (print) | LCCN 2023056268 (ebook) | ISBN 9798887194608 (hardback) | ISBN 9798887194615 (paperback) | ISBN 9798887194622 (adobe pdf) | ISBN 9798887194639 (epub)
Subjects: LCSH: Whitman, Walt, 1819–1892–Criticism and interpretation–History–20th century | Whitman, Walt, 1819–1892–Appreciation–Soviet Union. | Whitman, Walt, 1819–1892–Appreciation–Russia.
Classification: LCC PS3237.4.R8 R86 2024 (print) | LCC PS3237.4.R8 (ebook) | DDC 811.3–dc23/eng/20240129
LC record available at https://lccn.loc.gov/2023056267
LC ebook record available at https://lccn.loc.gov/2023056268

Copyright © Academic Studies Press, 2024
ISBN 9798887194608 (hardback)
ISBN 9798887194615 (paperback)
ISBN 9798887194622 (adobe pdf)
ISBN 9798887194639 (epub)

Book design by Lapiz Digital Services
Cover design by Ivan Grave.
On the cover: Cover of Uot Uitman, *Pionery*, trans. M. S. (Petrograd: Segodnia, 1918), by Vera Ermolaeva. *The National Library of France*.

Published by Academic Studies Press
1577 Beacon Street
Brookline, MA 02446, USA
press@academicstudiespress.com
www.academicstudiespress.com

The publication of this book is supported by:

Contents

List of illustrations	ix
Permissions	xii
Note on transliterations, names and translations	xiii
Acknowledgements	xiv
Foreword	xvii

Introduction — 1

Chapter 1. Whitman as a *primitive* (1880s–1910s) — 25
1. A neo-wanderer — 27
2. "Striking up for a New World" — 30
    - The Adamic Whitman — 30
    - The Greek Whitman — 32
3. The barbarian — 35
    - The Germanic Whitman — 35
    - Against "Latin" sclerosis — 36
4. Westward: another direction for the quest of the *primitive* in Russia — 39
5. Appropriation and separation — 43
    - Transatlantic barbarians: Whitman and Verhaeren — 43
    - Volte-faces — 45

Chapter 2. The Futurist poet (1910s–1920s) — 51
1. The poetry of modern chaos — 52
    - Poet of the metropolis — 52
    - A rebel against hierarchy — 55
2. A precursor of Futurism — 58
    - A "propeller" of Western avant-gardes — 58
    - Korney Chukovsky's "first real Futurist" — 61
3. Whitman and (post-) Russian Futurist poetry — 63
    - Velimir Khlebnikov: from circumspection to kinship — 64
    - Vladimir Mayakovsky: from anxiety of influence to anxiety of impotence — 65
    - Post-imperial Whitman (the Baltic states and Ukraine) — 71

Chapter 3. Whitman the prophet (1880s–1930s) — 80
1. **The prophet of the body** — 81
   - "I believe in the flesh and the appetites": the anti-Victorian Whitman — 81
   - The passion of the body (Konstantin Balmont) — 83
   - Yiddish poets and the female body — 85
2. **The poet as "kosmos"** — 87
   - The prophet's heart as a cosmos (Morris Rosenfeld) — 88
   - Cosmic consciousness (Richard Maurice Bucke) — 89
   - A "chronic mystical perception" (William James) — 90
   - From the Milky Way to Russian iconostasis (Balmont and Grigoriev) — 91
3. **The seer and the guide** — 96
   - New American and British churches — 97
   - The Russian *prorok* — 100
   - The prophet of the Promised Land — 104

Chapter 4. From democrat to socialist (1880s–1919) — 112
Foreword: the impact of the British editions — 113
1. **"The institution of the dear love of comrades"** — 115
   - Whitman and British ethical socialism — 115
   - The transatlantic socialist fellowship — 116
   - Continental European Whitmanites — 119
2. **The Russian democrat** — 123
   - Selected poems, from Whitman and not from Whitman — 124
   - The poetry of "struggle" versus the poetry of "future democracy" — 128
3. **War and peace** — 133
   - "An example of war poetry" — 133
   - Whitman the wound-dresser — 135
   - Love and reconciliation — 136

Chapter 5. The extraordinary adventures of Walt Whitman in the land of the Bolsheviks (1918–1936) — 141
1. **A wide circulation** — 142
   - The 1920s: (re)-translating, (re)-publishing Whitman in Russian — 142
   - The anthology of the revolution: highly selected poems — 146
   - *Korenizing* Whitman — 149
   - The 1930s: becoming a classic — 152
2. **Whitmanian agitprop** — 155
   - Celebrating the revolution with Whitman in 1918 — 155
   - The Proletkult shows: "the first experiments of poetic theatre" — 157
   - The Whitman club: "to kiss, to work and to die *Whitman's way*" — 165
   - Whitman and Soviet film: from kino-eye to montage — 167

Chapter 6. Between the wars: a transatlantic fellow traveler (1919–1938) — 171
1. **In Europe: the relative decline of the socialist Whitman** — 172
   - The 1919 celebrations — 172

	Foiled European revolutions	173
	In the press: the Comintern of translators	176
	Turning "Salut au Monde!" into a parody	178
2.	**In the US: Proletarian Whitman**	180
	Turning more partisan	180
	Whitman for the workers	181
	"Towards Proletarian Art": Whitman among leftist intellectuals	183
	In Yiddish: "Salut au Monde!" as a marching hymn	187
	Whitman and the Great Depression	191
3.	**Supplementing Whitman's America**	195
	"The other America"	195
	Black Whitman, Red Whitman	197
Coda: Three American intermedial "Salut au Monde!"		201

Chapter 7. Pioneers and Pionery: political transfers (1886–1944) — 205

1. Preamble: the British marches of the "Pioneers" — 207
2. **Russian and Soviet Pionery** — 209
   - Fake Pioneers — 209
   - Avant-garde *Pionery* — 212
   - From "frontline fighters" to pionery — 214
3. **In the US: "O New Pioneers"** — 217
   - *Pionern: a velt fun marsh un arbet* — 217
   - The pioneers during the Great Depression — 218

Chapter 8. Anti-fascist Whitman (1936–1945) — 223

1. **"Against war and fascism"** — 223
   - "Spain 1873–74," Spain 1936–1939 — 224
   - León Felipe: from "Song of Myself" to "Salut au Monde!" — 225
2. **World War II: The Whitman pact** — 232
   - A "wartime Whitman" in the US — 232
   - Looking for Whitman on the White Sea — 236
   - The honor of poets (the French Resistance) — 239
   - 1945: Singing the spring — 241

Chapter 9. "Salut au Monde!" across the Iron Curtain (1946–1956) — 244

1. "Salut au Monde!": a French comeback — 245
2. *Saludo al mundo*: from Neruda to Mir — 249
   - Pablo Neruda's *Let the Rail Splitter Awake* — 250
   - Rendering unto Whitman what belongs to Whitman — 258
   - Pedro Mir's *Countersong to Walt Whitman* — 260
3. **The centennial of *Leaves of Grass* in 1955** — 266
   - New Soviet translations, critics and responses — 266
   - The World Peace Council and the 1955 celebrations — 267
   - Yevtushenko and Neruda: watermelons and strawberries — 271

Chapter 10. Back from the USSR (1955–1980s)   276
1. **A Soviet classic**   276
2. **Pablo Neruda as Whitmanian go-between**   283
   Nerudean repercussions   283
   A final companion   285
3. **Whitman and the counterculture**   287
   Walter Lowenfels: American and Soviet dialogs   287
   Lawrence Ferlinghetti: Goodbye, comrade?   289
   Allen Ginsberg: Hello again, *camerado*!   290
4. **From transatlantic to transmediterranean: new paths**   293

Coda   299

Appendix   306
Bibliography   317
Index of Walt Whitman's Poems and Works   344
Index of Names   345

List of illustrations

0.1. Korney Chukovsky in Odesa. October 19, 1902. Photograph by V. G. Chekhov. Source: https://prodetlit.ru/.
0.2. Korney Chukovsky in his Kuokalla Study, 1910s. Source: https://www.chukfamily.ru/.
0.3. Valentin Serov, *Portrait of the Poet Konstantin Balmont.* 1905. Pastel on paper mounted on cardboard. The Tretyakov Gallery. Wikipedia Commons.
0.4. Korney Chukovsky's cabinet in his Peredelkino House. Photograph by Delphine Rumeau.
0.5. Walt Whitman, "Salut au Monde," *Shriftn* no. 1 (1912). Author's collection.
2.1. Cover of *Dzintars*, no. 1, 1918. National Library of Latvia.
2.2. Walt Whitman, "Salut au Monde!," *Dzintars*, no. 1 (1918), 35. National Library of Latvia.
2.3. Cover of Johannes Semper, *Walt Whitman*, Talinn: Varrak, 1920. Illustration Ado Vabbe. © Adagp, Paris [2023]. Author's collection.
2.4. Mykhail' Semenko, "Sistema," *Kobzar'* (Kyiv: Golfstrom, 1924), 615.
3.1. *Vispe*, no. 3 (1923), 86. Joe Fishstein Yiddish Poetry Collection, Rare Books and Special Collections, McGill University Library.
3.2. Boris Grigoriev, *Portrait of Walt Whitman*, 1918, oil, 90 x 57 cm, Pskov Museum. Wikipedia Commons.
3.3. G. Frank Pearsall, *Walt Whitman, half-length portrait, seated, facing left, left hand under chin*, ca. 1869. Charles E. Feinberg Collection, Library of Congress.

3.4. "Uot Uitmèn," *Plamia*, no. 21 (September 22, 1918), 4. Russian State Library.
3.5. Karl Bulla, *Repin reading the news of Lev Tolstoy's death*. With K. Chukovsky and N. Nordman-Severova (Repin's wife), in Kuokkala. Next to Chukovsky hangs Repin's *Portrait of Poet Korney Ivanovich Chukovsky*, 1910. Wikipedia Commons.
4.1. Cover of *Mother Earth*, no. 1 (1906). Project Gutenberg.
4.2. Cover of the first issue of *Signal*, November 1905. University of Southern California Digital Library. Russian Satirical Journals Collection.
4.3. Cover of Uot Uitmèn, *Poèziia griadushchei demokratii* (Moscow: Sytin, 1914). Russian State Library.
4.4. Guillaume Apollinaire, Detail from the calligram "2e Canonnier Conducteur," *Der Mistral* (Zürich), no. 1 (March, 3, 1915).
4.5. Jean Lurçat, Ornamental composition. Illustration in Walt Whitman, *Six poèmes*, Paris, A.-G. Gonon, 1919. © Fondation Jean Lurçat, Adagp, Paris [2023]. National Library of France.
4.6. and 4.7. Frans Masereel, Woodcuts. Illustrations in Walt Whitman, *Calamus* (Geneva: Éditions du Sablier, 1919). © Adagp, Paris [2023]. National Library of France.
5.1. Cover of Uot Uitmèn, *List'ia Travy* (Petrograd: Vsemirnaia Literatura, 1922). New York Public Library.
5.2. Cover of Kornei Chukovskii, *Uot Uitmèn. Poèziia griadushchei demokratii* (Moscow, Petrograd: Gosudarstvennoe Izdatel'stvo, 1923). Illustration Evgeny Belukha. Author's collection.
5.3. Cover of *Plamia*, no. 35 (January 5, 1919). Illustration by Sigismunds Vidbergs. Russian State Library.
5.4. Cover of *Walt Whitman*, trans. Gurgen Haykuni (Moscow: Hammer and Sickle, 1923). National Library of Armenia.
5.5. Cover of Ivan Kulyk, ed., *Antolohiia amerykans'koï poeziï, 1855–1925* (Kharkiv: Derzhavne vydavnytstvo Ukraïny, 1928). Dartmouth Library. Rauner Special Collections.
5.6. Boris Grigoriev, Sketches for the decoration of the English Embankment during the Petrograd 1918 festival. State Russian Museum, Saint Petersburg [SPB 742-746].
5.7. Members of the Petrograd Proletkult performing a collective reading of Walt Whitman's "Europe" at the House of Proletarian Culture, Petrograd. *Plamia*, no. 21 (September 22, 1918), 4. Russian State Library.
5.8. Members of the Petrograd Proletkult performing a collective reading of Walt Whitman's "Years of the Modern." Slava Katamidze Collection.
5.9. Cover of Uot-Uitmèn, *"Evropa": Instsenirovannoe stikhotvorenie s prologom.* (Arkhangelsk: Prosvet. otd. pol.-prosv. upr. Bel. voen. okr., 1920). Russian State Library.
5.10. First colophon of the publishing house Vsemirnaia Literatura, by Yuri Annenkov.

6.1. Cover of Antonina Sokolicz, *Walt Whitman* (Warsaw: Wyd. Zw. Robot. Stowarzyszeń Spółdź, 1921). "We demolish the creation." National Library of Poland.
6.2. First lines of Reuben Ludwig, "Symposium," in *Gezalmete Lider* (New York: Aroysgegeben fun kolegn un fraynt mit der hilf fun Y.L. Perets shrayber-fareyn, 1927), 53.
6.3. Linoleum cut by Vojtěch Preissig, in Walt Whitman, *Salut au Monde!* (New York: Random House, 1930), 9. Berlin State Library.
6.4. Richard Halls, *Federal Dance Theatre presents Salut au Monde adapted from a poem of that name by Walt Whitman*. 1936. New York City: Federal Art Project. Library of Congress.
7.1. Introduction to *The Poems of Walt Whitman*, by Ernst Rhys (London: Walter Scott, 1886), ix.
7.2. Cover of Uot Uitman, *Pionery*, trans. M. S. (Petrograd: Segodnia, 1918). Illustration by Vera Ermolaeva. *Public Domain Review*.
7.3. Inside of Uot Uitman, *Pionery*, trans. M. S. (Petrograd: Segodnia, 1918). Illustration by Vera Ermolaeva. National Library of France.
7.4. Detail from Uot Uitmèn, *Peredovye boitsy*, trans. K. Chukovskii (Petrograd: Gosudarstvennoe Izdatel'stvo, May 1, 1923). Russian State Library.
7.5. Detail from Uot Uitmèn, *List'ia Travy*, trans. K. Chukovskii (Moscow: Ogonëk, 1931), 9. Russian State Library.
8.1. "Spain," by Walt Whitman, illustrated by Rockwell Kent. *New Masses* 21, no. 4 (October 20, 1936), 11. Rights courtesy of Plattsburgh State Art Museum, State University of New York, USA, Rockwell Kent Collection, Bequest of Sally Kent Gorton. All rights reserved.
8.2. Cover of *A Wartime Whitman*. William Aiken, ed. (New York: Armed Services Editions, 1945). Author's collection.
9.1. "Salut au monde par Walt Whitman," *Défense de la Paix*, no. 1 (1951), 6. Bibliothèque Nationale de France.
9.2. Cover of Walt Whitman, *Saludo al mundo*, trans. G. Gasman (Santiago de Chile: Ediciones de Librería Neira, 1949). Illustration Ernesto Barreda. Author's collection.
10.1. Cover of Walt Whitman, *Lyrik und Prosa* (Berlin: Volk und Welt, 1966). Author's collection.
11.1. Alexander Burganov, *Monument to Alexander Pushkin*, 2000, bronze. Washington University Campus. Photograph Julia Mendova.
11.2. Alexander Burganov, *Monument to Walt Whitman*, 2009, bronze. Moscow State University Campus. Photograph Anna Shvets.
11.3. Mural with Boris Grigoriev's *Walt Whitman*, Kiselev Street 11, Pskov. *Pskovskaia Lenta Novostei*, October 29, 2022.

Permissions

Extract from Manuel Maples Arce, *Super-poema bolchevique en 5 cantos*, translated by K. M. Cascia, in *Stridentist Poems* (Storrs: World Poetry Books, 2023). World Poetry Books. Used with permission.

Extracts from Charlotte Douglas, ed. and Paul Schmidt, trans., *The Collected Works of Velimir Khlebnikov: Volume I—Letters and Theoretical Writings* (Cambridge, MA.: Harvard University Press). Dia Art Foundation. Used with permission. All rights reserved.

Extract from Leivick, "Tsu Amerike," trans. Richard J. Fein, in *With Everything We've Got. A Personal Anthology of Yiddish Poetry* (Austin: Host Publications, 2009). Host Publications. Used with permission.

Extracts from Pablo Neruda, *Let the Rail Splitter Awake*, trans. Waldeen (International Publishers). English translation © International Publishers. Used with permission.

Extracts from Pedro Mir, *Contracanto a Walt Whitman*, in *Poemas* (Madrid: Ediciones La Discreta, 2009). © Ediciones de La Discreta, S. L. Used with permission.

Extracts from Adonis, "A Grave for New York," in *A Time Between Ashes and Roses: Poems*, trans. Shawkat M. Toorawa (Syracuse: Syracuse University Press, 2004). English translation © Syracuse University Press. Used with permission.

Note on transliterations, names and translations

Russian and Ukrainian words have been translated according to the Library of Congress (ALA-LC) system. Yiddish words have been translated according to the YIVO tables. In the main text, however, I have not used transliteration for names, given in their form most usual to the reader.

If no reference is indicated, it means that the translation is mine.

Acknowledgements

It is a great pleasure to thank the people who were involved in this research. I was helped and supported in so many ways that the completion of this book sometimes felt like collective work.

I have considerably benefited from discussions and collaborations with my much-missed colleagues at the University of Toulouse. Claire Gheerardyn has been involved with this book from the start and very helpfully read parts of it. Collaborating with her on various projects has been tremendously stimulating and uplifting. Among other things, she has taught me to look at monuments and to take images seriously. Christophe Imbert never failed to share references to Whitman and, time and time again, read the French prequels of this book. Modesta Suárez provided many opportunities for discussion of my work at her poetry seminar and Hélène Beauchamp showed me the way to Whitmanian agitprop.

I am much indebted to the community of Whitman scholars and learned a lot from the "Whitman weeks" and Whitman conferences that I attended in Dortmund, Tours, Exeter and Créteil: many thanks to Walter Grünzweig, Peter Riley and Éric Athenot for organizing these Whitman feasts. I also benefited from exchanges with Ed Folsom, Kirsten Harris, Dara Barnat, Vincent Dussol, Jacques Darras and Betsy Erkillä (who welcomed me at her Northwestern seminar almost fifteen years ago). I express particular gratitude to Walter Grünzweig for his extensive review of my book *Fortunes de Walt Whitman*, which sparked the impulse to prolong this research, and for his supportive follow-up. I am very grateful to Tatiana Venediktova for her invitation to the Moscow Whitman conference in 2019: Yuri Orlitsky's and Olga Panova's contributions were significant sources of knowledge and inspiration for this project. Many thanks to Anna Shvets for her warm presence at the conference and for her many photographs of Whitman's monument on MSU campus. I also thank Tatiana and Olga for bringing attention to *Fortunes de Walt Whitman* in the journal *Literatura Dvukh Amerik*.

Various other discussions with colleagues and friends have supplied precious research leads. I am indebted to Ko Iwatsu for alerting me to Benjamin Fondane. Galyna Dranenko came to Grenoble with the wonderful gift of the "Whitman Bezmezhniki" and indicated many Ukrainian sources. I am grateful to Daria Sinichkina for sharing her unpublished talk "Celebrating the 'revolutionary ego' in Russian poetry after 1917 as a tribute to Walt Whitman's visionary cosmism" and for so many fruitful conversations about Russian poetry. Svetlana Dreyer was a wonderful companion in Moscow: we visited Chukovsky's house in Peredelkino and took a memorable metro ride at night to the aptly named Mezhdunarodnaia Station in search of a Whitmanian treasure.

Even though digitalization has radically changed research practices, a lot of the material covered in this book was not within easy reach. Access was facilitated by the dedicated librarians of the University of Grenoble, in particular Isabelle Laty and Valérie Chambon, and by the staff at McGill University Library and at the Vernadsky National Library of Ukraine in Kyiv. I am grateful to Anastasia Gladoshchuk for getting so much material from the Russian State Library after it was no longer possible to go there. She graciously pretended that I was bestowing upon her an opportunity to become acquainted with rare books and papers—even when it necessitated a trip to Khimki. The meticulously collected and organized files that she sent whenever I needed something were miraculous.

This research sometimes pointed to domains where I had limited access, for lack of linguistic skills. Many thanks to Inna Volkovynska for going through Ukrainian material with me and to Stéphane Cermakian for his enthusiasm in translating what was inside an intriguing chapbook kept at the Armenian National Library. Laurent Dedryvère devotedly read many pages and checked all the German and Hungarian quotes. Karolina Szymaniak's excellent Yiddish classes enabled me to continue this work, but the complex poetic texts that I came across sometimes remained beyond my reach. I am grateful to Raphael Koenig for sharing some of his expertise, and I don't have enough words to thank Arnaud Bikard, who edited all the pages on the Yiddish Whitman with immense care and diligence.

The process of getting permissions for quotes and images was convoluted, but also sometimes surprisingly rewarding. Many thanks to Julia Sycheva and Daria Avdeeva for their incredible work on the Chukovsky website and for letting me quote their material and use their images. I am grateful to Classiques Garnier for allowing me to translate and adapt parts of *Fortunes de Walt Whitman*, and to Dany Savelli, the editor of *Slavica Occitania*, for her permission to translate my article "Agitprop whitmanienne à Petrograd." I received a generous grant from the research center LLA-Creatis at the University of Toulouse, as well as from my current research center Litt&Arts at the University of Grenoble. I must warmly thank Alessandra Anzani at Academic Studies Press for her immediately enthusiastic response to the project and Stuart Allen for his virtuoso editing work.

I am lucky to be surrounded by the most supportive family and friends. My parents have always done everything in their power (and more) to help me. My son Paul, quick to comment on Whitman's oddities, offered enthusiastic encouragement. Laurent Folliot has read every word of this manuscript with the unconditional generosity that characterizes him as a friend. His feedback was invaluable. Finally, I cannot thank my husband Francis Guévremont enough. He has followed each minute detail of this work, has taken interest in each tiny discovery and has read each chapter with unwavering focus. I owe him more than he knows.

Foreword

This book is the result of many years of research into Walt Whitman's reception. It started with a study on Whitman's epic legacy in the Americas, which investigated Pablo Neruda's "debt" towards his precursor.[1] It expanded in another book, *Fortunes de Walt Whitman*, published ten years later.[2] My aim was to shed a transnational light on the ideas and forms of modernity that Whitman incarnated in Europe and the Americas. I showed that the most innovative interpretations were elaborated in transatlantic and hemispheric dialogues: Whitman was read as a gay poet in turn-of-the-century Britain well before Allen Ginsberg made him an iconic figure; Latin American poets debated whether his America was truly inclusive and representative years before African American writers did so. Even the idea of Whitman as a "national poet" resulted from multiple transatlantic interactions.

In following the circuitous paths of Whitman's transatlantic reception, I came to locate a fascinating crossroads in Soviet Russia, where political interpretations of his poetry shifted. However, the scope and length of *Fortunes de*

---

1 Delphine Rumeau, *Chants du Nouveau Monde. Épopée et modernité (Whitman, Neruda, Glissant)* (Paris: Classiques Garnier, 2009).
2 Delphine Rumeau, *Fortunes de Walt Whitman. Enjeux d'une réception transatlantique* (Paris: Classiques Garnier, 2019), 717.

Walt Whitman (over seven hundred pages) did not allow at that point for a more detailed analysis of these particular aspects. The following book therefore focuses on them and reverses the perspective of *Fortunes de Walt Whitman*: instead of forming extensions of the transatlantic field, Russia and the Soviet Union are the core of this investigation. As I kept discovering new material, I expanded the pages on the Russian and Soviet political reception in the first half of the twentieth century and split them into several chapters (4, 5, 7). The Soviet reception after World War II was added, thus filling what had remained a lacuna (Chapters 8 and 9). In the course of this research, I realized how crucial it was to take into account the multicultural and multilinguistic realities of the Russian Empire and of the Soviet Union—the limits of my linguistic skills did not enable me to cover as much as needed for a comprehensive study, especially in Central Asia, but I hope to have opened new paths just as much as I have explored uncharted territories. The Yiddish reception also came to the fore, especially since it was sometimes a bridge between Russian and US socialist readings of Whitman.

While refocusing on the Russian and Soviet reception, I have kept, however, a transnational framework, which was all the more necessary as the idea of world literature loomed large in the first decade of the twentieth century and was then central to the definition of the Soviet canon. Internationalism remained an ideological tenet in the USSR, regardless of the nuances and limits of its implementation, and had a vast impact on transnational literary networks. I therefore condensed a long chapter of the French book on "the primitive Whitman" to provide contextual material for an in-depth study of the primitivist and Futurist Russian Whitman (Chapters 1 and 2). I also kept developments on the socialist and communist Latin American Whitman after World War II, but reshaped them and connected them to the Soviet story of Whitman's reception.

Another difference with my previous research is methodological. While my approach was then mostly textual, the stress on the political side of Whitman's reception demanded a more historical perspective, a shift from a comparatist approach to the methods of cultural transfers, with their emphasis on evident historical contacts and various instances of mediation (in the case of literature, translators especially). I have also embraced a new intermedial approach, since Whitman's political reception did not only materialize in critical discourses and literary texts, but in adaptations for the stage and in multiple images for various visual arts. Illustrations played an important role as well and the place that they hold in this book bears witness to this.

Part of the research that was done after the publication of *Fortunes de Walt Whitman* was used in conferences and articles, in particular in the French journal

Slavica Occitania, with a contribution on the *primitive* and Futurist Russian Whitman and another one on agitprop adaptations.³ They have not simply been translated into English for the present book, but reworked and adjusted to its perspective.

---

3 Delphine Rumeau, "Primitif américain et primitivisme russe. Deux cas de réception (Longfellow, Whitman)," *Slavica Occitania*, no. 53 (2021): 249–275; "Agit-prop whitmanienne à Petrograd," *Slavica Occitania*, no. 57 (2023): 83–112.

Introduction

The American poet Walt Whitman was the author of a single collection of poems, *Leaves of Grass*, first published in 1855, then constantly revised and expanded over the course of almost forty years. While the first edition contained twelve poems, which followed one another without titles, the last one, known as the "deathbed" edition, comprised more than four hundred poems, divided into clusters. The development and transformation of the text was in phase with the expansion and construction of the nation, whose territorial completion, at the end of the nineteenth century, practically coincided with the last edition in 1891. While the book had limited success during Whitman's lifetime, it had an immense posterity, including internationally: Whitman became a major reference point, first in Europe at the turn of the century, and then on an increasingly global scale.

Many of the "poets to come," whom Whitman invoked at the threshold of his book, answered his call, and their responses formed a conversation, a platform to discuss the meaning of poetry. Whitman kept addressing his future readers, both as individuals and as communities. In that regard, his gesture was profoundly modern: as Walter Benjamin argues, modern writers and artists claim to rely on "posterity" to recognize their value whereas "all previous ages were unanimous in their conviction that their own contemporaries held the keys that would open the doors to future fame."[1] Whitman wished for an audience both in the long term and on a vast scale. The famous 1855 preface to *Leaves of Grass* essentially defined a "national" bard, but an international readership would contribute to the poet's legitimization.

In her book *Atlantic Citizens*,[2] Leslie Eckel has shown how sensitive Whitman was to British reviews of his poetry and how he used them to enhance the credibility of his posture as national bard. As Lawrence Buell has proposed, such attention characterized most American Renaissance writers and reflected a postcolonial anxiety.[3] However, Whitman hailed countries other than the former colonizer, and, more broadly, the "world." In the inaugural poem, which would finally be entitled "Song of Myself," Whitman sounded "his barbaric yawp over the roofs of the world," a line that Matt Cohen calls "the most catchy" of many attempts Whitman made to "broadcast" widely.[4] One poem in particular epitomizes the global scope of Whitman's address, "Salut au Monde!"—one of the most quoted and translated pieces outside the US. First called "Poem of Salutation" in 1856, it took on its present French title in 1860.[5] As he revised the poem throughout the various editions of *Leaves of Grass*, Whitman edited out the most conspicuously American references, thus making it all the more accessible to his international audience. In 1865, the poem "Years of the Unperform'd" asked: "Are all nations communing? is there going to be but one heart to the globe?"[6] This poem too became a favorite of Whitman's internationalist reception. In 1871, the inscription "to foreign lands" declared:

---

[1] Walter Benjamin, "The Path to Success in Thirteen Theses," in *Selected Writings*, vol. 2, trans. Rodney Livingstone (Cambridge, MA: Harvard University Press, 1999), 145. The essay was originally published in *Frankfurter Zeit*, September 22, 1928.

[2] Leslie Eckel, *Atlantic Citizens: Nineteenth-Century Writers at Work in the World* (Edinburgh: Edinburgh University Press, 2013).

[3] Lawrence Buell, "American Literary Emergence as a Postcolonial Phenomenon," *American Literary History* 4, no. 3 (Fall 1992): 411–442.

[4] Matt Cohen, *Whitman's Drift: Imagining Literary Distribution* (Iowa City: University of Iowa Press, 2017), 187.

[5] According to Walter Grünzweig, "Salut au Monde!" reflects the internationalist discussions of European revolutionaries (especially Giuseppe Mazzini's views), see "'For America—For All the Earth.' Walt Whitman as an International(ist) Poet," in *Breaking Bounds*, ed. Betsy Erkkilä and Jay Grossman (Oxford: Oxford University Press, 1996), 241. Thoren Opitz reads it less as a sign of internationalist awareness than "a megalomaniac outreach" after the lack of national success of the 1855 edition. See "World Wide Walt: Making and Marketing Whitman's Global Persona," in *The New Walt Whitman Studies*, ed. Matt Cohen (Cambridge: Cambridge University Press, 2019), 69. Opitz argues that it was not so much the case afterwards, since Whitman "uncoupled the value of his self from recognition by the mass-market" (81). However, calls to a global audience persisted.

[6] The poem, later entitled "Years of the Modern," borrowed many sentences from an early prose text, "The Eighteenth Presidency" (1856 too) about the future elimination of frontiers and boundaries, as well as the new interlinking of the inhabitants of the Earth.

> I heard that you ask'd for something to prove this puzzle the New
>   World,
> And to define America, her athletic Democracy,
> Therefore I send you my poems that you behold in them what
>   you wanted.⁷

It was therefore not only a postcolonial gesture, but, as Pascale Casanova writes, the response of a "provincial":⁸ from the margins of the dominant literary space, Whitman sought to reach the center, and even to relocate it. His strategy was to wipe the slate clean by declaring the birth of modernity in 1855, in America. From then on, the "Greenwich meridian" of modernity would pass through Brooklyn, NY.

In many ways, this strategy proved successful. What Grünzweig describes as "an international Whitman movement"⁹ came into existence early. The first (albeit anecdotal and unsuccessful) Whitman society was founded by Sadakichi Hartmann in 1887 and was comprised of Europeans.¹⁰ Horace Traubel (the son of a Jewish German immigrant) then founded the "Walt Whitman Fellowship International," open to European Whitmanians. The latter considered themselves to be a cosmopolitan circle:¹¹ Léon Bazalgette, the great intercessor of Whitman in France, dreamed of the United States of Europe on the model of Whitman's America, and maintained close links with his English and German counterparts, Johannes Schlaf especially. Valery Larbaud, the other major French Whitmanian of the beginning of the century, envisioned a "society of literati," "one and indivisible in spite of borders."¹² Whitman's success went beyond the circles of his admirers. Ezra Pound, one of his great respondents, was impressed when Richard Henri Riethmuller, his German professor at the University of

---

7 Walt Whitman, *Leaves of Grass and Other Writings*, ed. Michael Moon (New York: Norton, 2002, based on the "deathbed" edition), 5. I will refer to this edition as LG.
8 Pascale Casanova has argued that the "provincial" as a recurring theme is a symptom of "unequal representation" in the literary world (*La République des lettres* [Paris: Points/Seuil, 2008], 145).
9 Grünzweig, "'For America—For All the Earth,'" 243.
10 Sadakichi Hartmann was American, born in Japan of a Japanese father and a German mother. He wrote in German about Whitman. He named Canadian Richard Maurice Bucke as president of the society and Thérèse Bentzon from Paris, Rudolf Schmidt from Copenhagen and Enrico Nencioni from Florence as honorary members. See Sadakichi Hartmann, *Conversations with Walt Whitman* (New York: E. P. Coby & Co., 1895), 35–37.
11 See Walter Grünzweig, "'Salut au Monde!': Walt Whitmans weltliterarische Programmatik und sein globales Netzwerk," in *Vergleichende Weltliteraturen / Comparative World Literatures*, ed. Dieter Lamping and Galin Tihanov (Berlin: Metzler, 2019), 163–182.
12 Valery Larbaud, *Ce vice impuni, la lecture: Domaine anglais* (Paris: Gallimard, 1936), 11.

Pennsylvania,[13] told him that Whitman was better known in Denmark, even by the "peasants," than in Camden, New Jersey, where Whitman lived his last twenty years and was buried. (The anecdote was reported much later in the *Cantos*.) The Danish peasants' appreciation of Whitman remains to be proven, and, as Matt Cohen points out, the now common assumption that "until well into the twentieth century . . . Whitman was more highly regarded and more widely read in several European countries than he was in the US" is difficult "to demonstrate empirically in the absence of definitive broad-scales histories of literary distribution and reception for most countries."[14] I still contend that many innovative interpretations of Whitman were elaborated outside the US, or in dialogue with it: Whitman was read abroad as "the American poet" before he belonged to the national canon, and his poetry was converted into radical politics through this transatlantic back-and-forth.

Whitman's reception abroad has of course already been the object of many studies, and I am much indebted to several of them. In his seminal work on Whitman in 1946, Gay Wilson Allen has a long chapter on "Whitman and World Literature,"[15] which he revised and augmented throughout new editions, and which was the matrix for a major collective work *Walt Whitman and the World*, published in 1995[16] and still a reference book. However, like most other contributions,[17] it compartmentalizes Whitman's national receptions and does

---

13 Richard Henri Riethmuller, *Walt Whitman and the Germans* (Philadelphia: Philadelphia Americana Germanica Press, 1906).
14 Cohen, *Whitman's Drift. Imagining Literary Distribution*, 135.
15 Gay Wilson Allen, *Walt Whitman Handbook* (Chicago: Packard & Co., 1946). Allen later wrote that the discovery in 1936 of a book on Whitman in Danish by Frederik Schyberg, prompted him to learn Danish and was what led him to become a Whitman scholar. Schyberg "had done two things that surpassed any book written in English": he took into account the successive editions of *Leaves of Grass* and discussed Whitman's place in world literature. See Gay Wilson Allen, "A Backward Glance. History of My Whitman Studies," *Walt Whitman Quarterly Review* 9, no. 2 (1991): 93.
16 Gay Wilson Allen and Ed Folsom, eds., *Walt Whitman and the World* (Iowa City: University of Iowa Press, 1995).
17 Some of them were early, like the book by Riethmuller mentioned above and Harold Blodgett, *Walt Whitman in England* (Ithaca: Cornell University Press, 1934). They were followed by Fernando Alegría *Walt Whitman en Hispanoamérica* (Mexico: Studium, 1954) and Betsy Erkkilä, *Walt Whitman among the French* (Princeton: Princeton University Press, 1980). To mention only a few of the most recent works: Walter Grünzweig, *Constructing the German Walt Whitman* (Iowa City: University of Iowa Press, 1994); M. Wynn Thomas, *Transatlantic Connections, Whitman U. S., Whitman U. K.* (Iowa City: University of Iowa Press, 2005); Marta Skwara, *Polski Whitman: O funkcjonowaniu poety obcego w kulturze narodowej* (Krakow: Towarzystwo Autorów i Wydawców Prac Naukowych Universitas, 2010); Benham M. Fomeshi, *The Persian Whitman: Beyond a Literary Reception* (Leiden: Leiden University Press, 2019); Caterina Bernardini, *Transnational Modernity and the Italian Reinvention of Walt*

not focus on intercultural dynamics, on the multiple networks of people and exchanges of ideas that shaped them. A number of studies on national receptions hint at the need for a connected and global approach, in particular Walter Grünzweig's *Constructing the German Whitman*, which emphasizes the idea of interculturality and understands reception as a *"collaborative* phenomenon,"[18] or Marta Skwara's *Polski Whitman*, which often connects the Polish reception with the Soviet one and casts light on how intricate reception phenomena are. While the title of Skwara's book fails to suggest that the Polish Whitman she portrays is in fact not a strictly national figure, Caterina Bernardini puts this aspect to the fore in her *Transnational Modernity and the Italian Reinvention of Walt Whitman*. In my own previous study on Whitman's reception,[19] I focused on the "transatlantic" field, more precisely between Europe and the Americas. As I have narrowed the scope on the political reception for the present book, I have come to prefer "international," and even "internationalist," to "transnational": the international Whitman that I consider does not result so much from the recent emphasis on the "transnational" in scholarship, as from a political construction shaped by the very history of the concept of "internationalism" and its uses by political organizations and institutions throughout the twentieth century.

The Comrade and the Icon

From the beginning, the reception of Whitman's poetry was determined not merely by aesthetics, but also by strongly political issues and implications. Quite early on, Whitman was appropriated for political purposes and became a "prophet" of the Left. His watchword, "Democracy," underwent numerous inflections, especially socialist and, later, communist. Whitman regularly addresses his reader as a *camerado*, a word coined after the French *camarade* or the Spanish *camarada*. *Camerado* resembles the older version of the French *camerade*, in which the etymology of the word is even more apparent: it comes from the Latin *camera* (chamber) and designates those who sleep in a same room. This was

---

Whitman. 1870–1945 (Iowa City: University of Iowa Press, 2022). There are also several contributions on the Chinese reception in Ed Folsom, ed., *Whitman East and West. New Contexts for Reading Walt Whitman* (Iowa City: University of Iowa Press, 2002). For a critical overview, see Ed Folsom's chapter "Impact on the World," in Cohen, *The New Walt Whitman Studies*, 232–247.

18 Grünzweig, *Constructing the German Walt Whitman*, 2.

19 Delphine Rumeau, *Fortunes de Walt Whitman. Enjeux d'une réception transatlantique* (Paris: Classiques Garnier, 2019).

particularly apt for Whitman's ideal readers, with whom he wanted to share not only ideas and words, but a certain intimacy: the poem "Starting from Paumanok" ends with the apostrophe "O Camerado close." Although Whitman's refusal to acknowledge the homoerotic implications of his poetry disappointed some of his admirers, he became a major reference in discussions about homosexuality, as well as a gay icon later on. The homoerotic connotation would combine with the political meaning of the word "comrade" that started to emerge at the end of the nineteenth century. This was certainly the case in the writings of Edward Carpenter, one of Whitman's great British intercessors. But throughout the twentieth century, the politically radical Whitman was seldom aligned with socially and culturally liberal values, at least not until the 1960s. Indeed, the camerado became more and more a partisan comrade after the Russian Revolution and the institutionalization of communism. "Camerado" also anticipated *kamarado*, the translation of "comrade" in Esperanto, the new language of internationalism developed at the turn of the century.[20] This book will focus on Whitman the comrade, understood as a political poet and a legendary figure.

It is difficult to separate the poet from his poetry, in part because the critical context of the early reception was conducive to such a confusion, with a flurry of studies on Whitman's "life and work," such as those by Henry Bryan Binns or Léon Bazalgette. However, it was not only the poet's life that fascinated his readers but his very person: his figure, his face and his body. Certainly, Whitman largely programmed the phenomenon, or at least encouraged it. In the first edition of 1855, there is no author's name on the cover of the book, but inside, there is a daguerreotype, which shows not just a face, but a body emerging from the white of the page. The testamentary poems, grouped in the "Songs of Parting," section, state that the book itself is a body. "So Long!," the last poem in the final version of *Leaves of Grass*, contains the famous lines: "Camerado, this is no book, / Who touches this touches a man." (LG 424) This confusion was embraced and hyperbolized by many readers. It explains in part why admiration for Whitman often bordered on fetishism—for example, his beard could function as a kind of relic, concentrating the vitality of the man, the power of the bard and the organic growth of his poetry. This should be borne in mind when approaching Whitman's reception: while the material I use is mostly textual (translations, reviews, commentaries, poems), it is important to take into account other media, especially images. Of course, any comprehensive reception study should be intermedial, and Whitman's musical reception

---

20 Oddly, Whitman was translated into Esperanto only very recently (a few poems in magazines in 2008 and 2013 and "Song of Myself" translated by Jamie Pesadilla in 2019).

would also make for a fascinating chapter—I will hardly mention it, however, admittedly for lack of musical expertise, but also because iconography played a more crucial part across the corpus I am concerned with. Whitman used photographs of himself in groundbreaking ways, and these images have in turn been central to his reception: the vast majority of editions, especially in translation, contain reproductions of one or several of his portraits. In the Slavic and Yiddish versions, G. Frank Pearsall's portrait of a pensive Whitman was systematically used, and it contributed to the construct of Whitman "the prophet" as much as it illustrated it. These photographs became objects of ekphrases, inspired artists and provided a matrix for other images. Because images transcend language barriers, they are an essential medium of global communication. The word "icon" has suffered from being overused, especially when discussing anything Russian, but it is relevant, in its both senses, for Whitman. His fame exceeded the literary sphere, and he became a figure whose image and aura fascinated people and conveyed a sense of the sacred, even in antireligious contexts.

Russian, Soviet, Transatlantic, Internationalist

In 1944, Samuel Sillen, an American communist critic, wrote: "In view of Whitman's special interest in the Russian people, it is worth noting that his greatest foreign success was to be in Russia."[21] This remark is clearly biased, but it is revealing of the importance of Whitman's Soviet reception for the American Left, and much more generally, for the internationalist Left. It is also interesting that in a letter to an Irishman planning to translate *Leaves of Grass* into Russian, Whitman links the common fates of the US and of Russia with the dream of an "internationality of poems." It is worth quoting this letter at length, as it has often been mentioned in Russia:

> You Russians and we Americans;—our countries so distant, so unlike at first glance—such a difference in social and political conditions, and our respective methods of moral and practical development the last hundred years;—and yet in certain features, and vastest ones, so resembling each other. The variety

---

21 Samuel Sillen, *Walt Whitman: Poet of Democracy* (1944, repr., New York: International Publishers, 1974), 45. As far as Whitman's interest in Russia was concerned, Sillen had in mind the letter quoted hereafter and the fact that Whitman kept notes of his readings on Russian history.

of stock-elements and tongues to be resolutely fused in a common Identity and Union at all hazards—the idea, perennial through the ages, that they both have their historic and divine mission—the fervent element of manly friendship throughout the whole people, surpassed by no other races—the grand expanse of territorial limits and boundaries—the unformed and nebulous state of many things, not yet permanently settled, but agreed on all hands to be the preparations of an infinitely greater future—the fact that both peoples have their independent and leading positions to hold, keep, and if necessary fight for, against the rest of the world—the deathless aspirations at the inmost centre of each great community, so vehement, so mysterious, so abysmic—are certainly features you Russians and we Americans possess in common.

And as my dearest dream is for an internationality of poems and poets binding the lands of the earth closer than all treaties or diplomacy—As the purpose beneath the rest in my book is such hearty comradeship for individuals to begin with, and for all the Nations of the earth as a result—how happy indeed I shall be to get the hearing and emotional contact of the great Russian peoples![22]

My focus is precisely the Russian and Soviet reception, in relation to this "internationality" of poems and poets, but also of thinkers and artists. My aim is twofold. First, I intend to introduce new material and shed new light on this reception, the study of which has suffered from biased approaches and now stands in need of an update. Second, I would like to illuminate, through these lenses, the ways in which Whitman was constructed as an international poet and thereby earned his place in world literature, a category whose meaning changed tremendously throughout the twentieth century and was largely influenced by the equally changing conceptions of internationalism on the communist and Soviet agendas.

In short, this history consists in two parts, corresponding to the tsarist and Soviet periods. Between the end of the nineteenth century and the revolutions of 1917, Whitman's Russian reception was essentially a large outlet for the

---

22 Walt Whitman, "Letter to John Fitzgerald Lee, December 20, 1881," Walt Whitman Archive, accessed November 21, 2022, https://whitmanarchive.org/biography/correspondence/tei/yal.00254.html#yal.00254_n1. Whitman agreed to the translation, but there was no follow-up.

Western one, which it integrated and transformed. Some reviews appeared as early as 1883; an essay by P. Popov[23] presents his poetry as an image of "American life," and already emphasizes the political Whitman (insisting on the poems about "labor," such as "Song of the Broad-Axe," "A Song for Occupations," and "Pioneers! O Pioneers!"). It was reviewed in the American magazine the *Critic*, a fact that confirms the importance of foreign appreciation in the construct of the "national poet." However, it was not until the beginning of the twentieth century that Whitman's Russian reception gained momentum. Its two leading figures were then Konstantin Balmont and Korney Chukovsky, whose backgrounds were different and whose trajectories diverged after the Bolshevik Revolution. Chukovsky was born in 1882 and grew up in Odesa, the illegitimate child of a Jewish father and Ukrainian mother.[24] His father did not recognize him (his patronym was forged), which had consequences on his education: as an illegitimate child, he was expelled from the gymnasium. Essentially, he was a self-taught man, and he learnt English by himself. He discovered Whitman on the docks of Odesa, at the age of eighteen:

> One day when I was working on the docks a foreign sailor beckoned to me and thrust a thick book into my hands, demanding 25 kopeks for it. He glanced furtively about as he did so, as if the book were a banned one. Sailors on foreign ships often brought forbidden literature into Tsarist Russia.
>
> That evening after work I took my book to the lighthouse at the end of the jetty. It was a book of poetry written by a certain Walt Whitman, whose name I had never heard before.
>
> I opened at random and read:
>
> My ties and ballasts leave me, my elbows rest in sea-gaps,

---

23 P. Popov, "Uolt Guitman," *Zagranichnyi Vestnik*, March 1883, 567–580; reviewed in the *Critic*, June 16, 1883, 278–279. The year before, the magazine had published a lecture by John Swinton (a friend of Marx and a Whitman enthusiast); Whitman kept the *Critic* review and thought that Popov was actually Swinton himself (see N. A. Abieva, "Nachalo znakomstva s Uoltom Uitmenom v Rossii," *Russkaia Literatura* 1986 [no. 4]: 187). Before Popov, Ivan Turgenev translated as a draft "Beat! Beat! Drums!" in 1872. The manuscript was found much later at the National Library of France (see I. Chistova, "Turgenev i Whitman," *Russkaia literatura*, 1966 [no. 2]: 196-199; translation in *Walt Whitman Quarterly Review* 13, no. 1–2 [1995]: 68–72).

24 Chukovsky asked in his journal: "Who am I? Ukrainian, Russian, Jewish?" His biographer Irina Luk'ianova comments that he was Ukrainian on his mother's side (she spoke Ukrainian), Jewish on his father's side (because he was introduced to the Jewish intelligentsia quite young and was friends with Vladimir Jabotinsky), and Russian through language—*Kornei Chukovskii* (Moscow: Molodaia Gvardiia, 2006), 84.

> I skirt sierras, my palms cover continents,
> I am afoot with my vision...
> Under Niagara, the cataract falling like a veil over my countenance...
> Walking the old hills of Judea with the beautiful gentle God by my side,
> Speeding through space, speeding through heaven and the stars...
> I visit the orchards of spheres and look at the product,
> And look at quintillions ripen'd and look at quintillions green...
>
> Never before had I read anything like this. Clearly it had been written by an inspired madman who, in a state of trance of delirium, fancied himself absolutely free of the illusions of time and space. The distant past was to him identical with the present moment and his native Niagara Falls was neighbor to the millions of suns whirling in the void of the universe.
>
> I was shaken by these poems as much as by some epoch-making event. The chaos of my emotions at that time was in perfect harmony with the chaotic composition of the poetry. I seemed to have climbed to dizzying heights from which I looked down upon the ant-hill of human life and activities.[25]

Chukovsky writes that "for a whole year, [he] could not part from that amazing book" and that he carried it with him at all times, to work, to the seashore—he even lifted the spirits of a blind fisherman by reading Whitman to him. It was a life-changing experience: "Very young readers have a precious ability to live from the book they read, and it shapes the structure of their lives. This happened to me. I began to look at the world through the eyes of Walt Whitman and even, as it were, I was transformed into him." Chukovsky then set out to translate Whitman, in 1902 or 1903, but later judged his efforts to embellish his poetry with rhythms and rhymes as "cumbersome."[26] His first translations were not published until after he came back from London, where, on Vladimir

---

25 Kornei Chukovskii, "Uoltu Uitmenu, Blagodarnost' i slava," *Literaturnaia Gazeta*, May 28, 1969, 8; translation in Allen and Folsom, *Walt Whitman and the World*, 333–334. (My translation for the next quotes.)
26 "Now I am ashamed to admit this naive and pernicious act, but it must be taken into account that I was a lonely self-taught person who had no idea about the methods of literary translation." Ibid.

Jabotinsky's recommendation, he had been sent as a correspondent for *Odesa News*. They were first gathered in a chapbook in 1907.

FIGURE 1. Korney Chukovsky in Odesa. October 19, 1902. Photograph by V.G. Chekhov. Source: https://prodetlit.ru/.

FIGURE 2. Korney Chukovsky in his Kuokalla Study, 1910s. Source: https://www.chukfamily.ru/.

Three years earlier, in 1904, Konstantin Balmont, already a famous Symbolist poet, had also started translating Whitman. Born in 1867, Balmont was older than Chukovsky and came from a noble family. He learnt several foreign languages at a young age. He, too, however, was once expelled from the gymnasium, and later from university, but for political reasons. His collection *Burning Buildings* (*Goriashchie zdaniia*) made him very famous in 1900: it experimented with form but also displayed Nietzschean overtones in its exploration of the self. His political activism forced him into exile in 1905. He came back in 1913 only after his Whitman collection was published in 1911 by Skorpion, the Symbolist publishing house founded by Valery Bryusov and Sergey Polyakov. Both Chukovsky and Balmont wrote essays on Whitman in the 1910s and 1920s, which I will comment upon in detail later.

FIGURE 3. Valentin Serov, *Portrait of the Poet Konstantin Balmont*. 1905. Pastel on paper mounted on cardboard. The Tretyakov Gallery. Wikipedia Commons.

By then, Whitman's reception in Western Europe was in full swing. "Whitmania," as the British poet Algernon Swinburne called it, started early in Britain, with Michael Rossetti's 1868 edition, which, as Caterina Bernardini notes,[27] was a benchmark for all the European receptions. Quite often, Whitman's poems continued to bear the titles of that edition (based on the 1867 American one). Whitmania reached Western Europe (especially Italy, France and Germany) at the turn of the century, the belle époque—a period of intense transnational exchanges—through journals and magazines, especially. At that point, the Russian translators and readers did not participate

---

27 Bernardini, *Transnational Modernity*, 22–23.

in the Western European Whitmanian network, but they were fully aware of it. In 1906, Korney Chukovsky published an article entitled, in Latin script, "Whitmaniana," in which he expresses the need for a Russian Whitman. All of his editions of Whitman between 1907 and 1923 contain a section entitled "Russkoe o Uitmane" (Russian discourse on Whitman). Significantly, it includes foreign authors, such as Knut Hamsun or William James, as if they belonged to the Russian reception: both had been translated into Russian (by Polyakov in the case of Hamsun) and were considered by Chukovsky an integral part of the Russian debate. During that period, the Russian reception could be described as large sound box, a resonating chamber for American and European discourses, from which a Russian Whitman emerged. As Michel Espagne argues, cultural transfers often involve a triangulation, with one cultural sphere operating as a relay, a mediation, between two others.[28] For Whitman, the French reception often played that role (for French Canada or Brazil, but also for Iran).[29] Yet in this case, the hub connecting America and Russia was Britain. While Balmont read and spoke several languages, Chukovsky only knew English. All the texts in his bibliography are in English, and the great majority are British. That said, even Balmont mainly refers to British works: as Chukovsky shows (and with some contempt), his writings on Whitman borrow images and metaphors from the art historian John Addington Symonds.[30]

The second phase is the Soviet one. While Whitman's poetry had been censured under the tsar for being "pornographic," it was largely distributed right after the revolution, in 1918 and 1919. It was appropriated for propaganda purposes and often featured in anthologies of revolutionary poetry. Balmont left Russia in 1921, and for a long time, Chukovsky remained the country's sole translator and authority on Whitman. Even though he was at times attacked (especially in the late 1920s), he became a major figure of Soviet literary life. He is especially known for his children's books, but he was also a critic, translator, scholar (his work on Nekrasov was highly regarded) and a publisher, collaborating with the World Literature publishing house, founded by Maxim Gorky. From 1938 to his death in 1966, Chukovsky had a dacha in the writers' colony of Peredelkino (his

---

28 See Michel Espagne, "Comparison and Transfer: A Question of Method," in *Transnational Challenges to National History Writing*, ed. Matthias Middel and Lluis Roura (New York: Palgrave MacMillan, 2013), 36–53.
29 For Canada, see Rumeau, *Fortunes de Walt Whitman*, 274–285; for Brazil, see Maria Clara Bonetti Paro, "Walt Whitman in Brazil," in Allen and Folsom, *Walt Whitman in the World*, 128–146; for Iran (that is, on Nima Yooshij and Whitman), see Fomeshi, *The Persian Whitman*, 92.
30 Chukovsky put side by side quotes by the two in Uot Uitmèn, *Poèziia griadushchei demokratii* (Petrograd: Izdanie petrogradskogo soveta rabochikh i krasnykh deputatov, 1919), 111.

neighbor was his friend Boris Pasternak).[31] The Whitman shelves bear witness to the centrality of the American poet in his life and work. Somehow, the series of volumes represent the remarkable continuity of Chukovsky's career and of Whitman's fame in the USSR.

FIGURE 4. Korney Chukovsky's cabinet in his Peredelkino House. Photograph by Delphine Rumeau.

The 1920s and 1930s were also years of profound redefinitions of world literature as a concept. Katerina Clark proposes that, in line with Marx's condemnation of cosmopolitanism as an aspect of capitalist expansionism, "the international left, and the Soviet and Comintern platforms a fortiori, promoted 'internationalism' as an antidote and successor to cosmopolitanism."[32] It built a new canon, which defined the classics of world literature from the perspective of the revolution. This canon was much less Eurocentric than Goethe's conception of *Weltliteratur*, but it was not exactly global either at that point. As Clark demonstrates, in the 1920s and 1930s, the Soviet idea of world literature was

---

31 Chukovsky wrote that in the 1930s, Pasternak sent him a poem with a dedication that read: "For the gift of Whitman, / I send you my bearish compliments." Chukovskii, "Uoltu Uitmenu, Blagodarnost' i slava."
32 Katerina Clark, *Eurasia without Borders: The Dream of a Leftist Literary Commons, 1919–1943* (Cambridge, MA: Harvard University Press, 2021), 11.

very much oriented towards Asia. But it also foregrounded North American literature and gave it more and more weight, even connecting the US and Asia. While a major point of reference in these decades, Whitman reached a peak of significance in the '20s, before the more nationalist turn of the next decade. The '30s, however, cannot be covered in "a single narrative,"[33] since they combined the national and the international in complex ways. By that time, the Soviet reception was no longer reliant on external discursive elaborations and provided in its turn a critical springboard, which gave a renewed impulse to leftist readings of Whitman. While the Western and Russian socialist Whitmanians had been on parallel tracks until the mid-1920s, the American Left was by then more and more receptive to Soviet interpretations and relayed them. That was particularly true for minorities in the US, Jews and African Americans, for whom Moscow was a beacon of antiracism and anti-imperialism.

After World War II, as new translators and commentators of Whitman emerged in the Soviet Union, the geopolitical situation changed: communism spread to other regions and countries, which contributed to a Whitmanian revival in countries where he had lost momentum in the interwar period, such as Eastern Europe or France. Conceptions of internationalism and world literature changed too, and became more global. As the Third World turned into a major space of anti-imperialist struggles, cultural connections between the Second and the Third World also developed, as shown by Rossen Djagalov.[34] As far as Whitman's reception was concerned, this meant a renewed circulation in China and a boom in Latin America, on which I will especially focus.

Latin America became indeed an essential stage for the militant Whitman. In fact, the poet had been much celebrated there before, essentially as a continental voice. His reception really started in 1887 with an enthusiastic piece by the Cuban writer José Martí,[35] which inspired a sonnet to Rubén Darío, establishing the image of Whitman as prophet for Latin America.[36] Shortly after, Whitman became a major point of reference, as the inventor of American poetry, who embraced for the first time the vast dimensions of the continent and its wilderness. The sense of belonging to the New World waxed strong in late modernismo (Rubén Darío came to write long poems, with enumerations of the riches

---

33 Katerina Clark, *Moscow, the Fourth Rome: Stalinism, Cosmopolitanism, and the Evolution of Soviet Culture, 1931–1941* (Cambridge, MA: Harvard University Press, 2011), 7.
34 Rossen Djagalov, *From Internationalism to Postcolonialism: Literature and Cinema between the Second and Third Worlds* (Montreal: McGill-Queen's University Press, 2020).
35 José Martí, "El poeta Walt Whitman," *La Nación* [Buenos Aires], June 26, 1887.
36 Rubén Darío, "Walt Whitman," *Azul... Cantos de vida y esperanza* (2nd ed. 1888; this poem, 1890).

of America, especially in his *Canto a la Argentina*) and in a movement that was to be aptly named nuevomundismo (literally new worldism). Among the poets who admired Whitman were the Argentine Leopoldo Lugones, the Peruvian José Santos Chocano and the Uruguayan Armando Vasseur, his first substantial translator into Spanish (in 1912). As the Chilean poet Pablo Neruda writes, Whitman was a decisive model for continental poetry: "In truth, it was he, Walt Whitman, the protagonist of a truly geographical personality, who stood up for the first time in history with a continentally American name."[37] However, to claim Whitman's legacy was seldom a mere declaration of affiliation. Latin American Whitmanian poets did not intend to be mere followers: they wanted to emulate him, while taking into account the specificities of their lands and cultures, namely their Native American past, the idea of miscegenation for Brazil and of hispanidad for Spanish-speaking countries, especially after Spain lost Cuba to the United States in 1898. The Spanish-American War changed perspectives, as the US, once a colony, became in its turn a colonizing power. This explains in part the shift from the euphoric idea of a united continent to the more conflictual opposition of two Americas. In this context, Latin American poets, including Rubén Darío, began to use Whitman against his own country: since his democratic ideals were betrayed in the US, he was resurrected to restore them, with help from the South. After World War II, there was a remarkable convergence of these Latin American uses of Whitman and Soviet discourse on the poet. The "hemispheric" Whitman turned into an internationalist one and "Salut au Monde!" the hymn of Latin American leftist poets. Neruda, who became a communist in 1945 and remained a great friend of the USSR until his death, played a central role in this relocation of Comrade Whitman.

A need for new narratives

As Samuel Sillen's remark suggests, the Russian and Soviet Whitman has been the object of a number of studies, in the form of essays and articles, mostly in Russian and English. However, most of these studies not only require updating, but are in need of revision. As is often the case for Soviet reception studies, the powerful ideological filters that colored them in the first place were never removed; on the contrary, they tended to accumulate, to grow thicker as time went by. Even though Chukovsky was never a fanatical propagandist, he was a

---

37 Pablo Neruda, *Obras completas*, 5 vols., ed. Hernán Loyola (Barcelona: Galaxia Gutenberg, 2002), 5:359.

Soviet critic, belonging to a certain time and place.[38] Like all his contemporaries, he largely emphasized the watershed represented by the October Revolution for Whitman's reception: while Whitman had been censored and banned before that date, he became a Soviet favorite after it. This idea was repeated over and over in his prefaces to Whitman's translations. In Sillen's words:

> In view of Whitman's special interest in the Russian people, it is worth noting that his greatest foreign success was to be in Russia. Under the Tsar, he had to be read surreptitiously, of course. In 1905, Korney Chukovsky was tried for printing a translation of "Pioneers! O Pioneers!," and in 1911 his book of translations was ordered destroyed. But following the Socialist Revolution of 1917 Whitman became a best-seller and exerted tremendous influence on Soviet poetry.[39]

There is truth to this summary: Chukovsky's first book-length translation was banned in 1914 (and not 1911), while the new 1918 version was immediately republished in 1919 in a print run of fifty thousand copies. The contrast is indeed striking, and I do not intend to underestimate it—in fact, the revolutionary period is the center and pivot of the present study. But this story also contains exaggerations and mistakes: it was not "Pioneers! O Pioneers!" that Chukovsky printed in 1905 but a poem of his own, with only one line from Whitman; the 1911 book was not by Chukovsky but by Balmont. In other words, this narrative also served Chukovsky's own agenda and erased Balmont's translations from the history of Whitman's Russian reception.

Chukovsky's insistence on Balmont's flaws was obsessive: having begun his attacks in the journal *Vesy* in 1906,[40] his hostility was still ostensible in his later books on the "art of translation." In the prefaces or addenda to his own

---

38 In his work on Pushkin, Abram Reitblat has emphasized how Soviet scholarship was particularly prone to discrepancies between topics and periods that were overstudied and others that were left in the dark (*Kak Pushkin vyshël v genii* [Moscow: NLO, 2001]). It produced tremendous bibliographies, which had the advantage of being ideologically neutral, without exploiting all the data that they mentioned. Indeed, Valentina Libman's bibliography of American Literature in Russia and the USSR has provided a very precious tool for this work (*Amerikanskaia literatura v russkikh perevodakh i kritike. Bibliografiia 1776–1975* [Moscow: Nauka, 1977]).
39 Sillen, *Walt Whitman*, 45.
40 Balmont was defended by his friend and future wife Elena Tsvetkovskaya; the polemics can be found at Chukfamily.ru, accessed February 4, 2023, https://www.chukfamily.ru/kornei/pro-et-contra/polemika-chukovskogo-i-balmonta-o-perevodax-uolta-uitmena.

translations of Whitman, Chukovsky relentlessly points out his predecessor's errors and criticizes his choices of archaic words and unfit rhythms. It was even a matter of principle for him to transliterate differently the name of the poet (as Uot Uitman or Uitmèn): he insisted that the "l" was not pronounced in English. In the 1910s, critics were divided in their judgment. For example, in 1907, Alexander Blok agreed that Chukovsky was closer to the original, but noticed that Balmont's translations were easier to remember and were the work of a poet: he preferred an "elevating deception" (obman vozvyshaiushchii) to "inferior truths" (nizkie istiny).[41]

But Chukovsky's strategy eventually paid off, especially as Balmont was discredited after his exile: his translations were not reprinted after 1927 and were considered poor. In 1920, Mikhail Kuzmin blamed Balmont for "balmontizing" Whitman,[42] and forty years later Efim Etkind still lamented the "balmontisms," which cancelled the surprise that any reader should experience when discovering Whitman.[43] It took someone like Joseph Brodsky to go against the grain and claim his preference for Balmont's version.[44] I will not analyze and compare their translations: the case was reopened in the 1990s, especially by British and American scholars, and the issue has been quite thoroughly examined.[45] What I want to reevaluate is Balmont's more general contribution to Whitman's reception. Indeed, while Chukovsky won the battle for the title of Whitman's ambassador, he repressed a whole section of his reception at the beginning of the twentieth century, but also during the first years of Soviet Russia. A closer examination of Balmont's essays in the 1910s will reveal that his Whitman is actually much more revolutionary than Chukovsky's. And Balmont's translations, probably because they were versified, which made memorizing easier,

---

41 Aleksandr Blok, "O sovremennoi kritike," in *Sobranie sochinenii*, 8 vols. (Moscow: Khudozhestvennaia Literatura, 1962), 5:204.
42 Mikhail Kuzmin, "K. D. Bal'mont," *Zhizn' iskusstva*, no. 399 (March 16, 1920), 1–2.
43 Efim Ètkind, *Poèziia i perevod* (Moscow: Sovetskii Pisatel', 1963), 421.
44 In 1963, when Brodsky met Chukovsky's daughter, Lydia Chukovskaya, for the first time, he got straight to the point and told her that her father's translations revealed a lack of talent (Lidiia Chukovskaia, *Zapiski ob Anne Akhmatovoi*, 3 vols. [Moscow: Soglasie, 1997], 3:71); elsewhere (entry of August 31, 1940 [1:189]), one learns that, for her part, Anna Akhmatova, to whom Chukovsky read his translations of Whitman, found them "velikolepnye" (beautiful).
45 Lauren Leighton still sides with Etkind and sees in Balmont's Whitman a "Whitmont." *Two Worlds, One Art: Literary Translation in Russia and America* (De Kalb: Northern Illinois University Press, 1991). However, different views are expressed in Rachel Polonsky, "Translating Whitman, Mistranslating Bal'mont," *Slavonic and East European Review* 75, no. 3 (1997): 401–21 and Barry Scherr, "Dalliance with Language: Chukovsky and Bal'mont Translate Whitman," in *Stikh, iazyk, poèziia: pamiati Mikhaila Leonovicha Gasparova*, ed. Khenryk Baran et al. (Moscow: RGGU, 2006): 654–665.

continued to be used throughout the first half of the 1920s, the most intense period of Whitman's reception.

Balmont was not the only victim of this expunging process: Chukovsky never mentioned alternative translations and was particularly disdainful of Whitman's adaptations by the Proletkult, who staged his poetry and went on tour during the civil war, contributing to the poet's fame in the most unexpected places. Chukovsky's contempt for their work, combined with the early official disapprobation of the Proletkult, has left this whole side of the reception unexamined, and it is only recently that it has begun to be reevaluated, with an important contribution by the Russian scholar Yuri Orlitsky.[46] Many of Chukovsky's assertions have been relayed and sometimes exaggerated, like the idea that Whitman had a great influence on the Futurists (Khlebnikov and Mayakovsky, for example), and more generally on Soviet poetry.[47] In retrospect, it turns out that there was no strong correlation between Whitman's fame as "the prophet of Democracy" and his "influence" on Russian poetry. In fact, the editorial and critical reception appears quite disproportionate to the creative one. Compared with the rich tradition of talking back to Whitman in different languages, there have been few poetic addresses to Whitman in Russian. The gap between the two aspects of the reception should not be filled by hasty analogies between Whitman and Russian poets, but rather should be taken into account and explained. Was free verse difficult to accommodate in Russian poetry? Did Whitman become an official poet too early, and, as a result, lose some of his appeal for poets?

Of course, Chukovsky is not to blame for all the omissions in the history of the Russian Whitman. The need for revision also simply stems from changes in approaches to reception theory and literary history. One of the striking aspects of existing studies is that they have ignored the multilingual complexities of the Russian Empire and the Soviet Union. As the dominant language of the empire, Russian has obfuscated other languages in the history of Whitman's reception. But if one takes into account this multilingual reality, a number of facts that have been taken for granted need to be reevaluated. For instance, the Latvian

---

46 Iurii Orlitskii, "Poèziia Uolta Uitmena v russkoi revoliutsionnoi perspektive," in *Stikh i proza v kul'ture Serebrianogo veka* (Moscow: Iazyki slavianskikh kul'tur, 2018), 858–876.

47 See Stepan Stepanchev, "Walt Whitman and Russia," in Allen and Folsom, *Walt Whitman and the World*, 300–338, a very well-documented essay, which relays many of Chukovsky's views and agrees with Yassen Zassoursky, "Whitman's Reception and Influence in the Soviet Union," *Mickle Street Review* 9 [part 2] (1988). At times, Elena Evich simply copies and pastes parts of Chukovsky's essay "Maiakovskii i Uitman" ("Uolt Uitmen v russkikh perevodakh. Uitmenovskii 'sled' v russkoi poèzii" (2007), accessed October 5, 2023, https://yarcenter.ru/articles/culture/literature/uolt-uitmen-v-russkikh-perevodakh-uitmenovskiy-sled-v-russkoy-poezii-5869/).

translations were quite pioneering, with a small volume appearing in 1908, and another in 1911. The Ukrainian Whitman, ignored by Soviet criticism, has only recently been drawn forth by Ukrainian scholarship.[48] The same can be said about translations—let alone creative reception—in other Soviet languages. In the late 1980s, Yassen Zassoursky mentioned translations in "twelve languages beside Russian,"[49] without providing any details. My linguistic skills do not permit me to investigate all of these Soviet Whitmans, but I have endeavored to take them into account as much as I can. A little known 1923 Armenian translation will provide a new piece of the puzzle. Most other translations in Eastern Soviet languages were published in the late 1950s and 1960s. While they are often the work of important translators or poets and offer a rich field of investigation, which the present study does not claim to explore thoroughly, I do intend to map out their connection with the Russian reception.

There is yet another Russian-related internationalist Whitman that I want to bring to light: the Yiddish-speaking Whitman. Indeed, Whitman's reception in Yiddish is a very rich chapter. Few poets have been translated and advertised so much in Yiddish, especially in the United States, by immigrants who mostly came from the Pale of Settlement in the Russian Empire. Joseph Bovshover (the author of a 1897 essay on Whitman) was from Lyubavichi, I. J. Schwartz was from Lithuania, many others from Ukraine: Ruben Ludwig from Kyiv, Louis Miller[50] from Lanivtsi. This Yiddish Whitman has been the object of several important essays or chapters,[51] which focus mostly on his meaning within a Jewish framework or from a Jewish American perspective. While I am aware that Yiddish American poets were somehow "quarantined within their alien language" and that their work developed "concurrently with the Yiddish literary Renaissance in Europe,"[52] I still aim at placing their contribution on a

---

48 Les' Herasymchuk, *Amerykans'kyi bard v Ukraini.* (Kyiv: IVNVKP Ukreliotekh, 2009). A twenty-page essay published as a chapbook.
49 Zassoursky, "Whitman's Reception and Influence in the Soviet Union," 48.
50 Louis Miller (or Miler), author of the main translation of Whitman into Yiddish (1940), not to be confused with the more famous Louis Miller (1866-1927), editor and political activist
51 A pioneering work on the Yiddish Whitman is Leonard Prager's "Walt Whitman in Yiddish," *Walt Whitman Quarterly Review* 1, no. 3 (1983): 22–35. Also see the chapter "Going Native, Becoming Modern," in Rachel Rubinstein, *Members of the Tribe: Native America and the Jewish Imagination* (Detroit: Wayne State University, 1990), 59–86, and the chapter "From Heine to Whitman: the Yiddish poets come to America," in Julian Levinson, *Exiles on Main Street: Jewish American Writers and American Literary Culture* (Bloomington: Indiana University Press, 2008), 125–142.
52 Benjamin and Barbara Harshav, ed., *American Yiddish Poetry: A Bilingual Anthology*, 2nd ed. (Stanford: Stanford University Press, 2007), 31–32.

transatlantic and internationalist map. The majority of Whitman's American translators into Yiddish were also Russian-speaking and translated from Russian as well: many anthologies of poetry in Yiddish include American and Russian poetry (German is also well represented, especially Heine). They contributed to establishing Yiddish as a literary language and building a transatlantic and internationalist canon. Because so many of the Yiddish-speaking emigrant writers moved in socialist circles, they also had a political agenda: the diasporic Jewish reality combined with political internationalism. To translate Whitman, to write poems about him, to address him, was not only a pledge of allegiance to the American national poet, but also a way to connect the Yiddish transnational identity with a cosmopolitan vision of the United States, and to blend them into internationalism.

It is no coincidence that "Salut au Monde!" was the first poem by Whitman translated into Yiddish, in 1912. It was published in *Shriftn*, a New York Modernist journal, edited by David Ignatov, whom Rachel Rubinstein characterizes as "cosmopolitan and internationalist," and at the same time "self-consciously American."[53] The magazine published mostly poets from the Di Yunge group,[54] as well as translations (ranging from the *Kalevala* to Tagore's poetry). As Rubinstein contends, *Shriftn*'s dialogue with *Poetry: A Magazine in Verse* reveals a similar negotiation between the local and the global. Whitman was part of that negotiation: while his line "To have great poets, there must be great audiences, too," featured on every title page of *Poetry*,[55] "Salut au Monde!" was translated by I. J. Schwartz in the very first issue of *Shriftn*, and his portrait was printed in the 1913 one, next to a poem by Peretz Hirshbein "Dos lid fun dem nar" (Song of the fool), which can be read as a parody. Both Leonard Prager and Julian Levinson describe Schwartz's translation of "Salut au Monde!" as vernacular, written in a less *daytshmerish* (Germanized) Yiddish than most contemporary translations from poetry.[56] Of particular interest is the mix of Hebrew and Latin scripts (other translators later chose to translate the French title and thereby unify the alphabets). In all likelihood, Schwartz used an early American edition of the poem, maybe the 1860 edition with its mix of fonts

---

53 Rubinstein, *Members of the Tribe*, 70.
54 Mani Leyb, Zishe Landau, and more punctually Joseph Opatoshu, Moyshe Leib-Halpern.
55 Alice Corbin Henderson's essay "A Perfect Return" in the first issue of *Poetry*, documents Whitman's influence on French and English poetry, and predicts Whitman's return to America.
56 Levinson, *Exiles on Main Street*, 131–132. For more on Schwartz and Whitman, especially *Kentucky*, Schwartz's American epic in Yiddish, see 132–138.

(the title "Salut au Monde" is printed in cursive). Schwartz own translation radicalizes this heterogeneity with different alphabets.

וואלט וויטמאן:
Salut au Monde
אידיש : י. י. שװארץ.

FIGURE 5. Walt Whitman, "Salut au Monde," in *Shriftn* no. 1 (1912). Author's collection.

More generally, I will often hint at a Jewish Whitman in languages other than Yiddish. Indeed, many of the translators and commentators that I will discuss were Jewish, which is hardly surprising considering the fields covered by this study, where Jews were more present than in other parts of the world: the Russian Empire and the USSR, the US, pre-Nazi Germany and central Europe. They were also well represented in the leftist international circles that I will often evoke, like the Bund in the early twentieth century, which advocated a diasporic and lay Jewish identity.

The supplements and revisions that I intend to bring to the history of the Russian, Soviet and internationalist Whitman will obviously introduce new biases, sometimes willingly so, like the emphasis on the Yiddish Whitman, sometimes more arbitrarily. As I happen to have more expertise on Latin America than on China, I will inevitably introduce an imbalance between Whitman's spheres of reception West and East of Moscow. I certainly do not intend to write a definitive history, but a different narrative that will reveal some hitherto little-known circuits. I will follow a chronological order, with three major periods: from the belle époque to World War I (Chapters 1–4); the interwar period, starting in 1917 with the Russian revolutions and including World War II (Chapters 5–7); after 1945, until the mid-1980s and the end of the Cold War (Chapters 8–9). There will be some chronological overlaps between chapters, especially in the first part, which lays the foundations for my discussion of Whitman's reception as a revolutionary poet, in a broad European context, while dealing with thematic elements: Whitman "the primitive" partly became Whitman "the futurist," but the two categories interfered with one another; Whitman "the prophet" became the herald of the revolution and of new dawns, but his prophetic aura remained, even after World War II in some cases. While I have tried to decompartmentalize national receptions, Chapter 5 encompasses the Soviet 1920s and 1930s, while Chapter 6 focuses on Europe and the US between the wars: the Soviet reception also had a logic of its own and, for the sake of clarity, it made sense to maintain a form of continuity here. Chapter 7 is more of an interchapter, which will bring a coda to Chapters 4, 5 and 6: I wanted to focus on one particular poem, "Pioneers! O Pioneers!," a favorite of Whitman's leftist reception from the end of the nineteenth century to World War II, as a case study of internationalist circulation. And while "Salut au Monde!" became the anthem of communist Whitmania after World War II, it definitely provided the refrain of "The Internationale" à la Whitman, throughout the entire twentieth century. Accordingly, it will be the leitmotiv of this book.

Chapter 1

Whitman as a *primitive* (1880s–1910s)

Whitman's European reception coincided with the development of primitivism as a major trend in European thought and art. Primitivism is a vexed and complex phenomenon, but one of its central and stable tenets was a desire to reconnect with something lost, in particular nature or a sense of the sacred. Johannes Schlaf, one of Whitman's first German translators, emphasized the value of his poetry as an antidote to modern life, to the feeling of fragmentation and the lack of spirituality that it induced.[1] But primitivism was also an aesthetic category, and art historians have often been at odds over its definition—whether it is a transhistorical, anthropological notion (a "preference for the primitive,"[2] as Ernst Gombrich puts it) or whether it was a specifically Western movement which emerged at the end of the nineteenth century and reached full bloom at the beginning of the twentieth. Primitivism is all the more complex because it encompasses a variety of fields, from cultural and philosophical history to visual arts and literature, and draws from heterogeneous references—from local crafts to non-European artefacts (especially in the context of colonization).

---

1   Johannes Schlaf, "Walt Whitman," *Freie Bühne für den Entwicklungskampf der Zeit*, 1892 (no. 3), 977–988.
2   Ernst Gombrich, *The Preference for the Primitive: Episodes in the History of Western Taste and Art* (New York: Phaidon, 2002).

The *primitive*[3] was a versatile category, which encompassed seemingly contradictory referents and definitions. One could even argue that such flexibility is a characteristic trait of a notion that is polemical and programmatic rather than analytic and historical. In a way, the *primitive* had the same "protoplasmic" quality that Edmund Gosse ascribed to Whitman's poetry: "literature in the condition of protoplasm—an intellectual organism so simple that it takes the instant impression of whatever mood approaches it."[4] Not only was it redefined according to specific aesthetic agendas, but it could also carry multiple meanings at the same time—again, much like Whitman's poetry, which embraced contradictions.

The core paradox is that primitivism is above all a *modern* aspiration. Whitman himself kept defining and implementing modernity, while presenting himself as among the naked "Children of Adam" and declaring in "Song of Myself": "I speak the pass-word primeval." (LG 46) He represented himself as a *primitive*, but also as a primitivist: he wrote that his only essential readings were the Bible, Homer (especially the *Iliad*), the *Mahabharata*, Ossian and the *Nibelungen*.[5] Not only did the pervasive idea of primitivism shape the way in which he was read and understood, but he triggered commentaries and debates that fueled the momentum of literary primitivism—which has been relatively understudied in comparison to its visual and musical expressions.[6]

Like a magnifying lens, Whitman's reception reveals a tension at the core of primitivism: on the one hand, the *primitive* related to an origin—or at least a beginning; on the other, it was a destructive force that challenged civilization. In other words, it was associated with Adam or the ancient Greeks, but also with barbarians, and, in a Russian context, the Scythians. Whitman was the very incarnation of this Janus-faced *primitive* in European readings. Depending on the definition that was most operative for a given culture, the emphasis would fall on the Adamic side or on the barbarian. What I identify as two conflicting

---

3   I adopt Philippe Dagen's use of italics to signal distance from a word freighted with ideology and ambiguity (*Le Primitivisme: Une invention moderne*, Paris: Gallimard, 2019).
4   Sir Edmund Gosse, *Critical Kit-Kats* (New York: Dodd, Mead, 1896), 97.
5   Walt Whitman, *Poetry and Prose* (New York: Library of America, 1996), 665.
6   One of the few studies of the topic is Ben Etherington's *Literary Primitivism* (Stanford: Stanford University Press, 2017), which views primitivism as a utopian project rather than a purely colonial fantasy. Even though he deals with later authors (Césaire, Fanon, Lawrence, McKay), Etherington makes an interesting distinction between "philo-primitivism" (primitivism as a theme) and "emphatic primitivism" (an "aesthetic project," aiming at "a process of transformation toward the primitive" [10], at reactivating a "primitive remnant" [xiii]). One could argue that Whitman implemented emphatic primitivism and provided a model for its twentieth century promoters.

poles were, however, not mutually exclusive and often combined in various ways. Maurice Maeterlinck, the Belgian Symbolist poet and playwright, wrote profuse remarks on Whitman in his *Notebooks*, which are themselves a good example of such heterogeneousness. In them, Whitman ran the whole gamut of primitivist references: he incarnated "the opaque germination of a new Germanic world," "the Scald and the Scandinavian transplanted to America," while accomplishing "the dream of Adam" and embodying the "Homer of the New World."[7] Maeterlinck insisted that Whitman's world was still "a draft" and that his poetry had an "embryonic" quality. This chapter will highlight this dialectic between Whitman's work and the cultural backgrounds of its reception. Its scope is European and its approach comparatist, since its aim is to situate the Russian reception within a larger picture.

1. A neo-wanderer

Beneath the numerous declensions of the *primitive*, the most common root was the search for the lost link with Nature. Primitivism was indeed a criticism of civilization, which had driven man away from his original strength and power. More than Thoreau, whose work remained relatively unknown in Europe at the turn of the century, Whitman provided an American model, both as a poet and as a man (this was obviously a construct that had little to do with the poet's biography). The radically primitivist versions describe Whitman as a Titan, a "true son of Sky and Earth,"[8] in the words of the Russian Symbolist poet Konstantin Balmont, or, in those of the German poet Arthur Drey, a "blazing Titan of the virginal forest."[9] According to British art historian John Addington Symonds, he was even the sacred tree Yggdrasil itself: "He is a gigantic elk or buffalo, trampling the grasses of the wilderness, tracking his mate with irrepressible energy. He is an immense tree, a kind of Yggdrasil, stretching its roots deep down into the bowels of the world, and unfolding its magic boughs through all the spaces of the heavens."[10] As Martin Bidney observes, Balmont borrowed the image from

---

7 Maurice Maeterlinck, *Le Cahier bleu*, ed. Joanne Wieland Burston (Ghent: Éditions de la Fondation Maurice Maeterlinck, 1977), 155, 157, 150.
8 "Istyi syn Neba i Zemli," in Konstantin Ba'lmont, *Belye Zarnitsy* (Saint Petersburg: Izd. Pirozhkova, 1908), 102.
9 "Lodernder Titan des keuschen Urwalds!" Arthur Drey, "Walt Whitman," *Die Aktion*, no. 24 (September 4, 1911), 907. On the forest as the site of a *primitive* German identity, see Simon Schama, *Landscape and Memory* (New York: Knopf, 1995).
10 John Addington Symonds, *Walt Whitman: A Study* (London: John C. Nimmo, 1893), 155–156.

Symonds[11] and elaborated on it: Whitman was powerful enough to thrust the "young shoots of the mighty forests of the future."[12] Symonds's quote appeared again, quite later, in Sergei Eisenstein's writings.[13]

More frequently, Whitman was associated with the "wild," or with the "savage," as evidenced in Edward Carpenter's writings. Carpenter played a crucial part in the history of Whitman's British reception, not only for his accounts of his visits to Whitman, but also for his own collections of ostensibly Whitmanian writings, especially poetry.[14] The epigraph of his essay "Civilisation, its cause and its cure," is from Whitman: "The friendly and flowing savage, who is he? Is he waiting / for civilisation, or is he past it, and mastering it?"[15] The essay itself develops ideas often reminiscent of Emerson's "Nature": "Man has to undo the wrappings and the mummydom of centuries, by which he has shut himself from the light of the sun and lain in seeming death.... —and Nature must once more become his home, as it is the home of the animals and the angels." (35) For Carpenter, Whitman is that very man, who can undo "the mummydom of centuries." Whitman the wanderer tramping the "open road" was associated with Tolstoy, especially in Britain. The two writers were often mentioned together as two representatives of "the simple life," at a time when Tolstoy circles and societies had been springing up.[16] The periodical the *Tolstoyan* (1901–1902) was renamed the *Crank* (1904–1907) and finally the *Open Road* (1907–1913). Not only was that last title very Whitmanian, but the magazine featured a series on Whitman and emphasized his idea of poetry as a direct canal of experience, as opposed to "musical verbiage."

In France too, Whitman was primarily seen as a poet of Nature. The Naturistes (a group of thinkers and poets gathered around Maurice LeBlond) were indeed

---

11 Martin Bidney, "Leviathan, Yggdrasil, Earth-Titan, Eagle: Bal'mont's Reimagining of Walt Whitman," *Slavic and East European Journal* 34 (Summer 1990): 176–191.
12 Konstantin Bal'mont, *Belye Zarnitsy*, 101.
13 Sergei Èizenshtein, "Montazh" (1937), in *Izbrannye proizvedeniia*, vol. 3 (Moscow: Iskusstvo, 1964), 112.
14 See the chapter on Edward Carpenter in Kirsten Harris, *Whitman and British Socialism: "The Love of Comrades"* (London: Routledge, 2016), 31–64.
15 Edward Carpenter, *Civilisation: Its Cause and Its Cure and Other Essays* (London: Swan Sonnenschein & Co.,1891), 1.
16 See the "Modern Worlds, Simple Lives" section in Rebecca Beasley, *Russomania: Russian Culture and the Creation of British Modernism, 1881–1922* (Oxford: Oxford University Press, 2020), in particular 94–134. Beasley challenges the common assumption of a French genealogy for British Modernism: against this trend, which literary history retained as dominant, was a powerful Russophile movement, which valued life rather than art. One could argue that American literature played that role for French Modernism. But even in the case of British Modernism, "russomania" could sometimes converge with "whitmania."

very fond of Whitman. They presented the French American poet Francis Vielé-Griffin as his heir, or even his "grand-son," bringing with him all the joy of the "new world."[17] Vielé-Griffin was born in the US, but spent most of his life in France. He was at first much closer to Mallarmé than to Whitman, and *Les Cygnes* (The Swans), a volume that he sent to Whitman in 1888, was in fact very Mallarmean. In return, Whitman sent a copy of *Leaves of Grass* to Vielé-Griffin, who translated several poems from it. A year later, Vielé-Griffin published the collection *Joies* (Joys), written in free verse (with a preface explaining its use), praising the reconciliation of life and art through the recording of natural sensations. Yet another collection, *Chansons de la route* (Songs of the road), reads as an homage to Whitman, the poet of the "open road."

This Whitmanian quest is even more salient in Stuart Merrill's poetry. Born in Long Island (like Whitman), Merrill grew up in France (like Vielé-Griffin) and was at first close to Mallarmé. He met Whitman in 1887, in New York, after listening to his talk on Lincoln, and offered him a copy of the journal *La Vogue*, featuring Jules Laforgue's French translations from *Leaves of Grass*. Like Vielé-Griffin again, Merrill distanced himself from Mallarmé and turned more and more to *vers-librisme*. The collection *Une voix dans la foule* (A voice in the crowd), while dedicated to Émile Verhaeren, abounds with Whitmanian references. It shows the path that leads to the acceptance of modern life: the path of nature, available to the wanderer (*vagabond*). In "The lesson," Merrill seems to write his own variation on the ending of "Song of Myself" and ventures, post mortem, on the open road: "I know ... That I will live again, even if my flesh dissolved / In the songs of a poet coming after me / And with the impetus of hope which launches on the road, / In search of happiness, the rough wanderers."[18]

The figure of the wanderer, quite different from its Romantic version, and inspired by the Whitmanian companion searching for both nature and comradeship on the open road, was common to the French vers-libristes and to the German expressionists, especially Franz Werfel, as evidenced in the poem "The Wanderer Throws Himself into the Grass."[19] Some ten years later, Whitman was still depicted along similar lines by the Swedish poet Artur

---

17 Maurice LeBlond, *Essai sur le naturisme* (Paris: Mercure de France, 1896), 103.
18 Stuart Merrill, "La leçon," *Une voix dans la foule* (Paris: Mercure de France, 1909), 191. "Je sais ... / Que je revivrai, malgré ma chair dissoute, / Dans les chants d'un poète après moi survenu / Et dans l'élan d'espoir qui lance sur la route, / En quête du bonheur, les âpres vagabonds."
19 Franz Werfel, "Der Wanderer wirft sich ins Gras," *Der Weltfreund* (Leipzig: Kurt Wolff, 1918), 75.

Lundkvist: he is a "powerful wanderer" (starke vandrare), a "morning wanderer" (Morgonvandrare).[20] Even though Merrill wrote of "rough" wanderers, this construct of a poet able to restore a direct contact with nature was on the side of what Lovejoy and Boas called "soft primitivism,"[21] or what we could call Modernist pastoral.

2. "Striking up for a New World"

Though aboriginal, the *primitive* was not without models and preexisting representations. As far as "soft primitivism" was concerned, two categories dominated Whitman's reception, that of the Adamic and that of the Greek.

The Adamic Whitman

Whitman was often portrayed as a biblical prophet or as Adam himself. While the prophetic side of the analogy will be studied in a later chapter, the adamic relates directly to the *primitive*. The comparison is explicit in George Santayana's essay "The Poetry of Barbarism" (a title which, in itself, indicates the compatibility of the Adamic and the barbarian):

> We find the swarms of men and objects rendered as they might strike the retina in a sort of waking dream. It is the most sincere possible confession of the lowest—I mean the most primitive—type of perception. All ancient poets are sophisticated in comparison and give proof of longer intellectual and moral training. Walt Whitman has gone back to the innocent style of Adam, when the animals filed before him one by one and he called each of them by its name.[22]

---

20 Artur Lundkvist, "Porträtt: Walt Whitman," *Clarté*, nos. 4–5 (May 1929), reprinted in *Naket Liv* (Stockholm: Bonniers, 1929); English translation in Allen and Folsom, *Walt Whitman and the World*, 351–352.
21 Arthur Lovejoy and George Boas, *Primitivism and Related Ideas in Antiquity* (Baltimore: Johns Hopkins Press, 1935): "soft primitivism" refers to an agrarian Golden Age, when the land yielded milk and honey effortlessly, while "hard primitivism" refers to an age when man has to struggle to survive and has no time for the pursuit of other goals.
22 George Santayana, "The Poetry of Barbarism," in *Interpretations of Poetry and Religion* (New York, Scribner's Sons, 1900), 178.

This biblical Whitman was particularly (but not exclusively, as the example of Santayana shows)[23] represented in Southern Europe, especially in Italy and Spain.

The Italian scholar Pasquale Jannacone published a stylistic study on Whitman in 1898. In a chapter entitled "Comparison between Walt Whitman's poetic forms and the forms of primitive poetries,"[24] Jannacone lists repetition and parallelism as the main devices of *primitive* poetry. According to Jannacone, Whitman was not acting as a *primitive* poet but was truly one: America was indeed a "new world," whose people produced a *primitive* art, comparable with the poetry of Pindar or the Bible. Such a naïve reading of Whitman's primitivity is exactly what Cesare Pavese challenged in his thesis on Whitman. Written much later (in 1930), it argues that Whitman never achieved the "primitive poem that he dreamed of" but, rather, "the poem of such a dream" and that "he made poetry about making poetry" (egli fece poesia del far poesia).[25] In other words, Whitman was not a *primitive*, but a primitivist.

One of the most remarkable texts of the early Spanish reception is Miguel de Unamuno's 1906 "El canto adámico" (The Adamic song).[26] Unamuno begins by mentioning the circumstances in which he read Whitman—the staging of the reading, usually outdoors, as Whitman himself would have had it, is a topical proem of such accounts. It happened "during a biblical evening," in the company of a friend, for whom he translated a few lines. Since his friend marveled at Whitman's enumerations and wondered if that was indeed poetry—a central question in Whitman's reception, often discussed within dialogues[27]—Unamuno launched into a more general theory of lyric poetry: "When lyric poetry turns

---

23 To be more precise, Santayana belonged to two worlds: he was an American philosopher and professor, but he always claimed his Spanish Catholic cultural heritage (he was born in Spain and arrived in the US at the age of eight).
24 Pasquale Jannacone, *La poesia di Walt Whitman e l'evoluzione delle forme ritmiche* (Turin: Roux Frassati & Co.,1898), 10.
25 Cesare Pavese, "Whitman," *La Cultura*, June–September 1933, reprinted in *La letteratura americana e oltre saggi* (Turin: Einaudi, 1990), 131. This article is an abridged version of his thesis (*tesi di laurea*), which Pavese did not publish; excerpts can be read in Lawrence G. Smith: *Cesare Pavese and America* (Amherst: University of Massachusetts Press, 2008), 135–168.
26 Miguel de Unamuno, "El canto adámico," *Los Lunes de El Imparcial* [Madrid], August 6, 1906.
27 One of the prime examples is George Santayana's "Walt Whitman: A Dialogue," *Harvard Monthly*, May 1890, 85–91. In this dialogue, too, the question of primitivity was central (but rather on the "barbarian" side of it—Whitman's "barbaric yawp" was a key element of discussion) and the debate between the two characters (with meaningful names: Van Tender and McStout) focused on what defines beauty: Does beauty lie in things (Whitman's position) or in the form that poetry gives to it? In the first case, beauty is everywhere and the task of the poet is to draw attention to it. In the second case, beauty is rare and is a result of aesthetic activity.

sublime and spiritual, it ends in sheer enumerations, sighs of cherished names." He remembers watching children as they repeated with delight the word "horse" when they saw one: "They were creating the word as they repeated it: it was a song of genesis." Unamuno refers to Genesis 2, insisting that "to give a name to something is to gain spiritual hold on it" and that Whitman could have added as a conclusion to "Song of the Parting Sun": "To name things, what a powerful miracle." Unamuno relates the power of the biblical name to that of Homeric heroes, but adds an interesting distinction: to sing names with epithets is the product of a "reflexive exaltation," whereas to sing the names alone, the "naked names," is the result of "an irreflexive exaltation," which is the "supreme one." He also insists that Adam began naming things and animals around him before Eve ever existed: man needs names even before he feels the need to communicate. Naming is therefore lyric poetry in its purest form.

One could convincingly argue that this Adamic posture also triggered interest for Whitman in poets such as Paul Claudel and Pierre Jean Jouve in France. Claudel deemed Whitman the only artist who had understood the stakes of all the changes brought by the nineteenth century,[28] and even though his own poetry does not explicitly refer to him, it is hard not to be struck by the similarities between Whitman's catalogs and some of Claudel's enumerations in his *Odes*. Both poets salute the world in an effort to capture the pristine light and the pure energy of beginnings. The Adamic Whitman represented the poetry of wonder[29] and exaltation, or what Joachim Gasquet called at the time "lyrical realism."[30]

The Greek Whitman

Against the general European appreciation, Whitman was not considered in Britain as the prophet of America. M. Wynn Thomas writes that "Whitman's Americanism was, for Carpenter, not a neutral factor, nor a positive (let alone an inspirational) one, but an actual obstacle." [31] This is true of most British Whitmanians: for Edward Carpenter, John Addington Symonds or D. H. Lawrence, the US did not represent a new or *primitive* world, but rather an

---

28 Paul Claudel, "Richard Wagner. Rêverie d'un poète français," *La Revue de Paris*, July 15, 1934, 272.
29 On the poetics of wonder (*émerveillement*), see Michael Edwards, *Le Bonheur d'être ici* (Paris: Fayard, 2011); Edwards establishes connections between Whitman, Paul Claudel and Francis Jammes.
30 Joachim Gasquet, *L'Art vainqueur* (Paris: Nouvelle librairie nationale, 1919).
31 M. Wynn Thomas, *Transatlantic Connections*, 186.

extension of Britain, where the disease of capitalism had spread out of control. To make sense in Britain, Whitman needed to be decontextualized and then recontextualized in a less American and a more positive frame. It should also be added that Matthew Arnold's thinking had a strong impact on the British reception. In *Culture and Anarchy*, Arnold distinguishes three classes: the "Barbarians" (i.e., the aristocrats, preoccupied with appearances and forms), the "Philistines" (the middle class, with its strict moral code, obsession for material success and no interest in culture) and the "Populace." According to Arnold, culture makes circulation between these classes possible and is necessary for the renewal of civilization. Unsurprisingly, Arnold does not admire Whitman: the American's originality is his main flaw, a "demerit."[32] Regardless, *Culture and Anarchy* draws a valuable distinction between two opposed trends in history: Hebraism, which promotes the "strictness of conscience," and Hellenism, which values knowledge and "the spontaneity of consciousness." This opposition provided solid grounds for the construct of a Hellenic Whitman, who would offer a tremendous counterweight to the Hebraic burden of Victorian morals.

In Edward Carpenter's *The Intermediate Sex*, Whitman is said to be able to "imagine a new world of democratic ideas," precisely because he is "the most Greek in spirit and in performance of modern writers."[33] This vision of a Greek Whitman appealed to John Addington Symonds, who, contrary to most British Whitmanians, was neither a social nor political thinker, but an art historian. In *Studies of Greek Poets*, Symonds diagnoses the decay of civilization:

> The Greeks had no past. . . . The world has now grown old; we are gray from the cradle onwards, swathed with the husks of outworn creeds, and rocked upon the lap of immemorial mysteries. The travail of the whole earth, the unsatisfied desires of many races, the anguish of the death and birth of successive civilisations, have passed into our souls. . . . How shall we, whose souls are aged and wrinkled with the long years of humanity, shake hands across the centuries with those young-eyed, young-limbed immortal children?[34]

---

32 Letter to W. D. O'Connor, September 16, 1866, quoted in *Walt Whitman*, ed. Harold Bloom (New York: Infobase Publishing, 2009), 24.
33 Edward Carpenter, *The Intermediate Sex: A Study of Some Transitional Types of Men and Women* (London: George Allen & Unwin Ltd., 1908), 75.
34 John Addington Symonds, *Studies of Greek Poets* (London: Smith, Elder, 1873), 398.

The remedy is quite simple: "we must imitate the Greeks, not by trying to reproduce their modes of life and feeling, but by approximating to their free and fearless attitude of mind." Some contemporaries, especially Walt Whitman, already embody such an outlook:

> Strange as it may seem, Walt Whitman is more truly Greek than any other man of modern times. Hopeful and fearless, accepting the world as he finds it, recognizing the value of each human impulse, shirking no obligation, self-regulated by a law of perfect health, he, in the midst of a chaotic age, emerges clear and distinct, at one with nature, and therefore Greek. (422)

In his poem for Whitman "Of Love and Death, A Symphony," Symonds chooses a Greek theme—the plague of Athens.[35] But the "Greek" reincarnated by Whitman is not Apollonian: he emerges from archaic Greece, with all its (fantasized) Dionysian energy. Symonds invokes the "First Muse and mistress of primeval Pan." Other major references to a Greek Whitman include Oscar Wilde's remark that "there is something so Greek and sane about his poetry, it is so universal, so comprehensive,"[36] and, a little bit later, D. H. Lawrence's comment: "What a great poet Whitman is: great like a great Greek."[37]

In addition to the Arnoldian dismissal of the "Barbarian," another fact accounts for the prevalence of a Greek Whitman in Britain: all the authors mentioned above—Carpenter, Symonds, Wilde and Lawrence—were either gay or bisexual. Eve Sedgwick has shown how late Victorian and Edwardian British writers valued Greek homosexuality as a noble and virile model, the opposite of what they regarded as the prevailing effeminate and weak version of

---

35 This poem was reprinted as the opening piece of *In Re Walt Whitman*, a large collection of homages published after Whitman's death: Richard Maurice Bucke, Thomas B. Harned and Horace Traubel, eds., *In Re Walt Whitman* (Philadelphia: David McKay, 1893).
36 Oscar Wilde, "A Talk with Wilde," *Philadelphia Press*, January 17, 1882, 2.
37 David Herbert Lawrence, *Studies in Classic American Literature*, ed. E. Greenspan, L. Vasey and J. Worthen (Cambridge: Cambridge University Press, 2002), 414. Lawrence was one of Whitman's most thought-provoking readers. While he paid homage to Whitman as the seizer of "the quick of time," and as the "first White aboriginal"—high praise from someone deeply engaged with the idea of primitivity—he also aggressively challenged some of Whitman's claims, especially the American's will to incarnate everything and everyone. Lawrence's essay underwent several versions. The appreciation of Whitman as a Greek belongs to the 1921 version.

homosexuality.[38] Whitman was read as a gay poet much earlier in Britain than anywhere else, and the construct of a *primitive* Whitman should also be seen in light of the valorization of Greek homosexuality.

The Greek Whitman was not, however, exclusively British or gay. Comparisons were sometimes more specifically literary: in 1908, the Italian poet and critic Gian Pietro Lucini called Whitman "today's Homer" (l'Omero dell'oggi).[39] According to Johannes V. Jensen, his Danish translator, he was a primitive on a par with Pindar:[40] just like him, he was free from rhythmical constraints. In the case of Jensen, a vitalist and racist writer, who wrote extensively on the superiority of the Goths, the search for the *primitive* was neatly articulated with a discourse on renaissance, as evident in the title of some of his works: *Den gotiske Renaessence* (The Gothic Renaissance, 1901), *Den nye verden* (The new world, 1907): Jensen saw in Whitman the guide to the New World, a place of regeneration and renewal for the Goths. I shall now turn more specifically to this Germanic reception, for which the concept of the barbarian was, for the most part, more important than that of the Adamic or the Greek.

3. The barbarian

The barbarian could appear as the exact opposite of the Greek or of the biblical: instead of offering a model for new beginnings, he is associated with destruction and chaos. But in the context of a general questioning of Western civilization, the barbarian became the agent of a necessary destruction, an indispensable phase prior to any new form of society or art. The contradiction between emergence and destruction turned out to be dialectical and productive.

The Germanic Whitman

The barbarian Whitman was particularly strong in Germany, where the "Barbar" was central to the national self-image. In 1907, Gustav Landauer stated that, according to Whitman himself, the American people lived in

---

38 Eve Kosofsky Sedgwick, *Between Men: English Literature and Male Homosocial Desire* (New York: Columbia University Press, 1985).
39 Gian Pietro Lucini, *Ragion poetica e programma del verso libero: Grammatica ricordi e confidenze per servire alla storia delle lettere contemporanee* (Milan: Edizione di Poesia, 1908), 64.
40 Since the seventeenth century, Pindarism has designated poetry that values enthusiasm and inspiration rather than form. See H. T. Kirby-Smith, *The Origins of Free Verse* (Ann Harbor: The University of Michigan Press, 1996), 81–102.

an age of barbarism.[41] He drew a parallel between the modern US and the Germanic tribes of Arminius (a key figure for German Romantics and nationalists): they were both familiar with Greco-Latin culture, but also faced radical change. Around the same time, in 1908, Hermann Bahr published an essay entitled "Barbaren," which, while a review of G. B. Shaw and of the Danish poet J. V. Jensen, ended with a discussion of Whitman.[42] According to Bahr, "barbarism" had become a conscious choice rather than a predicament. Like Landauer, Bahr insisted on the need to restore sensation as the prime means to apprehend reality (for Landauer, this essentially meant nature, and for Bahr, the whole world, including urban and technological realities). For both of them, Whitman offered an example. Their position was developed and amplified in Stefan Zweig's famous essay "Das neue Pathos."[43] For Zweig as well, Whitman was an example of the original pathos that literature should seek and express.

Identification with the barbarian opened a possibility for a nationalist appropriation of Whitman, as Jensen's use of Whitman for a "Gothic Renaissance" had already suggested. Published in 1904, two German translations had clear nationalist overtones. One was the work of Karl Federn, for whom Whitman was an "anti-decadent," and the other, by Wilhelm Schölermann, was published by Eugen Diederichs, a press known for its nationalist leanings. According to Schölermann, Whitman was an example of Germanic achievement—had he been European, he certainly would have been German! That same year, an essay published in the antisemitic journal *Der Hammer* presented Whitman as the "Germanic interpreter of Life," the antidote to "Levitic elucubrations" (levitischer Klugkoserei).[44]

Against "Latin" sclerosis

The figure of the barbarian was also valued in cultures where it did not convey the same sense of national identity. In France, Whitman was seen as an antidote to the poison of civilization. Edward Carpenter's works on the necessity

---

41 Gustav Landauer, "Walt Whitman," translated in Allen and Folsom, *Walt Whitman and the World*, 189–193. The essay, first published in the *Vossische Zeitung*, was later reprinted as an introduction to Landauer's translation of Whitman's poems in 1921.
42 Hermann Bahr, "Barbaren," *Die Neue Rundschau* 19, no. 12 (1908), 1774–1781.
43 Stefan Zweig, "Das neue Pathos," *Das literarische Echo*, September 15, 1909, 1701–1707.
44 Samitasa (pseudonym of Willy Schlueter), "Walt Whitman, ein germanischer Lebensdeuter," *Der Hammer. Blätter für deutschen Sinn* (1904); quoted in Grünzweig, *Constructing the German Whitman*, 167.

of a cure for the ills of Europe were translated into French, as well as his poetry and his commentaries on Whitman. The causes of the illness were the same according to Carpenter and his French counterpart, Léon Bazalgette, who translated *Leaves of Grass* in 1909, and wrote *Le "Poème-Évangile" de Walt Whitman* (The Gospel Poem of Walt Whitman):[45] the weight of Christian morals, the contempt for the body and the separation from nature. In France, however, this decay of vitality was seen more specifically as the result of a sclerotic "Latin" culture. For Bazalgette, Catholicism was a decayed version of Roman culture. And even when the continuity between Catholicism and what was often called the Greco-Roman order was not so strictly established, the idea of a corrupt Latin civilization was pervasive. In his long study on Whitman (1889), Gabriel Sarrazin insisted on the need to rejuvenate humanity and literature simultaneously. The United States would provide a youth serum, since it was a world "populated by a race that used to be old and that became young again from the contact with a new soil."[46] Whitman was a pure product of that land of vigor, and, with his superb contempt for "proportion and composition," he would bring revitalizing energy. Unfortunately, his influence was hindered by the "genius" of Latin people, so austere and hostile to profusion. Some thirty years later, the poet Jean Richepin still wrote of American literature as having nothing to do with "Greco-Roman culture, where reason and critical thinking rule and order everything."[47] In his 1903 essay "Le Problème de l'avenir latin" (The Problem of Latin future), Léon Bazalgette excoriates Latin Europe's inability to reform and outlines a program of drastic change, based on sport and science. Soon after, he started a translation of *Leaves of Grass* into French.

Associating a quest for the barbarian with a wish for a renaissance was also frequent in nations with a strong historical identity but of rather low cultural and political status in Europe, such as Catalonia and Portugal. In 1900, Joan Pérez i Jorba, editor of the journal *Catalònia* (founded in 1898, in reaction to the development of the decadent movement and inspired by vitalism) wrote an enthusiastic piece on Whitman, stressing his "Homeric qualities."[48] In 1909, Cebrià Montoliu published in Barcelona translations from *Leaves of Grass* into

---

45 Léon Bazalgette, *Le "Poème-Évangile" de Walt Whitman* (Paris: Mercure de France, 1921).
46 Gabriel Sarrazin, *La Renaissance de la poésie anglaise* (Paris: Perrin et Cie, 1889), 248. According to Betsy Erkkilä, Whitman read that chapter and told Horace Traubel it was the most relevant piece ever written about him (*Walt Whitman among the French*, 94).
47 Jean Richepin, *L'Âme américaine à travers quelques-uns de ses interprètes* (Paris: Flammarion, 1920), 242.
48 Joan Pérez i Jorba, "Whitman," *Catalònia*, no. 6 (February 10, 1900), 52–54.

Catalan (three years before the equivalent in Spanish). Montoliu was an architect who also translated, among others, Emerson and Ruskin. In his preface, he associates modernity and democracy with a barbarian energy:

> Would you like in a single breath the triple essence of this new ideal, this new dream of an intense and democratic industrialization, of national exaltation and universal fraternity, which, coming from barbarian tempests [brumes barbres], came to wake you up, o Catalans, from a secular medieval spell, with a shock so great that your social life is seriously shaken? Read Walt Whitman.[49]

In 1913, Montoliu published a book-length study of the American poet,[50] which emphasized again the equivalence between Whitman and the United States, and heralded Whitman as the prophet of the "Barbarian Renaissance."

Such a paradoxical concept also loomed large in Portugal. The aim of the *Renascença portuguesa* was to support the new republican regime with a literary and cultural revival. Both Fernando Pessoa and his friend Mário de Sá-Carneiro were drawn toward this movement in their early years, and Pessoa published some of his first poems in journals such as *Renascença* and *Nova Renascença* (1914). Pessoa and Cesario Verde developed a philosophy called sensationism, close to French vitalism, which advocated sensation over rationality. Two of Pessoa's heteronyms, Alberto Caeiro (the sheep keeper) and Álvaro de Campos (the engineer), were heralds of primitivity as an antidote to civilization. In a poem subtitled "Sensationist ode," Álvaro de Campos screams his ferocious desire to live and celebrates the joy of throwing oneself onto grass. Such a stance is even more explicitly Whitmanian in "Salutation to Walt Whitman" (1915), with its Dionysian claim: "I belong to your Bacchic orgy of sensations-in-liberty."[51] Civilization fetters sensation and life: "Let me take off my tie, unbutton my collar, / You can't have a lot of energy with civilization looped around your neck."[52] Pessoa, who wrote that "the

---

49 Walt Whitman, *Fulles d'herba*, trans. Cebrià Montoliu (Barcelona: Biblioteca popular de "L'Avenç," 1909), 5.
50 Cebrià Montoliu, *Walt Whitman, l'home i sa tasca* (Barcelona: Societat Catalana d'Edicions, 1913).
51 "Orgia bacchica de sensações-em-libertade." Campos plays on Marinetti's "parole in libertà."
52 "Deixa-me tirar a gravata e desabotoar o colarinho. / Não se pode ter muita energia com a civilização à roda do pescoço . . ."—Álvaro de Campos, *Obra completa*, ed. J. Pizarro and A. Cardiello (Lisbon: Tinta-da-China, 2014), 84.

essential thing about the barbarian is that he is essentially modern,"⁵³ was one of Whitman's most acute readers.

In Italy, fascination for the barbaric *primitive* was less associated with the call for a renaissance and appeared to be less prevalent. However, the barbarian was also an operative aesthetic category, as evidenced in the title of Giosuè Carducci's *Barbarian Odes*. Carducci later discovered Whitman through the reviews of Enrico Nencioni, and appreciated his poetry. Gabriele D'Annunzio was greatly influenced by the *Barbarian Odes*, which, combined with the discovery of Nietzsche, largely provided the impetus for the *Naval Odes* (1893), with direct quotes from Whitman and prosodic experiments drawn from Carducci's "barbaric hexameters" and Whitman's free verse.⁵⁴ At that time too, in 1892, Enrico Thovez wrote about the need he felt to imitate Whitman: "Down with rhyme and meter."⁵⁵ Breaches of rhythmic patterns were the formal corollaries of the fascination for the *primitive*. This topic will be further investigated in the next chapter, as Whitman became a more specific type of *primitive*, that is, a precursor of Futurism.

4. Westward: another direction for the quest of the *primitive* in Russia

Before that, let us turn to the Russian primitivist reception of Whitman, which appears to be an extraordinary sound board for Western European discourses, but also a space of reconfiguration, integrating its own developments. Primitivism, a major trend during the Russian Silver Age, was elaborated in relation with its Western European manifestations but also presented distinctively national traits—it tended to be more reflexive and prone to theory, as evident in manifestos like Aleksandr Shevchenko's *Neo-Primitivizm*,⁵⁶ and put more emphasis on national popular traditions as sources of *primitive* inspirations. Art historians have usually stressed Russian primitivism's attraction to the East. While this was certainly the dominant trend, Russian primitivist discourse also

---

53 Fernando Pessoa, *Erostratus*, in *Páginas Íntimas e de Auto-Interpretação*, ed. Georg Rudolf Lind et Jacinto do Prado Coelho (Lisbon: Ática, 1966), 211.
54 On D'Annunzio, see Caterina Bernardini's chapter "'My big sympathy,' Whitman and Gabriele D'Annunzio," in *Transnational Modernity*, 89–118.
55 Enrico Thovez, *Diario e lettere inedite* (Milan: Garzanti, 1939), 244. For more on Thovez and Whitman, see Caterina Ricciardi, "Walt Whitman and the Futurist Muse," in *Utopia in the Present Tense: Walt Whitman and the Language of the New World*, ed. Marina Camboni (Rome: Il calamo, 1994), 271–273.
56 Aleksandr Shevchenko, *Neo-Primitivizm: Ego teoriia, ego vozmozhnosti, ego dostizheniia* (Moscow: Tipografiia 1-i Moskovskoi Trudovoi Arteli, 1913).

looked to American literature, especially the work of Henry Longfellow and Walt Whitman.[57]

It would be difficult to assign the Russian Whitman to either of the poles mentioned above, since primitivist references were used liberally and intermingled in commentary on his poetry. In a 1905 entry of the Brokhaus and Efron *Encyclopedic Dictionary*, Zinaida Vengerova placed Whitman next to the biblical prophets, while comparing his poetry to that of Homer. She called him a product of the American soil—a country where advanced civilization encountered primitive (pervobytnaia) agricultural life.[58] Some fifteen years later, in "The Nature of the Word," Mandelstam also used both biblical and Greek paradigms, referring to Whitman as a "new Adam," who offered a model of *primitive* poetry equal to Homer:

> America, having exhausted the philological supply it had carried over from Europe, panicked, as it were, then took some thought, and suddenly started growing its own personal philology, dug Whitman up from one place or other; and he, like a new Adam, began to give names to things, provided a standard for a primitive, nomenclatural, poetry [obrazets pervobytnoi, nomenklaturnoi poèzii], to match that of Homer himself.[59]

The other Greek analogue for Whitman was, as elsewhere in Europe, Dionysus, with strong Nietzschean overtones—the impact of Nietzsche on Russian thought and lexicon at the time was indeed considerable.[60] A long part of Korney Chukovsky's essay "Personality and Democracy" (1906) explains that Nietzsche himself never found his way to Dionysus and remained, with all his questions, doubts and problems, highly Socratic. According to Chukovsky, the real guide to Dionysus is none other than Whitman; Zarathustra himself would recommend Whitman as the ultimate model, the closest reincarnation of

---

57 For different reasons, Longfellow's *Hiawatha* was also (maybe even more so) commented as a *primitive* work. See Delphine Rumeau, "Primitif américain et primitivisme russe. Deux cas de réception (Longfellow, Whitman)," *Slavica Occitania*, no. 53 (2021): 249–275.
58 Zinaida Vengerova, "Valt Vitman," *Entsiklopedicheskii slovar'*, vol. 6a (Leipzig and St. Petersburg: Brokhauz and Èfron, 1892), 573.
59 Osip Mandel'shtam, "O prirode slova" (1922), in *Sobranie sochinenii*, 4 vols. (Moscow: Art-Biznes-Tsentr, 1993), 1:224–225; "On the nature of the word," trans. Sidney Monas, *Arion: A Journal of Humanities and the Classics*, n.s., 2, no. 4 (1975): 515.
60 See for example Ned Grillaert, *What the God-Seekers Found in Nietzsche: The Reception of Nietzsche's Übermensch by the Philosophers of the Russian Religious Renaissance* (Amsterdam: Rodopi, 2008).

Dionysus, only more astute (*khitree*).⁶¹ Dionysus stands halfway on the primitivist spectrum of references: while obviously Greek, he can generate chaos and a more destructive energy. Chukovsky insists on both the Americanness and the primitiveness of Whitman's poetry: it is awkward, rough and primitive (*neukluzhaia, grubaia, pervobytnaia*). However, Whitman himself was no primitive, he was *acting* as a primitive—more exactly he was wearing "the mask of savagery, of literary savagery" (lichinu dikaria, literaturnogo dikaria). This should certainly not prevent the reader from enjoying the show, for one has to appreciate a good play without paying attention to the prompter. Chukovsky's observation is remarkable since most commentators at the time saw Whitman as a first-degree *primitive*, and not as a primitivist, conscious of his own effort to return to a state of primitivity.

Next to Adam, Homer and Dionysus, stood the barbarian. Russian late Symbolism and early Futurism were indeed very much drawn toward a barbarian imagery. Vyacheslav Ivanov developed the concept of a "barbarian renaissance" (varvarskoe vosrozhdenie), which he considered "predominantly Anglo-Germanic" and defined as "an impulse to rewrite differentiated cultural forces into a new synthetic worldview."⁶² William Morris, John Ruskin, Walt Whitman and Henrik Ibsen liberated the energies of "new life." Chukovsky also referred to Whitman as a barbarian: in a 1913 essay,⁶³ he writes that Whitman created new forms "with the brazenness of a barbarian" (s derzost'iu varvara); in 1919, in the preface to his translation, he calls him a "barbarian bard" (varvar bard),⁶⁴ and a little bit later, he coins a Homeric epithet to refer to the "barbarianly straightforward" Whitman (varvarski-priamolineen).⁶⁵ More often than not, however, the Russian version of the barbarian was Eurasian rather than Germanic—the Hun, as in Valery Bryusov's poem "The Future Huns" (Griadushchie gunny) and the Scythian, as in the almanac entitled "The Scythians" (Skify) or in Alexander Blok's long poem bearing the same title. In the essay "The first futurist," Chukovsky gave voice to imaginary detractors of Whitman, who claimed that "the Huns, the Vandals" were coming to crush everything.⁶⁶ They did come, Chukovsky writes, and did not crush anyone.

---

61 Kornei Chukovskii, "Uot Uitman. Lichnost' i demokratiia v ego poèzii," *Maiak*, 1906 (no. 1).
62 Viacheslav Ivanov, "O veselom remesle i umnom veselii" (1907), *Sobranie sochinenii*, vol. 4 (Brussels: Foyer Oriental Chrétien, 1987), 73–74.
63 Kornei Chukovskii, "Poèziia budushchego," *Russkoe Slovo*, July 5, 1913.
64 Uot Uitmèn, *Poèziia griadushchei demokratii* (1919), 60.
65 Uot Uitmèn, *Poèziia griadushchei demokratii*, trans. Kornei Chukovskii (Moscow: Petrograd, Gosudarstvennoe Izdatel'stvo, 1923), 58.
66 Kornei Chukovskii, "Pervyi futurist," *Russkoe Slovo*, June 4, 1913.

Instead, they proclaimed, through their herald poet, Whitman, that everyone was a saint. Some twenty years later, Sergei Eisenstein still mentioned that Whitman's "cosmic all-encompassing pathos" was not "devoid of a touch of barbarism [varvarstva] in its primitive power."[67]

Finally, a reference to a prehistoric—more precisely Neanderthal—Whitman appeared in a short unpublished poem by Velimir Khlebnikov. It features side by side with a mention of Homer (not as a direct analogue of Whitman though):

> Внимательно читаю весенние мысли бога на узоре пестрых ног жабы.
> Гомера дрожание после великой войны, точно стакан задрожал от телеги.
> <Уота Уитмана> неандертальский череп с вогнутым лбом.
> И говорю: всё это было! всё это меньше меня![68]

> I read carefully the springtime thoughts of the god in the patterns of the dappled legs of the toad.
> Homer shaking after the great war, like a glass that shook when a cart went by.
> The Neanderthalian skull of Walt Whitman with its sunken forehead.
> And I say: all this was! all this is less than me!

This text, written in March 1921, condenses motives from Khlebnikov (the skull, the violent images of war, the interpolation of times) and from Whitman (the reading of natural signs, the affirmation of an all-encompassing "I"). The manuscript is difficult to interpret, since it could be read as <Uota Uitmana> or as <Uota u menia>, thus meaning: "I have Walt's Neanderthal skull, with its curved forehead," making the identification much more explicit:[69] Khlebnikov would then be presenting himself as one of Whitman's avatars on the wheel of Time.

The prevalence of a *primitive* Whitman in the Russian reception certainly bears witness to the close connections between Western European and Russian constructions of the American poet, but it also qualifies the mainstream idea

---

67 Sergei Èizenshtein, "Pafos," in *Neravnodushnaia priroda*, vol. 2 (Moscow: Muzei Kino, Èizenshtein Tsentr, 2006), 109.
68 Velimir Khlebnikov, *Sobranie sochinenii*, vol. 2 (Moscow: Nasledie, IMLI RAN, 2001), 22.
69 It is the version chosen by Ronald Vroon ("I have the same Neanderthal skull, the same curving forehead as you, old Walt"), in Velimir Khlebnikov, *Collected Works*, vol. 3, ed. Ronald Vroon and trans. Paul Schmidt (Cambridge, MA: Harvard University Press, 1987), 91.

that Russian primitivism was essentially an Eastern-oriented affair. And while Whitman was caught in the same net of references as in Western Europe, he was also invested with a particular primitivist aura and authority, which eventually translated into Futurist aesthetics.

5. Appropriation and separation

While the *primitive*, and especially the barbarian Whitman appeared as an exogenous source of inspiration which would bring new energy to a declining European culture, he was also subject to appropriation. An obvious way to incorporate Whitman into European poetry was to draw parallels and to find him counterparts. On the other hand, a number of poets who were at first attracted to Whitman later distanced themselves from him.

Transatlantic barbarians: Whitman and Verhaeren

Reception involves comparisons. In order to situate Whitman and to evaluate the degree to which he could be integrated into European poetry, critics and poets often drew parallels. These were sometimes meant to differentiate Whitman from European poets, as in the case of the frequent comparison with Mallarmé, who was allegedly the poet of the separation between life and art, while Whitman was the poet of their reconciliation.[70] But some writers also attempted to show that Whitman was a model for European poetry, as he already had counterparts (and not just followers). Among them, the Belgian poet Émile Verhaeren stood out.

Even though Whitman and Verhaeren were not directly linked and do not seem to have read each other, they were constantly associated in Europe as the two main poets of a new world, emerging from the ruins of the old. Verhaeren, who was born in 1855, the year *Leaves of Grass* was first published, was often labeled the European Whitman. Léon Bazalgette and Johannes Schlaf devoted

---

[70] See in particular Georges Duhamel, "Rubrique Les Poèmes," *Mercure de France*, April 13, 1913, 576. Duhamel opposed Whitman ("the powerful doorway to poetic life," leaving "an imperfect and confused work, like the minutes of a cordial, generous and adventurous life") to Mallarmé (the "solitary philosopher," leaving "a perfect and scant work where the fear to trust appearances is so heightened that it almost becomes a refusal to touch realities"). For more on this opposition, see Delphine Rumeau, "Whitman, antidote à Mallarmé," *Revue des Sciences Humaines*, no. 340 (2021): 85–100.

almost as much attention to his work as they did to Whitman's.[71] Bazalgette felt that Verhaeren's nationality and language[72] were accidents: "Verhaeren, so vast and so intense, was born for the New World."[73] "Verhaeren is essentially a barbarian who had to write his visions in a language rather meant to convey the delicate and refined sensations of utmost civilization." (36) The French writer and editor Philéas Lebesgue published an essay entitled "From Whitman to Verhaeren and beyond."[74] He later expatiated on their similarities, arguing that Whitman and Verhaeren were singers of the heroic race of the "Blond Europeans," "the Gauls, the Germans and the Normans," prone to adventures and conquests, whose feats the modern poets would celebrate:

> Appropriation by intelligence and settlement, by industrial and commercial exploitation, by iron and gold, is the great epic feature of our times.
> It needs singers and bards.
> An American, a Yankee from the people, first understood this. His name is Walt Whitman.
> A European, a Fleming of French culture and expression, has understood it as well and is steering the evolution of our literature, carrying into the future the prow designed by Symbolism. His name is Verhaeren.[75]

Stefan Zweig also insisted on the parallels between the two poets, especially in his biography of Verhaeren, whom he presented as "Walt Whitman's congenial brother."[76] Zweig noticed Verhaeren's popularity in Russia—where Whitman and Verhaeren were indeed often spoken of in the same breath and drew interest from the same commentators (such as Anatoly Lunacharsky). For the Spanish Ultraist poet Guillermo de Torre, Whitman and Verhaeren were both precursors

---

71 Johannes Schlaf published *Walt Whitman* with Schuster & Loeffler (Berlin and Leipzig) in 1904 and *Émile Verhaeren* in 1905.
72 Even though Dutch was the language of his native town, French was spoken and encouraged in his family.
73 Léon Bazalgette, *Émile Verhaeren* (Paris: E. Sansot, 1907), 5.
74 Philéas Lebesgue, "De Whitman à Verhaeren et au-delà," *Les Visages de la Vie*, no. 6 (1909), 372.
75 Philéas Lebesgue, "Walt Whitman et la poésie contemporaine," in Philéas Lebesgue, Alphonse Marius Gosser and Henri Strentz, *Essai d'expansion d'une esthétique* (Le Havre: Éditions de la Province, 1911), 11–12.
76 Stefan Zweig, *Émile Verhaeren, sa vie, son œuvre*, trans. from the manuscript by P. Morisse and H. Cherver (Paris: Mercure de France, 1910), 334.

of the "futurist lyricism" that he advocated. Verhaeren turned industry and the machine into literary themes, but he did not change the fundamental form of poems; on the other hand, Whitman experimented with form and "I Sing the Body Electric" might have inspired Marinetti.[77]

Volte-faces

While Whitman's reception was usually split between enthusiasm and rejection, it also had an interesting pattern: a number of poets who were at first very much drawn toward his poetry later turned away from it, as if it had proved impossible to assimilate completely, as if the *primitive* energy it communicated were not entirely fit for European poetry. I will focus on several cases, where the question of the *primitive* appears as central to understanding such volte-faces: Algernon Swinburne, Jules Laforgue, Valery Larbaud, and Fernando Pessoa.

Swinburne's contradictory relation to Whitman has been the subject of several studies and was even the starting point of Edmund Gosse's essay on Whitman as protoplasm. I do not aim to bring new material to the topic, but would like to locate it within a larger European framework and to show that this relation is quite typical of an ambivalent stance, between attraction and repulsion. As early as 1868 (the year Rossetti's anthology was published in Britain), Swinburne concluded his study on William Blake with a comparison of the Romantic with Whitman, "a poet as vast in aim, as daring in detail, as unlike others." His appreciation was ambiguous from the start, since he considered both poets as "at times noisy and barren and loose, rootless and fruitless and informal ... in the main fruitful and delightful and noble, a necessary part of the divine mechanism of things."[78] In 1871, he wrote a long laudatory address "To Walt Whitman in America," asking for "a song oversea," "in measureless onset," "with the sea-steeds footless and frantic."[79] The poem shows the already powerful song strengthening while crossing the ocean and concludes: "Let the flight of the wide-winged word / Come over, come in and be heard, / Take form and fire for our sakes." (136) Interestingly, this call is expressed in rhymed septets. This ambiguity, in a context of overall admiration, turned into acrimony in later comments. In the essay "Under the Microscope," written the following year,

---

77 Guillermo de Torre, "Filiación del lirismo futurista," in *Literaturas europeas de vanguardia* (Madrid: R. Caro Raggio, 1925), 253–255.
78 Algernon Charles Swinburne, *William Blake: A Critical Essay* (London: John Camden Hotten, 1868), 300–301.
79 Algernon Charles Swinburne, *Songs before Sunrise* (1871; Portland, ME: Thomas B. Mosher, 1901), 135.

Swinburne criticizes the very primitiveness of Whitman's poetry, which poured names onto the page without any order or form:

> It is one thing to sing the song of all trades, and quite another thing to tumble down together the names of all possible crafts and implements in one unsorted heap; to sing the song of all countries is not simply to fling out on the page at random in one howling mass the titles of all divisions of the earth, and so leave them. At this rate, to sing the song of the language it should suffice to bellow out backwards and forwards the twenty-six letters of the alphabet.[80]

In his essay "Whitmania" (1887), Swinburne attacked Whitman's disciples for writing terrible poetry. But the accusation did not spare Whitman himself entirely: in spite of some qualities, his rhetorical grandiloquence was unacceptably awkward. The main accusation was that of formlessness and an overfondness for juxtaposition: "Mr Whitman can only accumulate words."[81]

French "Whitmania" peaked a little after its British manifestation, but also started in the late nineteenth century. In 1886, Jules Laforgue published the first translations into French of whole poems from *Leaves of Grass*. The three pieces, which appeared in the Symbolist review *La Vogue*, were followed by a poem written by Laforgue himself, in which, for the first time, he experimented with free verse.[82] Whitman's liberating power translated into formal innovation. Two years later, in 1888, Laforgue wrote the poem "Albums," which formulated the dream of reconnecting with one's homeland and past (he was born in Uruguay) while projecting a future of innocence and freedom:

> On m'a dit la vie au Far-West et les Prairies
> Et mon sang a gémi : «Que voilà ma patrie!...»
> Déclassé du vieux monde, être sans foi ni loi,

---

80 Algernon Charles Swinburne, *Under the Microscope* (1872; Portland, ME: Thomas B. Mosher, 1899), 47.
81 Algernon Charles Swinburne, "Whitmania," *Fortnightly Review*, August 1, 1887, 170–176, reprinted in Bloom, *Walt Whitman*, 68.
82 See Éric Athenot, "1886, année vers-libriste: Laforgue, traducteur de Walt Whitman," in *L'Appel de l'étranger. Traduire en langue française en 1886*, ed. Sylvie Humbert-Mougin, Lucile Arnoux-Farnoux and Yves Chevrel (Tours: Presses Universitaires François-Rabelais, 2015), 107–123, and Carla Sofia Ferreira, "Seeing through French Eyes: 'Vers Libre' in Whitman, Laforgue, and Eliot," *Cambridge Quarterly* 45, no. 1 (2016): 20–41.

> *Desperado!* Là-bas je serai roi! . . .
> Oh! là-bas, m'y scalper de mon cerveau d'Europe![83]

> I was told about life in the Far West and Prairies
> And my blood moaned: "Now, this is my homeland! . . ."
> An outcast from the Old World, faithless and ruthless,
> *Desperado!* Over there I will be king!
> Oh! over there, to scalp myself of my European brains.

On is a complex impersonal French pronoun: it remains unclear where the account of life in the American West comes from. Indeed, Laforgue's poem bristles with literary reminiscences, from Rimbaud's "Drunken Boat" to Verlaine's "Languor." The word "desperado" evokes the mythology of the West but also encapsulates contradictory literary associations: it resonates with the melancholy of Gérard de Nerval's "desdichado" while bearing an echo of Whitman's "camerado." The poet expresses the Whitmanian dream of going back to a state of nature, "to become a virgin antelope again," "with no literature." However, Laforgue's barbaric call is ambiguous since the desire to be scalped eventually mellows into a wish for a quiet retreat: "And, once old, the farm in the sunrise / a milk cow and grandchildren."[84] The last line refers to such reveries as fragile "joujoux," a childish word for "toys," and casts a doubt on the very possibility of getting rid of one's "European brains." The poem therefore seems to summarize and foresee the future of the barbarian side of Whitman's French reception: it was passionately highlighted at first, but then it appeared as an impossible, if not dangerous, fantasy.

A similar pattern can be observed in Valery Larbaud, a central figure of early twentieth-century French literary life and a promoter of literary cosmopolitanism. Larbaud envisioned himself as the vanguard of the troops of Americans and Englishmen (and maybe also of Australians and Canadians later on!) about to storm and re-energize French literature.[85] The hero of that invasion was undoubtedly Whitman, even though Larbaud finally played a smaller part than he had wished in translating Whitman—Léon Bazalgette carried out the task sooner.

---

83 Jules Laforgue "Albums," in *Des fleurs de bonne volonté,* in *Œuvres complètes,* vol. 2 (Lausanne: L'Âge d'homme, 1995), 186.
84 "Et, devenu vieux, la ferme au soleil levant, / Une vache laitière et des petits-enfants . . ."
85 "With us, more exactly brought by us, the Barbarians entered literature. More exactly: the Barbarian. But what a Barbarian!" (Henry Jean-Marie Levet, *Cartes postales et autres textes, précédés d'une conversation de Léon-Paul Fargue et Valery Larbaud* [Paris: Poésie/Gallimard, 2001], 43).

Nonetheless, Larbaud confronted his Whitmanian model early, in his own poetry. In 1908, on July 4—a highly meaningful day that Whitman had already chosen for his first edition of *Leaves of Grass*—he published a volume entitled *Poésies*, under the name A. O. Barnabooth. It contained a fictional biography of a fictional author, provided by a fictional publisher: Barnabooth was supposedly born in South America and later granted the no less fictitious citizenship of the "State of New York." The poems were written in free verse and were reminiscent of Whitman's poetry in several stylistic aspects (enumerations, juxtapositions) and in their urge to encompass a vast geography. Some of them clearly expressed the will to get rid of form and art in order to gain access to the "real" itself:

> Assez de mots, assez de phrases! ô vie réelle,
> Sans art et sans métaphores, sois à moi,
> Viens dans mes bras, sur mes genoux,
> Viens dans mon cœur, viens dans mes vers, ma vie.[86]

> Enough of words and sentences! o real life,
> With no art and no metaphors, be mine,
> Come into my arms, on my knees,
> Come into my heart, come into my verse, my life.

The very first poem, "Borborygmi," offers a startling opening and praises the noises of the body as utterly poetic. This impertinent beginning is nonetheless slightly different from Whitman's audaciousness: a "borborygmus" is indeed a very mellow version of a "barbaric yawp." As with Laforgue, the appeal of the barbarian, however strong, seems to be toned down or tinged with distance and a sense of irony. The second edition of *Poésies* (1913) gave more room to such a reflexive mood and excluded some of the most obviously Whitmanian pieces (such as "Song of the Visible Variety"). When Larbaud finally published a volume of Whitman's poems, gathering together several translators, including himself, his enthusiasm had turned into a more complex and antagonistic relation. In the preface, he praised Whitman's ability to magnify everything, but he also stated that all catalog poems were failed ones: no matter what Unamuno (whom he quoted) thought, they were not the apex of lyric poetry, but the result of powerlessness, dreadful falls into allegory.[87] Larbaud also shifted from aesthet-

---

86 A. O. Barnabooth, *Poésies* (1913), in Valery Larbaud, *Œuvres* (Paris: Gallimard, "Bibliothèque de la Pléiade," 1957), 57.
87 Walt Whitman, *Poèmes. Feuilles d'herbe* (1918; Paris: Gallimard, 1922), 254.

ics to politics: he questioned Whitman's silence on slavery and his imperialist tendencies, even quoting Rubén Darío's poem. He concluded that Whitman's "mistake was to believe that America alone would take the intellectual, moral, etc. primacy of the world."

With Pessoa's heteronym, Álvaro de Campos, fascination for Whitman was not followed by a rebuff, but rather by the expression of doubts. In "Salutation to Walt Whitman," the *primitive* seemed to be the object of a mere wish, rather than an actual source of life and energy. The poem remained unfinished and fragmentary, thus making any final interpretation difficult. Still, incompleteness is precisely a key component of this text, whose publication was announced for the third issue of *Orpheu*, but never happened. Moreover, it keeps reiterating the imperative to go forward, as if departure and movement were never actual but remained optative. In several passages, "I want" (Quero) is repeated as if to exhaust will and desire by voicing them over and over again, until the subject declares his impotence and failure to fulfill his "excessive aspirations." Campos assesses his own failure as well as that of Whitman himself:

> Heia? Heia o quê e porquê?
> O que tiro eu de heia! ou de qualquer coisa,
> Que valha pensar em heia!?
> Decadentes, meu velho, decadentes é que nós somos...
> No fundo de cada um de nós há uma Bizâncio a arder,
> E nem sinto as chamas e nem sinto Bizâncio
> Mas o Império finda nas nossas veias aguadas
> E a Poesia foi a da nossa incompetência para agir...[88]

> Heia? What, heia? Why heia?
> What do I get out of heia! or out of anything,
> What is the point of thinking about heia?
> Decadents, old man, decadents, that's what we are...
> Within each of us there is a Byzantium on fire,
> And I don't even feel the flames or feel Byzantium
> But the Empire ends in our water-filled veins
> And Poetry came from our incompetence for action...

The renaissance that Whitman was supposed to bring about did not happen: instead of the return of a golden age, modernity sees the triumph of decadence.

---

88 Álvaro de Campos, *Obra completa*, 116-117.

Instead of young and healthy blood, insipid water runs through the veins of poets. Unlike many critics,[89] I would argue that such a failure does not result from Campos's inability to identify with Whitman, but rather from a hypersensitivity to Whitman's own moments of doubt and dysphoria. In the very same poem, attraction and enthusiasm give way to disillusion and powerlessness.

Campos's relation to Whitman is characteristic: for a number of European poets (one could add D. H. Lawrence), the barbarian—and its manifestation, Whitman—was a strong magnet, which played a major inspirational role—both thematically and formally—but whose power of attraction faded. After World War I especially, the *primitive* lost some of its appeal and Whitman's optimism appeared somewhat naïve and obsolete. However, another face of the *primitive* Whitman needs to be considered—one that looked less at nature and more at modern urban life, that was less drawn toward the past and more toward the future, and that was also more apparent in the Russian reception.

---

89 Pessoa's relation with Whitman is a vast and complex topic. It involves a personal "anxiety of influence" and very fertile answers to such an anxiety, which have been studied in depth, especially in Eduardo Lourenço, *Pessoa revisitado* (Porto: Editorial Inova, 1973) and *Fernando, Rei da Nossa Baviera* (Lisboa: Imprensa Nacional—Casa da Moeda, 1986); Irene Ramalho Santos, *Atlantic Poets: Fernando Pessoa's Turn in Anglo-American Modernism* (Hanover: University of New England Press, 2003). I have also written more extensively on it in *Fortunes de Walt Whitman*, 579–597 and 623–629.

Chapter 2

The Futurist poet (1910s–1920s)

Futurism can be seen as one of the offshoots of primitivism which developed within a number of avant-garde movements. Primitivism was indeed a broad and transversal category that could paradoxically combine with Futurism: going back to primitive sensations and approaches to art was not incompatible with searching ahead a revitalized future. Chronological time was challenged by both primitivism and Futurism. Other shared aspirations were the suppression of hierarchies and the reinvention of forms. The evolution of Korney Chukovsky's viewpoint is quite revealing: while he insisted on Whitman's Dionysian side in his early essays, he later emphasized the more experimental and avant-garde side of the American. This shift, concomitant with the development of Futurism in Russia, involved major changes in translations, from versified lines to free verse. Futurism, however, might on some level appear quite different from primitivism, or even at odds with it. The main difference lies in the opposition between the celebration of nature in most primitivist trends and the embrace of technology and urban life in Futurism. However, since Whitman was, in Leo Marx's terms, a poet of both "the machine" and "the garden,"[1] he could be claimed by both primitivists and Futurists alike. As the following discussion will show, while

---

1 Leo Marx, *The Machine in the Garden: Technology and the Pastoral Ideal in America* (Oxford: Oxford University Press, 1964).

the Futurist Whitman was not exclusively Russian—he was also Italian and Spanish—the shift from *primitive* to Futurist was most spectacular in Russia, where it was both emphasized and implemented in the works of Futurist artists, especially Vladimir Mayakovsky. The period covered here is mostly the 1910s, but it extends into the 1920s, especially with regard to the American continent.

1. The poetry of modern chaos

Poet of the metropolis

While the first primitivist version of Whitman cast him as a poet of nature, his Futurist avatar was, rather, a poet of cities and machines. For Whitman, a machine could enter a garden without ruining it—that is, to use Whitman's imagery, an axe could fell trees without endangering the beauty and richness of the land. Such a reconciliation was also sought by a poet like Khlebnikov; but more often than not, modernity was split between the country and the city, and Whitman's reception bears witness to this chasm. Roughly speaking, Whitman was at first more salient as a poet of nature, and was hailed somewhat later (in the 1910s, 1920s) as a poet of the city—which coincides with the development of American Modernism and European Futurism.

The urban Whitman reverberated in various parts of Europe— in poems by the Basque author Ramón de Basterra,[2] for example, or in Álvaro de Campos's odes. If Campos was mostly the primitivist and "sensationist" heteronym of Pessoa, he was also an engineer, very much drawn toward technology. In other words, Campos harbored the very same contradictions as Whitman. His urban side was manifest in poems published in the transatlantic review *Orpheu*, such as "Triumphal Ode," a paean to modernity, city life, technology, trade and crowds, and characterized by Whitmanian enumerations:

> Fraternidade com todas as dinâmicas!
> Promíscua fúria de ser parte-agente
> Do rodar férreo e cosmopolita
> Dos comboios estrénuos,
> Da faina transportadora-de-cargas dos navios,
> Do giro lúbrico e lento dos guindastes,
> Do tumulto disciplinado das fábricas,

---

2 Ramón de Basterra, "Inquilino de Bilbao. Oda a la Villa," *Hermes*, no. 16, April 1918.

E do quase-silêncio ciciante e monótono das correias de transmissão!³

Fraternity with all the dynamics!
Promiscuous fury to be part-agent
Of the iron and cosmopolitan wheeling
Of the strident trains,
Of the cargo-carrying labors of ships,
Of the slow, lurid turn of the cranes,
Of the disciplined tumult of factories,
And of the monotonous humming quasi-silence of the transmission belts!

Whitman as a poet of the modern city can be traced down several transatlantic paths. In 1916, the first issue of the American Modernist review the *Soil* displayed together an extract from "Crossing Brooklyn Ferry," the beginning of a poem by Arthur Cravan (the poem "Sifflet," translated into English, but with no title),⁴ a photograph of Manhattan by the Brown brothers and a drawing by Abraham Walkowitz. This disposition sets Whitman as a precursor of modernism, represented by poetry and the visual arts. Cravan's poem celebrates the hustle and bustle of the city and seems to prolong Whitman's words into a Modernist vision:

New York! New York! I should like to inhabit you!
I see there science married
To industry,
In an audacious modernity,
And in the palaces,
Globes,
Dazzling to the retina
By their ultra-violet rays
The American telephone
And the softness of elevators . . .⁵

---

3 Fernando Pessoa, *Poesias de Álvaro de Campos* (Lisboa: Ática, 1944), 144. (Written in 1914, first published in *Orpheu*, no. 1, 1915).
4 Arthur Cravan was English but wrote in French.
5 Arthur Cravan, "Sifflet," *Soil* 1, no. 1 (December 1916), 36 (previously published in French in *Maintenant*, April 1912).

The Brown brothers' photograph, with its view from above, seems to have been set into motion in the short film "Manhatta," shot in 1920 by Paul Strand (a photographer who belonged to Stieglitz's circle) and Charles Scheeler (a painter who, like Walkowitz, participated in the Armory Show in 1913). The film interwove shots of the city with quotes from Whitman's urban poems ("City of Ships," "A Broadway Pageant," "Manahatta," "Crossing Brooklyn Ferry"). It was first shown on Broadway in 1921, with the title "New York the Magnificent," and then in Paris in 1923 at a Dada evening (the notorious "Soirée du coeur à barbe," which led to the secession of part of the group).

Whitman inspired many artists and writers who travelled or emigrated to the US—in the latter case, largely settling in big cities. Such was the case with a number of Italian immigrants. The painter Joseph Stella, who emigrated to the US in 1896, painted the Brooklyn Bridge twice in 1919-1920, and explained how Whitman had modeled his vision of it (even though Whitman really was the poet of the Brooklyn ferry and wrote little about the structure):

> Meanwhile the verse of Walt Whitman—soaring above as a white aeroplane of Help—was leading the sails of my Art through the blue vastity of Fantasy, while the Fluid telegraph wires, trembling around, as if expecting to propagate a new musical message, like aerial guides leading to Immensity, were keeping me awake with an insatiable thirst for new adventures.[6]

Emanuel Carnevali, a poet who wrote in English after migrating to the US, invoked Whitman in his poem "Evening."[7] At the heart of the text a line in italics stands out, an address to the city itself: "O city, there lived in you once, O Manhattan, a man WALT WHITMAN." In almost the same way, the Ukrainian poet Mykola Tarnovsky later entitled his New York piece "U misti, de zhyv Uot Uitmen" (In the City where Walt Whitman Lived).[8] It was also the case for several American Yiddish poets. After "Salut au Monde!" in 1912, a 1919 issue of *Shriftn* published a picture of Walt Whitman (on page 1), a translation of "O Captain! My Captain!" and parts of "Song of Myself" by Louis Miller, along with cityscapes by Abraham Walkowitz—a combination quite reminiscent of the 1916 issue of the *Soil*. Since Yiddish-speaking poets often lived in big cities,

---

6   Joseph Stella, "The Brooklyn Bridge (A Page of My Life)," *Transition*, June 1929, 8–88.
7   On Carnevali and Whitman, see Caterina Bernardini, *Transnational Modernity*, 159–163.
8   In Ostap Kin, ed., *New York Elegies: Ukrainian Poems on the City* (Boston: Academic Studies Press, 2019), 18–19. The preface of the anthology refers to Whitman as a "Virgil" in New York for Ukrainian poets (xivx–xv).

especially New York, it is no surprise that Whitman, who often summed up the promises of America for immigrants, would appear in urban settings, from the "towers and the streets" of Aaron Nissenson's "Ballad of Walt Whitman" (1930)[9] to a short poem by B. Alkvit (Eliezer Blum), "Your Grass," published in 1931:

> Kh'trakht fun dayne grozn, Vitman,
> Un her dem roysh fun groysn
> Shteynernem vald Manhetn.[10]

> I think of your grass, Whitman,
> and hear the stir of the great
> stone forest Manhattan.

Nature fuses with the metropolis in this vignette. *Grozn* (the grasses) and *roysh* (the stir, the roar) combine in *groysn* (big, great), while *vald* (wood, forest) hints at *Walt*. *Manhetn*, though not rhyming with "Whitman," associates the sounds of the city and of the name of its poet. This piece is often quoted in anthologies of American Yiddish poetry.

This emphasis on the urban Whitman involved a shift from the search of a lost natural harmony to an embrace of chaos and fragmentation. When Pasternak's Doctor Zhivago writes that only the big city is able to inspire "a truly modern and new art," he mentions the "disorderly enumeration of seemingly incompatible notions and objects," typical of Blok, Verhaeren and Whitman, as a new form of perception, and not a mere stylistic device.[11] This comment leads us to another central element in Whitman's reception, equally important if one is to account for his presence in the Futurist pantheon: the refusal of order and hierarchy in perception and expression.

A rebel against hierarchy

> "A bored cow chewing the cud is as beautiful as the Venus de Milo"
>
> Kornei Chukovsky

The device of "disorderly enumeration" triggered compelling polemics. A gentle version can be read in the epistolary exchange between two Italian writers,

---

9   Aaron Nissenson, *Dos lebn vil mayse hern* (New York: A. Biderman, 1930), 97–98.
10 Eliezer Blum (B. Alkvit), *Vegn tsvey un andere* (New York: Farlag Inzikh, 1931), 34.
11 Boris Pasternak, *Doktor Zhivago* (1957; Moscow: Eksmo, 2003), 560.

Giovanni Papini and Ardengo Soffici. In 1918, Papini wrote an enthusiastic essay in which he declared that he discovered the meaning of poetry through Whitman (and not Dante or Petrarch), and concluded that it was necessary to "become a little bit barbaric again," for the sake of poetry.[12] He defended such ideas in his letters to Soffici, who, conversely, lamented the excess of immediacy and spontaneity in Whitman's poetry, arguing that "greatness" lies in restraint and in the creative will that commends "style."[13]

A much more aggressive position was that of the Norwegian writer Knut Hamsun, who abhorred the US. In a conference on American culture, he ridiculed Whitman's "original primitiveness" (oprindelige Primitivitet):[14] the American was able to feel but not to write. He thought with images, like an "Indian," but as he wrote, he replaced them with a hodgepodge from the Old Testament. He certainly could not be compared with a folk poet. Hamsun particularly insisted on the unbearable "columns of words," the "regiment of words." While his zeal for cataloging made Whitman unique, it also made him unreadable. This text was translated into Russian by Korney Chukovsky, who considered that Hamsun's only excuse was to have written this pamphlet while very young.[15]

This topic was indeed important for Chukovsky. In "Walt Whitman, First Futurist," he insisted on the absence of hierarchies in Whitman's poetry, where everything is seen, felt and collected directly, outside the frame of the intellect or the constraint of poetic forms, and where everything is thus equally beautiful: "a bored cow chewing the cud is as beautiful as the Venus de Milo; and a blade of grass is no less than the paths of the celestial planets; and to see a pea pod with an eye surpasses all the wisdom of the ages."[16] Chukovsky partly quoted "Song of Myself," but also added references that gave a Futurist flavor to the American poet, such as the Venus de Milo, an emblem of the classical canon of beauty that the avant-gardes challenged. Chukovsky analyzed the catalogs, with their heaps of chaotic images and endless lists, as the best expression of the urge to name every component of the world as equally worthy. Poetry and beauty are not a result of art, but lie in things themselves.

---

12 Giovanni Papini, "Walt Whitman," *Nuova Antologia*, 16 June 1908, reprinted in *24 Cervelli, Saggi non critici* (Milan: Lombardo, 1917), 367.
13 Letters of December 1907, January 1908 and July 1908, in Giovanni Papini, Ardengo Soffici, *Carteggio I, 1903–1908, dal "Leonardo" a "La Voce,"* ed. Mario Richter (Rome: Edizioni di Storia e Letteratura, 1991).
14 Knut Hamsun, *Fret det moderne Amerikas aandsliv* (Copenhagen: Philipsens Forlag, 1889), 76.
15 Uitmèn, Uot, *Poèziia griadushchei demokratii*, 1919, 107–108.
16 Kornei Chukovskii, "Pervyi futurist."

This debate on what Jacques Rancière would call a "redistribution of the sensible" was fueled by the antagonistic replies of the philosopher Vasily Rozanov. In 1915, Rozanov wrote negative reviews[17] of Whitman's poems in Chukovsky's translation. Whitman was simply "blind and deaf." Rozanov focused on the line "A mouse is miracle enough to stagger sextillions of infidels," which, along with "Song of the Exposition," provided prime examples of what he considered to be a lack of common sense. Whitman simply put words side by side and wrote "formalistic nonsense" (formalisticheskaia chepukha). In response, Chukovsky listed similarities between Whitman and Rozanov, juxtaposing quotes from the two authors (from *Specimen Days* and from *Solitary Thoughts*).[18] In his preface to the 1923 edition of Whitman, he again drew the same parallel: Whitman's conversational syntax was in fact "Rozanovian." The study following the translation insisted that both writers shared a prophetic inspiration and common themes (the soul and sex), even if Rozanov was "coquettish and cunning" (koketlivo-lukaviashchii pisatel) while Whitman was "barbarian and straightforward" (varvarski-priamolineen).[19] If Chukovsky's replies bore witness to Whitman's enduring power to catalyze polemics, they did not address Rozanov's main objection: What is the aesthetic and moral value of poetry that refuses to select and order the components of the world?

The question of whether poetry should discriminate was also central to D. H. Lawrence's appreciation of Walt Whitman. As noted previously, Lawrence had strong affinities with Whitman in his primitivist phase. His enthusiasm later switched to harsh criticism, particularly of the Whitmanian "I" and the poet's claims to universal identification. A more subtle objection was raised about the absence of selection in the poem "Leaves of Grass, Flowers of grass": "Leaves of grass, what are leaves of grass, when at its best grass blossoms." Lawrence asked. How could one want sheer, plain leaves of grass when grass can blossom into exquisite flowers? "Only the best matters; even the cow knows it."[20] Even the cow would admit that it is not as beautiful as the Venus of Milo, especially when chewing the cud.

---

17 Vasilii Rozanov, "Poèziia griadushchei demokratii. Uolt Uitmen," *Novoe vremia*, August 10 [23], 1915. A few days later, Rozanov published another piece on the same topic: Vasilii Rozanov, "Eshchë o demokratii, Uitmene i Chukovskom," *Novoe vremia*, August 13 [26], 1915.
18 Kornei Chukovskii, "Rozanov i Uolt Uitmen," *Petrogradskoe èkho*, March 29, 1918.
19 Uot Uitmèn, *Poèziia griadushchei demokratii* (1923), 56–58.
20 D. H. Lawrence, *Nettles* (1930), in *The Complete Poems* (Hamondsworth: Penguin Books, 1993), 587.

2. A precursor of Futurism

A "propeller" of Western avant-gardes

As a poet of modern and urban life, Whitman was bound to be of interest to Futurist artists. The American's importance was seldom proclaimed, however, since Futurism was more prone to self-advertising than to acknowledging precursors. In Western Europe, there was indeed a place for a proto-Futurist Whitman—but in manifestos or critical writings rather than in poems. Marinetti thus included Whitman in a list of "five or six precursors" whose "illuminating work" was accepted by the Futurists.[21] Whitman could stand by the side of Gustave Kahn and Émile Verhaeren. Papini, who considered Futurism "an Italian blossoming of exotic seeds," stated that "the first great Futurist poets" were Whitman and Verhaeren.[22] Paolo Buzzi, once a Futurist, paid homage to Whitman in 1922 for bringing "the overseas, the other world / barbarism, the great mother of civilization," and "the sound of the broad-axe" in his syntax and rhythm.[23] Basil de Sélincourt too considered him as a precursor of Futurism,[24] while the American Benjamin de Casseres hailed him as one of the "fathers of cubists and futurists."[25]

Even though he was not necessarily labeled as Futurist, Whitman was well represented in the Spanish avant-garde. The first substantial translations of his poetry appeared in the review *Prometeo* (founded by Javier Gómez de la Serna), the aim of which was to reverberate the "magic waves of new life."[26] It featured rather eclectic authors, but it was the main channel for Spanish futurism: Marinetti's manifestos were published there in 1909, at the same time as Whitman's poem "Dioses," translated by Enrique Díez Canedo.[27] In 1912, Julio

---

21 "Nous renions les maîtres les symbolistes, derniers amants de la lune," a text written in French in 1910, delivered at a series of lectures and published in *Le Futurisme* (Paris: Sansot, 1911); reprinted in Giovanni Lista, *Le Futurisme. Textes et manifestes (1909–1944)* (Ceyzérieu: Champ Vallon, 2015), 226. Caterina Bernardini has noticed that, in 1913, Marinetti sent a copy of the anthology *I poeti futuristi* to Luigi Gamberale with a dedication to "the author of a magnificent version of *Foglie d'herba*," in *Transnational Modernity*, 65.
22 Giovanni Papini, *L'esperienza futurista (1913–1914)* (1919; repr. Florence: Vallecchi, 1927), 103; 164.
23 "L'oltremare, l'oltremondo, / la barbarie gran madre delle civiltà," Paolo Buzzi, "Whitman," in *Poema dei quarantanni* (Milan, Edizioni futuriste di "poesia," 1922), 154.
24 Basil de Selincourt, *Walt Whitman: A Critical Study* (London: M. Secker, 1914).
25 Benjamin de Casseres, "The Renaissance of the Irrational," *Camera Work*, June 1913, 23.
26 "Prólogo," *Prometeo*, no. 1 (1908).
27 *Prometeo*, no. 36 (1912), 1–13 for "¡Gloria al mundo!" Enrique Díez Canedo was an important translator, especially from English and French. He wrote reviews of Whitman's translations

Gómez de la Serna (Javier's brother) translated several poems, starting with "Salut au Monde!," on the front page, with the title "¡Gloria al mundo!"[28] He radically reorganized Whitman's poem, regrouping lines into long prose-like stanzas, but only at the beginning of the poem (four pages). Whitman also loomed large in the review *Cervantes*, which moved from *modernismo* to *ultraismo* (although it remained, like *Prometeo*, quite eclectic). In 1919, on the occasion of Whitman's centennial, it published a long essay by Eugenio Montes, who drew parallels with William James's ideas but also evoked the "dynamic superdionysiac fluid" and the song of "the multitudes, drunk with tentacular vitality, new democratic directives, with the progressing war onwards, the skyscraper longing for height, craving for the stars, the locomotive, fast as an electric message."[29] According to Montes, the Italian Futurists received "ardent impulses" from Whitman.

Guillermo de Torre also paid attention to Whitman in his study on European avant-gardes. He presented the American as a beacon for European poetry and as the great conductor of Futurist world traffic: "Standing above the roads of the world, he commands the track switches for the new lyrical trains."[30] His long and experimental poem *Hélices* (1923, Propellers) referenced Whitman in the epigraph of the first part "Versiculario ultraísta" (Ultraist Versicle) and the opening of the section "Canto dinámico": "'Take my hand Walt Whitman'—as said the Atlant, the good old gray poet, in his stirring 'Salut au Monde'. / Oh the exhilarating roundtheworld trajectory [trayectoria perimundial]!"[31]

In Spanish-speaking America, even though he was chiefly read as the poet of continental geography, Whitman was also occasionally hailed as forefather of the avant-gardes. This was especially true of the Mexican Stridentist poet Manuel Maples Arce. His long "Bolshevik" poem *Urbe* paid homage to Whitman (and to J. M. W. Turner):

> Oh ciudad toda tensa
> de cables y de esfuerzos,
> sonora toda
> de motores y de alas.

---

into Catalan by Montoliú, into Spanish by Vasseur and into French by Bazalgette. In 1919, he edited an interesting centennial issue on Whitman in the journal *España*, no. 139 (June 5, 1919), with poems and a critical anthology (Martí, Larbaud).

28 For a thorough examination, see Kelly Scott Franklin, "A Translation of Whitman Discovered in the 1912 Spanish Periodical *Prometeo*," *Walt Whitman Quarterly Review* 35, no. 1 (2017): 115–126.

29 Eugenio Montes, "En el centenario de Walt Whitman," *Cervantes*, May 1919, 72–74.

30 Guillermo de Torre, *Literaturas europeas de vanguardia* (Madrid: R. Caro Raggio, 1925), 341.

31 Guillermo de Torre, *Hélices: Poemas, 1918–1922* (Madrid: Editorial Mundo Latino, 1923), 15.

> Explosión simultánea
> de las nuevas teorías,
> un poco más allá
> En el plano espacial
> de Whitman y de Turner
> y un poco más acá de Maples Arce.
>
> Los pulmones de Rusia
> soplan hacia nosotros
> el viento de la revolución social.
>
> Oh city all tense
> with wires and effort
> all noisy
> with motors and wings.
>
> Explosion of the new
> theories combined,
> a little further
> On the spatial plane
> from Whitman and Turner
> a little closer
> to Maples Arce.
>
> Russia's lungs
> blow the wind
> of the revolution
> in our direction.[32]

If Whitman and Turner are ultimately overtaken and blown away by the winds from Russia that roar in the following stanzas, they stand as benchmarks for Maples Arce. Let us go back and towards the East to examine the origin of those "Russian winds."

---

32 Manuel Maples Arce, *Super-poema bolchevique en 5 cantos* (Mexico City: Editorial Andrés Botas e Hijo, SUCR, 1924), first section, no page number. Whitman was spelled "Witman." Translated by KM Cascia in *Stridentist Poems* (Storrs: World Poetry Books, 2023). The poem was also translated by John Dos Passos in 1929.

Korney Chukovsky's "first real Futurist"

As he was turned into a precursor of the Futurists, Whitman became a poet of "language experiment" rather than a poet of life and sensation. Several essays published by Chukovsky between 1913 and 1914 (and partly recycled in the 1914 edition of Whitman translations) show this newly constructed Futurist Whitman. "Walt Whitman, First Futurist"[33] quotes the poem "Song of the Exposition"—one of the most debated in the early European reception[34]—, which contains an apostrophe to the Muse (epiclesis), summoned to leave the poetically barren lands of Europe and find new topics in America:

> Come Muse migrate from Greece and Ionia,
> Cross out please those immensely overpaid accounts,
> That matter of Troy and Achilles' wrath, and Aeneas', Odysseus' wanderings,
> Placard "Removed" and "To Let" on the rocks of your snowy Parnassus,
> Repeat at Jerusalem, place the notice high on Jaffa's gate and on Mount Moriah,
> The same on the walls of your German, French and Spanish castles, and Italian collections,
> For know a better, fresher, busier sphere, a wide, untried domain awaits, demands you.
> ....
> I say I see, my friends, if you do not, the illustrious emigré,
> (having it is true in her day, although the same, changed, journey'd considerable,)
> Making directly for this rendezvous, vigorously clearing a path for herself, striding through the confusion,
> By thud of machinery and shrill steam-whistle undismay'd,
> Bluff'd not a bit by drain-pipe, gasometers, artificial fertilizers,
> Smiling and pleas'd with palpable intent to stay,
> She's here, install'd amid the kitchen ware! (LG 167)

---

33 Chukovskii, "Pervyi futurist."
34 In 1908 Soffici wrote a "Reply to Walt Whitman regarding his Song of the Exposition." He addressed his brother Whitman, "Walt fratello," to inform him that the Muse who had crossed the Atlantic had now come back to her native lands, where old themes and old poets still appealed to her. Ardengo Soffici, "Risposta a Walt Whitman per il suo canto dell'esposizione," in *Il Commento* (1908), in *Opere*, vol. 4 (Florence: Vallenchi, 1961), 701.

This poem can be related to the tradition of the mock-epic, but should also be taken seriously: the insistence on the very prosaic qualities of the new themes is not a burlesque inflexion, but rather a democratic mark of the new American epic. Chukovsky highlighted this poem in his first editions: it opened the 1907 and 1914 collections. He commented on it using language that could have come straight from a Futurist manifesto: "Old poetry lies in a coffin [grob]." Chukovsky connected Whitman's call to place a sign saying "Remove" on the Parnassus with the Futurists' injunction to throw Pushkin overboard the ship of modernity. Locomotives and streets in Chicago sounded differently from meadows in Arcadia, so that Whitman had to prompt a brazen rebellion (*bunt*) against all past canons of beauty. In his harsh review of Chukovsky's translation, Rozanov also focused on "Song of the Exposition" and its request to the Muse. He ironically wondered why Whitman did not add a sign reading "We don't need anything" on Italian museums and Spanish or German castles. Such declarations were worthy of Kuzma Prutkov (Aleksey Tolstoy's character, famous for his absurd aphorisms), he stated. Whitman's poem could only be compared with *Èneida naiznanku* (Inside out Aeneid)[35] and Chukovsky was a fool to take it seriously.

Chukovsky took it seriously indeed. In "Poetry of the future," he insisted again that Whitman was the first "real futurist."[36] In "Ego-futurists and Cubo-futurists,"[37] he commented extensively (and critically) on the primitivist tidal wave that was engulfing Russia and the world. In his view, a certain kind of primitivism was not compatible with Futurism. Chukovsky mocked esthete poets, such as Nikolay Gumilev, who had suddenly declared themselves Adamists, akin to wild animals, and founded a sect of primitive people (*pervobytnye*). Chukovsky also mentioned *The Shaman and Venus* by Khlebnikov, but his main target was Igor Severyanin, who claimed that his soul was "drawn toward the Primitive," while writing about a viscountess drinking wine in a yurt. "Champagne in the tundra" could be the motto of these would-be primitives, Chukovsky sneered. Severyanin later wrote a homage to Whitman, a rhyming sonnet, which exemplified such contradictions: its refined and non-Whitmanian forms conflict with a violent vision of heaps of bodies, which might refer to Whitman's civil war poems, whilst being also reminiscent of the pyramids

---

35 This is probably *Virgilieva Èneida, vyvorochennaia naiznanku*, a burlesque poem by Nicolay Osipov (first volume 1791); there is also a nineteenth-century Belarusian poem (*Èneida navyvarat*), composed by Vikenti Rovinski.
36 Kornei Chukovskii, "Poèziia budushchego."
37 Kornei Chukovskii, "Ego-futuristy i Kubo-futuristy," *Al'manakh izdatel'stva "Shipovnik,"* vol. 22 (Saint Petersburg: Shipovnik, 1914), 95–125; republished under the title "Futuristy," in Kornei Chukovskii, *Litsa i maski* (Saint Petersburg: Shipovnik, 1914).

of bodies after Genghis Khan's massacres.[38] The "primitive" Whitman thus appears to be contained within the sonnet as in a "candy box," an expression that Chukovsky liked to use about Severyanin. Chukovsky contrasted this bogus primitivism with the "real" one, which involved rebellion, spontaneity, and whose two real agents were Mayakovsky and . . . Whitman, the "great biblical bard," "cyclopean prime prophet" and "first futurist poet," "first sign of the future." Another Whitmanian "Ego-futurist," whom Chukovsky spared more than Severyanin, was Ivan Lukash (better known then as Ivan Oredezh). His first collection of poetry, *Tsvety iadovitye* (Poisonous flowers), contains several pieces with hallmark Whitmanian features. The poem "Ia slavliu" (I adore) enumerates the most diverse things, linked with anaphors. In "Clamor Harmoniae," the poet exclaims: "All is mine and there is nothing but me. I created the universes and I will create myriads of universes because they are in me."[39] Chukovsky also saw resemblances between Whitman and Sergey Neldikhen, who indeed, mentioned Whitman as a possible model for Russian poetry.[40]

3. Whitman and (post-) Russian Futurist poetry

Whitman was occasionally a reference in avant-garde Russian visual arts: Mikhail Larionov quoted the short poem "Beginners" as an epigraph in his manifesto "Rayonnist painting."[41] But it was, quite predictably, among poets that Whitman's presence was most conspicuous, as Korney Chukovsky consistently emphasized.[42] Chukovsky tended to aggregate both Khlebnikov and

---

38 Igor' Severianin, "Uitmen" (1926), in *Medal'ony* (Belgrade: Izd. Avtora, 1934). As the title indicates, the whole collection consists of "medallions," namely sonnets paying homage to writers. There is a tradition of writing sonnets for Whitman, from Rubén Darío's poem "Walt Whitman," part of a series in fact entitled "Medallones" (in *Azul*, 1889) to Jaroslav Vrchlický's "Walt Whitman" (in *Nové sonety samotáře*, 1891) and Jorge Luis Borges's moving "Camden, 1892" (in *El otro, el mismo*, 1964). Both Vrchlický and Borges translated Whitman (Vrchlický translated into Czech a selection of *Leaves of Grass* as early as 1906).
39 "Все мое и нет ничего кроме меня. Я создал вселенныя и я создам мириады вселенных ибо они во мне."—Ivan Lukash, *Tsvety iadovitye* [1910] (n.p.: Salamandra PVV, 2018), 24.
40 Sergei Nel'dikhen, "Puti russkoi poèzii" (1921) in *Organnoe Mnogogolos'e* (Moscow: Ogi, 2013), 321. Nel'dikhen advocated "literary synthetism" (the convergence of poetry and prose).
41 Mikhail Larionov, "Luchistaia zhivopis'," in *Oslinyi khvost' i michen'* (Moscow: Izd. Ts. A. Miunster, 1913), 85.
42 The first sentence of the essay "Mayakovsky and Whitman" is peremptory: "In the history of Russian Symbolism, the poetry of Walt Whitman played a very insignificant role." Interestingly, whereas Verhaeren and Whitman were constantly associated in the 1910s and 1920s (by Lunacharsky or Chukovsky himself), in this late essay, Chukovsky saw in Verhaeren a major source of inspiration for the Symbolists, and in Whitman one for the Futurists.

Mayakovsky as heirs of Whitman, but a closer examination reveals diverging trends: Khlebnikov's relation with Whitman grew from suspicion to strong interest, while Mayakovsky took the opposite path, going from fascination to a form of antagonism. Whitman was also claimed by Ukrainian Futurist poets, in contradistinction to their Russian counterparts.

Velimir Khlebnikov: from circumspection to kinship

Khlebnikov's relation with Whitman has been much less studied than Mayakovsky's and usually merely relays Chukovsky's interpretation of "Zverenie" (The Zoo), a 1910 poem, as echoing section 33 of "Song of Myself," with its long anaphoric enumeration. Chukovsky convincingly drew the two poems together in his 1914 preface to Whitman. Much later, in 1941, he reiterated this analysis and added that, according to D. Kozlov, Khlebnikov highly enjoyed readings of Whitman in English, even though he did not understand them very well.[43] However, Chukovsky did not mention that Kozlov had met Khlebnikov in Baku, in 1921, some ten years after "The Zoo" was written. In fact, I would argue that Khlebnikov was really drawn toward Whitman in the last phase of his life and art. Indeed, in 1913, when Khlebnikov mentioned Whitman in his prose, he lumped him together with Chukovsky in a hostile apostrophe:

> You waves of filth and vice, you storms of spiritual abomination! You Chukovskys, Yablonovskys! Know that we steer by the stars, we have a firm hand on the helm, and our vessel does not fear
> The word pirate Chukovsky, waving Whitman's battle-ax, has leapt onto our docks during the storm, trying to seize the helm and capture the prizes of our struggle.
> But can't you see his corpse already floating on the waves?[44]

Khlebnikov blames Chukovsky's attempt to hijack the Futurists' struggles by simply brandishing Whitman, more exactly his "battle-ax." Such an effort is condemned with the violence of Futurist manifestos: Chukovsky's corpse lies on the waves (possibly with the corpses of all the writers whom Mayakovsky and the Burliuk brothers threw overboard in a "A Slap to the Public"). Chukovsky reappears, however, not as a "word pirate" anymore, but as a "patrolman" trying to bring the Futurist battle to a halt:

---

43 Kornei Chukovskii, "Maiakovskii i Uitman," *Leningrad*, 1941 (no. 2), 18–19.
44 Velimir Khlebnikov, *Collected Works*, vol 1, ed. Charlotte Douglas and trans. Paul Schmidt (Cambridge, MA: Harvard University Press, 1987), 259.

> Patrolman Chukovsky yesterday proposed that we take a rest,
> curl up for a nap in a jail cell with Whitman and some *-cracy*
> or other. But Przewalski's proud horses snorted disdainfully
> and refused. The Scythian bridle—the one you see on the
> Chertomlyk vase—remained hanging in the air. (259)

The Scythian referent is striking: the wild horses, characteristic of a native primitivism, refuse the tamed American variant offered by Chukovsky.

Only later did Khlebnikov return to Whitman, with a much more positive appreciation. In 1919, he mentioned him in "Wheel of Births," referring to Bucke's *Cosmic Consciousness* (see p. 89–90), in which an equivalence between Jesus and Whitman was first established. Khlebnikov added to Bucke's correspondences his own technological vision: "So Whitman is identical with Jesus, spattered by sparks from the factory work bench rather than by seaspray and the dust of the road. Industrial workers in grimy clothes have replaced gray-haired fishermen." (411) In 1921, while in the Caucasus, Khlebnikov seems to have read Whitman more than ever. At that time, he was close to A. Borodin, who published in Baku a translation of "Memories of President Lincoln."[45] An interesting testimony of Khlebnikov's renewed interest for Whitman is provided by Olga Samorodova, who stayed with him in Zheleznovodsk:[46] Khlebnikov liked that Chukovsky had called him "the Russian Whitman" and took pride in showing resemblances between some of Whitman's lines and his own. When Khlebnikov left Zheleznovodsk for good, the only book that he carried with him was Whitman. Indeed, the short poem quoted above, with the "Neanderthal skull," dates from 1921.

Vladimir Mayakovsky: from anxiety of influence to anxiety of impotence

Mayakovsky's relation to Whitman has received much more emphasis. In December 1919, Sergey Yesenin performed satirical ditties (chastushki) at the Café of the Union of Russian Writers, aimed at various poets. Mayakovsky was presented as a shameless imitator of Whitman:

> Ах, сыпь, ах, жарь,
> Маяковский – бездарь.

---

45 A. Borodin, *Uot Uitmèn* (Baku: Rubiny, 1922).
46 Olga Samorodova, "Poèt na Kavkaze," *Zvezda*, 1972 (no. 6); written in 1928.

> Рожа краской питана,
> Обокрал Уитмана.⁴⁷
>
> Ah, go get him, ah, harder,
> Mayakovsky is a hack.
> He is red in the face,
> He robbed Whitman.

The question is obviously much more complex than Yesenin's sally allowed for and deserves closer scrutiny.⁴⁸ In his first essays on the topic, Chukovsky, much as he did for Khlebnikov, displayed the similarities between Whitman and Mayakovsky's poetries and established a lineage with futurism. His later analyses were more subtle. In his memoirs, as well as the 1941 essay, he confirmed that, contrary to what his contemporaries thought, Mayakovsky was not a poet without roots (*bezrodnyi*) and that he had powerful ancestors (*predki*), Whitman among them. Still, Mayakovsky was no imitator, and saw Whitman not as a teacher but as an older brother and a comrade (*soratnik*).⁴⁹ When Chukovsky and Mayakovsky met for the first time in 1913, the American poet was one of the first topics they discussed: Mayakovsky criticized Chukovsky's translations for belonging in a "candy box" (*bonbon'erochno*), just like Balmont's. Chukovsky replied that he had drastically changed his method since his first attempts, especially regarding versification, and read some of his as yet unpublished new translations. Mayakovsky remained skeptical: even the new translations were too soft, full of "molasses" (*potoka*). He suggested that "flesh" should have been translated as *miaso* (meat). In other words, he suggested that Whitman should have been translated into his own Mayakovskyan idiom ("meat" is indeed a characteristic word of his poetry).⁵⁰ In a later encounter in the winter of 1914, Mayakovsky asked only for specific biographical information: How did Whitman perform his poetry? How did he read on stage? Was he booed? Did he wear extravagant costumes? Did he subvert Shakespeare and Byron? In July 1915, while Chukovsky hosted Mayakovsky and Nikolay Kulbin in Kuokkala, Whitman was again a recurring topic. By then, Mayakovsky was not only critical of Chukovsky's translations but of Whitman himself: while still appreciating

---

47 The ditty was written and published a little bit earlier, in the paper *Golos trudovogo krest'ianstva*, no. 127 (May 19, 1918).
48 I am much indebted to Clare Cavanagh's essay, "Whitman, Mayakovsky, and the Body Politic," in *Rereading Russian Poetry* (New Haven: Yale University Press, 1999), 202–222.
49 Chukovskii, "Maiakovskii i Uitman."
50 The comment was made by Clare Cavanagh; see her *Rereading Russian Poetry*, 211–212.

some aspects his poetry, he found it "sluggish" on the whole. He, Mayakovsky, would have written on similar themes with more energy.

One of the most interesting points in Chukovsky's account of these discussions is a list of lines from Whitman that Mayakovsky particularly enjoyed and was able to recite by heart. As Chukovsky mischievously observed, Mayakovsky was mainly interested in what he felt he could have written (only better!). The line "The scent of these arm-pits is aroma finer than prayer" resonates with Mayakovsky's epiphany about the body—one can think of a line from *A Cloud in Trousers*, stating that "veins and muscles are more faithful than prayers" (Zhily i muskuly—molitv vernei).[51] The emphasis on the body—fleshy or meaty—is probably the central primitivist element in both poets, who valued howling as a form of poetic expression and the tongue as its organ. The word "tongue" appears regularly in "Song of Myself," from the beginning of the poem onwards: "My tongue, every atom of my blood, form'd from this soil, this air." (LG 26) In Russian, *iazyk* designates, as in English, both language and the organ, and it is also central to Mayakovsky's poetry—for example, in this passage from *Man* (*Chelovek*) in 1918:

Покоится в нем у меня
Прекрасный
красный язык.
«О-го-го» могу –
зальется высоко, высоко.
«О-ГО-ГО» могу –
и – охоты поэта сокол –
голос
мягко сойдет на низы.[52]

In me lies a
beautiful
red tongue.
"Oh-oh-oh" I can—
it will go high, high.
"Oh-oh-oh" I can—
and—a chasing poet hawk
my voice
will softly go down.

---

51 Vladimir Maiakovskii, *Oblako v shtanakh* in *Polnoe sobranie sochinenii*, 13 vols. (Moscow: Khudozhestvennaia literatura, 1955–1961), 1:184.
52 Maiakovskii, *Chelovek*, in *Polnoe sobranie sochinenii*, 1:248.

Not only does the poet praise his own tongue, but he also compares his voice, like Whitman, to that of a hawk. The difference is that Mayakovsky's hawk-like voice descends from high-pitched notes, while Whitman projects his "barbaric yawp" over the "roofs of the world."

Another (half) between other and line that Mayakovsky knew by heart and liked to quote, also from "Song of Myself," was: "[I] am not contained between my hat and boots." (LG 31) Indeed, Whitman and Mayakovsky implemented a complete revision of the poetic "I," which had strong political implications. They both emphasized the "I" and sought to extend its limits, to have it *incarnate* the whole of humanity: the self, as a plastic entity, was the locus of democracy for Whitman and of the revolution for Mayakovsky. Chukovsky pointed to a passage in *Man* which was indeed utterly Whitmanian, including in its use of the word "miracle" (chudo):

> Как же
> себя мне не петь,
> если весь я –
> сплошная невидаль,
> если каждое движение мое –
> огромное,
> необъяснимое чудо. (1:247)

> How
> could I not sing myself,
> when all of me is
> a continuous wonder,
> when each of my moves
> is a huge
> unfathomable miracle.

One could add to Chukovsky's selection another passage, from the tragedy *Vladimir Mayakovsky*, which articulates the connection between the self and the mass, between the "I" and the "we":

> я вам открою
> словами
> простыми, как мычанье,
> наши новые души,

гудящие,
как фонарные дуги.⁵³

I open for you
   with words
     as simple as moos,
   our new souls,
   humming,
     like curved lamps.

Ia vam (literally: I to you) rather than *ia sam* (I myself, a recurring phrase in Mayakovsky). The very sounds carry the shift from the singular to the plural: in *slovami* (with words), one can hear *vam* (to you) and the ending *mi* later resonates with a phonetic variation *my* (we). This modulation of sounds (from a softened consonant to a hard one) prepares the semantic shift to the plural with the mention of "our new souls" (*nashi novye dushi*). These lines combine primitivist motifs (simplicity, the animal cry) and infuse them with political meaning.

The extension of the self involves the capacity to incarnate plurality but also to stretch to cosmic dimensions. A third quote that Mayakovsky appreciated was "Dazzling and tremendous how quick the sun-rise would kill me / If I could not now and always send sun-rise out of me." Chukovsky's translation made the identification with the sun even more explicit: "If I didn't have such a sun in myself." Mayakovsky went further in his poem "An Extraordinary Adventure Which Befell Vladimir Mayakovsky in a Summer Cottage," when he claimed to be wearing the sun as a monocle. Though not mentioned by Chukovsky as one of Mayakovsky's favorites, other lines from section 33 of "Song of Myself" resonate strongly with Mayakovsky, such as: "My ties and ballasts leave me, my elbows rest in sea-gaps, / I skirt sierras, my palms cover continents, / I am afoot with my vision." (LG 53) Like Whitman who becomes a meteor, Mayakovsky merges with the sky: "I stretch into a rainbow, then undulate into a comet's tail" (*To perekinus' radugoi, / to khvost zav'iu kometoiu*).⁵⁴ In *The Fifth International*, the survey of the world, including "the marvels of America," turns into an ascent to "celestial things."

---

53 Maiakovskii, *Vladimir Maiakovskii*, in *Polnoe sobranie sochinenii*, 1:154.
54 Maiakovskii, *Chelovek*, in *ibid.*, 265.

However, this vision of a triumphant and solar subject needs to be nuanced, for both poets. From the very first edition of *Leaves of Grass*, the poetic "I" experiences moments of collapse and fragmentation. His plasticity is at times dysphoric, engendering a sense of dissolution or of being overwhelmed. The awareness of how dangerous it is to stretch the "I" indefinitely might be what Whitman and Mayakovsky shared most intimately. In this light, one can better appreciate the odd passage where Whitman appears in the long poem *150. 000. 000*, at the "Cheaple Strong Hotel" in Chicago. As it turns out, in this proclaimed land of democracy, all citizens, including Whitman, are subjected to President Woodrow Wilson:

> Все ему
>   американцы отданы,
> и они
>   гордо говорят:
>   Я –
>   американский подданный.
> Я –
>   свободный
>   американский гражданин.
> Под ним склоненные
>   стоят
>   его услужающих сонмы.
> Вся зала полна
>   Линкольнами всякими.
>   Уитмэнами,
>   Эдисонами.
> . . . .
> В тесном смокинге стоит Уитмэн,
> качалкой раскачивать в невиданном ритме.[55]

> All Americans
>   are subjected to him
> and they
>   say proudly:
>   I am
>   an American subject.
> I am

---

[55] Maiakovskii, *150. 000. 000*, in *Polnoe sobranie sochinenii*, 2:135.

                         a free
                                    American citizen.
     Under him stand
                         the bent crowds
                                    that serve him.
     The whole room is full
                         Of all sorts of Lincolns.
                                    Of Whitmans
                                               of Edisons.
     ....
     In a tight tuxedo stands Whitman,
     Rocking to an unprecedented rhythm.

The Americans proclaim their freedom, their "I" (*ia*, which constitutes a line of its own). But they appear to be subjects in the etymological sense of the word: they are subjugated. The Russian term *podannyi* is polysemic: it refers to citizenship, but in a more archaic sense it means subjected to (a meaning reinforced by the echo with *otdanny*). Whoever proclaims to be an American citizen is in truth the subject of the president. Similarly, Whitman, who appeared on the famous 1855 daguerreotype as a free man, wearing the casual clothes of a worker, is now squeezed into a ridiculous tuxedo. The discrepancy between illusion of freedom and actual servitude, between the proclamation of a powerful poetic "I" and the danger of being turned into a political puppet, was a real preoccupation for Mayakovsky. In 1921, he was already writing a more official poetry, and three years later, in 1924, he would write a funeral homage for Lenin. The vision of a grotesque Whitman at a presidential party can be read as the expression of such a fear, rather than as the hostile result of an anxiety of influence.

Post-imperial Whitman (the Baltic states and Ukraine)

Avant-garde movements developed in different regions of the Russian Empire, and therefore in languages other than Russian, especially at a time when local cultures and languages benefited from various degrees of support after a period of intense Russification ended in 1905; when some countries gained their independence, like the Baltic states in 1918; or when a policy of *korenizatsiia* (indigenization) was advocated by the Soviet power in the 1920s. The most salient achievements, as far as Whitman's reception is concerned, were the Latvian and Estonian translations of selected poems and multiple allusions in Ukrainian avant-garde poetry. This was of course a time of when numerous borders were radically redrawn in Europe: the Estonian translation was published after independence from Russia in 1919. But while the colonial and postcolonial stakes are not to be overlooked, all the Eastern avant-gardes were connected throughout the period and form a complex, if not homogeneous, network.

The Baltic Whitman: the national and the global

The first Baltic language into which Whitman was translated was Latvian. In 1908, the very young poet Kārlis Jēkabsons published a selection, which was followed by another in 1911;[56] in 1918, "Salut au Monde!" was published in the first issue of the Latvian journal *Dzintars* (Amber), translated by Rūdolfs Egle, who later became a prolific translator. The name of the journal indicates its politics (amber is a typical Latvian product and a national symbol). Again, the cosmopolitan "Salut au Monde!" combines with national claims: through translation, Latvia establishes its place in world literature. As was the case with the Yiddish translation in 1912, different elements combine visually: Latvian folk patterns, Fraktur characters still in use in Latvia, and the modern font of the title and refrain "Salut au Monde!"

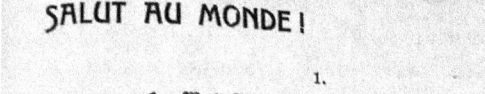

FIGURE 2.1. Cover of *Dzintars*, no. 1, 1918. National Library of Latvia.

FIGURE 2.2. Walt Whitman, "Salut au Monde!," *Dzintars*, no. 1, 1918, 35. National Library of Latvia.

Whitman was then translated into Estonian in 1920, by the writer Johannes Semper. Semper was a member of Siriu, a literary group whose members were often drawn toward Futurism. Semper published an anthology entitled *Walt Whitman*, which contained, once again, "Salut au Monde!," in an abbreviated version. He selected sections 5 and 9, which list Eastern and Northern European toponyms (the Volga, the Dnieper rivers, Moscow, Cracow, Warsaw, Christiania [Oslo] and Stockholm). The choice bears witness to the entanglement of

---

56 Volts Vitmens, *Zāļu stiebri* (Spears of Grass), trans. Robert Skargas, pseud. of Kārlis Jēkabsons (Riga: Imantas apgāds, 1908), 38 pages; *Brīvā teka* (Free run), anonymous trans. (Riga: ģeralkomisija pee A. Golta, 1911), 32 pages.

localism and globalism common to both the reception of "Salut au Monde!" and the Baltic avant-gardes. The cover was illustrated by Ado Vabbe, an important artist, known for bringing abstraction to Estonian painting.

FIGURE 2.3. Cover of Johannes Semper, *Walt Whitman*, Talinn: Varrak, 1920. Illustration Ado Vabbe. © Adagp, Paris [2023]. Author's collection.

Whitman and Ukrainian Panfuturism: an American Kobzar

The case of Ukraine, which did not become an independent state, was different. Whitman was translated into Ukrainian later, and he was known mostly through Russian translations.[57] Still, he was also claimed as a precursor by Ukrainian Futurism. While Mayakovsky cast Pushkin into the sea, Ukrainian Futurists often included Taras Shevchenko (the "Kobzar," the bard, the national poet) in their pantheon. In his 1921 collection *V kosmichnomu orkestri* (In the

---

57 See Chapter 5: a few translations of poems appeared in a journal in 1924, and then in Ivan Kulyk's anthology of American poetry in 1928, but Whitman was not primarily known via Ukrainian translations. In the preface to his anthology, Kulyk noticed Whitman's popularity and poetic influence in Ukraine thanks to Chukovsky's translations.

cosmic orchestra), Pavlo Tychyna associated the Ukrainian bard with Whitman and Verhaeren:

Людськість промовляє
трьома розтрубами фанфар:
Шевченко – Уїтмен – Верхарн.
Мов кабелі од нації до нації,
Потужно революції диктують на землі:
Шевченко – Уїтмен – Верхарн.⁵⁸

Humanity speaks
three fanfare bells:
Shevchenko—Whitman—Verhaeren.
Like cables from nation to nation,
They strongly dictate revolutions on earth:
Shevchenko—Whitman—Verhaeren.

The addition of Shevchenko to the Whitman/Verhaeren dyad gives it a distinct national stance.

Around 1921 or 1922, in Uman, an avant-garde group was formed around Andrii Chuzhyi.⁵⁹ They called themselves the "Walt Whitman Boundless" (Bezmezhnyky). Chuzhyi was particularly enthusiastic about the American poet. Born in 1897, he came from a working-class family and he worked, among many trades, at the "United National library," which held a copy of Whitman.⁶⁰ He wrote poetry in Ukrainian and Russian and was close to Yiddish poets (in particular Moyshe Khashchevatski and Leib Kvitko). Together with Ezra Fininberg, they created the literary journal *Ekzekutsiia* (Execution), with poems in Ukrainian, Russian and Yiddish. The journal was handwritten and its pages had the shape of butterfly wings.⁶¹ Whitman's name features on the first page,

---

58 Pavlo Tychyna, *V kosmichnomu orkestri* (1921, repr. Lviv: Nova kultura, 1923), 6. The first three lines (which open a section of the poem) are repeated on the next page, to close the section.
59 Chuzhyi's real name was Andrii Storozhuk. "Chuzhyi" means "strange" or "stranger."
60 In a letter to Miron Petrovsky, Chuzhyi later recalled how Leib Kvitko visited him at the library and taught him some Yiddish and Hebrew. Kvitko would "caress" the books—among them, Shevtchenko, Lesya Ukrainka, Dante and Whitman. In Iryna Berliand, ed., *Ekzekutsiia: Zbirnyk umans'kykh bezmezhnykiv* (Kyiv: Dukh i Litera, 2023), 105.
61 In 2022, a copy kept in the Fininberg archive in Israel was turned into the book mentioned above by the Ukrainian publisher Dukh i Litera.

and even in the first line of the "editor's note" (in Russian, but the word "bez-mezhnyk" is Ukrainian):

> Именем мойсея и христа, будды и сократа, уитмана и конфуция.
> Мы, великие безмежники, открываем экзекуцию.
> Ляг!⁶²

> In the name of Moses and Christ, Buddha and Socrates, Whitman and Confucius,
> We, the great boundless, start the execution,
> Lie down!

The association of Whitman with Christ, Buddha and Confucius was quite common in the European and Russian receptions (see Chapter 3). In this case, it combines with futuristic explosions.

In a poem, Andrii Chuzhyi stages his first encounter with Mykhail Semenko and Les Kurbas (major Futurist poets) in Sofiyivska Park (a scenic landscape park which is one of Uman's attractions). They could feel "the warm hands" of Shevchenko, Whitman, Blok and Tychyna. Chuzhyi himself claims to write under the combined influence of "Taras [Shevchenko], and Lesya [Ukrainka], Voloshin and Semenko, Whitman and Blok."⁶³ One of the poems that best shows this influence is "I am a shepherd" (1923), in which the poet walks barefoot on the grass:

> я ходжу ногами босими,
> вмиваюсь росами.
> Під моїми ногами
> не стогне трава,
> не плачуть квіти,
> як не плачуть вони
> від бджіл і метеликів,
> як не плачуть діти і квіти,
> коли їх топчуть
> своїми обережними поцілунками-позірами
> матері й зорі.⁶⁴

---

62 Ibid., 38.
63 Andrii Chuzhyi, "Davno nema ni Lesia, ni Mykhailia . . . ," in *Poeziï: Virshi ta poemy* (Kyiv: Radians'kyi pys'mennyk, Kyiv, 1980), 70.
64 "Ia – pastushok," in ibid., 10.

> I walk barefoot,
> washing my face with dew.
> Under my feet
> the grass does not wail,
> the flowers do not cry
> nor do they cry
> from the bees and butterflies,
> nor do children and flowers cry,
> when they are crushed by
> the careful kisses and stares
> of their mothers and the stars.

Even though Chuzhyi was part of a Futurist group and was committed to communism, his poetry was less experimental and political than most of his fellows'. He found in Whitman a model of cosmic poetry and of extension of the self. He later wrote that while he was a poet "forgotten by God," some called him a "Whitman from Uman" (Umans'kyi Uïtmen).[65]

In 1922, Mykhail Semenko himself mentioned Whitman in several of his works. Semenko was a main actor in dissident Ukrainian Futurist movements, especially Panfuturism (also known as Quero-Futurism, it united the Aspanfut, the Komunkult and other grouplets). His manifesto poem "Promova" (Speech) begins by establishing a Whitmanian filiation:

> Коли Уот Уїтмен вмер
> (1892)
> народивсь
> я[66]

> When Walt Whitman died
> (1892)
> I
> was born.

In "System," Semenko brings Shevchenko and Whitman (and himself) together with several Ukrainian Futurists (Tychyna, Oleksa Slisarenko), and other

---

65 Andrii Chuzhyi, *Tvory*, ed. V. T. Polishchuk (Cherkasy: Siiach, 1997), 41.
66 Mykhail' Semenko, *Kobzar'* (Kyiv: Gol'fstrom, 1924), 617. This volume collects all the works published between 1920 and 1922.

Modernists and Futurists (Marinetti, for example). While Moscow appears (though in smaller type than Paris and New York), Mayakovsky is carefully avoided.

FIGURE 2.4. Mykhail' Semenko, "Sistema," *Kobzar'* (Kyiv: Golfstrom, 1924), 615.

Oleksa Slisarenko, at first associated with the Symbolists, then joined Panfuturist organizations. The poem "Walt Whitman" belongs to his first Futurist collection *Poèmy* in 1923 and can read as a correction of Mayakovsky's Whitman. The opening line, "Ia cholovik" (I am a man), seems to come straight from Mayakovsky's *Chelovek*; and the following ones emphasize Whitman's integrating powers, the ages "rustling their wings" above him:

> Я чоловік.
> Такий звичайний, що аж смішно –
> Ріка кришталева у смердючих берегах,
> Віки
> Шелестять надо мною крилами.
> Тремтіння і жах
> Перетоплюю на сміливість у своїх гамарнях,
> Слухаю шуми вітру, машин і дихання коханої женщини;
> Бачу хмари, землю, димарі, звірів і людей;
> Мацаю речі, нюхаю запахи:
> Я такий звичайний, що аж смішно.
> І день мій розцвітає, як лотос.

> I'm a man
> So simple it's funny—
> The river flows crystal-clear between reeking banks.
> The ages
> Rustle their wings above me.
> I melt down
> Shivering and horror into courage in my forges,
> I listen to the noise of the wind and cars, and
> The breathing of a loving woman,
> I see clouds, the land, chimneys, animals and people;
> I touch things; I inhale smells.
> I am so simple it's funny—
> And my day blossoms like a lotus.[67]

---

67 First published in the Kharkiv journal *Chervonyi shliakh*, 1923 (no. 4–5), 5. Translated in Kin, *New York Elegies: Ukrainian Poems on the City*, 12–13. The poem was republished in 1955, in New York, in *Obirvani Struny* (Broken Strings), an anthology of Ukrainian poets murdered during the Soviet Terror, and again in the anthology *Rozstriliane vidrodzhennia* (The Executed renaissance), published in Paris in 1959.

Whitman's days were no lotuses in Mayakovsky and Slisarenko's "simple man" appears as a more pacified version of the American poet.

The rebuttal of academic tradition, the valorization of intuition and of corporeal experience had explicit and revolutionary implications in Futurist poetry. In Europe, Whitman's political reception was firmly grounded in that primitivist and Futurist field of the early twentieth century.

Chapter 3

Whitman the prophet (1880s–1930s)

In the preface to *Leaves of Grass*, Whitman largely appealed to a Romantic conception of the poet-magus, making use of religious terms and redefining them: poets were guides who showed people the way, therefore replacing priests: "There will soon be no more priests. Their work is done. They may wait awhile.... perhaps a generation or two ... dropping off by degrees. A superior breed shall take their place ... the gangs of kosmos and prophets en masse shall take their place." (634) The "prophets en masse" would be powerful but transient and would eventually fade away: "A new order shall arise and they shall be the priests of man, and every man shall be his own priest." Most enthusiastic receptions of Whitman in the late nineteenth century seized upon this thinking and made it their touchstone. The semantic elasticity of the idea of the prophet, as outlined by Whitman, matched the complex cultural and religious changes of the times. The word "prophet" itself underwent significant fluctuations and ran the whole gamut from sacred to secular.[1]

---

1 On the political secularization of religious discourse, see the classic works of Walter Benjamin, Gershom Scholem (who was also interested in Whitman, see Allen and Folsom, *Walt Whitman and the World*, 391–392), Ernst Bloch and Michael Löwy; more specifically on poetry, see Paul Bénichou.

When it comes to Whitman the prophet, the confusion between the poem and the poet is at its greatest. Whitman's poems themselves can provide mystic or cosmic experiences and be read as new Gospels. But there was also a physical cult around Whitman—as when his English worshippers drank from the "love cup" that had belonged to him, or when his admirers had locks of his hair enshrined in jewelry like relics.[2] Quite often, after Whitman's death, the inspiration was a photograph of the poet, usually one of the "good old gray," his beard a metonymy of his prophetic stature. Many examples can be found in the pages of the *Conservator* and in tribute volumes, such as *In Re Walt Whitman* (1893) and *Walt Whitman, Yesterday and Today* (1916). More generally, many poems addressed to Whitman in fixed forms can be read as analogous to icons. I will look at the intricate and entangled meanings of Whitman "the prophet," and at the different media, textual and visual, through which his legend was constructed and conveyed. Whitman sometimes appeared at odds with established creeds, especially when he was heralded as the liberator of the body and its appetites. He could be associated with mystical and individual forms of religious experience, as well as considered as a guide and a seer for new churches and new communal ideals.

1. The prophet of the body

Whitman was considered as the poet of the body by readers with different agendas. As I proposed in Chapter 1, this was part of the construct of Whitman as a *primitive* poet. In Western Europe, however, especially in Britain, the emphasis on the liberation of the body often resulted in homoerotic readings: Whitman was a "Uranian," a Greek and virile homosexual, quite different from other "effeminate" types. But the promotion of the body as a sacred entity was also of interest to religious philosophies and spiritual discourses aiming at redefining the relations between the body and the soul, especially in Russia.

"I believe in the flesh and the appetites": the anti-Victorian Whitman

The British reception particularly highlighted Whitman's glorification of bodily appetites. In the context of a strict Victorian society, Whitman announced

---

2   See Michael Robertson, *Worshipping Walt: The Whitman Disciples* (Princeton: Princeton University Press, 2008); for photographs of the enshrined "relics," see Susan Jaffe Tane and Karen Karbiener, *Poet of the Body: New York's Walt Whitman* (New York: Grolier Club, 2019).

the liberation of stifled, especially homoerotic, desires. For John Addington Symonds, Whitman was the archetype of the Uranian and "Calamus" was "the gospel of comradeship"—though it was a pity that Whitman himself failed to perceive the "inevitable points of contact between sexual inversion and his doctrine of comradeship."[3] Edward Carpenter developed his views on the relation of soul and body in *Pagan and Christian Creed: their Origin and their Meaning* and in *Towards Democracy*. The poem "The Ocean of Sex" is a good example of Whitmanian rewriting:

> To hold in continence the great sea, the great ocean of Sex, within one,
> With flux and reflux pressing on the bounds of the body, the beloved genitals,
> Vibrating, swaying emotional to the star-glint of the eyes of all human beings,
> Reflecting Heaven and all Creatures,
> How wonderful![4]

Henry Bryan Binns, who was close to Carpenter, also saw in Whitman the great herald of the emancipated body, of "Man the Divine Being."[5] Carpenter's writings reached Khalil Gibran, the Lebanese writer who had emigrated to the United States.[6] His famous essay "The Prophet" (1923), which asserted the central role of poetry in religious prophecy, often had Whitmanian overtones.

Back in Britain in the early 1920s, D. H. Lawrence's praise was certainly more ambiguous, but partly based on similar grounds. Lawrence's encounter with Whitman was crucial, leading to a conflicting relation of mixed admiration and virulent criticism—the kind of relationship that was to interest Harold Bloom in his study on the "anatomy of influence."[7] Lawrence's essay on Whitman in *Studies in Classical American Literature* was heavily edited throughout its four versions (between 1919 and 1923), with an increasingly biting style. Nonetheless, Lawrence reiterated his tribute to Whitman as liberator of the body. In its first

---

3   John Addington Symonds, *A Problem in Modern Ethics* (London: 1896), 119.
4   Edward Carpenter, *Towards Democracy* (1905; New York: Kenneley 1912), 383.
5   Henry Bryan Binns, *The Great Companions* (London: A. C. Fifield, 1908), 58–59.
6   See Robin Waterfield, *Prophet: The Life and Times of Khalil Gibran* (New York: St Martin's Press, 1998). Lebanese émigrés in the United States, such as Gibran, but also Ameen Rihani, played an important role in the Arabic reception of Whitman.
7   See Harold Bloom, "Near the Quick. Lawrence and Whitman," in *The Anatomy of Influence* (New Haven: Yale University Press, 2011), 255–265.

version, the essay contained esoteric developments on parts of the body as seats of emotions and thoughts (the coccygeal plexus was, for example, the home of consciousness). In the following version, Lawrence added comments on the repression of sensuality in Western history, which Christianity did not initiate but carried to its end (a vision of civilization in fact close to that of Carpenter). Whitman's tremendous contribution was the reversal of that historical course. The final version of the essay dwelt on this achievement, explaining that the function of art was not aesthetic, but moral, as long as it was not didactic and sought to change "the blood," not "the mind." In that regard, "Whitman was a great moralist. He was a great leader. He was a great changer in the veins of men."[8] Lawrence emphasized his pioneering role: "Whitman was the first to break the mental allegiance. He was the first to smash the old moral conception, that the soul of man is something 'superior' and 'above' the flesh," the first to say to the soul, "Stay there. Stay in the flesh. Stay in the limbs, the lips, the belly. Stay in the breasts and in the womb and the phallus. Stay there, soul, stay in your place." (156) Whitman delivered the great message of American heroism: the soul, reunited with the body, must not withdraw from the world, but must go out on the open road and seek contacts. Lawrence did have reservations, however, as he deemed that Whitman did not follow through on the moral revolution that he initiated: he sometimes still confused empathy with "the love of Jesus" and "the charity of Paul." While Lawrence's critique of Christian values was sharper than Carpenter's, and while he set limits to Whitman's accomplishments, his reading exemplifies a post-Victorian reception of Whitman as a great liberator of the body.

The passion of the body (Konstantin Balmont)

As far as Whitman's homosexuality was concerned, the poet's Russian reception was very different: references to a gay Whitman were quite scarce. In his diary, Chukovsky relates a conversation with Kropotkin, who saw in Whitman a "pederast" and a "homosexual" (like Wilde and Carpenter, both of whom he knew personally) and expressed the strongest disapproval.[9] Chukovsky mentioned the European polemics about Whitman's homosexuality in his 1918 edition, only to take sides in a peremptory way: "An excellent rebuke to these writers was given by the German novelist Johannes Schlaf, author of a monograph on Walt Whitman. He titled his article 'Is it true that Walt Whitman was a homosexual?,'

---

8 Lawrence, *Studies in American Literature*, 155.
9 Kornei Chukovskii, *Dnevnik*, vol. 1 (Moscow: Sovetskii Pisatel', 1991), 85 (July 31, 1917).

and utterly defeated the notorious Dr. Bertz, who argued that Whitman, like Shakespeare, like Plato, was an adept of same-sex love (Jahrbuch für sexuelle Zwischenstufen, 1905)."[10] In the 1923 edition, Chukovsky observes that intense friendship is a frequent thing among young people and that for Whitman such "friendship" also existed between women.[11]

However, there was a place for the "liberator of the body," especially in Balmont's commentaries. In an early essay, "Poet of personality and life," he translated "Like Adam early in the morning" and noted that male and female beauties were equally celebrated. Before Whitman, there had been "no such bold and selfless and encompassing singer of the human body."[12] Balmont celebrated Whitman's body itself, the body of a "gladiator," "full of the forces of nature." In "Poetry of struggle," Balmont insists on the sacredness of the "body":

> We do not feel that our body is divine. We do not feel or know that the movements of passion associated with our bodies are a poem of Beauty to be cherished. Deeply perverted by historical Christianity, full of senseless disrespect, neglect, self-contempt, we incarnate spirits with disproportionate parts, with the head some kind of monster independent from the other parts of the body, inhabiting them, crushing them, raping them, distorting them, and we are almost incapable of understanding the beauty of a *living body*, magnificent in all its movements and impulses, healthy, complete, spiritual, passionate, attractingly-invitingly-passionate.[13]

Balmont reiterates the very founding word of Christianity, *strast'* (passion), and subverts its meaning, associating it with the appealing beauty of the body. In terms reminiscent of Symonds, whom he mentions, he adds that "Whitman restores the body in his own rights," and includes long excerpts from "I Sing the Body Electric." In his 1911 anthology of Whitman's poetry, he translated several poems from the "Children of Adam" cluster, including the whole of "I Sing the Body Electric," "A Woman Waits for Me" (which states that "sex contains all, bodies, souls"), and "Spontaneous me" (with its "love-juice" and "love-odor").

---

10 Uitmèn, *Poèziia griadushchei demokratii* (1918), 71.
11 Ibid. (1923), 67.
12 Bal'mont, "Pevets lichnosti i zhizni" (1904), in *Belye zarnitsy*, 71.
13 Bal'mont, "Poèziia bor'by" (1907), in ibid., 109.

Later anthologies would not be that inclusive: even though Chukovsky translated "A Woman Waits for Me," he consistently avoided "I Sing the Body Electric."

Interestingly, Balmont very clearly associated the "poet of the body" with the "poet of Democracy." According to him, Whitman was "free" and "freed," he was the messenger of the liberation of all people (*vestnik osvobozhdeniia*). The link was also established in the writings of the Polish poet Julian Tuwim, who was an enthusiastic reader of Whitman in his early years and combined primitivist and mystic tropes: Whitman was Dionysiac and full of cosmic energy. Above all, he was the poet of the identity of the soul and the body, an important theme of Tuwim's early (and unpublished) poems.[14] The association between democracy and the liberation of the body existed in most British readings (especially Carpenter), but not in all other European receptions—in France, the two sides were even split apart: while Gide valued the homosexual Whitman (and stayed away from any political implication), the unanimists (Duhamel, Romains) celebrated the democratic persona.

Yiddish poets and the female body

While slightly moving away from the prophetic Whitman, I would like to linger on the poet of the body and draw attention to Yiddish contributions on this aspect. They are all the more interesting because they do not come from emigrants to the US, but from writers who lived in former parts of the Russian Empire: Lithuania and Poland. In 1923, Kalman Zingman founded the Yiddish literary journal *Vispe*. He was a belletrist and publisher, who had lived in Kharkiv and Berlin before returning to his native Kaunas, the capital of newly independent Lithuania, where Jews were granted some autonomy. *Vispe* (islet) was a local word designating the sand banks of the Neman River. The tension between the local and the global was indeed central to the journal's project: the manifesto of the first issue expressed the frustration of living on an islet while the world was so full of movement.[15] Translations were an integral part of *Vispe*. Whitman was featured with a photograph that often appeared in Russian publications (see below) and a poem.

---

14 The relation between Tuwim and Whitman is a substantial one, which has been extensively documented by Marta Skwara (*Polski Whitman*, 190–221).

15 All the information on Kalman Zingman comes from Gennady Estraikh, "Utopias and cities of Kalman Zingman, an uprooted Yiddishist dreamer," *East European Jewish Affairs* 36, no. 1 (June 2006): 31–42.

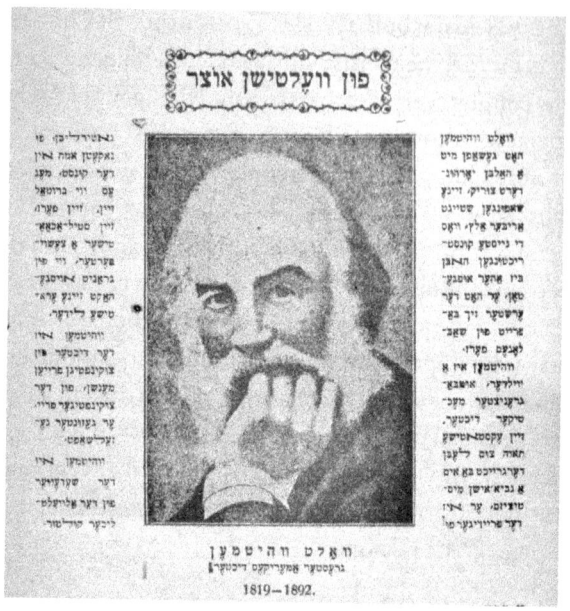

FIGURE 3.1. *Vispe*, no. 3 (1923), 86. Joe Fishstein Yiddish Poetry Collection, Rare Books and Special Collections, McGill University Library.

Interestingly, instead of the expected "Salut au Monde!," the poem that Dovid Grinshpan translated into Yiddish was "A Woman Waits for Me."

The second instance is Melech Ravitch, a Yiddish poet from Eastern Galicia who lived in Lemberg (Lviv), Vienna and Warsaw before emigrating in the 1930s (he would finally settle in Montreal). In the early 1920s, he belonged to the Modernist group Di Khalyastre (The Gang), with Uri Zvi Greenberg and Peretz Markish. At a time when Whitman was a conspicuous reference in the Polish literary world (Tuwim himself was Jewish, though coming from an assimilated family), Greenberg read him with enthusiasm. Ravitch did not write explicitly about Whitman, but his poem "Song to the Human Body" almost reads as a combination of translated lines. It sings in praise of the body, especially the female body, because "the belly is holy" (vayl der boykh iz heylik).[16]

> Ikh bin mit ir
> Vayl ikh bin der dikhter fun der neshome fun froyen
> Un der dikhter fun zeyer layb
> Vayl zeyer layb un neshome iz eyns. (22)

---

16 Melech Ravitch, "Gezang tsum mentshlekhn kerper," in *Di fir zaytn fun mayn velt* (Wilno: B. Kletskin, 1929), 19.

> I am with her
> Because I am the poet of the soul of women
> And the poet of their body
> Because their body and soul are one.

In "Song of Myself," Whitman wrote: "I am the poet of the Body and I am the poet of the Soul" and "The body and the soul are one," while often stating the equal beauty of the male and female body. In Ravitch's poem, the association of the Hebraic word *neshome* (soul) and the Germanic *layb* (body) makes the equation striking. The word *geshlekht* (sex) is also repeated and emphasized. Melech Ravitch was one of the rare poets who used Whitmanian (translated) language to praise the female body.

I will finally quote Abraham Walkowitz's brief but interesting comment on Whitman's "body electric." As previously mentioned, Walkowitz's cityscapes featured alongside Whitman's poem in *Shriftn* and therefore belong to the story of the urban Jewish American Whitman. But Walkowitz had a stronger, albeit less visible link to Whitman: he was fascinated by the dancer Isadora Duncan, whom he drew on many occasions. As is known, Duncan herself was a major actor in Whitman's reception, and invented ways to transfer his poetry to dance. In a late interview, Walkowitz thus discussed the impact of Duncan on his own creation: "So, she was a Muse. She had no laws. She didn't dance according to the rules. She created. Her body was music. It was a body electric, like Walt Whitman. His body electrics. One of our greatest men, America's greatest, is Walt Whitman. Leaves of Grass is to me the Bible."[17] Walkowitz's words betray a recurrent confusion of the poet and his work but also the multiple and intricate layers of Whitman's reception.

2. The poet as "kosmos"

"Cosmos" (or "kosmos" in Whitman's spelling) is an important word in *Leaves of Grass*, and one that would resonate in the early twentieth century. Because of the elasticity of its meaning, it lent itself to all sorts of interpretations and semantic realignments. "Cosmic" might refer to space (the Earth, the luminaries) but also to more spiritual realities. It merged pagan, Hindu[18] and Christian experiences,

---

17 Smithsonian Collections, accessed September 27, 2023, https://www.aaa.si.edu/collections/interviews/oral-history-interview-abraham-walkowitz-13176.

18 I will not insist on this aspect, but there was a whole tradition of reading Whitman in terms of Hindu pantheism and mysticism. A remarkable example is Romain Rolland's chapter on Whitman in *Prophets of the New India* (*Essai sur la mystique et l'action de l'Inde vivante*, 1929). Rolland related Whitman to Vivekananda.

thus speaking to the syncretism of the times. The "cosmic" Whitman was essentially mystical, but could be invested with a more mundane collective dimension. As an example, the Austrian Expressionist poet Franz Werfel made references to Whitman's "cosmic democracy" or to the "all-encompassing dimension of his cosmic feeling of comradeship [kosmischen kameradschaftsgefühl]."[19] Again, experience, religion and politics were entangled.

The prophet's heart as a cosmos (Morris Rosenfeld)

Rosenfeld was one of the first Yiddish poets to emigrate to the US: born in Russian Poland, he settled in New York in 1886. Not long after, he wrote the poem "Walt Whitman," a loose sonnet (14 lines without rhymes), with the subtitle "America's greatest poet" (*dikhter*). As for many immigrants, addressing Whitman was a declaration of belonging to the US, but also an act of appropriation. Rosenfeld would become famous for his *Songs from the Ghetto*, but in the ode to Whitman, surprisingly, it was not the social or political that came to the fore. Rosenfeld focused on the poet's heart:

> O du in vemes shtarker zinger-brust
> es hobn zikh tsvey opgrundn fareynt:
> di tiefkeyt fun farklerten himel un
> di shtil farvigte tiefkeyt fun der erd;
> in vemes harts es hot geshaynt di zun,
> der mond un vu es hobn hel geglantst
> di shtern, gantse veltn ohn a tsol[20]

> O you, in whose powerful singer's breast,
> two abysses intertwined:
> the deepness of the thoughtful sky and
> the softly cradled deepness of the earth;
> within whose heart arose the sun,
> the moon and where the stars brightly
> shone, countless entire worlds

Light permeates the poem and reveals Whitman's heart as a microcosm containing the universe. In the second half, it harbors the buds of May, and

---

19 Quoted in Grünzweig, *Constructing the German Walt Whitman*, 128, 132.
20 Morris Rosenfeld, *Gezamelte lieder* (New York: Aroysgegeben fun der Internatsyonaler bibliotek ferlag kompani, 1904), 232.

blends the rumble of thunder with the song of the nightingale. At the end, the poet declares his allegiance: "prophet, immortal, I praise thee; I kneel / upon the dust, before the dust, and sing." While Whitman "bequeathed himself to the dirt," Rosenfeld kneels upon that dirt and takes inspiration from it. The poem was included in the 1919 anthology of Yiddish poetry by Zishe Landau (a Modernist poet):[21] it was the first of four pieces by Rosenfeld, as if Whitman were his guardian. Given the importance of Rosenfeld for American Yiddish poets, establishing such a lineage was quite meaningful. Not too surprisingly, it was also a favorite of anthologies of American Yiddish poetry[22] and of Yiddish poetry in English translation, such as Joseph Leftwich's pioneering *Golden Peacock* (first edition 1939). The poem was also reprinted at the opening of Abraham Asen's translation of twenty-five poems by Whitman in 1934.[23]

Cosmic consciousness (Richard Maurice Bucke)

After Whitman visited him in Canada, the psychiatrist Richard Maurice Bucke wrote a hagiography of the poet, simply entitled *Walt Whitman*.[24] Whitman performed miracles during the civil war and endured a true Passion: the hostile criticism he had to face was comparable to the Crucifixion. Bucke figured himself as St. Paul, explaining the revelation. His interpretations were indeed rooted in an evangelical logic and he read the poems as parables. However, even if Bucke started from the New Testament, his religious conceptions were very personal and gave the evangelical Whitman a "cosmic" slant. In fact, Bucke was interested in the phenomena of revelation and illumination, in what he called, after Edward Carpenter, "cosmic consciousness." In his famous book on the topic (1901), he listed many mystical experiences as ways of accessing this higher form of consciousness. According to Bucke, such experiences were becoming more and more frequent: there were few from biblical times to the Renaissance (Moses, Socrates, Jesus, Paul, Dante, Las Casas), but many in the nineteenth century (Blake, Balzac, Carpenter, among others), with Walt Whitman as the most representative example of all periods.

---

21 Zisha (Zishe) Landau, ed., *Antologye: di Idishe dikhtung in Amerike biz yohr 1919* (New York: Farlag Idish, 1919).
22 Nayman Mayzel, ed., *Amerike in Yidishn vort antologye* (New York: Ikuf, 1955).
23 Valt Vitman, *Finf un tsvantsig lider* (New York: Idish lebn, 1934).
24 Richard Maurice Bucke, *Walt Whitman* (Philadelphia: David McKay, 1883).

Cosmic Consciousness had a huge impact.²⁵ It was translated into Russian in 1915, much earlier than into other languages.²⁶ Khlebnikov mentioned Bucke's work and drew a parallel with his own construct of an equivalence between Jesus and Whitman. Chukovsky commented on it at the end of the 1918 and 1919 editions of *Poetry of the Future Democracy*. He referred to it as a "curious" book and praised the richness of materials in Bucke's collection of cosmic experiences. Since Chukovsky concluded with a quote, Bucke's words turned out to be the very last of the book, emphasizing Whitman's "full cosmic consciousness."

A "chronic mystical perception" (William James)

Another influential appreciation of Whitman was that of William James. In *The Varieties of Religious Experience*, James quoted a long passage from Bucke as an introduction to his section on Whitman.²⁷ He observed that Whitman was often considered the "restorer of the eternal natural religion" and sometimes referred to as a "pagan," which he believed to be inaccurate. While the Greeks and Romans clearly separated good from evil, Whitman stated that even "what is called evil is equally perfect";²⁸ while the pagans were well aware of their mortality, Whitman rejected the idea. Even if James found that Whitman's gospel had a "touch of bravado"²⁹ that diminished its impact on many readers, he saw a cosmic quality in his poetry. James equated "cosmic consciousness" with what he called "chronic mystical perception." He came back to Whitman and Bucke in his lecture on mysticism, finding "the same recurring note" "in Hinduism, in Neoplatonism, in Sufism, in Christian mysticism, in Whitmanism": "Perpetually telling of the unity of man with God, their speech antedates languages, and they do not grow old." (411) Whitman's mysticism, however, was quite specific, with its "naturalistic pantheistic" version of the same creed. In *Pragmatism*, James also quoted at length the

---

25 The work was frequently reprinted in English, in accessible paperback editions. Bucke has thus done a lot for the dissemination of Whitman to a wider audience. The spiritualist and esoteric current of Whitman's reception remains quite strong today in the United States outside academic circles. The friendship between Bucke and Whitman was the subject of the film *Beautiful Dreamers* (1991), by the Canadian John Kent Harrison.
26 Richard Moris Biok, *Kosmicheskoe soznanie* (Petrograd: Novyi chelovek, 1915). Chukovsky indicated 1914 in his essay, but I could not locate an earlier version than the 1915 one.
27 William James, "The religion of healthy-mindedness," *The Varieties of Religious Experience* (1905; New York: The Modern Library, 1936), 84–87 for the pages on Whitman.
28 In "Burial Poem," *Leaves of Grass*, 1856 edition.
29 James, *The Varieties of Religious Experience*, 87.

poem "To You," and suggested two interpretations: the "monistic way" or "mystical way of pure cosmic emotion," and the "pluralistic way of interpreting," which attributes diverse meanings to "you." James stated that "both ways satisfy; both sanctify the human flux. Both paint the portrait of the *you* on a gold-background. But the background of the first way is the static One, while in the second way it means possibles in the plural, genuine possibles, and it has all the restlessness of that conception."[30]

The Varieties of Religious Experience made a considerable impression in Western Europe and in Russia. It was translated into French in 1905 (*L'Expérience religieuse*) and quoted by Régis Michaud in his chapter on Whitman as a "cosmic poet" in *Anglo-Saxon Mystics and Realists*. According to Michaud: "In Anglo-Saxon countries, where the distinction between the mystical and the poetic order has never been as clear as in France, many people find in Whitman a prophet and a Bible. He is the Bible of absolute optimism."[31] In Russia, it was translated in 1910, and even before that date, exerted influence on the intellectuals who shaped the idea of "God-building" (Maxim Gorky admired James).[32] *Pragmatism* was also translated in 1910. Chukovsky read the book that very year and commented on it in a letter, writing that James's remarks about Whitman made him want to resume his own work on the American poet.[33] In his 1914 (and then 1918 and 1919) edition of *Poetry of the Future Democracy*, a whole page is devoted to James's readings of Whitman, both in *The Varieties of Religious Experience* and in *Pragmatism*, with substantial quotes.

From the Milky Way to Russian iconostasis (Balmont and Grigoriev)

Balmont's assessment of Whitman as a cosmic poet might appear quite different. In fact, it needs to be understood in the context of Russian cosmism, a broad theory which combined science, philosophy, religion and ethics. Its most famous theorist was Nikolay Fyodorov. However, the similarities between Balmont's, James's and Bucke's respective lexicon and imagery are rather striking.

---

30 William James, "Pragmatism and Religion," in *Pragmatism* (Cambridge, MA: Harvard University Press, 1975), 133.
31 Régis Michaud, *Mystiques et réalistes anglo-saxons, d'Emerson à Bernard Shaw* (Paris: Armand Colin, 1918), 103.
32 See Joan Delaney Grossman and Ruth Rischin, ed., *William James in Russian Culture* (Landham: Lexington Books, 2003), especially Barry Scherr, "Gorky and God-Building," 189–210.
33 Kornei Chukovskii, letter to P. B. Struv, Summer 1910, *Sobranie sochinenii*, vol. 14 (Moscow: Agentstvo FTM, Ltg, 2013), 229.

From his first essay on Whitman, "Singer of Personality and Life," Balmont used the adjective "cosmic." He wrote that "Whitman sees the One Whole" (Edinoe Tseloe), adding,

> Whitman's religion is cosmic enthusiasm, that inexhaustible universal delight, for which it is neither tiresome, nor difficult, nor tedious to create more and more clusters of planets, and to continuously bless the generative darkness, filled with mystery, and to create every minute in each new flower the first morning of the Universe.[34]

Again, the *primitive* and the cosmic are intertwined. A later essay, "Poetry of the struggle," also insists on the "cosmic" element. Whitman is called an "apostle of a new humanity"[35] and features as an intermediary between the lights of the Milky Way and the Earth:

> It is said that everyone is born under their own Star. I would say that Walt Whitman was born under the multistellar influence of the Milky Way, which is why he was so eager to bind all souls in clusters of stars. We must bring forth Mankind's deeply hidden light, and, thus transferring Heaven to Earth, and truly throwing the transfigured Earth into the cosmic dance of the luminaries. (107)

The adjective "transfigured" (preobrazhennoi) carries strong spiritual overtones (it refers to Christ's appearance in radiant glory in front of three of His disciples). Such cosmic powers bear collective and even universal significance. Like James, Balmont saw a certain timelessness in this sensitivity to the universe, to the "not I":

> Whitman argues that the basic elements of a decent life and national greatness are a strong character, an independent personality, a sincere religiosity—it is not church religiosity, of course, which is meant here, but a reverent appreciation of all the senses of existence, a harmonization of our dissonances, a

---

34 Konstantin Bal'mont, "Pevets lichnosti i zhizni" (1904), in *Belye zarnitsy*, 83.
35 Konstantin Bal'mont, "Poèziia bor'by" (1907), in ibid., 100.

free fusion of individual sounds and melodies into one universal Symphony. (120)

The "cosmic" Whitman was also visual. In 1913, as one learns from Chukovsky's *Correspondence*, the painter and theosophist Nicholas Roerich had agreed to draw the cover for his new book of translations from Whitman.[36] Unfortunately, the project was not carried out: the 1914 cover did not bear any illustration and no draft has been found. In 1918, however, Boris Grigoriev painted a large portrait of Whitman, on the occasion of the Petrograd revolutionary celebrations.

FIGURE 3.2. Boris Grigoriev, *Portrait of Walt Whitman*, 1918, oil, 90 x 57 cm, Pskov Museum. Wikipedia Commons.

---

36 Kornei Chukovskii, letter to A. V. Rumanov, early September, in *Sobranie Sochinenii*, 14:311.

The portrait was clearly inspired by a photograph of Whitman by G. Frank Pearsall that was popular in Russia:

FIGURE 3.3. G. Frank Pearsall, *Walt Whitman, Half-length portrait, seated, facing left, left hand under chin.* ca. 1869. Charles E. Feinberg Collection, Library of Congress.

FIGURE 3.4. "Uot Uitmèn," *Plamia*, no. 21 (September 22, 1918), 4. Russian State Library.

In the original photograph, Whitman, dressed in loose-fitting casual clothes, adopts a pose somewhat reminiscent of Albrecht Dürer's *Melencolia*. In a later print, the framing is different, leaving out the bohemian clothes and focusing on the face. It is the print Horace Traubel used at the opening of *With Walt Whitman in Camden*. In 1918, it could be found in Chukovsky's edition[37] and in the Proletkult journal *Plamia*. In the latter case, it was framed by a paean to Whitman, entitled "A man with an open heart," which turned Whitman into a proletarian idol. But the colorization seems inspired by Balmont's words in "Poetry of struggle": "Lit by a blush, blue-eyed, with an attentive and penetrating face, he is a true son of Heaven and Earth." (102) The rosy and blue hues of the face irradiate the surrounding world in Grigoriev's painting. The portrait also seems to illustrate Balmont's words in "Singer of Personality": "The face of Walt Whitman is not the face of a spirit or a demon, but the luminous face of a mighty inhabitant of the earth, in love with the earth, the face of a giant who can play with fragments of cliffs as with a ball, and can pile mighty stones one upon another."[38] *Lik* is a more poetic word for face than *litso* and also refers to the beaming face on an icon. Indeed, Balmont was writing at a time when icons had been rediscovered and were major sources of inspiration for primitivist art. As Tatiana Victoroff points out, Grigoriev's Whitman "seems to be God the Father observing men taking over the continuous Creation of the world."[39] This portrait of a saint's *lik* seemed almost lost in the massive propagandistic display of the Petrograd festival. It stood as a reminder of a not-so-distant past, when the religious and the political would easily mesh.

Another cosmic work inspired by Whitman is of particular interest to our Russian-American circuit. In 1927, the Amaravella group was invited to the first exhibit of Soviet painting in New York. They were "cosmist" painters, close to Nicholas Roerich[40]—*amaravella* is a Sanskrit word meaning expansion, creative energy. The exhibit at Corona Mundi (the International Center for Arts) in New York gathered painters from different parts of the world, from Paul Gauguin to Norman Rockwell, and the USSR was represented by Amaravella. One of the paintings, "Song of Myself," by Pyotr Fateev, was inspired by Whitman. According to a review, it was "a magnificent dramatic

---

37 It is featured in the preface, precisely when Whitman's "religion" is discussed (31).
38 Bal'mont, "Pevets lichnosti i zhizni," in *Belye zarnitsy*, 84.
39 Tatiana Victoroff, "Visages de Russie. Grigoriev et Bounine," *Slavica Occitania*, no. 53 (2021): 175–176.
40 They were presented in the Americanized versions of their names as: Alexander Sardan, Boris Smirnoff-Rusetsky, George Schigolev, Runa and Peter Fateyef. They all died during the Great Terror, except for Fateev.

depiction of mountains against the night sky, in subtle transitions of shadow and light; gradually, the body of the Earth appears."[41] The painting was also shown in Chicago in 1928, but unfortunately I was not able to trace it after that date nor find any copy of it.

3. The seer and the guide

In this last section, I would like to consider more broadly the collective mission of the prophet Whitman. As in the etymological sense of "religion," it was about establishing a link between man and the sacred, but also between men themselves. What religion meant varied greatly: while some used its lexicon and imagery to advocate a secularized version, others kept the sacred dimension at the center. The first option was especially represented in Germany. Karl Knortz was, as Walter Grünzweig observes, anti-religious, and yet he saw in Whitman the embodiment "of the Gospel according to Matthew,"[42] while Johannes Schlaf considered Whitman "the first poet-seer of a third gospel" (der erste Dichter-Seher eines dritten Evangeliums).[43] This was even more the case in France, with Léon Bazalgette's essays, such as "Le Poème-Évangile de Walt Whitman" in 1921. Bazalgette's writings found readers in Russia and in Poland.[44] The second option, on which I will focus, was more common in Britain, Russia and the US—both in English and in Yiddish. This version of religious interpretations of Whitman has been studied in depth regarding the American "disciples" and the British reception,[45] but much less so in other areas, especially Russian and Yiddish. It is useful, however, to first summarize the core elements of the Anglo-American reception, which were later diffracted and appropriated.

---

41 Zinaida Gribova, *Khudozhniki "Amaravelly": sud'by i tvorchestvo* (Moscow: MBA, 2009), 92. Gribova quotes from the *Philadelphia Record*. The appendix of her study lists all the works by Fateev; the only indications for the Whitman painting (no. 149 on the list) are "Pesn' o sebe (po poème Uitmena), 1920, USA."
42 Grünzweig, *Constructing the German Walt Whitman*, 21.
43 Johannes Schlaf, "Review of Karl Knortz, *Walt Whitman, der Dichter der Demokratie*," quoted in Grünzweig, *Constructing the German Walt Whitman*, 38.
44 In 1921, Stanisław Vincenz published the essay "The Religion of Walt Whitman" in the Polish journal *Naród* (no. 23), which, together with a translated text by Bazalgette ("The Art of Walt Whitman"), formed the introduction of a volume of translations.
45 Whitman's British reception has been studied thoroughly by Kirsten Harris, whose book *Walt Whitman and British Socialism* offers an extensive analysis of texts and archives. I only select and summarize here what is most relevant to my comparative perspective.

New American and British churches

The rich yet changeable religious terrain of nineteenth-century America was perfect for Whitman's reception. He was considered a renovator, a founder, or a prophet, with constant semantic shifts, which were not so much due to a lack of a lucidity on the part of his "disciples" as to the complexity of this religious context. All the "hot little prophets," as Bliss Perry called them,[46] saw Whitman as a figure of religious renewal. Quite expectedly, the images most frequently used in the United States and Canada were those of Christ and the Messiah. As early as 1867, William O'Connor, one of the very first disciples, published "The Carpenter: A Christmas Story" in *Putnam Magazine*. John Burroughs, Whitman's faithful friend (who wrote no less than two books and fifty articles about him between 1866 to 1920) compared him with a god and welcomed the advent of a new religion: "Whitman, it means a life as much as Christianity means a life."[47] The most fervent and best-known disciple, Horace Traubel, created the journal the *Conservator* (the source of so many tributes to Whitman) as the organ of "the Liberal Conference," whose aim was to bring together various liberal religious movements.

The ground was equally fertile in England, where religion would combine with social and political outlooks. Edward Carpenter's essay "Civilisation: Its Cause and Its Cure" is quite representative of the conflation of religion and socialism conducive to the sanctification of Whitman: "This is the Communism which Civilisation has always *hated*, as it hated Christ. Yet it is inevitable; for the cosmical man, the instinctive elemental man accepting and crowning nature, necessarily fulfils the universal law of nature."[48] However, contrary to other British disciples, Carpenter's enthusiasm declined over time, especially after his second visit to Whitman in 1877. In Kirsten Harris's words, "he retained his faith in *Leaves of Grass* as a prophetic text throughout his life but increasingly Whitman's personal flaws became problematic."[49] Other followers were keener on building communities around Whitman's gospel.

One of the places where the figure of the poet-prophet of socialism appeared earliest and was hailed most fervently was undoubtedly the Eagle Street College, a reading group in Bolton, in the industrial north of England. Formed in the early 1870s, the group's identity changed radically in 1885, when its founder

---

46 Bliss Perry, *Walt Whitman* (Boston: Houghton and Mifflin, 1906), 286.
47 *Notes on Walt Whitman as Poet and Person*, quoted in Robertson, *Worshipping Walt*, 50.
48 Carpenter, *Civilisation*, 67.
49 Harris, *Whitman and British Socialism*, 61

James William Wallace discovered Whitman in a moment of revelation.[50] The Eagle Street College then became the circle of English Whitmanians (the address changed as Wallace moved to Adlington, but the name remained). They held an annual "Whitman Day" on May 31, the poet's birthday. Wallace visited Whitman shortly before his death in 1891, Whitman's American friends visited Bolton, and so did Richard Maurice Bucke in 1894. The college was a place of transatlantic exchange, contributing not only to the spread of Whitman's poetry in England, but also to the diffusion of socialist ideas among American Whitmanians.

It was also in northern England, in Manchester, that the first Labour Church was founded, in 1891, by John Trevor. The church expanded to other towns, like Bolton, where it was in close contact with the Eagle Street College. It also expanded across the Atlantic, into Massachusetts. The Labour Church has been debated among historians: Eric Hobsbawn sees it as a typical example of secularization, of the reinvestment of religious structures and rhetoric in a political cause, while Marc Bevir nuances this Marxist position by insisting on the religious component really at work in the movement.[51] In Trevor's words: "Socialism is to our corrupt age what Christianity was to the world at the beginning of our era."[52] Trevor presented Whitman as "nearer to God than any other man on earth"[53] and a prophet superior to Jesus because he delivered his words directly in the poems, without the mediation of the Gospels. Whitman was read at meetings, and his name frequently appeared in the *Labour Prophet*, the press organ of the Labour Church. Each issue reaffirmed this principle: "That the Labour Movement is a Religious Movement." Whitman was the subject of long articles, but only one poem was printed in its pages, which generally preferred contemporary British working-class poetry.

While the Labour Church dwindled after Trevor left it in 1900, and disappeared altogether with World War I, the Eagle Street College continued its activities well into the 1920s, until Wallace's death in 1926. Even after that, the Whitmanian C. F. Sixsmith (he held an important position in the cotton industry and built a collection of Whitman-related artefacts) continued May 31 celebrations. Another late disciple was Will Hayes, a pastor in Chatham, southern England, who published *Walt Whitman: The Prophet of the New*

---

50 Wallace is one of the cases studied by Richard Maurice Bucke in *Cosmic Consciousness*.
51 See Mark Bevir, "The Labour Church Movement, 1891–1902," *Journal of British Studies* 38 (April 2, 1999): 217–245.
52 John Trevor, "Perfidious Albion," *Labour Prophet*, April 1896, 57.
53 Quoted by Harris, *Whitman and British Socialism*, 158.

Era in 1921, with chapters like "The Christ of Our Age" and "The Carpenter of Brooklyn."

Though far from being a disciple of Whitman, or anyone else for that matter, the British writer G. K. Chesterton was fascinated by the American poet early on. His account provides an interesting glimpse of the kind of prophetic aura that surrounded Whitman:

> My whole youth was filled, as with a sunrise, with the sanguine glow of Walt Whitman. He seemed to me something like a crowd turned to a giant, or like Adam the First Man. It thrilled me to hear of somebody who had heard of somebody, who saw him in the street; it was as if Christ were still alive. I did not care about whether his unmetrical poetry were a wise form or no, any more than whether a true Gospel of Jesus were scrawled on parchment or stone.[54]

Chesterton's point is to explain that Whitman's "sanguine glow" was somehow delusive and that, no matter how appealing his poetry was, it contained a major flaw: it was based on emotions rather than principles, and therefore was not valid as theology. Poets like Shelley and Whitman

> had really taken out of the old Catholic tradition one particular transcendental idea; the idea that there is a spiritual dignity in man as man, and a universal duty to love men as men. . . . They took it for granted that this spiritual idea was absolutely self-evident like the sun and moon; that nobody could ever destroy that, though in the name of it they destroyed everything else. They perpetually hammered away at their human divinity and human dignity, and inevitable love for all human beings; as if these things were naked natural facts. And now they are quite surprised when new and restless realists suddenly explode, and begin to say that a pork-butcher with red whiskers and a wart on his nose does not strike them as particularly divine or dignified, that they are not conscious of the smallest sincere impulse to love him, that they could not love him if they tried, or that they do not recognize any particular obligation to try. (153-154)

---

54 G. K. Chesterton, "Is Humanism a Religion," in *The Thing: Why I Am a Catholic* [1929], *Collected Works*, vol. 3 (San Francisco: Ignatius Press, 1990), 147–148.

Faith in men, rather than in Man, reliance on emotions instead of ideas or principles, meant that Whitman's gospel remained a poetic one, not a religious one. In that regard, Whitman was quite different from Tolstoy, to whom Chesterton paid even more attention. Chesterton hailed Tolstoy for his "colossal faith," "his vast fearlessness and vast knowledge of life," but observed that he was deficient in "poetry" and was in no way a "mystic." I will now turn to this Whitman-Tolstoy parallel, which was often drawn in Britain.

The Russian *prorok*

At the time when Balmont was writing about Whitman the cosmic prophet, Chukovsky began using prophetic imagery too, but in a more subdued and individual way, with less insistence on the "cosmic." In 1909, he called Whitman a singer of psalms (*psalmopevets*).[55] In 1913, he repeated Apollinaire's joke on Whitman's funeral,[56] but changed the end of the narrative. In Apollinaire, after the lamb, whiskey and watermelon festival, drunk men on all fours carried Whitman's coffin into his mausoleum. Chukovsky replaced this grotesque ending by a solemn moment of homage, which conformed with most accounts of the funeral: "There were no priests, but at the grave, one of the friends read passages from various sacred books: from the Bible, the Koran, the Zend-Avesta, Confucius, and also from the book of that great bard-prophet [*bard-prorok*], whom they were now burying so strangely."[57] As a cliffhanger, he asked: "What is this sacred book? Why haven't we heard of it? What are its prophecies [*prorochestva*]?" and promised more details to come. *Prorok*, the Slavic-rooted word for prophet has strong cultural and literary connotations in Russian and is the title of a famous poem by Pushkin (1828).[58] Parallels with Tolstoy and comments by Repin contributed to the construction of Whitman as *prorok*.

---

55 Kornei Chukovskii, "Mirovoi vostorg," *Rech'*, July 18, 1909.
56 On April 1, 1913, Apollinaire published in *Mercure de France* an account of Whitman's funeral, based on "an anonymous witness." It was a parody of Bazalgette's version (which emphasized the solemnity of the ceremony): there were barbecues, huge kegs of whisky, beer and lemonade, heaps of watermelon, everyone was drunk and ended up fighting. A Russian translation was published.
57 Kornei Chukovskii, "Poèziia budushchego." All these texts were indeed read at Whitman's funeral.
58 In Polish too, Whitman was referred to as "prorok," by Antoni Lange, as early as 1892. Lange drew a parallel with Adam Mickiewicz (see Skwara, *Polski Whitman*, 169–178).

Tolstoy and Whitman: "great souls"

The parallel between the two writers was often made on the basis of their prophetic and religious aura. It had been a quite common association—from Whitman's obituary, "American Tolstoy," in the Russian journal *Knizhki Nedeli* (Books of the Week), to William James's contrasting approach in *The Varieties of Religious Experience*.[59] Tolstoy himself was well aware of Whitman's poetry. His appreciation grew more positive with time and with a more thorough knowledge of it, but his first impression in 1889 was negative: Whitman's poems were "ridiculous" (nelepye).[60] However, when he was offered Ernst Rhys's edition, Tolstoy read it carefully and marked a number of poems (such as "I Dream'd in a Dream" and "Europe").[61] He sent a note to Lev Nikiforov, the editor of *Posrednik*,[62] recommending this "original" and "brave" poet. According to Aylmer Maude, his British translator, Tolstoy still had reservations and said: "with all his enthusiasm, he yet lacks a clear philosophy of life. On some vital issues he stands at the parting of two ways and does not show us which way to go."[63]

Notwithstanding these criticisms, Whitman and Tolstoy were often paired, especially in Britain, where Whitmania coincided with Russomania.[64] The Eagle Street College can be compared with other literary societies with social ambitions, such as the Tolstoyans in Purleigh or the Ruskinians in Liverpool. Even though these societies and literary churches focused on one author, they shared the same canons. In the words of Charlotte Alston, those who were reading Tolstoy "were likely also to be reading other 'prophets' of the day: John Ruskin, Edward Carpenter, Thomas Carlyle, Walt Whitman or William Morris."[65] Other British figures, who were not disciples in any way, helped popularize and establish the parallel. Alfred Fletcher, a socialist journalist, wrote an article in the *New Age* entitled "Tolstoy and Whitman," emphasizing the Christlike

---

59 The case of Tolstoy was treated in the chapter "Sick Soul."
60 Lev Tolstoi, *Dnevnik*, June 11, 1889 in *Polnoe sobranie sochinenii*, 90 vols. (Moscow: Khudozhestvennaia Literatura, 1928–1958), 50:116.
61 The information is provided by Korney Chukovsky in "L. Tolstoi ob Uolte Uitmane," *Literaturnaia Gazeta*, August 25, 1940.
62 Tolstoi, *Polnoe sobranie sochinenii*, 65:130. *Posrednik* (The Mediator), which belonged to the publisher Sytin, was very much dedicated to the education of the masses and Tolstoy was quite involved with them; Nikiforov was also John Ruskin's translator.
63 Quoted by Chukovsky in the little section "Tolstoy and Turgeniev on Whitman," at the end of his 1919 edition of Whitman's poetry (starting at 114).
64 "Whitmania" is Swinburne's expression, while "Russomania" refers to Rebecca Beasley's book (on Tolstoy and Tolstoyan movements, see especially 98–116).
65 Charlotte Alston, *Tolstoy and His Disciples: The History of a Radical International Movement* (London, New York: I. B. Tauris, 2014), 5.

qualities of Whitman. Comparable associations were made in the US, especially between Tolstoy, Whitman and Carpenter. One of the most fervent disciples of Whitman, Ernst Crosby, wrote several essays on the Russian. In *Tolstoy and His Message* (1903), he used Whitman's poetry to illuminate Tolstoy, quoting Whitman's answer to those who accused him of destroying institutions: what he was building was the institution of "the Dear Love of Comrades." Like Tolstoy, who advocated Christianity and brotherhood outside the Orthodox Church, Whitman sought to create a community based on love.

Another example appeared in a 1921 collection of essays *Groyse neshomes* (Great souls), by the Yiddish writer Shemarye Gorelik. Gorelik was born in the Ukrainian part of the Russian Empire, he lived in Vilna, contributed to the *Yidisher Almanakh* in Kyiv, moved to Switzerland during World War I and then to Berlin, thus participating in a trans-European network of poets. His twenty-page chapter on Whitman[66] is between one on Ruskin and another on Tolstoy. Gorelik's main concern is how Whitman can lead us to happiness; his essay contains several passages in translation, such as the poem "Me imperturbe."

The Whitman-Tolstoy connection is therefore not so much a direct one as the result of cross-readings and comparisons by the two writers' disciples. A more immediate link can be established between Whitman and another admirer of Tolstoy, the painter Ilya Repin.

Ilya Repin's Whitman: "the second sun of Christianity"

The 1914 edition of Chukovsky's translation contained a remarkable preface by Repin, which went against the grain of the primitivist reception. Repin hoped that with the advent of Whitman, "modern pagan individualism" and "the modern cult of personality" would come to an end, as well as the epidemic of "savagery" that struck Russia. Repin abhorred Nietzsche and considered Whitman as his finest opponent. He presented him as the "second sun of Christianity" (vtoroi solntse khristianstva), as the poet of "church, community, love" (sobornost', sodruzhestvo, liubov'). The term *sobornost'* belongs to the Orthodox vocabulary and has Slavophile connotations: it designates a spiritual community, opposing Western individualism. Repin prophesizes: "Soon the cultured mob will see the disgusting banality [poshlost'] of their narcissistic heroes, and they will all bow down willingly to the World of Peace."[67]

---

66 Sch. Gorelik, "Vot Vitman," in *Groyse neshomes* (Dresden: Wostok, 1921), 102–120.
67 Uot Uitmèn, *Poèziia griadushchei demokratii*, trans. K. Chukovskii (Moscow: Sytin, 1914), 5–6.

The edition was immediately censured and forbidden, under the charge of "pornography." Chukovsky was outraged. He protested in the press, quoting Repin's words (and slightly distorting them): "He was a God-seer, a prophet [prorok]! He is the new sun of Christianity!"[68] Whitman was a new apostle, censored for bringing about a new religion. The main argument was that not only Repin, Balmont and Gorky, but the whole world had recognized Whitman as a god-seer and that Russia, by banning him, was an outcast. Chukovsky also quoted Edward Carpenter (who compared Whitman with Lao-Tzu, Ezekiel and Isaiah),[69] mentioned Léon Bazalgette's reading of Whitman as a "religious prophet" and listed several European translations that spread Whitman's "psalms." A copy of Whitman was in every home in America, Australia and England; special magazines were published to disseminate his ideas; societies and colonies of students were developing. At the end of his plea, Chukovsky returned to his usual primitivist language: Whitman was "crude" (grud), indeed, but "like a titan, like a Cyclopean bard." His endorsement of Repin's view was probably more strategic than revealing a deeply felt conversion to the Christian Whitman, but it provides yet another interesting example of the semantic flexibility and efficacy of the prophet/*prorok* construct.

FIGURE 3.5. Karl Bulla, *Repin reading the news of Lev Tolstoy's death*. With K. Chukovsky and N. Nordman-Severova (Repin's wife), in Kuokkala. Next to Chukovsky hangs Repin's *Portrait of poet Korney Ivanovich Chukovsky*, 1910. Wikipedia Commons.

---

68 Kornei Chukovskii, "Anekdot," *Rech'*, February 22, 1914.
69 In his otherwise lukewarm 1907 review of Carpenter's *Days with Walt Whitman*, Chukovsky appreciated the comparisons between *Leaves of Grass*, the *Upanishads*, Lao-Tzu and the Gospel (in *Vesy*, 1907, no. 2).

The prophet of the Promised Land

As noted above, one of the earliest tributes to Whitman in Yiddish was Morris Rosenfeld's sonnet, which enshrined Whitman as a cosmic prophet. This poem was often included in essays about Whitman. So was the photograph of a meditative Whitman, by G. Frank Pearsall, used in the journal *Vispe* (see above) and in both Abraham Asen's (1934) and Louis Miller's (1940) translations. Indeed, it is perhaps in American Yiddish poetry that Whitman was most consecrated as a prophet: he was able to see and articulate the future, and also to gather around him a community. That prophetic Yiddish-speaking Whitman later found an extension in Hebrew.

The open road

For Jewish immigrants to the US, Whitman's inclusive vision of America was particularly meaningful. There were several reasons for this: the construct of Whitman the "prophet" could easily be appropriated and reshaped; many immigrants were close to socialist movements (especially the Bund), where Whitman's aura was tremendous; and for many Yiddish poets, Whitman embodied the very possibility of building a literary tradition from scratch.

Along with "Salut au Monde!" and "O Captain! My Captain!," one poem particularly appealed to Yiddish poets, "Song of the Open Road," which showed new paths across uncharted territories and exhorted readers to take them. It was the poem Moyshe Varshe chose to translate in his diary in 1912 (the year when Whitman's "Salut au Monde!" was translated in *Shriftn*). Born in 1887, in the Polish part of the Russian Empire, Varshe was a member of the Bund before he emigrated to the US in 1906; his friends were the members of the Modernist group Di Yunge who published *Shriftn*. Varshe translated a couple of sections from the poem (the second and the last ones).[70] Contrary to Schwartz, who emphasized multilingualism in "Salut au Monde!," he homogenized Whitman's language in Yiddish: "Allons" simply became *Kum* (Come), and "Camerado" became *Khaver* (friend, or comrade). Oddly, Varshe left out one line, though it might have resonated with Jewish experience in the US ("Let the tools remain in the workshop! let the money remain unearn'd").

In 1934, Abraham Asen published the first book-length Yiddish translation of Whitman's poetry, *Finf un tsvantsik lider* (Twenty-five poems). Born in

---

70 See Varshe's translation, annotated by Corbin Allardice, *Taytshworks*, accessed September 8, 2023, https://www.taytshworks.com/post/commonplace-book-3-walt-whitman.

Brest-Litovsk, Asen was a dentist in New York, as well as a prolific translator (of Shakespeare, Milton and the Bible). In his collection, Asen also gave a special place to "Song of the Open Road" ("Dos gezang fun dem frayen veg"): it was entirely translated and represented half of the book, while "Salut au Monde!" was represented by only a small fragment. He did not translate the last version of the poem, but a previous one, from 1871, which was longer (it comprised 17 sections instead of 15 from 1881 onwards). Still, he must have known the latest versions of the poem, since it is only in them that the final apostrophe is made to the "Camerado" (in the previous and longer versions, it was to "Mon enfant"). Asen translated it as *Kamerad*, in line with Whitman's Esperanto-like "Camerado." He kept the French "Allons," simply transliterated. Contrary to Varshe's, his "Song of the Open Road" was resolutely open to multilingualism.

Whitman the novi

Whitman the prophet of a new promised land could be compared with Moses. While Rosenfeld had used the European word *profet*, most Yiddish writers after him would rather refer to Whitman as a *novi*, using the Hebrew word. As an example, the title of an essay published in 1933 by Isaac Isaacson in Buenos Aires was "Amerikes groyser novi fun a banayter mentshhayt"[71] (America's great prophet of a renewed mankind).

Joseph Bovshover was among the prominent Yiddish poets who wrote about Whitman. Born in Lyubavichi in tsarist Russia, Bovshover lived in Riga, where he enthusiastically read Heinrich Heine (a poet often paired with Whitman), and emigrated to the US in 1891. He was one of the most popular Proletarian poets, along with Rosenfeld, Morris Winchevsky and David Edelstadt, and probably the most famous American Yiddish poet in the Soviet Union (a collection of his poems was published in Petrograd as early as 1918, and others followed in Moscow, Kyiv and Kharkiv). Bovshover wrote an essay about Whitman, along with others on Heine, Emerson and E. Markham. According to him, "Walt Whitman writes his poetry in the style, and very often in the tone, of the Bible. He sings, as the ancient prophets [novim] sang."[72] As Julian Levinson argues, Bovshover brought "Whitman into a Judaic frame of references."[73] Such a frame remained quite open to multiple references since Whitman was "a great,

---

71 Isaac Isaacson, *Eseyen un kritik vegn literatur un kunst* (Buenos Aires: Visn, 1933), 33.
72 Joseph Bovshover, *Gezamelte shriften poezye un proza* (New York: Fraye arbayter shtite, 1911), 330.
73 Levinson, *Exiles on Main Street*, 130.

bright, pleasant, but also prophetic person—a kind of Buddha or Moses of free thought, of eternal progress and eternal love. He stands at the highest level of time, as a great temple of truth and light, which he has built, and where the peoples will forever pilgrimage." (334) To illustrate "the zeal of a poet and prophet," Bovshover provided extensive quotes, from "Starting from Paumanok," "Song of Myself" (with the line "Be not curious about God") and "So Long!" These choices were different from the poems most quoted in Europe at the time. Bovshover concluded his essay on the many existing translations of Whitman's poetry, emphasizing his position in world poetry.

Several poems by Whitman can be found in a thick anthology assembled by Baruch Vladeck in 1917.[74] Born in Russia, a member of the Bund, exiled to Siberia, Vladeck emigrated in 1908 to the US, where he eventually became one of the most active promoters of the Yiddish press (he worked for the *Jewish Daily Forward*) and became highly involved in New York political life (he was elected councilman as a Socialist). The book was three hundred pages and contained a great variety of authors, from Rousseau and Danton to the regular guests of socialist anthologies, Ruskin, Morris and, of course, Whitman. The editorial work was hasty, the names of the translators seldom appeared and the pagination was inconsistent. One can assume that the main translator was Kolya Tepper, who is mentioned on the front page as "co-operating" with the edition and who was a well-known translator (especially from Russian). As far as Whitman was concerned, apart from the very last poem (an excerpt from "Salut au Monde!," in Schwartz's translation), there was no mention of the translator. The choice of poems is surprising, quite different from the favorites of British or Russian socialist anthologies: they all point to the prophet and the maker of miracles. At the beginning of the anthology is section 7 of "To Think of Time." Towards the end is "Miracles," in its 1860 version (it bears the title "What shall I give?"). The word *vunder* (miracle) is its leitmotif. A few pages later comes "City of my walks and joys" (later entitled by Whitman "City of orgies"), a poem about desire and love. The most intriguing poem, simply entitled "By Walt Whitman," is after the famous piece by Pushkin "The Prophet" (also "Novi" in I. Kisin's translation). This poem, about "the glorious world of a new bright future," "blurring the sight" of the poet like a "golden cloud," does not read as the translation of a text one could identify in *Leaves of Grass*, and its circular structure (the last stanza repeats the first) is untypical of Whitman. The result of pairing Pushkin's "Novi" with a prophecy attributed to Whitman is an unexpected diptych. Another interesting

---

74 Baruch Vladeck, ed., *Fun der tiefenish fun harts a bukh fun layden un kampf* (From heart's depth, a book of suffering and struggle) (New York: Miller & Hillman, 1917).

combination appears at the very end of the anthology, with the excerpt of "Salut au Monde!" (the French title was translated as "A bagrisung der velt") saluting the Slavic tribes and the Jews, followed by a poem by Vladeck himself. Whitman holds a strategic place in this wide-ranging anthology.

In his preface to Whitman's *Twenty-Five Poems*, translated by A. Asen, Abraham Reisen also designated Whitman as a *novi*, a prophet of the "New America." Reisen explained that Whitman was *the* national poet and that this very national quality boosted his international aura as well: the more rooted the poet, the more universal his poetry. In this case, the function of the *novi* was to articulate the local, the national and the global, an equation that was as essential to Yiddish poets as it was to Whitman (though not necessarily solved in the same way).

The powers of the *novi* lie essentially in vision and speech: as a prophet, the poet can foresee the future, but also utter and communicate his visions. In Aaron Nissenson's "Ballad of Walt Whitman," the "bright prophecy" is a source of light that illuminates the night and of words for those who are deprived of speech.[75] In Jacob Segal's poem "We," Whitman's song reverberates everywhere.[76] One of the most interesting pieces dedicated to Whitman was published in 1931 by the poet Broche Coodley. Born in Podolia, Coodley emigrated to the United States in 1913, settling in Los Angeles. In "Walt Whitman," she paid homage to the American poet with the heart of a *novi*, who sees "mankind blooming," "young sprouts of corn on the battlefield," as well as "winter in Switzerland."[77] The words *er zet* (he sees) and *er hert* (he hears) are the essential linkages of the poem. The "magnetic optimism" from the "vibration" of Whitman's speech is a manifestation of the poet's prophetic gifts. The end of the poem addresses Whitman as a "tremendous giant" (riziker gigant), the most impressive poet of his generation. This tribute has a strong social and political content and also belongs to the socialist story that I will develop in Chapter 6.

All these examples confirm Julian Levinson's conclusion in his pages on the American Yiddish Whitman (based essentially on Bovshover and I. J. Schwartz): responding to Whitman was not so much about becoming American as it was about constructing "a new *Jewish* discourse, using Whitman as a model," since "these poets also generally read Whitman as a modern version of the biblical prophet, a tradition they see as their own."[78]

---

75 Nissenson, *Dos lebn vil mayse hern*, 97–98.
76 Jacob Isaac Segal, "Mir," in *Lyrik* (Montreal: n.p., 1930), 190–191. Segal settled in Canada after some years in New York.
77 Broche Cooley, *Uzorn* (Los Angeles: Aroysgegebn fun a grupe fraynt, 1931), 57–58.
78 Levinson, *Exiles on Main Street*, 139.

The dream come true

This prophetic Whitman endured in both American Yiddish and Hebrew traditions. In Europe, Whitman the prophet lost much of his appeal after World War I, as the conflict had made Whitman's faith in mankind more difficult to adhere to. In America, as the next chapters will show, Whitman's prophecies also appeared to be contradicted by reality, especially after the Great Depression. This did not, however, necessarily invalidate the poet's dreams, but it did postpone them to an indefinite future or convert them into partisan discourses. As we shall see, most socialist poets tried to find a way to restore Whitman's visionary powers and to increase the probability of their fulfillment by clamping them onto Marxism.

Whitman's prophetic aura persisted for some Yiddish poets on other levels, however, especially after the foundation of Israel. H. Leivick, one of the most prominent figures in Yiddish poetry, turned to Whitman quite late. Leivick (born in Belorussia) escaped from Siberia where he was a prisoner and arrived in America in 1913. He ended years of contributions to papers like *Frayhayt* and *Der Hamer* after the communists refused to denounce the pogroms in Palestine; he was later involved with the Yiddisher Kultur-Farband, but left after the Molotov-Ribbentrop pact.

In a late poem, "To America" (1954), Leivick meditated at length on his relation with the country where he had "lived for forty-one years," carrying its "bounty of freedom," a freedom "sanctified and blessed by the blood of Lincoln's sacrifice / and in the hymns of Walt Whitman" and yet unable to sing it "with joy, with praise, with pure admiration." At the end of a meandering and poignant negotiation with his own feelings of guilt and longing, but also of doubts about America, he seems to come to terms with his qualms and to reconcile the "wonder places" of his dreams as a boy, Beersheba and Jerusalem, with the place where he will die. Just like him, America has spent time with Abraham and David:

> Oykh du, Amerike, bist noent mit zey arumgegangen,
> Oykh du host in dayn harts farnumen gots gebot un brokhe
> Tsu zayn a land vos rint mit milkh un honik,
> Tsu zayn filtsolik vi der zamd baym yam un vi di shtern oyfn himl,
> Tsu zayn neviish fray, vi s'hobn vegn dir gekhlumt dayne shefer.—
> O zol der kholem fun Volt Vitman un fun Linkoln oykh haynt dayn kholem zayn.

You too, America, have walked intimately with them,
for you have also taken to heart God's command and blessing
to be a land that flows with milk and honey,
to be as abundant as the sands of the shore and the stars in the sky,
to be a prophet of freedom just as your founders dreamed you could be,
O, let the dream of Walt Whitman and of Lincoln also be your dream.[79]

In the same years, Mattes Deitch (a poet born in the Ukrainian part of the Russian Empire, who lived mostly in Chicago), wrote quite a long poem entitled "Walt Whitman," included in a collection published in Tel Aviv in 1959.[80] It shows Whitman walking with God on the shore of Paumanok, compared with a Baal Shem (a healer, a miracle worker who makes use of practical Kabbalah), looking at his own dream come true: he sees Manhattan as he dreamed it, as Moses saw the Tabernacle before Bezalel built it. Deitch combines American toponyms with Jewish references. The Tabernacle (*Mishkn*) is the earthly dwelling of God, and Bezalel its chief conceiver. *Menhetn* (Manhattan) rhymes with *profetn* (prophets). Whitman then picks a pebble from the beach, licks it and speaks to it, addressing in his speech *Manahatta*, the "symbolical crown of his Lincoln-Jefferson America." He finally wades into the sea until "there is no dividing line to mark / the sea from his Leaves of Grass." The end of the poem hails Whitman in more conventionally American terms, as "a monument to a land of multiple peoples" (filfelkerdik land), a statue of liberty, the "poetic father of free spirit" (poetisher tate fun frayem geist). Interestingly, the translation of the poem into English for the 1961 edition of the anthology *The Golden Peacock*[81] emphasized its Americanness more than its Jewishness: Moses has visions "in the wilderness," an original American concept. It significantly changed the last two lines and separated them from the stanza where they belonged in the original version: "Walt Whitman stands, a monument, / Of all the nations into the one America blent!" In the American version, Whitman stands for unity rather than multiplicity and freedom.

---

79 H. Leivick, "Tsu Amerike," first published in the *Tog-morgn Zhurnal*, included in *A Blat oyf an eplboym* (Buenos Aires: Kium, 1955), 370; trans. Richard J. Fein in *With Everything We've Got. A Personal Anthology of Yiddish Poetry* (Austin, Host Publications, 2009), 60.
80 Mattes Deitch, *Tsum noentstn shtern* (Tel Aviv: Peretz Publ., 1959), 43–44.
81 Joseph Leftwich in *The Golden Peacock: A Worldwide Treasury of Yiddish Poetry*, 2nd ed., (New York: T. Yoseloff, 1961), 375.

Another avatar of the prophet emerged in Israel, where *Leaves in Grass* was translated into modern Hebrew in 1952. It was the work of Simon Halkin, whose biography takes us along paths this chapter has made familiar: born in tsarist Russia, he emigrated to the US in 1914 and lived in New York, where he studied Hebrew, and then in Chicago. Yet, contrary to most immigrants, who stayed in the US, he moved to Palestine in 1932; he went back to New York between 1939 and 1949 and then settled for good in Israel, serving as a professor of modern Hebrew literature at the University of Jerusalem.[82]

Translations were just as important for modern Hebrew literature at that time as they had been for Yiddish literature half a century before: they played a key role in establishing a literary language and a canon of world literature in Hebrew. Halkin's translation *'Ale 'eśev* fulfilled the will of Uri Zvi Greenberg, who in a 1928 manifesto, advocated the use of Hebrew against Yiddish and summoned Whitman:

> And I think that Whitman should have written in Hebrew, since he is moulded from the same substance as a Hebraic prophet. . . . In my "visionary leap," I transfer, as you know, Vilna, a city so like Jerusalem, from the soil of Poland and position it securely near Tiberias. Afterward, I also transport Walt Whitman to the living land of Israel.
>
> Rise up, our Hebraic Whitman, rise up![83]

Whitman provided an example of a national poetry able to invent its own forms. In the words of Jeffrey Einboden, who has thoroughly studied this translation, "Intersecting a seminal moment in Israeli self-definition, and reflecting the oscillating identity of its translator, the *'Ale 'eśev* of 1952 would also include renditions from Whitman that clearly gesture to issues of political independence and personal relocation—issues of contemporary relevance to Halkin, and much of his readership, in the early 1950s."[84] Einboden has also shown how Halkin enhanced "the prophetic and elliptical urgency" of *Leaves of Grass*

---

82 The translation of *Leaves of Grass* is his best-known accomplishment, but Simon Halkin also translated Yiddish poetry into Hebrew, in particular the poetry of his cousin Shmuel Galkin, a famous Soviet Yiddish poet and translator.
83 Uri Zvi Greenberg, *Kelape Tish'im Ve-tish'ah* (Tel Aviv: Sadan, 1928), 35. Translation by Ezra Greenspan in Allen and Folsom, *Walt Whitman and the World*, 388–389. The apostrophe could be translated as "Hebrew Whitman" rather than "Hebraic" (it is the same word in Hebrew).
84 Jeffrey Einboden, *Nineteenth-Century U. S. Literature in Middle Eastern Languages* (Edinburgh: Edinburgh University Press, 2013), 130.

and provided a "Hebrew amplification of Whitman's biblicism."[85] He did so by using many biblical equivalents (such "Garden of Eden" for "heaven" or "Valley of Hinnom" for "hell") and by emphasizing a number of stylistic aspects, such as parallels, symmetries and invocations. Einboden also notes that the title of the translation, in its unvowelled script, coincides with a phrase of the Hebrew Bible meaning "upon the grass." Of particular interest is the examination of "Salut au Monde!": like most translators before him, Halkin performed a number of appropriations (or "domestications," in Einboden's word), particularly regarding the lines relating to his culture or land: as an example, in the line "You Jew journeying in your old age through every risk, / to stand once on Syrian ground!," "Syrian ground" is translated as "holy land." The acme of the prophetic Judaic rendition of Whitman involved its relocation to Zion.

This examination of the prophetic Whitman has demonstrated how intermingled the religious and political were at the turn of the century. The British and the American Yiddish receptions are particularly revealing of this shift from religion to politics and of the use of a messianic imaginary for secular struggles. It is to this that I will now turn.

---

85 Ibid., 131, 132.

Chapter 4

From democrat to socialist (1880s–1919)

"Democracy" was Walt Whitman's watchword. As Kirsten Harris contends, the word had a special aura and meaning for him and his followers.[1] It also loomed large in Whitman's political reception, especially in the period that I will now consider, from the 1880s to World War I. Edward Carpenter, the most famous British Whitmanian, called his own collection of poems *Toward Democracy*, while Korney Chukovsky chose "Poetry of Future Democracy" as title for his translation of Whitman. In both cases, democracy was a goal, an ideal, or, in Whitman's terms, a "great word, whose history ... remains unwritten, because that history has yet to be enacted."[2] The lack itself was inspiring. Whitman's democracy remained full of potential, at a time when political ideas were bubbling, from the most utopian to the most action-oriented. Whitman himself had expressed support and sympathy for European revolutions: in 1850, he wrote the poem, "Resurgemus," for the victims of tyrants during the revolutions of 1848.[3] It was later included in *Leaves of Grass* (with no title in

---

1 K. Harris has a section on "The Word Democracy" in her chapter on Carpenter (*Whitman and British Socialism*, 51–61).
2 Whitman, *Poetry and Prose*, 984.
3 On Whitman and the 1848 Revolutions, see Betsy Erkkila, "'To Paris with my Love:' Walt Whitman among the French Revisited," *Revue d'Études Françaises Américaines*, 108, no. 2 (2006): 7–22.

1855, then "Poem of the Dead Young Men of Europe, the 72nd and 73rd Years of These States," and later "Europe, the 72nd and 73rd Years of These States"). Not too surprisingly, it became a favorite among the European revolutionaries who read Whitman (and was often referred to simply as "Europe"), along with "To a Foil'd European Revolutionaire." But while showing interest in socialist movements, Whitman never endorsed any of them. That did not stop European socialists and communists from using his poems, though, or simply his name, for their cause. Whitman was read as a poet of collective love, brotherhood, communality, which translated into diverse political uses. Paradoxically, given the internationalist agenda of socialist readers, national contexts mattered more than for the *primitive* or Futurist Whitman: different contexts shaped different political receptions. Whatever the flaws of the British, French or American democracies, they were indeed democracies, which was not the case with the German Empire, and even less so with the Russian Empire, especially before 1905. In Russia, notwithstanding the fact that socialist and anarchist ideas were thriving, the idea of democracy stood mostly as the opposite of autocracy and censorship—at least for Whitman's translators and commentators. The Italian case was slightly different: the recently unified kingdom was a nascent nation slowly implementing democracy. The challenge is to take into account such diverse economic and political contexts while mapping out the networks of socialist readers that formed along several lines. Socialism developed earlier in Britain, which was therefore at the vanguard of the political reception in many respects. The British and the Americans formed fellowships while European Whitmanites in France, Germany and Italy exchanged ideas. In this particular instance, the Russian reception appears to have been less connected to Western Europe.

Foreword: the impact of the British editions

It was often the British editions, more easily available—especially to a number of European revolutionaries exiled in London, from German Social Democrats to Russian Narodniks—that provided access to Whitman in Europe. The first two in particular, William Michael Rossetti's in 1868 and Ernest Rhys's in 1886, had a decisive impact. They were very different, separated by two decades and corresponding to distinct stages of Whitman's poetry. Ernest Rhys, a Welsh socialist, had much more of a political agenda than Rossetti. The choice of poems was different, and so were the paratexts. In contrast with Rossetti's epigraph from Michelangelo, Rhys began his preface with a stanza from Whitman's "Pioneers." Rossetti insisted on the originality of Whitman's poetry, Rhys on its impulse toward "love and comradeship."⁴ Yet, both emphasized "democracy." For Rossetti, the book taken as a whole was a "poem both of Personality and Democracy"⁵—Korney Chukovsky would use the exact same words as the title of one his first essays on Whitman. He quoted Thoreau, for whom Whitman "is Democracy." The title he chose for the first section of poems was "Chants Democratic" (already the title of a cluster in the 1860 *Leaves of Grass*). In Rhys's preface, Democracy also loomed large as an encompassing concept: he emphasized Whitman's faith in "the Democracy that is so unsettling the old feudal relations, in art as well as in political and social life."⁶

As Caterina Bernardini argues, Rossetti's "ideological stance was rooted in the Italian Risorgimento tradition,"⁷ since his father was an exiled Italian patriot. In return, Rossetti's edition shaped the initial Italian reception of Whitman. Enrico Nencioni, the Florentine critic, used it for his essays on Whitman,⁸ and, as Bernardini notes, promoted a Democratic Whitman directly aligned with Rossetti's own views, especially regarding his admiration for the revolutionary activist Mazzini: Nencioni characterized Whitman in Mazzinian terms, as a poet standing "with the people," rather than "for the people."⁹ Ferdinand Freiligrath, a German poet and activist who was often exiled in Britain (where he became Marx's friend), also encountered Whitman through Rossetti's translation in 1868: he published an essay along with the first translations of Whitman into German (from "Drum-Taps"). As Walter Grünzweig observes, Jakob Schabelitz, who published the first German book-length edition of Whitman in 1889, was a revolutionary democrat who had befriended Freiligrath in exile.¹⁰

Rhys's selection found its way to Russia—we know it was sent to Tolstoy. More importantly, it was after his stay in England that Chukovsky published the poem inspired by Whitman's "Pioneers," on which I will comment at length later. Admittedly, the poem was often quoted in socialist Britain, but its popularity originated precisely from Rhys's epigraph. Rhys's principle of a popular and cheap edition would inspire several other translators. In 1907, Johannes Schlaf published his work with the press Reclam in the form of an affordable

---

4   Michael Rossetti, *Leaves of Grass: The Poems of Walt Whitman, Selected, with an Introduction by Ernest Rhys* (London: Walter Scott, 1886), x.
5   Ibid., 5.
6   *Leaves of Grass*, ed. Rhys, xxxiii.
7   Bernardini, *Transnational Modernity*, 24.
8   Nencioni's essay in 1881 was reviewed in the *New York Times* (James Jackson Jarves, "Art and Poesy. Walt Whitman Held up as a Model to Italian Poets," *New York Times*, October 24, 1881, 2).
9   Bernardini, *Transnational Modernity*, 26.
10 See the chapter on Freiligrath in Grünzweig, *German Whitman*, 11–19.

book "which fit into everybody's pocket."[11] Caterina Bernardini has brought to light a similar edition by Luigi Gamberale, who, after completing his unabridged translation, worked on small and cheap volumes "intended to be popular and accessible to all."[12] She has shown how Gamberale cut the catalogues as he edited the poems for a working-class readership. The volumes were printed in his hometown, Agnone, in 1912. Chukovsky's translation for the publisher Sytin, in 1914, was ill-fated (it was banned by censorship), but the choice of Sytin can be explained by his strong commitment to educating the masses.

1. "The institution of the dear love of comrades"

Whitman and British ethical socialism

Fin de siècle Britain was awash with new political ideas.[13] Anarchism, socialism, messianism and utopianism combined easily before political parties were formed and theories converted into electoral manifestos. In the period between 1880 and 1914, often referred to as the "socialist revival," Marxist thought gained momentum while also generating counterproposals and more utopian ideas. There were many leagues and societies, from the most Marxist (the Social Democracy, established in 1880) to the least: William Morris's Socialist League, G. B. Shaw's Fabianism, and all those that formed the nexus of "ethical socialism." Whitman was important for the Socialist League, where the prophetic rhetoric was strong (its manifesto demanded "single-hearted devotion to the religion of socialism").[14]

Among the main figures in that busy intellectual landscape was J. W. Wallace, who regularly delivered lectures on Whitman's democracy, as a new form of religion. William Clarke was more involved in politics: he was the co-founder of the Fellowship of the New Life in 1883 (alongside Carpenter), and joined the Fabian Society in 1886, contributing to the *Fabian Essays in Socialism* (1889). In 1892, Clarke wrote one of his longest essays, a study on Whitman, for Swan Sonnenschein & Co., which published mainly socialist books. More prolific yet was Edward Carpenter, whose socialism was based on the idea of comradeship, with little concern for action or actual power. Carpenter's interest

---

11 Ibid., 53.
12 See Bernardini, *Transnational Modernity*, 66–70.
13 Again, the British political reception of Whitman has been studied thoroughly by Kirsten Harris, to whose book I refer.
14 William Morris and the Provisional Council of the Socialist League, "Manifesto of the Socialist League," *Commonweal*, February 1885, 2.

lay with political poetics rather than political theory. However, his idealism could embrace activism, since he contributed to the inclusion of poetry in the repertoire of socialist slogans and workers' hymns. His poem "England arise" is one of the classics of British socialist poetry: it was read at Labour Church meetings, sometimes together with poems by Whitman. In 1892, he collected texts and scores for the songbook *Chants of Labour*,[15] which included Shelley, Morris and Whitman. The book featured "For You O Democracy" (under Rossetti's title: "Love of Comrades"), "The Great City" and excerpts from "Song of the Broad-Axe" that removed the nationalistic parts of the poem. These choices are very similar to the later Russian socialist and communist ones. I don't wish to suggest that the Russians were necessarily aware of the British selection—more likely they simply picked the same overtly political pieces.

The transatlantic socialist fellowship

Wallace and Carpenter both visited Camden and were in close contact with their American counterparts through an extensive correspondence. The main representative of the American branch of the Whitmanian socialists was Horace Traubel, who compiled Carpenter's works. Traubel founded the journal the *Conservator*, whose purpose was to preserve Whitman's heritage,[16] but some articles had a fully political orientation, including, for example, attacks on major capitalists. Carpenter's writings were given an exceptional platform in the *Conservator*; he was the most conspicuous Whitmanite on its front page.[17]

Traubel was also the author of two collections of poems. *Chants communal* was first published in the socialist weekly the *Worker*, and then as a book in 1904. It contained some idealistic poems, quite Whitmanian in style, as well as long sequences of paratactic prose, which were more partisan: "We are learning a lesson. The lesson of inviolable unity.... We refuse longer to remain isolated. We have learned to stick together."[18] In the collection *Optimos*, published in 1910, the idea of struggle receded and gave way to grand prophetic declarations. In the poem dedicated to Whitman, "O my dead comrade. For W. W.," Traubel staged himself at Whitman's death-bed: "O my great dead! / You had not gone—you had stayed, in my heart, in my veins, / Reaching through me, through others

---

15 Edward Carpenter, *Chants of Labour* (London: Swan Sonnenschein & Co.,1892).
16 There were 352 issues; Gary Schmidgall provides an anthology in *Conserving Walt Whitman's Fame: Selections from Horace Traubel's Conservator, 1890–1919* (Iowa City: Iowa University Press, 2006).
17 See ibid., xxxiv.
18 Horace Traubel, "Of many voices one voice," in *Communal Songs* (Boston: Small, Maynard & Co.,1904), 27.

through me, through all at last, our brothers, / A hand to the future."[19] *Optimos* borrowed, except for the catalogues, all the great Whitmanian stylistic devices: apostrophes, questions, anaphora. The collection was therefore criticized for being a pale imitation of the master; in her apologetic work on Traubel published in 1913, Mildred Bain explained that the resemblance was unavoidable because Whitman's influence was "a root nourishment as impalpably strong as natural elements."[20]

Whitman was also a reference among activists and union members, especially the Wobblies (the members of the International Workers of the World). One of the most important figures was Emma Goldman, whose Whitmanian activism had started before World War I. Goldman was born in the Lithuanian part of the Russian Empire and emigrated to the US quite young. She became an anarchist and was jailed for being involved in a murderous conspiracy—she discovered Whitman at that time.[21] In 1906, she founded a magazine, which she planned to call *Open Road*. The name, already in existence, had to be changed to *Mother Earth*,[22] but the cover of the first volume showed that road.

FIGURE 4.1. Cover of *Mother Earth*, no. 1 (1906). Project Gutenberg.

---

19 Horace Traubel, "The people are the masters of life," in *Optimos* (New York: Huebsch, 1910), 248.
20 Mildred Bain, *Horace Traubel* (New York: Albert and Charles Boni, 1913), 28.
21 Timothy Robbins, "Emma Goldman Reading Walt Whitman: Aesthetics, Agitation, and the Anarchist Ideal," *Texas Studies in Literature and Language* 57, no. 1 (2015): 80–105.
22 *Mother Earth* 1, no. 1, 5.

The magazine regularly printed Whitman's poems[23] or published essays about him.[24] The poet was also important to a lesser-known figure, Marian Wharton, a feminist and socialist activist (incidentally, Meridel Le Sueur's mother). Wharton was much involved in the People's College, an alternative place of education that existed from 1914 to 1917 in Fort Scott, Texas. *Plain English*, the textbook she wrote for her English classes, abounded in examples taken from Whitman.[25]

Finally, Whitman was a reference for politicians, such as Eugene Debs, the founder of the American Socialist Party. Debs had a close relationship with Traubel, and their letters displayed signs of affectionate camaraderie, such as fraternal apostrophes and outpourings of "love-thoughts." Debs himself wrote about Whitman in the *Conservator*.[26] Ella Reeve Bloor (Mother Bloor), who would become a great figure of American communism, recounted in her autobiography that, as a child (she was born in 1862), she used to visit her aunt who lived in Camden, on Mickle Street, where Whitman lived. She explained how much she enjoyed taking the ferry, watching the people there, mingling with the crowd, soaking up the Whitmanian spirit: "Perhaps it was on those ferry-boat rides that the course of my life was determined, and that Whitman somehow transferred to me, without words, his own great longing to establish everywhere on earth 'the institution of the dear love of comrades.'"[27] She also quoted at great length her favorite Whitman poem "The Mystic Trumpeter."[28]

Another transatlantic connection developed in the late nineteenth century, between the US and Germany: an important German-speaking community

---

23 "Envy" in the third issue, two poems on the front page of a 1917 issue.
24 Elizabeth Burns Fern, "The Democracy of Whitman," *Mother Earth*, no. 11 (January 1907), 23–30; no. 12 (February 1907), 15–21.
25 Marian Wharton, *Plain English. For the Education of the Workers by the Workers* (Fort Scott, Kansas: The People's College, 1917). For example: "In the following quotations note the use of the pronouns and mark whether they are personal, relative or interrogative, whether they are used in the subject form, possessive form or object form: 'Camerado, I give you my hand, / I give you my love more precious than money, / I give you myself before preaching or law; / Will you give me yourself, will you come travel with me, / Shall we stick by each other as long as we live?'" (136). Another exercise consists of introducing punctuation in the sentence: "Walt Whitman who represents individualism at its best writes 'I sing the song of myself' To this the socialist replies "Inasmuch as my redemption is bound up in that of my class I sing the song of my class" (306).
26 Eugene Debs, "About Walt Whitman," *Conservator* 18, no. 5 (July 1907), 73; Debs also reviewed William English Walling's *Whitman and Traubel* in 1917.
27 Ella Reeve Bloor, *We Are Many* (New York: International Publishers, 1940), 22.
28 Much later, when Bloor died in 1951, Walter Lowenfels, then a Philadelphia correspondent for the *Daily Worker*, read this poem at her funeral. J. Edgar Hoover recounted this in his anticommunist book *Masters of Deceit: The Story of Communism in America and how to Fight it* (New York: Henry Holt and Company, 1958) and denounced the communists' appropriation of Whitman, especially their annual pilgrimage to Camden Cemetery (see 158, 171, 336).

had settled in the US, along with a number of German exiles. American and German Whitmanites corresponded and visited each other. The Americans were particularly enthusiastic about Freiligrath's essays and Johannes Schlaf's translations.[29] Karl Knortz's lectures in the US, delivered in German, were later published. His Whitman had a lot in common with the democratic poet outlined by Freiligrath. Conversely, Horace Traubel benefited from a unique dissemination in Germany. His poems were discussed in France, one appeared in Russian in *Pravda* in 1913, but this does not compare with his German reception: *Communal Songs* was translated in 1907[30] and poems from *Optimos* were translated by Johannes Schlaf in the magazine *Die Lese* (1913).

Continental European Whitmanites

A more broadly European network of socialist Whitmanites was also in existence, even though it remained interconnected with what I call the transatlantic fellowship. If Britain was its vanguard, Germany was its main hub at the beginning of the twentieth century, with Johannes Schlaf in close contact with Bazalgette and Traubel. Schlaf was not the only German figure from the Left to translate and comment Whitman. Gustav Landauer, a Jewish social anarchist, a friend of Martin Buber and Petr Kropotkin, was also a Whitmanite.[31] He developed an original conception of socialism, based on a revolution of human relations and the conviction that a community must be bound together by spiritual links—as Grünzweig points out, Landauer stressed Whitman's concept of "adhesiveness." His translation was only published in 1921, but he had worked on it before: its introduction was an essay written as early as 1907. Landauer compared Whitman with Proudhon, on the basis of their common search for a balance between "conservative and revolutionary spirits, individualism and socialism."[32] Whitman also featured in the German socialist press, as Grünzweig demonstrates in his chapter "Whitman and the Marxists," with an essay by Schlaf in the *Sozialistische Monatshefte* in 1904 or poems by Whitman and by Traubel in Clara Zetkin's socialist women's journal *Die Gleichheit* (Equality).[33]

---

29 See Grünzweig, *German Whitman*, 15–16.
30 Horace Traubel, *Weckrufe: Kommunistische Gesänge*, trans. O. E. Lessing (Munich, Leipzig: Piper & co, 1907).
31 See Grünzweig, *German Whitman*, 52–56. More generally on Landauer, see Eugen Lunn, *Prophet of Community: The Romantic Socialism of Gustav Landauer* (Berkeley: University of California Press, 1973).
32 Gustav Landauer, "Walt Whitman," in *Der werdende Mensch. Aufsätze über Leben und Schriften* (Postdam: Gustav Kiepenhauer Verlag, 1921), 190 (first published in *Vossische Zeitung*, 1907).
33 Grünzweig, "Whitman and the Marxists," in *German Whitman*, 151–154.

I also want to mention Kurt Tucholsky's use of "Salut au Monde!" Born in a Jewish family, Tucholsky was a very active satirical journalist. He used several pseudonyms, among which "Ignaz Wrobel." Under that name, he published in 1913 the poem "Salut au monde!," "freely inspired by Walt Whitman" (frei nach Walt Whitman). The first stanza is indeed a translation, except for the name: "Take my hand, Walt Wrobel." Afterwards, Wrobel turns Whitman's song of wonder into social criticism:

> *Ich höre die Hypothekenzinsen des Theaterdirektors auf den Tisch rollen und dazu den Gläubiger seufzen und sagen: "Sechzig Prozent – da sind Sie wieder billig weggekommen!"*
> . . . .
> *Ich höre, wie der gute alte Pariser vor Gericht vorwurfsvoll kreischt: "Herr Staatsanwalt, was fällt Ihnen ein? Bin ich vielleicht ein Wucherer?"*

> I hear the theater manager's mortgage interest roll onto the table and the creditor sigh and say, "Sixty percent—you got off cheap again!"
> . . . .
> I hear the good old Parisian screeching reproachfully in court: Prosecutor, what are you thinking? Am I perhaps a usurer?"

> *Ich sehe die Reporter, die Philologen, die Nigger in den Goldminen und alle Sklaven der Erde.*
> *Ich sehe, wie ein Theaterkassierer das Geld des Besuchers in der Hand hin- und herwendet und fragt: "Ist das Ihr Ernst?"*

> I see the reporters, the philologists, the negroes in the gold mines and all the slaves on earth.
> I see a theater cashier shake the visitor's money in his hand and ask, "Are you serious?"

The end of the poem goes back to translating (freely) Whitman, with the optimistic lines of section 11:

> *Salut au monde!*
> *Ein jeder von uns unvermeidlich!*
> *Ein jeder von uns, seis Mann oder sonst ein Weib, mit seinem Recht an die Erde!*

> *Ein jeder von uns mit seinem Teil hier ebenso göttlich wie irgend einer!*
> *Salut au monde!*
>
> Salut au monde!
> Each of us inevitable,
> Each one of us, whether man or woman, with their right to the earth!
> Each one of us with their part here is just as divine as anyone else!
> Salut au monde!³⁴

However, the context changes the meaning of Whitman's words: they are no longer a statement, a summary of all the enumerations that preceded, but rather a prophecy or a call for action. While reality and ideal coincided in Whitman, reality is now to be inverted to coincide with the ideal.

In the case of Italy, Bernardini has studied Ada Negri's relation with Whitman, in particular her essay "The giant of free America."³⁵ Negri's favorite poem was "Years of the Modern," a choice most Russian and Soviet Whitmanians would share. I will focus more on the French reception, where the socialist Whitman has been somehow overlooked,³⁶ probably because Whitman was essentially of significance only for the Group of the Abbey, a utopian community of writers and poets (among them, René Arcos, Charles Vildrac, Georges Duhamel, Jules Romains), which was mostly active between 1906 and 1908. They were often called the unanimistes, after Jules Romains's doctrine that literature should capture the collective life and spirit of men. Henri Ghéon even suggested changing unanimisme to whitmanisme.³⁷ The group and its members, though important at the time, have been quite forgotten in literary history, probably because they were formally and stylistically rather conservative, and therefore did not fit with the narrative of modernity. Léon Bazalgette's anthologies did not focus on the poetry of struggle and left out pieces like "Europe" or "Pioneers," which the British valued. Yet, Bazalgette was close to socialist circles and his translations were advertised in the left-wing press.

---

34 Ignaz Wrobel, "Salut au monde!," *Die Schaubühne*, no. 49 (December 4, 1913), 1205.
35 Ada Negri, "Il gigante della libera America," *Il figurinaio* 5, no. 8 (February 19, 1893), 2–3.
36 Betsy Erkkilä has extensively documented the unanimistes' relation with Whitman and Daniel Halévy's translations (*Walt Whitman Among the French*, 173), but has provided fewer details on Guilbeaux and on the socialist press.
37 Henri Ghéon, "Les Poèmes: le whitmanisme," *Nouvelle Revue Française*, no. 14 (June 1912), 1053–1071.

The way Whitman was featured in *L'Effort libre* is quite representative of the ambiguities of whitmanisme, of the tension between idealist unanimisme and more radical outlooks. First called *L'Effort*, the journal was founded in 1910 by Jean-Richard Bloch, who conceived it as a collaborative space between contributors and readers—subscribers often became contributors in their turn. In 1912, the *Anthology of the Effort* gathered poems by members of the Abbey. It ended with an essay on Whitman by Bazalgette and a selection of poems, mainly from "Autumn Rivulets." In 1914, *L'Effort libre* published a much more substantial selection of Whitman's poems. It was conceived as a popular, affordable book,[38] in the spirit of Schlaf's Reclam edition, but it left out many of the conspicuously political pieces. Yet, the "Autumn Rivulets" poems were published in the satirical anarchist journal *Le Bonnet rouge*.[39] The edition of 1914 was advertised on the front page of *L'Humanité* (Jean Jaurès's socialist newspaper), with a portrait of Whitman and a quote from "To a Foil'd European Revolutionaire."[40] *L'Humanité* chose the one poem that was highlighted by all European socialist Whitmanites.

In addition, Whitman was a reference for more radical readers than the unanimistes. In 1901 Daniel Halévy translated four "Chants démocratiques" in *Pages libres*, a magazine with socialist leanings and educational aims. "A Song for Occupations" was translated with the title: "Aux ouvriers" ("To the Workers"— Whitman's 1867 title, kept by Rossetti). It was followed by "À un révolté ou à une révoltée vaincue" ("To a Foil'd European Revolutionaire," again from Rossetti's version: "To a Foiled Revolter or Revoltress"). Halévy especially emphasized Whitman's interest for the 1848 Revolution. In 1908, in *Les Pages libres* again, an essay by Pierre Nicolas celebrated the "singer of virile friendship and of men's comradeship that leads to the comradeship of Democracies."[41] In 1907, Elsie Masson praised "Walt Whitman, ouvrier et poète" (worker and poet) in *Mercure de France*. Masson insisted on Whitman's "revolutionary propaganda" as a journalist: he "lambasted all the offences that were reported to him, did not spare the churches, fulminated against the death penalty."[42] Two years later, Valery Larbaud speculated that Whitman would have been greatly amused by Masson's text, especially the part where he is described as an "ardent revolutionary."[43]

---

38 Its price was 1.25 francs, compared with eight francs for Bazalgette's complete translation.
39 *Le Bonnet rouge*, July 31, 1914, 4.
40 *L'Humanité*, July 9, 1914, 1.
41 Pierre Nicolas, "Walt Whitman," *Les Pages libres*, July 1908, 40.
42 Elsie Masson, "Walt Whitman, ouvrier et poète," *Mercure de France*, August 1, 1907, 391.
43 Valery Larbaud, "Lettres anglaises: Walt Whitman en français," *La Phalange*, April 20, 1909, 952–955.

One of the most interesting contributions was a long essay by Henri Guilbeaux as part of the *Portraits d'hier* (Portraits of yesterday) series in 1910. Guilbeaux was close to Bazalgette and *L'Effort libre*, to which he contributed, but grew more and more radical: a member of the Anarcho-Communist Federation and a pacifist, he left France when the war began and then lived in the Soviet Union for a few years. Guilbeaux explained that he came to know Whitman thanks to Schlaf's cheap German edition (Reclam). He praised the poet as "a genius from the people, who loved the people and worked for the people."[44] But what makes Guilbeaux unique is his knowledge of the French reception and of Whitmanian activities in France at the time. He listed the various conferences delivered on Whitman in Belgian and French "Universités Populaires."[45] Guilbeaux called for the creation of a "fellowschip" (*sic*) of Whitmanians who would spread all over France the "Gospel of Modern Times" and "build the solid institution of the tender and proud affection of comrades." According to Guilbeaux, unanimisme—and by that he meant not only Rolland's doctrine but all the works of the Abbey—was the "complete negation of Whitmanisme": "their books might be appreciated by an over-literate elite but will never provide any thrill to the people whom Whitman always addressed directly."[46] Guilbeaux spared some of them, however, especially Philéas Lebesgue and Jean-Richard Bloch.

W. Grünzweig has mentioned the existence of (few) far-right Whitmanians in Germany. I could not locate them in France. To the contrary, a review of Bazalgette's translation in the nationalist *L'Action française* in 1909 displayed the utmost disgust for Whitman's "hodgepodge of nationalities," "social pandemonium," "ragbag of people."[47] While he was not as fiercely committed to the struggles of the people as in Britain, the French Whitman was nonetheless firmly grounded in the Left.

2. The Russian democrat

When it comes to the political implications of Whitman's poetry at the beginning of the twentieth century, the Russian reception stands further apart from the European and the North American ones. Whereas Whitman the *primitive* or Whitman the prophet were shared constructs, Whitman the democrat took on

---

44 Henri Guilbeaux, *Walt Whitman: Portraits d'hier* (Paris: H. Fabre, 1910), 1.
45 Sometimes called Folk high schools, they were institutions that provided an education for adults, without granting academic degrees. An example of a lecture on Whitman, by Joseph Lecomte, can be found in *La Vie intellectuelle* [Brussels], no. 1 (1908), 17–28.
46 Henri Guilbeaux, "Walt Whitman," *L'Effort libre*, May–June 1912, 576–577.
47 Pierre Lasserre, "Walt Whitman," *L'Action française*, April 27, 1909.

rather specific features in Russia. The writings of Carpenter were well known, the name of Traubel was familiar, but it was not their political comments that Chukovsky mentioned in his overviews of the Western reception. Indeed, Whitman was read with a more domestic agenda in tsarist Russia, where censorship was a key factor. The first translations of Whitman's poems were published in periodicals only after the 1905 Revolution, when some freedom of expression was granted. Collections and essays followed, by both Balmont and Chukovsky, which hosted fascinating debates on whether Whitman was a revolutionary poet or not.

Selected poems, from Whitman and not from Whitman

Extracts of Whitman's poetry were presented in P. Popov's review in 1883, but the first poem to appear as an integral translation was published in 1899 in the new journal *Nachalo*. Entitled "From Walt Whitman. Translated from English," by the so-called translator N. Tan, this poem has a quite puzzling story. Far from a translation, it is in fact an invention. Tan was the pseudonym of Vladimir Germanovich Bogoraz, a poet and activist. Born Jewish, Bogoraz converted for practical reasons and changed his first name, Nathan, to Vladimir—"Tan" was after "Nathan." A member of Narodnaia Volia, one of Russia's main radical movements, he was arrested in 1886 and exiled three years later to Yakutsk, Siberia, where he remained for ten years and carried out ethnographic research. Only a couple of months after his return to Saint Petersburg, he published the "translation" from Whitman. At the time, Bogoraz was leaning toward Marxism—*Nachalo* was the journal of the Legal Marxists. Thematically, the poem is an aggregate of revolutionary topoi. Formally, one could see a vague similarity with "Pioneers! O Pioneers!" and its syllabo-tonic quatrains, but above all, it resembles most of Bogoraz's poems at the time. The beginning reads:

> Не скорбным, бессильным, остывшим бойцам,
> Усталым от долгих потерь,
> Хочу я отважным и юным сердцам
> Пропеть свою песню теперь![48]

> Not to mournful, powerless and cold fighters,
> Tired of long losses,
> But to brave and young hearts
> Do I want to sing my song now!

---

48 I. S. Eventon, ed., *Poèziia v bol'shevistskikh izdaniiakh, 1901–1917* (Leningrad: Sovetskii pisatel', 1967), 58–59.

And the end:

> Да скроется сумрак, да здравствует свет!
> Мы вестники новых времен!
> Весна молодая идет нам вослед
> Под сенью несчетных знамен.

> Let the darkness disappear, long live the light!
> We are heralds of new times!
> A young spring is following us
> Under countless banners.

As Bogoraz later admitted, the translation was a fictitious one.[49] It still raises interesting questions, especially since this was not a practice Bogoraz was familiar with: Was the American poet famous enough among the narodniki that his name would amount to a revolutionary shibboleth? Or maybe pretending that it was a translation was simply a ploy to avoid censorship? But then, where did Bogoraz hear of Whitman? In Yakutsk or on his return to Petersburg? In 1902, Tan-Bogoraz (who was then in New York) published another poem "by Whitman," "Song of steel," together with a poem by Maxim Gorky "Song of the Petrel." While "Song of steel" went into limbo, the 1899 poem had an interesting fate after 1917. It was often included in anthologies of revolutionary poetry, as a poem by Bogoraz, sometimes under the title "Song of Spring." In 1951, Dmitri Shostakovich, who had just been severely criticized by Stalin, composed a number of official pieces to secure the position that he was beginning to regain. Among these works was a choral cycle of revolutionary poetry.[50] The final piece was Bogoraz's so-called translation, referred to in the score as "Song / lyrics V. Tan-Bogoraz (from W. Whitman)." The poem was also quoted by Antonina Koptiaeva in her novel about the civil war *Na Urale Reke* (On the Ural River, 1971). To go back to 1899, it is fascinating that Whitman's poetry (almost) made its (almost) first appearance in the radical press and that his name would thus be associated with revolutionaries.

This connection was strengthened in the context of the following translations. Both Balmont and Chukovsky were involved in political protests at the beginning of the century. Balmont's participation in demonstrations and

---

49 See *Poèty demokraty 1870–1880x godov* (Leningrad: Sovetskii Pisatel', 1968), 743.
50 *Desiat' poèm na slova revoliutsenykh poètov kontsa XIX – nachala XX stoletii: dlia smeshannogo khora bez soprovozhdeniia, soch. 88* (Ten choral poems to the words of revolutionary poets of the late nineteenth and early twentieth centuries, for a mixed choir without accompaniment). The premiere, conducted by A. V. Sveshnikov, head of the State Russian Song Choir, took place on October 10 in Moscow.

publication of a pamphlet against the tsar in 1901 got him exiled for a couple of years. As he explained in "Poliarnost'" (Polarity), it was upon his return that he started to translate Whitman, from the fall of 1903 to the fall of 1905, first on the Baltic Sea, in Meriküla and Sillamäe (Estonia), then in Moscow in 1905, with the "incessant music of rifle shots"[51] in the background. At the end of 1905, after participating in protests again, Balmont had to flee to Paris, and he did not come back to Russia until 1913. His book-length translation of Whitman was published during that time, in 1911.

Korney Chukovsky was in his hometown, Odesa, during the *Potemkin* mutiny. When he came back to Saint Petersburg, he founded the journal *Signal*, which was the first satirical paper after some freedom of the press had been granted. In the first issue, he published a rewriting of Whitman's "Pioneers! O Pioneers!" While only one line was indicated as being translated from Whitman, the whole poem was in fact an adaptation (see Chapter 7 on "Pioneers"). After three issues, Chukovsky was charged with insulting the tsar and sentenced to six months in jail; he was bailed out and the sentence was finally overruled. Chukovsky stopped his activities as a satirist after 1905, but he continued to translate and discuss Whitman.

FIGURE 4.2. Cover of the first issue of *Signal*, November 1905. University of Southern California Digital Library. Russian Satirical Journals Collection.

---

51 Konstantin Bal'mont, "Poliarnost'" (1908), repr. as the introduction to Uol't Uitman, *Pobegi travy* (Moscow: Skorpion, 1911), vii.

During the years 1906 and 1907, both Balmont and Chukovsky had a political agenda as they translated Whitman. Balmont's versions appeared in the periodicals of the publishing house *Znanie* (Knowledge), supervised by Maxim Gorky. In fact, when he visited the US in 1906, Gorky told the *New York Times*: "I will place Walt Whitman, also, as my favorite American poet. He is so absolutely original, so much a man of the people, and a democrat straight away."[52] The poems chosen were representative of what drew liberal readers to Whitman: "Years of the Modern," "O Star of France," "Europe" and "Beat! Beat! Drums!" Extracts from "Europe" were also translated by Chukovsky for the magazine *Narodnyi Vestnik* (the People's Messenger). In 1907, Chukovsky published the first collection in Russian—though still short and selective, with only forty pages of poems. It included parts of "Song of Myself" and excerpts from the "Calamus" section, along with more expected political poems ("Europe" again, but also "O Captain! My Captain!").

Moreover, some poems were translated into other languages in the Russian Empire. As noted in Chapter 2, a Latvian anthology was published as early as 1908. In 1911, an anonymous edition was published. Like the previous Latvian translation and like Chukovsky's 1907 anthology, it was about forty pages long. It has been attributed to Makonis (pseudonym of Jēkabs Kalniņš), a member of the Latvian Social Democratic Workers Party, who was sent from 1909 to 1917 to a penal colony in Smolensk, where he was allowed to write poems and stories. The poem "To a Foil'd European Revolutionaire" was translated into Lithuanian in 1909. It was published in the United States, where a Lithuanian press had existed since the "Lithuanian press ban"—the ban on the Latin alphabet which came into force in 1865 as part of the policy of Russification. Even though the counterproductive ban was lifted in 1904, Lithuanian publications abroad continued to thrive. Whitman's poem was published in *Vienybe lietuvniku* (Unity of the Lithuanians).[53] The translator was Julius Baniulis, a writer who had emigrated to the US in 1902 and collaborated with various socialist papers.

In 1910, the Vilna Polish journal *Wiedza* (Knowledge) published an essay on Whitman by Stefan Rudniański.[54] Like most socialist activists in the Russian Empire, Rudniański (who had been expelled from his gymnasium in 1905 for

---

52 "Maxim Gorky on the Russian Revolution," *New York Times*, April, 15, 1906, magazine section, 3.
53 "In patremtą Europos kovotoją," *Vienybe lietuvniku*, no. 43, September 27, 1909, 4. It was a weekly newspaper first published in Plymouth, PA, and then in Brooklyn. By 1909, it was a socialist periodical.
54 Stefan Rudniański (Ruber), "Walt Whitman. Życie i twórczość," *Wiedza: tygodnik społeczno-polityczny, popularno-naukowy i literacki*, 1910, no. 31, 157–160; no. 32, 189–192; no. 33, 220–224.

participating in student strikes) used a pseudonym, Ruber. As Marta Skwara has shown, he aimed at presenting Whitman to the working classes, beginning with a translation of "No Labor-Saving machine."[55] He mentioned the cheap German and Russian editions, presumably Schlaf's selection and Chukovsky's chapbook. Rudniański stood at cultural crossroads: born in Brest, he studied in Warsaw and Leipzig, and lectured for varied cultural organizations (the Polish Cultural Society, People's Universities and workers clubs), where he very likely talked about Whitman.

The poetry of "struggle" versus the poetry of "future democracy"

Even though Konstantin Balmont was less prolific on the politics of *Leaves of Grass* than Chukovsky, he put more emphasis on the idea of struggle. This has been much underestimated by Soviet critics: as I noted, while he strongly supported the February Revolution, Balmont disapproved of the Bolshevik coup and eventually fled Russia. It did not fit the Soviet narrative that an exile like Balmont read Whitman in a more radical way than Chukovsky. At the end of the essay "Poetry of struggle," Balmont wrote:

> We live in an evil house; its foundations lie on corpses, on half corpses, on tortured living beings. We must destroy this evil house and build another one. We—we, the people—, we are builders, have we not the power to build everything that our feelings and our thoughts conceive for us!
> The way to construction is struggle. The struggle of the isolated with themselves and the struggle of the isolated with the merging mass of united monsters who thrive on injustices.[56]

While Balmont's 1911 collection had the neutral title *Pobegi travy* (Spears of grass), it included many poems from "Children of Adam" and added to the repertoire of political poems "Salut au Monde!" (translating the title and keeping the French underneath) and "Song of the Broad-Axe." The preface characterized Whitman's democracy with two short sentences: "Idealized democracy. Enlightened power of the people."[57] Balmont repeatedly used the word *narod*

---

55 Skwara, *Polski Whitman*, 94–98.
56 Konstantin Bal'mont, "Poèziia bor'by" (1907), in *Belye zarnitsy*, 119.
57 Konstantin Bal'mont "Idealizovannaia demokratiia. Prosvetlennoe narodovlastie," in *Pobegi travy*, vii. The two words are synonyms for "democracy," but the second one is Slavic.

(people) in his translation, starting with the first inscription: "Yet utter the word Democratic, the word En-Masse" becoming "No slovo moe—dlia Naroda, moi lozung—Dlia Vsekh" (But my word—for the People; my motto—For All).

Chukovsky had a different standpoint. Despite his enthusiasm and his use of "Pioneers" in *Signal*, he was reluctant to read Whitman as a revolutionary poet, let alone a socialist one. Even though he evolved throughout the years, he remained mainly interested in one fundamental aspect of Whitman's political thought: the tension between the individual and the collective.

In the very first piece he published on Whitman, "Path to Reconciliation,"[58] in 1904, Chukovsky drew two versions of the poet, seemingly hard to reconcile: on the one hand, the civil poet (*poet grazhdanin*), the tribune of the masses, and on the other hand, the decadent poet of sexual love and Dionysian intoxication. "Where is the connection?" Chukovsky asks—an important question "especially for Russians at the present moment." Two paths can lead to the reconciliation of the two models: logic and "sensory perception." The second option, provided by Whitman, is the most efficient: it erases the separation between the "I" and the "not-I." In any case, Chukovsky, though acknowledging Whitman as a civil poet, one who calls for action (he quotes a stanza from "Pioneers"), is adamant that he cannot be compared with Ada Negri or even Nekrasov: "The poet—the citizen, the singer of the crowd, composing hymns to every average person—was the greatest individualist." In his following essay, "Personal identity and Democracy,"[59] Chukovsky expands on these two versions of the poet. He first defines Whitman's "all-encompassing" conception of democracy:

> Whitman creates the religion of the proletariat, its philosophy, poetry, science. He is not trying to raise the proletariat to the "true world" [istinnyi mir] but to extract the "true world" out of the proletariat, to recreate it out of the proletariat. This is a complex, multifaceted democratic theodicy, and not a narrow worldview, like the varied theories and systems that the working class has produced until now.[60]

---

58 Kornei Chukovskii, "O puti k primireniiu," *Odesskie Novosti*, November 26, 1904.
59 Kornei Chukovskii, "Uot Uitmen: Lichnost' i demokratiia ego poèzii." "Lichnost'" is a difficult word to translate, since it combines the ideas of personality, identity and individuality. As noted earlier it probably translates Rossetti's assessment of *Leaves of Graves* as a poem of "Personality and Democracy."
60 Chukovsky uses the expression *chertvertoe soslovie* (the Fourth Estate), roughly meaning the working class.

Then he turns to the question of individualism. After a long passage about the Dionysian quality of Whitman's *lichnost'*—and a long comparison with Nietzsche—Chukovsky asks again: "Now the question, perhaps the most accursed question of Russian philosophy: How can Whitman's democracy be connected with his deification of the individual"? He observes that the Russian reviewers widened the gap: Balmont took into account only individualism[61] while Mr Dioneo (Isaac Shklovsky) considered only democracy.[62] "In a word, the Russian reader is presented with two different Whitmans and does not know how to tie them together." Whitman did not know either and preferred to acknowledge his own contradictions, but it was precisely "by not trying to build artificial bridges of logic between the two edges of this deep abyss" that he showed the way. Again, Chukovsky suggests the value of feeling, intuition, "pathos," to reconcile the self and democracy.

In the years 1906 and 1907, he repeatedly presented Whitman as an "anarchist." First applied to Whitman's individualism, the word loomed large in the following essay, also published in 1906, "Revolution and Literature. The Poet Anarchist Walt Whitman."[63] The title is misleading since Chukovsky argues that Whitman was no revolutionary and that anarchism should not be understood in a strictly political sense. In fact, in a later essay in 1909, Chukovsky expressed strong disagreement with Mikhail Nevedomsky's view: "for some reason, Mr. Nevedomsky wants Whitman to be an 'anarcho-socialist,' although Whitman has stated many times that 'the natural course of things will lead to better results than any theory of socialism can promise.' He spoke out against strikes and demanded from the workers a spiritual struggle, and not an economic one, in a spirit close to Tolstoyism."[64] Chukovsky did not use the term "anarchist" in a social or economic sense, but rather as a rough equivalent of "democratic." His essay on the "poet anarchist" began by quoting "Europe" (in the very loose translation previously published), only

---

61 Chukovsky referred to Balmont's essay "Pevets lichnosti i zhizni" (Singer of personal identity and of life), published in 1904; his own essay was, as clear from the very title ("lichnost' i demokratiia," a dialogue with Balmont. Chukovsky right: at that point, Balmont was more interested in Whitman's embrace of life and cosmic consciousness; see Chapters 1 and 3). However, Balmont did relate Whitman's lichnost' to collective issues and insisted that his "I" was "the simple strong I of the new race."

62 In 1898, under the pseudonym "Dioneo," Isaac Shklovsky published two short essays on Whitman.

63 Kornei Chukovskii, "Revoliutsiia i literatura. Poèt-anarkhist Uot Uitman," *Svoboda i zhizn'*, September 24 [October 7], 1906.

64 Kornei Chukovskii, "Mirovoi vostorg."

to say that the poem was hardly representative and was, in fact, unique in Whitman's poetry. Indeed, Whitman was a "Protestant with no protest in his soul"; he found causes only for admiration and not for rebellion. Even slavery, which Beecher Stowe and Longfellow were able to denounce with "pathos," was an opportunity for writing hymns instead of cursing. Chukovsky cited the infamous lines from "I Sing the Body Electric" about the slave auction. His quote, however, was more a parody than a translation: "A stupid merchant does not know how to do his trade / Well, I'll help him! / Gentlemen, you see a miracle!" For Whitman, equality was not to be conquered but was already there: "people are equal now; and you have the very power to constantly enforce this present equality." What was hostile to democracy simply did not exist, or rather it was part of democracy. It was this very inclusiveness that Chukovsky called "an anarchist conception of the world" (anarkhicheskoe miroponimanie). Whitman's democracy was cosmic in essence: he saw "democratic unity" among the stars, the sea waves, the lilacs, and people were only an insignificant part of it. Whitman's "demos" did not involve a mere social class or group, nor a state, but absolutely everything. To support his stand, Chukovsky quoted P. Popov, who, in 1883, had referred to Whitman as "Goethe's Faust, but happier," "reveling in life as it is." What Chukovsky omitted was that Popov also referred to Whitman as "Milton's Satan" and mentioned his "spirit of indignation and pride."[65] At the end of the essay, he wondered if "Pioneers! O Pioneers!" was a counterexample. The answer was no, since the poem was about the promises of the prairies and not about revolutions: "this 'orgy' is not an orgy of political passions, it is not about the ruins of the old system," but about "an insane passion for creative, constructive work." The essay was included in the selection of poems published in 1907, bearing the same title, which drew the attention of the *New York Times* correspondent in Saint Petersburg.[66]

Six years later, Chukovsky prepared a larger collection for the renowned publisher Ivan Sytin, "Poetry of the Future Democracy."

---

65 In later references to Popov's essay, Chukovsky reintroduced the spirit of indignation and "Milton's Satan" (*Poèziia budushchei demokratii*, 1919), 103.
66 "POET-ANARCHIST WHITMAN. Title Given American Author by His Translator into Russian. Special Correspondence," *New York Times*, July 21, 1907, 2. "Naturally, the Russian reviewer I have quoted thinks that the best thing Whitman wrote was the 'Summons to Insurrection.'"

Figure 4.3. Cover of Uot Uitmèn, *Poèziia griadushchei demokratii* (Moscow: Sytin, 1914). Russian State Library.

This edition brought him excitement and disillusion. In 1913, his completed manuscript was briefly lost by the publisher—fortunately it was soon found again, but the incident caused Chukovsky "unheard-of pain."[67] When the book was released, it was condemned by the censors as "pornography." To Chukovsky's dismay, Sytin did not even send a lawyer to defend the book at the hearing—this was the only instance when he did not contest a suit against one of his publications, due to his efforts to gain the goodwill of the government.[68] All Chukovsky could do at the time was to protest in the press: "But here comes the strange, terrible, laughable, insane news: the book was arrested for pornography?! The poetry of the coming democracy turns out to be fornication, obscenity! It turns out that this inspired prophet, shaking the sky and earth with fiery volcanic words, was just a drooling old man, a lewd, trashy profligate!"[69] However, even if the book was censored, it was reviewed and contributed to further discussions on Whitman. The ban later gave prestige to Whitman, as Soviet critics liked to point out that previously censored writers were freely published by the Bolsheviks.

---

67 Letter to Sergei Botkin, September 8 [21], 1913, in Chukovskii, *Sobranie sochinenii*, 4:311.
68 According to Charles Rudd, *Russian Entrepreneur: Publisher Ivan Sytin of Moscow. 1851–1934* (Montreal: McGill-Queen's University Press, 1990), 151–152.
69 Chukovskii, "Anekdot."

In 1917, the February Revolution already made Whitman fashionable again and his work was included at poetry readings. For example, on April 13, 1917, under the provisional government, a poetry evening at the Petrograd Tenichevsky school featured the great names of contemporary Russian poetry (Yesenin, Klyuev, Akhmatova), as well as Whitman ("Beat! Beat! Drums!") and Verhaeren. The Whitman was read by a famous actress, Lydia Yavorskaya (Princess Bariatinsky), best known for her roles in Chekhov's plays. This unlikely mix was quite typical of the eclecticism of the times.

3. War and peace

Before returning to the political reception of Whitman in Russia after 1917, I want to focus on France and Germany during the war and its immediate aftermath. While the two countries were at the heart of the conflict, they developed quite a similar relation to Whitman. At first, the display of patriotism in his early civil war poems was inspirational, but the "wound-dresser" was ultimately much more appealing. Hopes to transform the horror of the war into a transcending ordeal found templates in Whitman's war poems.

"An example of war poetry"

Participation in the war was a point of contention for the European Left. While Jean Jaurès is known for his unapologetic pacifism, others traded internationalism for patriotism when the war broke out. In Germany, Whitman was held up by social democrats as "an example of war poetry"—the title of an essay by Franz Diederich, who explained that Whitman taught his readers not to turn away from hard realities and to "face the worst boldly."[70] Another instance was Max Hayek, who published an essay on "Whitman poet of war" and several translations in the socialist press (*Sozialistische Monatshefte*).[71] "The Mystic Trumpeter," a poem often quoted by socialists, became a call to arms.

There were no patriotic uses of Whitman in France at the beginning of the war, except perhaps in Guillaume Apollinaire. Whitman had been very much on Apollinaire's mind before the war—one remembers his hoax account of Whitman's funeral in 1913. At the beginning of the war, Apollinaire became a French citizen so as to enroll in the army. His early war poems were patriotic and

---

70 See Grünzweig, *German Whitman*, 58–59.
71 The translations were published as a book in 1919 (see ibid., 59–62).

bellicose. In "2e canonnier conducteur," he described "Victory" rejoicing at the soldiers' salvo; the poem alternates lines and calligrams, among which stands a defiant Eiffel Tower.

Figure 4.4. Guillaume Apollinaire, Detail from the calligram "2e Canonnier Conducteur," *Der Mistral* (Zürich), no. 1 (March, 3, 1915).

It reads as "Hail to the world (Salut monde), whose eloquent tongue I am, the tongue that your mouth O Paris sticks out and will always stick out at the Germans." It is tempting to read "Salut monde" as a reference to Whitman, whose benevolent greeting to the world seems to be reversed into a defiant gesture towards the Germans. Apollinaire's war poems were more complex than this calligram alone suggests. Other pieces were ambivalent and expressed the agonies of war, such as "Les Feux mouvants du bivouac" (1916), which title can read as an approximate translation of Whitman's "By the bivouac's fitful flame."

Whitman was not exploited by the French when the war broke out, but when the US entered the conflict. He was mentioned in unexpected places, such as a 1917 article in "The Watchman of consulates and international commerce," on a full page, starting with a quote from "Pioneers." The piece stated that, were he alive, Whitman would celebrate with ardent enthusiasm the program of the Allied nations—his war poems were in the hearts and on the lips of all the brave volunteers who were coming to liberate France.⁷² In 1918, at the very end of the war, another essay on Whitman⁷³ tried to reconcile the pacifist and the war poet: Whitman was a pacifist, but not a naïve one. He knew that war could be an ordeal that forced the righteous to overcome their weaknesses. He was an internationalist, but he made distinctions between nations—and France was special to him. The glorious soldiers of Soissons felt, like Ulysses Grant's troops, that they were on a just crusade. The essay ended with a call for reconciliation and quoted "O Star of France," written when the country was defeated by Germany in 1871, yet announcing the future triumph of freedom, justice and peace. Similarly, in 1918, Whitman was hailed in the US as a patriotic poet.⁷⁴

Whitman the wound-dresser

In spite of these instances, Whitman's civil war poetry was generally appreciated for its empathy with soldiers and its wish to soothe the nation's wounds. Léon Bazalgette himself had always been a pacifist and an advocate for the union of the Old Continent. *Europe*, published in 1913, was a manifesto against nationalism. The war reinforced his position and reshaped his relation with Whitman. In 1917, he published a translation of "O Star of France."⁷⁵ The gesture was ambiguous: Was it a patriotic demonstration—as the translation of the title, "Ode to France," could suggest—or a poem that anticipated a new defeat? In any case, it expresses hope for what will follow the war. This sense of hope is enhanced by the illustrations—a series of grey images ending with a colorful image of a valley, illustrating the return of the immortal star of France.

Of greater scope and circulation was *Le Panseur de Plaies* (the Wound Dresser), published that same year. It still featured "O Star of France," but also an anthology of Whitman's war writings, journalism, letters and poems—texts about the agonies of war and reconciliation. The war that was ravaging Europe appeared as a form of repetition of the American Civil War. Bazalgette wished for a similar outcome, the conversion of loss and bloodshed into unity:

---

72 Mathilde Parmentier, "Walt Whitman," *Le Moniteur des consulats et du commerce international*, June 30, 1917, 3.
73 Charles Cestre, "Walt Whitman, poète de l'Amérique en guerre," *Revue des Nations latines*, October 1918, 168–183.
74 A review of Walt Whitman's *Songs of Democracy* was entitled: "A Collection of 'Patriotic Poems' in Which the 'Good Grey Poet' Celebrates the Ideals for Which America Is Fighting Today," *New York Times Book Review*, June 16, 1918, 277.
75 Walt Whitman, *Ode à la France*, trans. Léon Bazalgette, with eleven woodcuts by Paul Combet-Descombes (Paris: À la Belle Édition, 1917). This was a luxury edition, in large format.

We will simply insist, at the beginning of these pages, on the meaning that Walt Whitman intended to give to the great war that transformed his life and his poems: that of an absolute victory of the Union over Secession. . . . As for us, fighting and living our great war, the civil war of Europe, fifty years after him, while the outcome is still uncertain, who would refuse to embrace the dream that millions of victims might also form the pedestal of the future Union, forever victorious over the forces of selfishness, mendacity and predation—that dream which alone is great enough to let us glimpse sometimes, like a promise floating above the mass graves, the redemption of its atrocity, its unfathomable hideousness?[76]

Published in 1919 in Switzerland, *Der Wundarzt* appears as an equivalent of the *Panseur de plaies* (or vice-versa).[77] It was brought together by the Alsatian René Schickele and contained translations of some poems (by Gustav Landauer) as well as letters and prose pieces from the war (translated by Ivan Goll). It was, however, quite different in tone: as the preface indicated, it lacked the "pathos" (*der pathetische Schwung*) once characteristic of Whitman and revealed instead the greatest "simplicity."[78]

Love and reconciliation

A striking feature of Whitman's reception in the years immediately after the war is the emergence, or rather acceptance, of homoeroticism. An important controversy had followed Apollinaire's joke in 1913, and for a whole year, the pages of the *Mercure de France* were filled with letters, from France, but also the US and Germany, taking sides on the question of Whitman's homosexuality. The beginning of the war put an end to it. Also, before the conflict, André Gide had wanted to translate Whitman and restore the text's homoerotic qualities, erased by Bazalgette. The *Nouvelle Revue Française* accepted the project of a collective translation, with Larbaud as coordinator, but it did not go smoothly: Claudel withdrew from it after becoming aware of Gide's sexual preferences, and when the war broke out, the book was postponed in order not to stir up unwanted

---

[76] Walt Whitman, *Le Panseur de plaies. Poèmes, lettres et fragments de Walt Whitman sur la guerre*, new translation by Léon Bazalgette, with two portraits of the poet (Paris: Édition de la Revue Littéraire des Primaires, "Les Humbles," 1917), 4–5.

[77] Walt Whitman, *Der Wundarzt. Briefe, Aufzeichnungen und Gedichte aus dem amerikanischen Sezessionskrieg* (Zürich: Max Rascher Verlag, 1919).

[78] "Vorbemerkung des Herausgebers" (editor's note), in Whitman, *Wundarzt*, 5.

polemics at a time of more pressing issues. In 1918, it was finally published, with Gide's and his friend Jean Schlumberger's translations of "Children of Adam" and all the "Calamus" poems (in Louis Fabulet's translation). No scandal ensued.

Better yet, Léon Bazalgette himself seemed to change his views on the matter. As he continued to spread the Whitmanian gospel after the war, with several books, often in collaboration with artists, he emphasized different poems. *Les Dormeurs* (The Sleepers) was published in 1919[79] as a quarto with sixteen woodcuts by Marcel Gaillard—one of them was an erotic female nude. The same year, Bazalgette again translated some of Whitman's most sexual pieces in *Six Poèmes*:[80] this time, "A Woman Waits for Me" was followed by a more homoerotic set. The folio was illustrated by Jean Lurçat, a young French artist who would later become famous for his tapestry work.

FIGURE 4.5. Jean Lurçat. Ornemental composition. Illustration in Walt Whitman, *Six poèmes*, Paris, A.-G. Gonon, 1919. © Fondation Jean Lurçat, Adagp, Paris [2023]. National Library of France.

In 1919, a new version of *Calamus* was published in Geneva by Éditions du Sablier, just founded by René Arcos (a French poet associated with the Abbey of Créteil) and Frans Masereel (a Belgian engraver, close to Henri Guilbeaux, whom he had joined in Switzerland). They published Romain Rolland along

---

79 Walt Whitman, *Les Dormeurs*, new translation by Léon Bazalgette, with sixteen woodcuts by Marcel Gaillard (Paris: François Bernouard, 1919).
80 Walt Whitman, *Six poèmes*, new version by Léon Bazalgette, ornamental compositions by Jean Lurçat (Paris: A.-G. Gonon, 1919).

with former poets of the Abbey, and had a strong pacifist agenda. In the preface, Bazalgette wrote that Whitman

> takes us "away from the noise of the world," to the retreats where the emblematic reed grows, to confide in us a secret that weighs heavily on him and that he would not dare to deliver other than surrounded by wilderness, solitude and silence: the need to cherish men like himself, virile and loving, natural and free, to be, for example, one of those two young, wild-blooded lads who pursue their adventure through the world hand in hand, or of those gentle males and companions who walk with their arms passed around each other's shoulders as if to support the precious weight of brotherly love.[81]

While still emphasizing Whitman as a poet of companionship, Bazalgette seemed, in a spirit of reconciliation, to accept the possibility of a homoerotic reading. The illustrations, ten woodcuts by Frans Masereel, do not exactly match this "boys in the woods" spirit. Masereel, who would later become a major artist and a communist fellow traveler, chose to illustrate the most political poems. His setting for the naked (or not naked) comrades was the city rather than nature.

81 Walt Whitman, *Calamus*, new version by Léon Bazalgette, with ten woodcuts by Frans Masereel (Geneva: Éditions du Sablier, 1919), 14–15.

FIGURES 4.6. and 4.7. Frans Masereel. Woodcuts. Illustrations in Walt Whitman, *Calamus* (Geneva: Éditions du Sablier, 1919). © Adagp, Paris [2023]. National Library of France.

In 1921, in *"Le Poème-Évangile"* [Gospel Poem] *de Walt Whitman*, Bazalgette, for all his circumlocutions, acknowledged that Whitman's conception of love was uncommon:

> Let us not be surprised by his proud and tender masculinity, nor by the fact that the impulses he confesses to us hardly evoke the usual faces of passion; the contrary would have been a dissonance. He loves the way Walt Whitman loves. He invites us to affirm the same spontaneity, the same insubordination in love, by not limiting ourselves to one or two of its provinces, but by exploring the others, perhaps the vastest still—witness those he himself has travelled to and of which he gives us wonderful accounts.[82]

He believed that the "strength of the appetites" expressed by this poetry, particularly the sexual instinct, could not be stressed enough. This was not exactly an endorsement of the homosexual Whitman, but it was as close as Bazalgette

---

[82] Léon Bazalgette, *Le "Poème-Evangile" de Walt Whitman* (Paris: Mercure de France, 1921), 192–193.

came to it. Similarly, his 1924 review of Gide's *Corydon* (a dialogue in which Whitman was clearly a gay password) contained some irony but also words of conciliation very much in the spirit of a "wound dresser."

A similar trend can be observed in Germany, with a renewed emphasis on democracy, in the context of the nascent Weimar Republic. Hermann Bahr defined Whitman's democracy as "erotocracy."[83] The link between eros and democracy was salient in Hans Reisinger's translation, published in 1922. Reisinger, a friend of Thomas Mann, had been working on the poems for ten years, publishing some of them in the leftist journal *Das Forum*. His introduction emphasized the concepts of "love" and "Eros."[84]

Whitman did not disappear from Western European socialist references in the 1920s, but the war did impact his reception, since his faith in love and comradeship could appear as somewhat naive. To the contrary, Whitman's Russian socialist reception gained momentum with 1917. Whitman's war poetry was summoned again, not for its pacifist and unionist pieces, but for its martial ones. It is time to consider this Bolshevik phase, which reorientated the trajectory of Whitman's reception.

---

83 Hermann Bahr, "Walt Whitman," *Die neue Rundschau* 30, no. 1 (1919), 555–564, trans. Walter Grünzweig, in Allen and Folsom, *Walt Whitman and the World*, 201.
84 See the introduction to Walt Whitman's *Werk* (Berlin: S. Fischer, 1922), trans. Horst Frenz and Walter Grünzweig, in Allen and Folsom, *Walt Whitman and the World*; see also Thomas Mann's letter to Reisinger.

Chapter 5

The extraordinary adventures of Walt Whitman in the land of the Bolsheviks (1918–1936)

The title of this chapter is almost an exact quote from Lev Kuleshov's 1924 film *The Extraordinary Adventures of Mr West in the Land of the Bolsheviks*. Though completely unrelated to Whitman, the film lends us its title, since Whitman's fortune in Soviet Russia was quite exceptional. The years that followed the October Revolution saw tremendous changes in cultural policies, arts, propaganda and publishing systems. Whitman was heralded as a revolutionary poet precisely at that time of intense creativity: his poetry was widely circulated, provided Proletarian anthems, was adapted for the stage and used in agitprop performances. Admittedly he was not the only foreign author to be adopted in this way, but among poets, he can only be compared with Émile Verhaeren,[1] and Whitman's success was much more lasting. This chapter focuses on the period between 1918 and 1923, when enthusiasm for Whitman peaked, and extends into the 1930s, when his place as a canonical author was consolidated.

---

1   See Iurii Orlitskii's chapter on Verhaeren and "proletarian free verse": "Russkii Verkharn do i posle revoliutsii: k probleme genezisa proletarskogo verlibra," in *Stikh i proza v kul'ture Serebrianogo veka*, 840–857.

1. A wide circulation

The 1920s: (re)-translating, (re)-publishing Whitman in Russian

Chukovsky's translation, which had been banned, was revised in the years following the revolution. In 1918, five thousand copies were printed by the publishing house Parus. The poem "Song of the Exposition," which opened the previous selection, was pushed back to the end. Instead, the collection started with a more political choice, "You, Felons on Trial in Court"—its last line ("And henceforth I will not deny them—for how can I deny myself?") being related to Dostoevsky in a footnote.

The edition included a postface by the high-ranked Bolshevik Anatoly Lunacharsky, head of the People's Commissariat for Education (Narkompros). He insisted that Whitman was a communist, and even criticized the title of Chukovsky's translation, *Poetry of Future Democracy*, on the grounds that the collectivist aspect of Whitman should be emphasized more than the democratic one. According to Lunacharsky, the power and the grandiose beauty of Whitmanism lay in "communism," "collectivism" and what Romain Rolland called "unanimism" (*edinodushie*). Like Verhaeren's poetry, it showed the victory of human unity over the individual. Lunacharsky also rejected the term "sympathy" to refer to Whitman's conception of friendship and love, and preferred "brotherhood" (*bratstvo*). He concluded with a definition of communism, which was not only political (the struggle against private property) but also spiritual (the "desire to throw off the pitiful shell of the 'I' and to fly out of it like a creature inspired by love, to become a giant, all-human, immortal and fearless like Whitman").[2] In 1919, fifty thousand copies were printed by the Press of the Petrograd Soviet (the spelling was changed, in accordance with the reforms). Lunacharsky's essay was still included, but not in its entirety and as part of a larger ensemble of texts about Whitman. Chukovsky disagreed with his analysis, replying (in the same volume) that socialism was completely alien to Whitman and that "democracy" was a "titanic" word that went hand in hand with the word "comradeship" (*tovarshchestvo*).

---

2 All quotes are from A. Lunacharskii, "Uitmèn i demokratiia," in Uot Uitmèn, *Poèziia griadushchei demokratii* (Petrograd: Izdanie petrogradskogo soveta rabochikh i krasnykh deputatov, 1919), 116–117.

In 1922, for the first time,[3] Chukovsky entitled his collection *List'ia travy* (Leaves of grass), for the World Literature publishing house. Founded by Gorky, the press was engaged in a very large project of translations into Russian. The most prominent writers and translators worked for it:[4] Zamyatin and Chukovsky were in charge of the English-language section. In 1921, after reading the *Nation and Athenaeum*, Chukovsky wrote in his diary:

> New material on Walt Whitman! And the main thing: how all parts of the world have come closer together: the English writing about the French, the French responding, the Greeks intervening—all nations tightly woven together, civilization becoming broad and unified. It was as if I had been pulled out of a puddle and thrown into the ocean! From now on I have decided not to write about Nekrasov, not to dig into literary squabbles, but to boldly join world literature.[5]

The metaphor of the ocean not only conveys the idea of immensity, but also of movement, of ebbing and flowing; it points at a transatlantic space, which translation will make it possible to cross. Whitman was published in the main collection (*osnovnaia seriia*), which was more academic than the popular one, as it included criticism. It contained all the pieces that had become by then Proletarian classics ("Years of the Modern," "Europe," "Beat! beat! Drums!"), Chukovsky's favorite "Song of the Exposition," but also new translations, from "Children of Adam" to "I Sing the Body Electric." Another lasting change in this 1922 edition was the inclusion of prose pieces (from *Specimen Days* and *Democratic Vistas*).

---

3 It seems that the work was already done by 1920 but that the publication process took longer than expected (in February 1922, Chukovsky wrote in his diary: "Yesterday I spent all day proofreading Whitman. World Literature had been putting this book together for two years, and now it is finally coming out." (*Dnevnik*, 1:189).

4 The catalog published in 1919 announced twelve hundred authors. Two hundred twenty titles were actually published between 1918 and 1924. Among the translators were: Zamyatin, Chukovsky, Mayakovsky, Zhirmunsky, Lozinsky, Gumilev (who was murdered in 1921). See Maria Khotimsky, "World Literature, Soviet Style," *Ab Imperio* 3 (2013): 119–154.

5 Chukovsky, *Dnevnik*, 1:161–162 (March 30, 1921).

Figure 5.1. Cover of Uot Uitmèn. *List'ia Travy* (Petrograd: Vsemirnaia Literatura, 1922). New York Public Library.

1922 was also the year when Balmont's translations were partly reprinted. The title of the collection changed from *Pobegi travy* (Spears of grass) in 1911 to *Revolutionary Poetry from Europe and America: Whitman*—a title, however, which may not have been Balmont's choice, since he had already left Russia in 1920.[6] The selection from Whitman was thinner by two thirds and only included the most revolutionary pieces. In his preface, written while still in Moscow, Balmont didn't use the same communist lexicon as Lunacharsky and remained vague in his presentation of Whitman as a seer and prophet, akin to Shelley (a poet whom he had often translated, and who was indeed a socialist reference). But he did compare Whitman to a worker, "raising his creative hammer."[7]

---

6 In 1921, after his exile from Russia, Balmont also published an anthology of world poetry in Berlin (*Iz mirovoi poèzii* [Berlin: Knigoizdatel'stvo Slovo, 1921]), which included Whitman's poems in a larger ensemble of Western literature, mostly European: British and German Romantic poets (Coleridge, Wordsworth, Blake; Heine and Goethe), Baudelaire and Leopardi (Whitman selection: 93–119). This a-political anthology contrasted with the one Balmont had been putting together for Soviet Russia.

7 Uol't Uitman, *Revoliutsionnaia poèziia Evropy i Ameriki. Uitman* (Moscow: Gosudarstvennoe izdatel'stvo, 1922), 4.

The following year, Chukovsky had yet another selection published, for State Edition (Gosizdat). He added "Song of the Open Road" and "O Captain! My Captain!," poems more rooted in the American experience. The cover of the book was illustrated by the artist Evgeny Belukha.

FIGURE 5.2. Cover of Kornei Chukovskii. *Uot Uitmèn. Poèziia griadushchei demokratii.* Moscow, Petrograd: Gosudarstvennoe Izdatel'stvo, 1923. Illustration E. Belukha. Author's collection.

The American and Russian flags are intertwined in a design that signifies not merely the international aims of the revolution, but also the literary connections that were developing over the Atlantic.

Though it was never published, another interesting translation was conceived during these years, by Alexander Krasnoshchyokov, a Bolshevik literatus like Lunacharsky. Born in Chernobyl, he emigrated to the US in 1903, was involved in trade unions and returned to Russia after the February Revolution. He played a major role in establishing the Far Eastern Republic, after which he moved to Moscow, where he had a decisive part in developing financial policies. He is also known for his love affair with Lili Brik (Mayakovsky's lover). In 1924, after the death of Lenin who protected him, he was falsely accused of corruption, arrested and put on trial—one of the first trials meant to set an example. While imprisoned (at a time when one could still receive books), he asked for a copy of *Leaves of Grass* and worked on his own translation.[8] Unfortunately, the translation appears to be lost, but it is quite extraordinary that a Soviet banker would translate Whitman while serving time.

The anthology of the revolution: highly selected poems

Chukovsky's and Balmont's collections were not the only means by which Whitman's poetry was circulated. During these same years (1918-1924), many poems were printed separately, in almanacs, in the press or as chapbooks and leaflets. The ones already published in the press before 1917 were reprinted and remained favorites. Chukovsky's editions also inspired essays on Whitman which sometimes included poems. In his 1919 essay,[9] V. Friche translated (in prose) the poem "I Dream'd in a Dream": Whitman's "new city of Friends" became "the city of comrades" (gorod tovorishchei). Friche referred to Whitman's poems as "hymns to the brotherhood of all people" and to "Salut au Monde!" as a "hymn to the solidarity of nations." The essay was followed by a selection of poems in Chukovsky's translation (though Friche didn't mention his name), among which, once again were "Europe," "Beat! Beat! Drums!" and "Years of the Modern." In 1919, an issue of *Plamia*, edited by Lunacharsky, displayed on its front page three lines from "Years of the Modern," in Chukovsky's translation, with a drawing by Sigismunds Vidbergs.[10]

---

8   See Bengt Jangfeldt, *Mayakovsky: A Biography*, trans. Harry D. Watson (Chicago: University of Chicago Press, 2014).
9   Vladimir Friche, "Uot Uitmèn," *Vestnik zhizni*, 1919 (no. 3–4), 67–70.
10 Sigismunds Vidbergs (1890-1970), a Latvian artist, illustrated *Plamia* during its two years of existence (1920–1922). Vidbergs is better known for his Art Deco and erotic drawings, such as illustrations for the *Kama Sutra*.

FIGURE 5.3. Cover of *Plamia*, no. 35 (January 5, 1919). Illustration by Sigismunds Vidbergs. Russian State Library.

Some poems were published in new translations, such as "Song of the Broad-Axe" and "In Cabin'd Ships at Sea" by Dmitri Maizels[11] and "Years of the Modern" by Sergei Farforovsky,[12] better known for his ethnographical work, but also the author of a collection of poetry. Farforovsky's version of "Years of the Modern" was entitled "From Whitman": it was indeed more an adaptation than a translation. It selected thirteen lines and put them in a different order, beginning with "I see the frontiers and boundaries of the old aristocracies broken." This line was translated literally as "See the destruction of the frontiers that the tsar and the tyrant endeavored to hold." It ended with the allegories of Democratic values: "I see Freedom, completely arm'd and victorious and very haughty, with Law on one side and Peace on the other." In Farforovsky's version, "Freedom" was not only accompanied by "Peace" and "Law" but also by "Brotherhood" (*Bratstvo*). Such editing processes were also at work in Chukovsky's version, which was less selective (with eighteen lines), but whose reordering was approximately the same. In all likelihood, Farforovsky did not translate from Whitman

---

11 "Stikhotvoreniia Uot Uitmena," trans. D. Maizels, *Plamia*, no. 30 (December 1918), 498.
12 "Iz Uitmana. Gody sovremennosti," trans. S. Farforovskii (Petrograd: *Literaturnyi al'manakh*, 1918), 7–8.

but rearranged Chukovsky's text[13] to make it more propagandistic, hence the addition of "Brotherhood," a key word in Lunacharsky's essay. The other main distortion was the recurring use of the word "proletarian" (as the equivalent, for example, of "average man").

Other poems were published separately, mostly from the writings of the civil war and of the early Reconstruction era, like "Pioneers! O Pioneers!" A poem was printed on a single page in 1918, like a tract, and distributed on the front line in Totma. In 1922, in Baku, A. Borodin, who was well acquainted with Khlebnikov, translated "When Lilacs Last in the Dooryard Bloom'd" in memory of President Lincoln.[14] Baku had turned into a cultural hub, and many poets and intellectuals fleeing the hardships of Moscow or Petrograd found relative shelter there. Some poems by Whitman were published in the magazine *Voemor*, and an editorial on "the Liberation of the Middle East" started with an epigraph from—once again—"Years of the Modern."[15]

Whitman's poems were included in anthologies of revolutionary poetry, especially in manuals (*sborniki*) of poems to be learnt by heart and recited. More often than not, Balmont's translations were used, a logical choice since they were versified and therefore easier to remember. And even though Balmont's *Whitman* received some really bad reviews upon its publication in 1922,[16] it probably contributed to a larger availability of the poems (there was no copyright regarding works that were considered as "revolutionary patrimony" and none for authors or translators who had gone into exile either). In 1927, an anthology offered a selection which even alternated Balmont's and Chukovsky's translations and was accompanied by Friche's essay.[17] "Years of the Modern," in Chukovsky's socialist adaptation, was still in a good position: it was definitely the anthem of the revolutionary wing of Whitmania.

---

13 Both versions were published the same year, which makes it difficult to establish a chronology. However, Chukovsky had been working on translating Whitman for a long time, and his book had quite a large circulation, while Farforovsky only published his translation in an almanac.
14 "Kogda siren' bliz' doma v sadike tsvela poslednim tsvetom" (Iz tsikla "Pamiati Prezidenta Lincol'na"), trans. A. Borodin (Baku: Rubiny, 1922; 28 pages, with a presentation of "Whitman's main works").
15 The editorial was written by the chief editor Andrei Zhubenko. See Sofiia Starkina, *Velimir Khlebnikov* (Moscow: Molodaia Gvardiia, 2007), 70.
16 Ivan Aksenov wondered why Balmont's translations were reprinted since they discredited "Old Walt"—see *Pechat' i revoliutsiia* 2 (1923), 232.
17 *Sotsial'naia i revoliutsionnaia poèziia Ameriki i Evropy* [Socialist and revolutionary poetry of America and Europe] (Moscow and Leningrad: Gosizdat, 1927), 7–21 (the book also contained poems by Verhaeren, Rolland, Becher). Friche was the editor of the series Rabochaia biblioteka po literature dlia shkol vtoroi stupeni (Workers' library of literature for secondary schools).

Korenizing Whitman

In the 1920s, a policy of *korenizatsiia* (indigenization) was implemented in the Soviet Union to gain support for the revolution from non-Russian populations. Teaching and publishing in local languages were encouraged, a reversal of decades of imperialist Russification. While Whitman's translations into other languages of the union cannot be considered as part of official policy, they are nonetheless to be understood in this context.

The first instance is a selection of poems translated into Armenian in 1923, by the poet Gurgen Haykuni, for the publishing house Hammer and Sickle. Born in the Ottoman Empire, Haykuni was involved in revolutionary movements in 1905, and again in 1917, when he participated in the foundation of the Communist Party of Armenia in Tbilisi. In 1918, he was people's commissar (*Narkom*) for nationalities of the North Caucasian Soviet Republic, and between 1922 and 1930 he led the group of Armenian writers in Moscow. Though Whitman's collection was published in 1923,[18] it was completed in April 1920, in Moscow, as indicated in the chapbook (each translated poem is precisely dated).

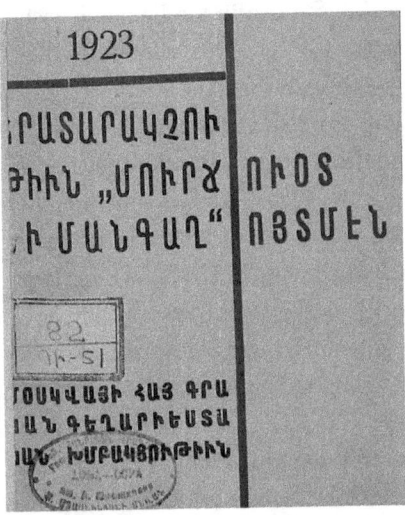

FIGURE 5.4. Cover of *Walt Whitman*, transl. Gurgen Haykuni (Moscow: Hammer and Sickle, 1923). National Library of Armenia.

Haykuni translated from Russian and specified which version he was referring to in each case (a practice uncommon enough with relay translations to deserve

---

18 *Walt Whitman*, trans. Gurgen Haykuni (Moscow: Hammer and Sickle, 1923). In Armenian.

notice). The first poems were translated from Chukovsky: "To You (whoever you are ...)," "To You ("Stranger, if you ...)," "You Felons on Trial in Court," "Beat! Beat! Drums!," "When I Read the Book" and "To a Cantatrice." The last ones were from Balmont's translations: "Race of Veterans," "Look Down Fair Moon," "As a Phantom Caressed Me," "To a Common Prostitute" and "One Self's I Sing." The last poem translated from Balmont was "Salut au Monde!," and it clearly stood apart: it was by far the longest piece and was introduced with a full title page. As was the case with the 1918 Latvian translation, the national and the international went hand in hand, but in this case, "international" meant internationalist rather than cosmopolitan. Yeghishe Charents, often considered the most important Armenian poet of the twentieth century, also translated two poems by Whitman: "Years of the Modern" and "Europe,"[19] the two main revolutionary successes staged by the Proletkult. Charents supported the Bolsheviks and joined the Red Army during the civil war. One can assume that this was also an indirect translation. Indeed, Charents translated mostly from Russian (Lermontov, Yesenin, Mayakovsky), German (Heine) and French (Hugo, Verhaeren). He also translated "The Internationale" into Armenian.

The second instance is Ukrainian, with the first translations from Whitman in the 1920s, by Ivan Kulyk. Born in a religious Jewish family, he grew up in Uman (known for its Jewish orthodox community).[20] The son of a teacher at the Talmud Torah School on Pushkin Street, Kulyk first spoke Yiddish and Russian. But he became more and more interested in Ukrainian language and traditions, which he studied extensively, until they became central to his work. After studying briefly at the Odesa Academy of Arts, he emigrated to the US, where he spent three years, mostly working in factories and engaging in political struggle. He came back to Ukraine in 1917, via Siberia, and was involved in the civil war. As Yohanan Petrovsky-Shtern writes, "his Bolshevik Revolution was an international phenomenon as long as it spoke Ukrainian."[21] He became quite an important political figure, and between 1924 and 1926 he was sent to Canada as Soviet consul. He developed a great interest in the country, which inspired several of his poems: he was particularly sympathetic to the cause of Native Americans and celebrated the revolt of the Métis Louis Riel.

---

19 Yeghishe Charents, *Erkeri žoġovaçow* [Collected Works], vol. 3 (Yerevan: Soviet Armenia Publishers, 1965), 323–325. In Armenian.
20 He was born in 1897, the same year as Andrii Chuzhyi, the "Whitman from Uman" (see Chapter 2): they went to the same school, were friends and began writing at the same age. See Nataliia Kostenko's introduction to Chuzhyi, *Poeziï*, 4.
21 Yohanan Petrovsky-Shtern, *Anti-Imperial Choice: The Making of the Ukrainian Jew* (New Haven: Yale University Press, 2009), 78. See the chapter "Between Two Fires. The National-Communist Utopia of Ivan Kulyk" for details on Kulyk's life and work.

It was during that period that he translated Whitman into Ukrainian for the first time (in one case, he mentioned Montreal as the place where he did the translation). All the "inscriptions" were published in 1924 in the Kharkiv "socio-political, literary and scientific" journal *Chervonyi shliakh* (Red way), which articulated the national (with poems by Shevchenko, but mainly by the young avant-garde) with the global (with many translations). Shortly after, "Starting from Paumanok" was published, without sections 8 and 10 (sections that refer to religion). At the end of the poem, Whitman's "camerado" simply became a *tovarishch*. Kulyk also translated the first nine sections of "Song of Myself" (which was printed just before a poem by Verhaeren) and poems by Horace Traubel in the same journal.²²

FIGURE 5.5. Cover of Ivan Kulyk, ed., *Antolohiia amerykans'koï poeziï: 1855-1925* (Kharkiv: Derzhavne vydavnytstvo Ukraïny, 1928). Dartmouth Library. Rauner Special Collections.

In 1928, he edited and translated a thick anthology of American poetry, which opened with Whitman. In his preface, he insisted that America had its own culture, different from Europe, a fact that Americans themselves were finally becoming aware of—he mentioned the 1912 issue of the journal *Poetry* as an example of that shift.²³ The process of emancipation was taking a long time,

---

22 "Inscriptions," *Chervonyi shliakh*, 1924 (no. 6), 84–89; "Starting from Paumanok," 1924 (no. 7–8), 99–106; "Song of Myself," 1924 (no. 10), 54–59.
23 Ivan Kulyk, ed., *Antolohiia amerykans'koï poeziï, 1855–1925* (Kharkiv: Derzhavne vydavnytstvo Ukraïny, 1928).

however, because of the country's lack of unity and poor material conditions; the bourgeoisie valued English models, while the rest of the population was illiterate. (The parallel with the Ukrainian situation is interesting, even though Kulyk did not make it explicitly.)

He explained the anticolonial principles that guided his choices and defined the periods during which American literature gained its independence from Britain. Interestingly, even though Whitman had a key role in this history, the decisive period for Kulyk was the civil war—again, an interesting parallel with recent Ukrainian and Soviet history. The anthology excluded the writers he judged too dependent on the English canon, like Poe and Longfellow. This preface seems to anticipate F. O. Matthiessen's definition of what constitutes the American canon—except for Kulyk's lack of appreciation for Emerson, whom he deemed an imitator of Carlyle. Another interesting element is Kulyk's ideas on translation, which, according to him, should be a creative process that primarily takes into account the reader: the meaning of the text relies largely on the receptor and is, thereby different in New York and Kharkiv (33). As for Whitman, he is especially valued for being "completely American," even if he was also "universal and cosmic." (21) He revolutionized form "in the same way that the industry changed everything in society." Kulyk specified which edition of *Leaves of Grass* he used (the 1919 one by Bucke, Harned and Traubel). The anthology contained 21 poems (or excerpts), starting with "O Captain! My Captain!," including parts of "I Sing the Body Electric," several war poems, and ending with several inscriptions, in particular "To Foreign Lands," "Poets to Come" and "To the Reader." Haykuni, Charents and Kulyk all suffered from the brutal shift of the regime and were victims of the Great Terror: Haykuni survived a ten-year term, but Charents and Kulyk were shot in 1937.

The 1930s: becoming a classic

Whitman was regularly republished in Russian in the following decade (1931, 1932, 1935), always in Chukovsky's translation. The 1931 edition was part of the Ogonëk library series: the books were very small (14 × 10 cm) and very cheap (fifteen kopeks), meant for the working class. It was quite similar to the German Reclam edition. The Whitman selection was only forty-three pages. On the copy held at Moscow State Library, the poem "Years of the Modern" was marked on the table of contents, a discreet anonymous confirmation that this poem was one of Whitman's Soviet favorites.

The 1935 edition is especially worth discussing for its preface, which struck a very different note from Lunacharsky or Friche's communist appreciations. Its author was D. S. Mirsky, a major figure of Russian criticism. Mirsky was a literate prince, close to the Acmeists, who was exiled in Britain after the revolution. He taught Russian at the University of London and was linked to the Bloomsbury group. He was the author of a famous and still authoritative history of Russian literature.[24] In the early 1930s, he "converted," joined the British Communist Party and asked to return to the USSR.[25] With Gorky's help, his request was accepted in 1932. He then befriended Chukovsky (who wrote about him in his diary)[26] and collaborated with him for the 1935 edition.[27]

Mirsky presented Whitman as an individualist, the last in a line of bourgeois poets. Moreover, "if on the one hand Whitman is a brother spirit to Dante and Goethe, his other affinities would include such individuals as Brigham Young, leader of the Mormon sect, and the founder of 'Christian Science,' Mrs. Eddy."[28] His poetry does have a collective dimension since "he is the poet of American democracy of the fifties and sixties," yet precisely for that reason, what he gives poetic voice to is "democracy's illusion that a new humanity has already been born . . . with all of his genius, he bears the indelible brand of that democracy's anti-revolutionary and provincial character." Also, "Whitman's democracy, organically and in deepest essence, was nationalistic. Democracy for him was something specifically American." Such an assertion contrasts with the prevailing vision of an internationalist Whitman. Mirsky also went against the grain when he wrote that he did not appreciate "Salut au Monde!," a poem marred by Whitman's "provincialism," a collection of clichés about unvisited places. Mirsky also observed that, even though Whitman had sympathy for revolutions, he remained a passive supporter; if he hated the slaveholders, it was mainly because

---

24 D. S. Mirsky, *A History of Russian Literature: From Its Beginnings to 1900* (London: Routledge, 1926–1927); reprinted by Northwestern University Press, 1999.
25 See Gerry Smith, *D. S. Mirsky: A Russian-English Life, 1890–1939* (Oxford: Oxford University Press, 2000).
26 "Mirsky is extraordinarily kind. He is a very cultured man, genuine and of great literary talent. He has an ugly beard and an English suit so dirty, worn and loose that it doesn't look like anything. He also has a particular way of listening to you: he punctuates each of your sentences with an *i-i-i* of sympathy (it sounds like the guttural yelp of a little pig). All this makes him a charming and amusing character. He is very poor. He is a staunch democrat, but he has inherited from his noble ancestors a strong penchant for good food. He ruins himself to satisfy his stomach. Every day he leaves his sad little shapka and slim coat with the guard at the National Hotel and heads for its luxurious restaurant, where he usually spends no less than forty rubles (for he eats, but he also drinks), leaving four rubles as a tip for the waiter and one for the guard" (Chukovskii, *Dnevnik*, 2:119–120 [January 27, 1935]).
27 Chukovsky stated that he first read Mirsky's preface in 1965 (*Dnevnik*, 2:440), which seems very unlikely, as he was involved in the publishing process; he appreciated it for its intelligence, even if it was incomprehensible to the average reader.
28 D. S. Mirskii, "Poèt amerikanskoi demokratii," preface to *List'ia travy* (Leningrad: Khudozhestvennaia Literatura, 1935), 9–30; trans. Stephen Stepanchev in Allen and Folsom, *Walt Whitman and the World*, 300–338.

they undermined American unity. But it didn't matter, according to Mirsky, because one shouldn't judge past writers through ideology. At a time when the debate about the arts had narrowed considerably and when "bourgeois" poets were being ostracized more and more fiercely, this preface had a certain aplomb. Mirsky made a concession to the lexicon of the time as he referred to Whitman's "realism," but such realism came with tremendous innovations: Whitman "constructed a new and unprecedented type of realistic ode, one springing out of an everyday and prosaic reality and catching up the myriad artistic threads of a highly variegated American life," while "breaking completely with the older poetry of a 'feudal' Europe and Asia (and its American imitators) a building up a new poetic art from a very beginning." Mirsky pointed out some flaws, especially a tendency toward abstract rhetoric, and it seemed to him that Whitman's epigones, for instance Sandburg, had retained only these weaker aspects, as they considered Whitman a prophet instead of a poet. At the very end of the essay, Mirsky made another political concession by relating Whitman to "constructive communism," a catchphrase quite unrelated to the ideas developed in the course of this preface. In 1937, Mirsky was arrested and sent to a gulag, where he died, near Magadan, in 1939.

Unlike Mirsky, Chukovsky survived the Great Terror and remained Whitman's Russian interpreter until the mid 1950s, with little competition. A parallel translation was written, however, by Dmitri Maizels, a poet who had lived in the US in his youth. As mentioned above, Maizels translated two poems for *Plamia* in 1918. These two pieces are were only the tip of the iceberg of a comprehensive translation, which he relentlessly tried to have published, to no avail. In 1927, he submitted the 450-page manuscript to the publishing house Zemlia i Fabrika, which specialized in popular series of Soviet and classic foreign literature. In his letters, Maizels lamented their lack of reply and the general difficulty of publishing poetry—all the more regrettable as *Leaves of Grass*, a "wonderful" and "strong" (krepkaia) book, was well adapted to the "violent times" people were going through.[29] Further attempts to have the translation published, in 1933 (with Academia) and 1935 also failed. In the latter case, his submission competed with a reprint of Chukovsky's translations. Maizels suggested that his translations could supplement Chukovsky's to make a complete edition of Whitman's poetry. But it seems that Chukovsky was not keen on this idea, and that he provided a negative report to the publisher. It is unclear

---

29 Lucas-v-leyden, "Leteiskaia biblioteka," *Lucas-v-leyden.livejournal*, accessed March 20, 2023, https://lucas-v-leyden.livejournal.com/96492.html.

whether this was for political reasons or because Chukovsky wanted to keep Whitman to himself—after all, three decades later he published a book entitled *My Whitman*.

2. Whitmanian agitprop

Whitman's poetry did not only circulate as written text and was adapted to other media. During the first years of Soviet Russia, it was especially available for agitprop,[30] which developed in various forms, particularly as posters, theatre and then cinema.

Celebrating the revolution with Whitman in 1918

During the October 1918 celebrations, for the anniversary of the revolution, a Whitman installation was created on the English Embankment (Angliiskaia Naberezhnaia) in Petrograd, on the banks of the Neva. These were huge celebrations, with an extraordinary abundance of demonstrations, cannonades, decorations and shows (such as the premiere of Mayakovsky's *Mystère Bouffe* and the Proletkult's staging of Romain Rolland's *Prise de la Bastille* [The Storming of the Bastille]).[31] The Whitman installation was only a small part of a huge project, but it was nonetheless remarkable, since no other foreign poet was given such a place. Whitman's portrait by Boris Grigoriev (see Chapter 3) was hung with the caption "SOCIALISM." Some of his lines were written on large red cubes, lit from inside, like lanterns: "My password: democracy" or "All things are equal."[32]

---

30 I do not refer to agitprop in the strict historical sense (directed by the agitprop department of the Central Committee of the Party), but in a slightly broader sense (art involving practices of agitation and propaganda, possibly emanating from the Party, but also simply supported by it).
31 See Natalia Murray, *Art for the Workers: Proletarian Art and Festive Decorations of Petrograd, 1917–1920* (Leyden: Brill, 2018).
32 According to Lev Pumpianskii, the portrait unfortunately did not look good in large format ("Oktiabr'skie torzhestva i khudozhniki Petrograda," *Plamia*, 1919 [no. 35], 14). The canvas (oil, pink and pale blue tones) hangs at the Pskov Museum (but its dimensions are 90 cm × 57 cm). The sketches of the entire installation are archived at the Russian Museum in Saint Petersburg (see reproductions in Murray, *Art for the Workers*, 170–171).

Figure 5.6. Boris Grigoriev. Sketches for the decoration of the English Embankment during the Petrograd 1918 festival. State Russian Museum, Saint Petersburg [SPB 742-746].

Whitman also took part in the Voronezh celebrations of 1918.[33] Among the events was a pantomime, conceived by a circus artist, Carlo Giovanni Faccioli, a Milanese who had emigrated to Voronezh,[34] renamed himself Karl Ivanovich Faccioli and founded a company called Cooperative. The show was called *Torzhestvo revoliutsii, ili sbitye okovy* (The Triumph of the Revolution, or the Broken Chains) and was inspired by Julien Tiersot's descriptions of French revolutionary celebrations: it consisted in the "agitation trial" (agitsud) of the "hydra of the revolution," followed by its execution. The hydra was a sixty-meter-long, eight-meter-broad, six-meter-high cardboard creature, with a wire tail that wagged in unison with its three heads. It was carried by forty guards, followed by two hundred caged counterrevolutionaries and by "living pictures." Once sentenced to death, the hydra was butchered, doused with kerosene and burned. Whitman's poems accompanied the ceremony. According to Maliuchenko, a crowd of no less than ten thousand people took part in the event, the most successful of its kind in Voronezh.

---

33 See James Von Geldern, *Bolshevik Festivals, 1917–1920* (Berkeley: University of California Press, 1993), 41. For a direct and detailed account, see G. S. Maliuchenko, "Pervye teatral'nye sezony novoi epokhi," in *U istokov: Sbornik statii*, ed. Dmitri Shcheglov (Moscow, VTO, 1960), 242–331, especially 272–282.

34 Many Italian circus artists had emigrated to Russia, like the Cinizelli family, which gave its name to a famous circus in Saint Petersburg.

The Proletkult shows: "the first experiments of poetic theatre"

The major form of Whitmanian agitprop, however, was the Proletkult show. Its main creator was Alexander Mgebrov, who, together with his wife Victoria Chekan, directed the theatre section of the Petrograd Proletkult. *La Prise de la Bastille* was Mgebrov's most famous show, but it was a commission, and he expressed regret about not following his "exclusive path of poetic theatre," especially "Whitman's way of involving everyone in a general rhythm."[35] While many poets were read or staged (Shelley with *Prometheus Unbound*, but mostly Soviet Proletarian poets, like Aleksei Gastev), two stood out: Vladimir Kirillov and Walt Whitman. Even though Whitman was not as obvious a choice as Kirillov, a member of the Proletkult, he was the very first poet Mgebrov staged and for whom he showed unabated enthusiasm. In his memoirs, Mgebrov dedicated a chapter to the birth of Proletkult, beginning with an epigraph, allegedly a quote from Whitman: "The days came when one began to realize that a brick lying in a pile on the road was no less worthy of praise than the most delicate and fragrant rose."[36] The same year, he also staged Émile Verhaeren's *La Révolte* (The Rebellion; Vosstanie): Whitman and Verhaeren were once again revolutionary comrades. Mgebrov insisted that the theatre be open to all, like Whitman's table,[37] and that the shows be completely free. Indeed, not only was the audience varied, but the actors themselves were workers, in accordance with the principles of the Proletkult. Mgebrov's portraits of the participants are often vivid and include children (like Lenochka Stepanova, the thirteen-year-old daughter of a worker).[38]

The Whitman evening premiered on July 10, 1918, in Petrograd, at the Palace of Proletarian Culture, a large building off Nevsky Prospect, which was once a club for nobles. It was attended by Meyerhold and presented by Lunacharsky. In his review, Alexander Kugel' noted: "There was, undoubtedly, something extremely original and unusual in the fact that the 'people's commissar,' let's say, 'in a bourgeois way,' a minister in a coat and a hat, stood on proscenium and clarified to the audience who the poet Walt Whitman was. It carried indeed a certain democratic

---

35 Aleksandr Mgebrov, *Zhizn' v teatre*, 2 vols. (Moscow: Academia, 1932), 2:408.
36 Ibid., 318.
37 Mgebrov used a quote from "Song of Myself" (19): "This is the meal equally set, this is the meat for natural hunger," which, in Chukovsky's translation reads as an invitation to an "open table"—"Ètot stol, nakrytyi dlia vsekh, dlia tekh, kto po-nastoiashchemu goloden".
38 The son of Alexandr Mgebrov and Victoria Chekan, Kotia Mgebrov-Chekan, became a myth: he acted as a child in *La Prise de la Bastille* and *The Legend of the Communard*, but died tragically at the age of nine in a tram accident as the troupe was touring the western front. He was buried on the Champ de Mars in Petrograd and was later the subject of literary works and of a film (*Byl nastoiashchim trubachom*, 1970). To my knowledge, he was not central to the Whitman evenings, but he may have participated in them.

simplicity, in the spirit of the American poet."[39] The show comprised three parts and eight extracts, including "Beat! Beat! Drums!" and "Years of the Modern," essentially in Chukovsky's translations. Mgebrov picked poems that had already received attention and had often been published separately. This might just have been an easy option, but maybe Mgebrov thought that recognizable poems would be more effective than new ones. The well-known poems were staged at the beginning of the show, which later on included less obvious pieces and an extract from "Song of Myself," a more complex and less directly political poem: in this case, it was precisely the poem's capacity to astonish that was valued (Mgebrov wrote of the Red Army soldiers in the front row, who had never seen anything quite like it).

The evening opened with the poem "Europe," which was well suited for revolutionary propaganda: the theme (the victims of the tyrants' repression during the revolutions of 1848), the message (the poet never despairs of liberty), and even the use of a different calendar, starting with the birth of American Democracy. Mgebrov's description in his memoirs provides a useful commentary of these photographs, published in *Plamia*:

FIGURE 5.7. Members of the Petrograd Proletkult performing a collective reading of Walt Whitman's poem "Europe" at the House of Proletarian Culture, Petrograd. *Plamia*, no. 21 (September 22, 1918), 4. Russian State Library.

---

39 Homo novus, pseud. of A. Kugel', "Zametki," *Teatr i iskusstvo*, nos. 26–27 (August 14, 1918), 268.

Imagine a bridge of fire. This bridge was created on a background of burning cardboard, as if it symbolized the path of humanity in the struggle for the future. To the right of the spectator, on a large platform, in the foreground, Europe was standing, a symbolic image of it, representing past revolutionary struggles. Silhouettes of girls and boys stood all over the stage, on a tiered platform, at varied heights. They formed, as it were, a tableau vivant, the beginning of an ecstasy, pointing towards something big and shiny, which suddenly radiated. The girls wore white clothes, the boys were in festive work coats. Music played in the distance behind the stage. A deep male voice suddenly broke the solemnity of the ecstatic silence and, with a gesture pointed toward Europe, said the first line.[40]

Choirs of voices resounded, first men, then women. The rhythm accelerated as the lines were said by running actors, and sometimes distributed among them: an actor would say one word, another one the next word. This dynamic tempo was meant to "reinforce the sense of solidarity of the masses." It was sustained by the lights: a "blood-red" light, which became more intense at intervals, especially when the figures of evil listed in the poem twisted and contorted onstage (in Mgebrov's words, a "macabre dance"), was followed by near-darkness and at the end by a radiant light, when dozens of young people in light-colored clothing invaded the stage, with laurel and palm branches. The whole poem took fifteen minutes, and Mgebrov insisted that the performance's success—that is, the rapture of the audience—well justified the substantial effort involved in this adaptation for the stage. Mgebrov wrote that this was the "very first experiment with poetic theatre" (346), and he was extremely proud that it played an important role in the subsequent development of the genre.

"Europe" was followed by "Years of the Modern," a great success in 1918, as we have seen, but with a different title ("Sterty rubezhi," literally "Borders erased"). The same setting was used.

---

40 Mgebrov, *Zhizn' v teatre*, 2:339.

FIGURE 5.8. Members of the Petrograd Proletkult performing a collective reading of Walt Whitman's "Years of the Modern." Slava Katamidze Collection. ("I see Freedom, completely arm'd and victorious and very haughty, with Law on one side and Peace on the other.")

Less expectedly, the poem "The City Dead-House," about a prostitute in the morgue, was also staged, as a monologue, recited by Mgebrov himself, who knelt before a corpse covered with a sheet. He pointed out that Ada Corvin (who was more famous as a dancer) loved to play the role of the corpse and would not let anyone else have it. During the Proletkult's tour in Latvia, Corvin fell ill with typhus and was abandoned by the troupe as the Whites were about to enter Riga; she died there, "as lonely as she was on stage as a prostitute's corpse." According to Mgebrov, this was quite an extraordinary coincidence, an example of the blurring of art and life (or in this case, death). He described more briefly the staging of "Song of the Banner at Daybreak" (the only poem in Balmont's translation)[41] and of "We Two Boys Together Clinging," referring to them as danced poems rather than recited ones. Victoria Chekan also indicated in her memoirs that "Song of the Banner" was soundtracked by "The Internationale."[42]

---

41 Lynn Mally points out that a specialty of the Petrograd Proletkult was allegorical theatre (in *The Legend of the Communard*, for example, the heroes were named "Wisdom" and "Truth"). "Song of the Banner at Daybreak" might have appealed to Mgebrov because it lent itself to such a staging. In Lynn Mally, *Culture of the Future: The Proletkult Movement in Revolutionary Russia* (Berkeley: University of California Press, 1990), 114.
42 Viktoriia Chekan-Mgebrova, *Zapiski*, quoted in David Zolotnitskii, *Zori teatral'nogo Oktiabria* (Leningrad: Iskusstvo, 1976), 305.

By contrast, Mgebrov went into detail for "Song of Myself," a poem too long and complex to withstand being read aloud by a single reader. He acknowledged that this was the case for many masterpieces, and considered it outrageous that they remained inaccessible to the masses. The Proletkult was indeed keener on bringing culture to the people than on creating it from scratch. Mgebrov developed his own solutions for this poem because he believed that they could be used more widely. The most important was to never let attention wane, hence the varied rhythms, with musical sequences, and the constant movement. Out of the many examples he provides, I will only select the first stanza of section 19:

> This is the meal equally set, this the meat for natural hunger,
> It is for the wicked just the same as the righteous, I make appointments with all,
> I will not have a single person slighted or left away,
> The kept-woman, sponger, thief, are hereby invited,
> The heavy-lipp'd slave is invited, the venerealee is invited;
> There shall be no difference between them and the rest.

The lines were spoken by different groups, and in the enumeration (in Chukovsky's rather loose translation: "the thief, the parasite, the kept woman"), each word was said by a different actor, while the final line was said in chorus. The director and actors aimed at provoking "ecstasy." One was meant to get caught up in the musical whirlwind of the whole poem.

Mgebrov concluded that the experience was a huge success (with soldiers rising enthusiastically at the reading of the last piece, "To You"), while regretting that it was not seen out to the end, because the civil war required too much of everyone's energy and deprived the show of many spectators. However, the Whitman evening was performed several times, including for the October 1918 celebrations in Petrograd, and a brochure was printed on that occasion. The show also went on tour—I mentioned earlier the performance in Riga, but there were many more places, among which, Kronstadt, Krasnoe Selo and Gatchina, Luga (where there was no time to set up the stage and the evening took place in the open air, under the moonlight). It was shown in Moscow for the conference of all the Russian Proletkults in September 1918. Mgebrov wrote:

> What can, be compared to, say, that time when, in the Kremlin,
> in the hall where the most terrible death sentences were passed,
> on the very table where these sentences were signed, Chekan,
> wearing a red dress and a Phrygian cap, holding in her hands

a red battle banner, read "Song of the Banner at Day-Break," in front of an iron squadron of harsh Latvians, the most advanced fighters on the most dangerous fronts of that time. These and similar moments are worth sacrificing, perhaps, a lifetime. (402)

After this first tour, the troop was sent to the front line, and began performances on the eve of 1919, in famine-stricken places: Pskov, Valk, Yuriev and Riga (where Corvin died). The tour continued for another year, alternating Kirillov, Whitman and *La Prise de la Bastille* for the most part. A brochure of the Whitman evening was printed in 1920 by "the direction of political agitation of the Belomorsk military district," with a prologue: the propaganda emphasis was even more heavy-handed for the staging of this poem on the White Sea, soundtracked by "La Marseillaise."

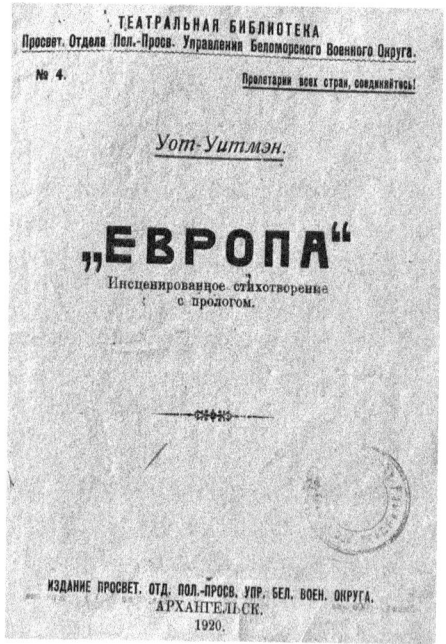

FIGURE 5.9. Cover of Uot-Uitmèn *"Evropa": Instsenirovannoe stikhotvorenie s prologom.* Arkhangelsk: Prosvet. otd. pol.-prosv. upr. Bel. voen. okr., 1920. Russian State Library.

It is difficult to appreciate the reception of such performances. Mgebrov regretted that, apart from Meyerhold, the intelligentsia did not attend his show. However, he was confident that it had an impact on the masses, who did not leave "printed words" but "printed deeds." For lack of traces of such printed deeds, one can only turn to the reviews, whose enthusiasm was hardly unanimous. The Whitman evening was generally reviewed favorably after it premiered in July 1918, but often with caveats. The *Krasnaia Gazeta* particularly enjoyed the chorus experiments, even though it thought the show was still a work in progress.[43] Sergei Proskurnin appreciated its novelty and its "freshness" (svezhest') but also found it lame in some respects.[44] The only piece of lavish praise came from Vladimir Kirillov, who was very close to Mgebrov. His essay "Walt Whitman and the Proletarian Theatre," published in the Proletkult's journal *Griadushche* (the Future), confirmed the enthusiasm of the audience.[45] Kirillov was delighted with this adaptation, never attempted before in the United States or in Europe, and felt that the attending comrades had experienced a very deep emotion, a "religious ecstasy," a pure "joy" (radost') as they listened to the words of Whitman, "prophet of the common future and of the brotherhood of all." The performance was a major break with the unbridled "vulgarity" (poshlost') of cabaret and cinemas—expressions of petit-bourgeois culture—and therefore an important step in the great process of liberation that Russia was implementing.

By contrast, Alexander Kugel, the famous theater critic and satirist, was appalled at the "decadent" and "modernist" spirit of the adaptation.[46] The harshest critic, however, was no less than Mikhail Gerasimov, a popular Proletarian poet.[47] He saw in the bridge of fire a "church blaze[48] in a cubist-futurist style," a mix of registers he found repugnant. But what Gerasimov deplored most of all were the "hysterical cries" punctuated by interjections that created a "shrill pathos." The scene was "boiling and belching" when the staging of Whitman required simplicity. Gerasimov insisted on that word: only simplicity was inspirational and it was with simplicity that workers died on barricades and battlefields. Mgebrov's affectation (*manernost'*) was alien to the mind of the worker—it conveyed the spirit of the petit-bourgeois intelligentsia. Gerasimov did appreciate Whitman's poetry, which sometimes made him feel like weeping or even "bellowing like a buffalo." But such passion was not easy to convey on stage and excessive pathos annihilated the original strength of the poem. What

---

43 "Vecher Uot Uitmena," *Krasnaia gazeta*, July 23, 1918, 3. Another very positive review was "Teatral'noe èxo," *Novaia Petrogradskaia gazeta*, July 23, 1918, 4.
44 Milii Stremin (pseudonym of Sergei Proskurnin), "Vecher tovarishcha Uitmena," *Vechernie ogni*, no. 77 (July 22, 1918), 4.
45 V. K[irillov], "Uot Uitmen i proletarskii teatr," *Griadushchee*, July 1918 (no. 5), 12.
46 Homo novus (Alexander Kugel'), "Zametki," 266–268.
47 Mikhail Gerasimov, "O vechere Petrogradskogo Proletkul'ta," *Gorn*, 1918 (no. 1), 56–57.
48 *Pech' ognennaia* refers to religious iconography.

was missing from Mgebrov's performance was artistic impetus (*poryv*) and inner strength.⁴⁹

Later Soviet critics showed little charity toward Mgebrov's poetical adaptations. Their harsh judgments are hardly surprising given that Alexander Bogdanov's arrest in 1923 destroyed the Proletkult's reputation. Dimitri Shcheglov, who had witnessed the show, was particularly critical of the "neurasthenic" reading of "A Woman at the Morgue": "There was something tasteless, decadent and ... provincial in this 'philosophy' and *in the way* it was presented."⁵⁰ The theater historian David Zolotnitsky recognizes that the Proletkult themes were revolutionary but laments that their aesthetics were not: the ladies wearing white, the statue-like poses, the lights, the danse macabre, were all infused with symbolism and belonged to the past. Even the reconciliation of the religious and the revolutionary, once advocated by Lunacharsky ("ecstasy" was then part of his lexicon), was already obsolete in 1918. Zolotnitsky concludes: "Mgebrov's spectacles undoubtedly played their role in fostering heroic feelings. But their time passed quickly."⁵¹ Similarly, Boris Alpers estimates that these "imperfect experiments had very little success" and that "none of the theater professionals seriously considered them."⁵²

Even though the "Whitman evening" stopped touring after 1919, there were later sporadic Whitman Proletkult events, as evidenced in Chukovsky's memoirs. In March 1922, he was invited to see a performance in Petrograd. His account is rather sketchy, but eloquently critical:

> Somehow Mgebrov (an actor) invited me to the Proletkult building on Ekaterininskaya Street, to see a production from Walt Whitman, staged by workers. As soon as the rehearsal began, the actors set up luxurious leather deep armchairs—taken from the Assembly of the Nobles—and jumped on them with their boots. I asked Mgebrov why they were doing this. "It's the ascending movement" [voskhozhdenie vvys']—he replied. I took my hat and walked away. I can't witness the spoilage of things. I respect them. And if you don't instill that respect to the artists, you won't get anywhere. Art begins with respect for things.

---

49 A note from the editors was added to say that they did not agree with all of Gerasimov's harsh comments, but that they published them since "fraternal criticism" (!) was helpful to Proletarian culture.
50 Shcheglov, *U istokov*, 33–34.
51 Zolotnitskii, *Zori teatral'nogo Oktiabria*, 308.
52 Boris Alpers, *Teatral'nye ocherki*, vol. 1 (Moscow: Iskusstvo, 1977), 35.

I left, and never came back. They got Whitman completely wrong.[53]

Chukovsky's late and random attendance at the show, his complete disapproval and utter disgust, apparently confirms Alpers's conclusion. It remains difficult, however, to assess the popularity of Mgebrov's performances. Zolotnitsky and Alpers's studies are both extremely well researched and provide highly valuable material, but they are also, especially in their conclusions, saturated with the Soviet ideology of the 1970s, which was not particularly favorable toward the aesthetics of ecstasy. Even if Mgebrov's work was not hailed enthusiastically by critics and intellectuals, it did contribute to Whitman's momentum in the early years of Soviet Russia.

The Whitman club: "to kiss, to work and to die *Whitman's way*"

Another sign of Whitman's popularity in the early 1920s was the creation of the Whitman Club (*kruzhok*) by students at the Polytechnic University, which was mentioned in Chukovsky's diary for the first time in February 1922. A few weeks later, he gave some details about the founder of the club, Boris Barabanov,[54] and inserted a note from him.[55] The most interesting part is the account of his visit to the club, which provides an insight on the passionate intellectual debates of the times:

> I went to the Whitmanian Club yesterday and came back full of shame. In truth, there was little whitmanism there: people argued, shouted, accused each other of insincerity, but what a thirst for an all-sacrificing "religion," what a reserve of fanaticism.

---

53 Chukovsky, *Dnevnik*, 1:197 (March 21, 1922). Ekaterininskaya Street was indeed the name of the Proletkult Street.
54 "He visited me several times. His overcoat is completely torn, in fact it consists of three or four separate parts; his face is beautiful, he has brown (but dirty) curls, his expression is that of someone with a toothache. I looked for him at the dorm on Basseinaia (the dorm of the Pedagogical Institute)—there, girls and boys scurry up and down the stairs, every room is full of people, and everyone knows Barabanov, he is very popular, a sort of leader, a 'talent'—and yet none of these girls would think of sewing up his overcoat." Chukovskii, *Dnevnik*, 1:193 (March 15, 1922).
55 Barabanov's note reads: "Kornei Ivanovich. Exactly a week ago we had our first meeting: that day was a great and unprecedented celebration for all of us. There were about twenty people (we believe that it is a lot of people to work with). The meeting lasted about four hours. We talked, read "You" and "The Open Road," my presentation "Modernity and Whitman," was planned but for lack of time and because of the complexity of the material, it was postponed, besides we wanted you to be present." (Ibid., 1:493)

I have become a man of pure literature in recent years, I had never imagined that any assessment of Whitman was possible except from a literary standpoint, and it turns out that, due to my purely *literary* work, young people's eyes were burning, people were sitting well past midnight and debating the question: how to live. One of them, like a man from Kostroma kept throwing up at me: "this is aesthetics!" As if "aesthetics" was a swear word. They don't need aesthetics—they are passionately interested in morals. Whitman interests them as prophet and teacher. They want to kiss and work and die *Whitman's way*. They instinctively smelled a "literary man" in me, and they turned their backs on me. (March 18, 1922; 1:195)

Chukovsky added more general ideas about Russia at the time; the country lacked irony and humor, was absolute seriousness, and had a thirst for faith. He made a similar comment about the "Whitmanians" (presumably the very same students) at a meeting of the World Literature publishing house. Events were organized to launch the publication of Whitman's *List'ia travy*, which Chukovsky documented in his diary. Again, they are worth mentioning for the intensity and the enthusiasm of the Whitman debates that they reveal:

On Tuesday, April 4, Whitman was honored at World Literature. . . . I read aloud a few passages from *Democratic Vistas*. Volynsky made a magnificent speech about it, which I listened to with rapt attention, though it was based on a great misconception. Volynsky picked on the word: "transcendental" social order, and began to argue that Whitman *was denying reality*, in the name of the metaphysical. In short, he made Whitman a spiritualist. I wrote to Zamyatin that Volynsky was wrong about many things. (April 7, 1922; 1:207)

Chukovsky's inserted a note written by Zamyatin: "But his religion is not at all rationalistic or cerebral, it is corporeal. His iconostasis does not consist in transcendental geometry, but in stones, steam engines, policemen, thieves, wires, grains, worms." Zamyatin's comment translates Whitman into Russian referents, while, again, insisting on the "prophet of the body." After Volynsky,

the Whitmanians spoke. They are all savages compared with us, but you can feel their wild power [dikarskaia sil'na]. They are naive, but strong in their naivety. One of them said of their society: "We learned of Whitman by accident. At first, we wanted to call our club the 'Society of True Men.' When we got to know Whitman, we saw that he was right for us. We had no criteria, no steering wheel. We had about twenty clubs and organizations at our institution, all of which were collapsing. We need a teacher and leader [*rukovaditel'*] like Whitman." (April 7, 1922; 1:208)

Whitman and Soviet film: from kino-eye to montage

Whitman's presence can also be recorded, though on a smaller scale, in cinema—the art that was, according to Lenin, most suited for agitprop. He was indeed a reference for the two major directors of the 1920s and 1930s, Dziga Vertov and Sergei Eisenstein, even though their aesthetics were opposed: while Vertov advocated the technique of the "kino-eye," aiming at recording acute perceptions and rhythmically quite close to the newsreel, Eisenstein was the master of "montage," which heavily edited the film material. Whitman's enumerations, which pretend to record the ebb and flow of things, while juxtaposing heterogeneous realities and establishing new relations, could fit into both aesthetics, however different.

Vertov, himself a poet, acknowledged that he enjoyed Whitman's poetry,[56] and the critic Naum Kaufman wrote in 1929 text about *Man with a Movie Camera* (*Chelovek s apparatom*) that Vertov was "the Soviet Whitman."[57] The reference to Whitman was most conspicuous in *One Sixth of the World* (*Shestaia chast' mira*, 1926). The film presents a sequence of shots, mainly of the vast Soviet territory, but also of the Western world, recalling the panoramic vision and enumerations of "Salut au Monde!" Indeed, the opening of the film shows an airplane flying and the whole landscape is seen from high above: Whitman's imaginary flight in section 33 of "Song of Myself" has become a technical achievement. The film is characterized by a large number of intertitles, which have no informational

---

56 See Ben Singer, "Connoisseurs of Chaos: Whitman, Vertov and the 'poetic survey,'" *Literature Film Quarterly* 15, no. 4 (1987). Singer refers to an interview with Mikhail Kaufman, Vertov's brother and director of photography, according to whom Whitman was indeed a decisive influence.
57 Naum Kaufman, "Chelovek s apparatom," *Sovetskii ékran*, 1929 (no. 5), 5. Jacques Rancière also notes that "the montage of *Man with a Movie Camera*, which brings the manicurist's gestures, the conjurer's tricks and the assembly line work into the same accelerated rhythm, owes more to 'A Song for Occupations' or 'Song of the Broad-Axe' than to *Das Kapital*." In *Aisthesis: Scènes du régime esthétique de l'art* (Paris: Galilée, 2011), 100.

necessity—the film has no plot, no dialogue. Better still, the intertitles are not intended to give referential details—about a particular place for example. The most recurrent one simply consists in the word *Vizhu* (I see), in large letters, and reads as the translation of the anaphora "I see" in "Salut au Monde!" (The poem was included in Balmont's 1911 translation, under the title "Privet miru", as well as in his anthology of "Revolutionary poetry" in 1922.) Other intertitles are apostrophes to the audience: sometimes *vy*, sometimes *ty*—the plural or the singular form of "you". Another sequence is punctuated by the anaphora *gde tam* (where), again recalling section 33 of "Song of Myself." The alternation of wide shots and close-ups is also quite typical of Whitman's metonymic apprehension of the world. The critics of the time noticed the literary and poetic aspects of the film, which they sometimes lamented (notably Victor Shklovsky and Ippolit Sokolov,[58] who wrote of a "Whitman-Derzhavin" anti-cinematic style).[59] The film as a whole seems to expand and detail the evocations of Russia or the Asian steppes in "Salut au Monde!": "You of the mighty Slavic tribes and empires! you Russ in Russia!" (LG 124), "I see the steppes of Asia, / I see the tents of Kalmucks and Bashkirs / I see the nomadic tribes with oxen and cows" (LG 122). At the same time, like Whitman, it crossed borders, whether to denounce capitalist countries or to pay tributes to the socialist movements of the West. The film was quite controversial, because it lacked the documentary quality that was expected (the places and the sources were not specified), and also because Vertov, who borrowed footages from Western newsreel, was accused of plagiarism.

Whitman was not directly quoted in Sergei Eisenstein's films,[60] but was a regular reference in his theoretical writings. Eisenstein developed a theory of ecstasy, a key term of the Proletkult, to which he gave new meanings, by articulating it to another concept: pathos. In "Pathos," Eisenstein reads Whitman's poems as "emotional [pateticheskie] hymns," based on ecstatic experience, namely,

---

58 Gippolit Sokolov, "O fil'me '*Shestaia chast' mira*,'" *Kino-front*, 1927 (no. 2), 11, trans. J. Graffy, in *Lines of Resistance. Dziga Vertov and the Twenties*, ed. Yuri Tsivan (Pordenone: Le Giornate del cinema muto, 2004), 236.
59 About the ode in the film, and its renewal by the Whitmanesque style, see Michael Kunichika, "'The ecstasy of breadth': The Odic and the Whitmanesque Style in Dziga Vertov's *One Sixth of the World* (1926)," *Studies in Russian and Soviet Cinema* 6, no. 1 (2012): 53–74.
60 Jacques Rancière relates Eisenstein's cinema to Whitman's style: "the dialectic of *The General Line* gains its demonstrative power only in the torrents of milk or the frenzy of the reapers carried away by the Whitmanian rhythm" (Rancière, *Aisthesis*, 100).

the experience of "unity in diversity."⁶¹ The poem he enjoyed most was "Song of the Broad-Axe," which he also quotes at length, in Balmont's translation, in the unpublished version of *Montage* (1937). He emphasizes how Whitman transforms an "object" into an "emblem," fragmenting a general frame into numerous shots which reveal everything that the axe can do.⁶² Whitman is thus both an example of pathos (which brings the diverse together into an ecstatic experience) and of montage (which unfolds the object to transform it into a series of tools). Interestingly, Eisenstein was one of the few Soviet commentators to point at some major issues with Whitman's conceptions of democracy: while Whitman saw America as an ideal of liberation from the colonial rule of Europe, he was blind to the "simultaneously enslaving role of the same pioneers in relation to the Redskins, later to Black people, later yet to the workers, and in a more distant future, to entire states behind the borders of America."⁶³ In spite of this qualification, Whitman is a recurring name in Eisenstein's copious writings, including in his *Memoirs*.

I would like to conclude this chapter on Whitman's association with the development of new Soviet conceptions of world literature. As Jérôme David observes,⁶⁴ two adjectives were used in Russian, with slight nuances, *vsemirnaia* and *mirovaia*: the former was rather associated with the study of literary networks (inter*national*), and the latter with establishing a canon (*inter*national). Vsemirnaia literatura was the name of the publishing house in existence from 1918 to 1924, while mirovaia literatura was the name of the Institute of Literature, founded in Moscow in 1936. The uses of the two adjectives were not always clear-cut: *mirovaia* was more common, and *vsemirnaia*, which can also translate as "universal," involved a canon-building process as well.⁶⁵ David's distinction is nonetheless helpful, since it roughly corresponds to two successive (albeit at times overlapping) trends, as Soviet world literature went from a *vsemirnaia* conception in the 1920s to a *mirovaia* one later on. Whitman's

---

61 Sergei Èizenshtein, "Pafos," in *Neravnodushnaia priroda*, 2:97.
62 Sergei Èizenshtein, "Montazh" (1937), in *Izbrannye proizvedeniia*, 2:423–424.
63 Ibid.
64 Jérôme David, *Spectres de Goethe: Les Métamorphoses de la littérature mondiale* (Paris: Les Prairies ordinaires, 2011).
65 See Galin Tihanov, *The Birth and Death of Literary Theory: Regimes of Relevance in Russia and Beyond* (Stanford: Stanford University Press, 2019), 175–185. Tihanov explains that Viktor Shklovsky objected to Gorky's project for the World Literature publishing house, as he saw "in it a coercive instrument of imposing a nonnegotiable canon."

reception reflected these evolutions. Before we follow up on Whitman's Soviet reception during World War II and the Cold War, however, it is necessary to return to Europe and then across the Atlantic again, where Whitman travelled back as a communist poet. The Vsemirnaia Literatura winged horse will take us westward for now.

FIGURE 5.10. First colophon of the publishing house Vsemirnaia Literatura, by Yuri Annenkov.

Chapter 6

Between the wars: a transatlantic fellow traveler (1919–1938)

Whitman did not disappear from the European cultural landscape during the interwar period, and he even made his debut in places where his reception was slightly belated. But in countries where he was popular before the conflict, especially Britain, Germany and France, he gradually lost some of his appeal. Regarding political reception, the context is key. Whitman remained a reference for Western European socialists and communists in the years immediately after the war, when hopes for an international revolution were still high. After the defeat of the Red Army in Poland and the last insurrections in Germany, his work tended to disappear into the general repository of idealistic socialism. As it waned in Western Europe, Whitman's visibility waxed globally: in 1919, his poetry was introduced in China,[1] as his centennial coincided with May 4 movements, which challenged traditional values. I will focus on the transatlantic and hemispheric routes, since political references to Whitman became increasingly frequent in South America, and even more so in the US itself. The detour through Europe helped establish Whitman as canonical, especially as

---

1   See Xilao Li, "Walt Whitman in China," *Walt Whitman Quarterly Review* 5, no. 3 (Spring 1986): 1–2, on the introductory essay by Tian Han and on Whitman's importance for Guo Muoro. Both of them discovered Whitman while in Japan or through Japanese writings: transnational Whitmanian connections also developed on the other side of the world.

a leftist poet: as Whitman travelled back from Europe and the Soviet Union, he was enrolled on the side of the workers and masses, and his internationalist aura spread.

1. In Europe: the relative decline of the socialist Whitman

The 1919 celebrations

Whitman's centennial was the occasion of many events and publications in Europe. They came after the war, after the Russian Revolution and often with the reestablishment of nations (Poland) or birth of new regimes (the Weimar Republic). An example of the impact of Whitman's centennial in Germany is Paul Hindemith's claim "to have taught himself English by reading *Leaves of Grass* as the celebrations of the Weimar Republic coincided with those for the centenary."[2] He set to music two poems translated by Johannes Schlaf.[3] In 1919 again, Hans Reisinger's translation was published (and regularly reprinted); in 1923, the Austrian composer Franz Schreker, at the height of his fame, adapted some poems.[4] Left-wing appropriations of Whitman were re-energized. As W. Grünzweig has commented, Johannes Becher, a German expressionist poet and a socialist, addressed Whitman in his 1918 poem "To Europe" as a model of anti-decadence, and called for a "socialist army" that would reply to the word "en-masse!"

Celebrations were also organized in France. In May 1919, *L'Humanité* advertised the "Fêtes du people" (people's celebrations) for the centennial. Georges Chennevière's review of the evening at a major trade union venue in the east of Paris was drenched in enthusiasm and pathos:

> Something new was just born, on May 31, 1919! Let's not forget that date!
>
> Something new was just born. Could any of those who were in attendance Saturday evening doubt it? ...

---

2 See Kim H. Kowalke, "For Those We Love: Hindemith, Whitman, and 'An American Requiem,'" *Journal of the American Musicological Society* 50, no. 1 (Spring 1997): 135–136.
3 Paul Hindemith, *Drei Hymnen von Walt Whitman, für Bariton und Klavier*, op. 14 (1919); premiered in Frankfurt on February 20, 1920.
4 Franz Schreker, *Zwei lyrische Gesänge, für hohe Singstimme und Klavier* (1923); became *Vom ewigen Leben* in its version for orchestra in 1927.

This was a communion, where all the "faithful" participated in the same cult. Let's recall this style with fervor.

Here: the chorus stands up. Three hundred voices intone the song of praise. How we breathed among you, standing trees! With what force did the song resonate in us! How lovingly did we follow the unending ascent! Whitman steps forward. His voice fills the air, large, healthy, tumultuous. It bursts out, rumbles, caresses, comforts; it commands us not to despair, although we have not triumphed yet; it foresees the day when real peace will be proclaimed.[5]

This kind of staging was quite reminiscent of the Proletkult adaptations touring in Russia at the same time.

Foiled European revolutions

Yet the Whitman celebrations were not always steeped in euphoria. They also came shortly after the crushing of the German Spartacist insurrection, which gave a particular meaning to the poem most quoted at the time: "To a Foiled European Revolutionaire." On May 30, *L'Humanité* published on its front page an article by Bazalgette with the epigraph: "Courage donc, révolté, révoltée d'Europe! Car vous ne devez cesser avant que tout ne cesse!"[6] In June 1919, Antonio Gramsci planned to publish in his socialist newspaper *L'Ordine Nuovo* a translation of the poem by Palmiro Togliatti (a future leader of the Italian Communist Party). But the poem was banned (a fact later highlighted by Soviet critics)[7] and could only be printed when censorship ended in July.[8] Caterina Bernardini argues that Gramsci's reaction to the censors' decision "deemphasizes the political value of Whitman's poetry to serve a specific rhetorical and ideological aim: that of showing how Communism cares about art."[9] A few months later, Togliatti published another translation, this time of the poem "Europe,"[10] with the abridged title commonly used in Russia. In France, there

---

5   Georges Chennevière, "'Les Fêtes du Peuple.' Commémoration du centenaire de Walt Whitman," *L'Humanité*, June 2, 1919, 2.
6   "Be brave, European revolter, revoltress! / For till all ceases neither must you cease."
7   Iasen Zasurskii, "Uitmen na stranitsakh *Ordine Nuovo*" (Whitman in the pages of *Ordine Nuovo*), *Ogonëk*, June 1955 (no. 27), 23.
8   "A un rivoluzionario vinto d'Europa," *L'Ordine nuovo*, July 12, 1919, 68.
9   Bernardini, *Transnational Modernity*, 107.
10 "Europa," *L'Ordine nuovo*, December 6–13, 1919, 226.

were other instances of Whitmanian Fêtes du peuple in 1921. Quite appropriately, "To a Foil'd European Revolutionaire" was read to commemorate the Paris Commune in March 1921. In November, Whitman was read, along with Blok, at a communist festival of Russian music.

1919 was also a decisive year for Whitman in Hungary. Seven poems were translated by the journalist and reporter Árpád Pásztor for the magazine *Nyugat* (West). Pásztor was a socialist (he wrote a poem for Lenin in 1917, before he became critical of the Soviet Union). He was also Jewish and, in the note that served as an introduction to the poems, he explained that he first heard of Whitman from Morris Rosenfeld in New York, in 1907. Rosenfeld told him that Whitman was the poet who most influenced him:[11] the Yiddish Whitman was a transatlantic agent. Pásztor insisted that Whitman used to be completely unknown to Hungarian readers.[12] But all of a sudden, he was like "a fashion item," though no one really knew how to "wear" him! Pásztor's choice of poems indicated a way: as the insignia of the despised and the vanquished. It began with "The City Dead-House" and ended with "To a Foil'd Revolutionaire," followed by the section of "Song of Myself" that hails "those who have failed."

The issue was published for Whitman's centennial, in June 1919. This happened to be an extraordinarily unstable and violent moment in Hungarian history: the communist leader Béla Kun seized power in Budapest in March and established a Soviet Republic. Months of "Red Terror" followed, with harsh repression and military disasters, until Kun fled in August and a phase of "White Terror" began. It was during these months that the Whitman issue was published. Did Pásztor translate the poems at that time or were they ready before? The fact that the introductory note bears the date May 31 and the emphasis on crushed hopes leads me to think that the translations were concomitant with the devastating events of the spring, which caused Pásztor's disillusionment with communism. Pásztor later published, in 1922, a book-length selection, with an essay;[13] the "Foil'd Revolutionaire" still had a strategic place but was preceded by "Salut au Monde!" In 1921, "Song of Myself" was translated into Hungarian by Endre Gáspár and published in Vienna. In 1922, the conservative and authoritarian government of Admiral Horthy declared a ban on Whitman's works. The news was reported in the *New York Times* (March 11, 1922) and

---

11 Árpád Pásztor, "Jegyzetek Walt Whitman századik születésnapjára" (Notes on Walt Whitman on his 100th Birthday), *Nyugat*, no. 11 (June 1, 1919).
12 Whitman had not been translated yet, but in 1914, the Jewish female poet Piroska Reichard, a regular contributor to *Nyugat*, had published an essay in praise of Whitman and his new religion of the "manly love of comrades" ("Walt Whitman. 1819–1892," Budapest: Franklin, 1914).
13 Árpád Pásztor, *Walt Whitman* (Budapest: Dick Manó kiadása, 1920).

in *L'Humanité*: "Horthy the butcher has ordered the sequestration of Walt Whitman's works ... Several hundred policemen have visited the bookshops of Budapest and seized the works of the American poet."[14] The book was reprinted the following year.[15]

In Poland, in 1921, the Cooperative of the Railway Workers published a booklet on Whitman by Antonina Sokolicz. The cover clearly indicated the proletarian perspective on the poet.

FIGURE 6.1. Cover of Antonina Sokolicz, *Walt Whitman* (Warsaw: Wyd. Zw. Robot. Stowarzyszeń Spółdź, 1921). "We demolish the creation." National Library of Poland.

This was also an extremely difficult and complex political situation, just at the end of the Polish-Soviet War (the Treaty of Riga was signed in March 1921). Sokolicz was an actress and a socialist activist from a young age: she had to leave the Russian Empire after the 1905 Revolution, in which she was involved, and lived in France until 1914, before traveling to Russia and Siberia. Back in Poland after the war, she co-founded a publishing house for radical books and became a member of the Communist Party. She was the author of a pamphlet

---

14 *L'Humanité*, March 19, 1922, 4.
15 An essay by Géza Szilágyi in *Nyugat* (no. 4, February 16, 1923) shifted the focus and discussed only the homoerotic aspects.

on the "artistic culture of the Proletariat" and Whitman had a part to play in it. The essay emphasizes the word "Democracy," and contains several excerpts of classic "socialist Whitman" poems:[16] section 11 of "Salut au Monde!," "Years of the Modern" (beginning with the line: "I see the frontiers and the boundaries of the old aristocracies broken," like most Russian translations), "For You O Democracy," and the first half of "Pioneers! O Pioneers!"

In the press: the Comintern of translators

The socialist and communist press continued to feature Whitman in the early 1920s. In France, one of the main contributors was Marcel Martinet, who was involved with *L'Effort libre* before the war. In 1922, he reviewed Léon Bazalgette's final edition of *Leaves of Grass* for *L'Humanité*. He emphasized Whitman's impact on post-Symbolist French poetry, as well as his own revelation when he first read him, ten years earlier, at a time of great despair: "Just as he resuscitated many, he resuscitated me. . . . His words were not the words of a writer, but the bearers of a true revolution, of the kind that puts a desperate man back on his feet like the discovery of a great Hope."[17] The poems "Song of Myself" and "Song of the Universal" were "the most beautiful lyrical transcript of our revolutionary communism." Martinet also paid homage to Bazalgette: "We are many who cannot separate Whitman from his translator, historian, and commentator." This might be read as a commonplace compliment to a friend, but it reveals something important about reception: the poet and his mediator are sometimes so entangled that they form a new entity.

Another interesting article is the preface by Leon Trotsky to Martinet's play *La Nuit*. While praising Martinet, Trotsky lashed out at other Whitmanians:[18]

> Martinet comes from Romain Rolland's school—Rolland and his hesitating brains crippled by the whims of a sensibility poisoned by skepticism. But Martinet does not share his aristocratic pretension, his intellectual height, his judgmental pedantry, his selfish indifference. Recently, Martinet told us about another

---

16 Sokolicz used several translations: Alfred Tom for "Salut of Monde," a certain "Halin" for "Years of the Modern," and mostly Ruber (Stefan Rudniański). Rudniański and Sokolicz's paths probably crossed many times: they belonged to the same circles and both taught at Warsaw's "People's University" (Folk High School). Rudniański was murdered in Lviv in 1941 and Sokolicz in Auschwitz in 1942.
17 *L'Humanité*, July 13, 1922, 4.
18 The play was published in Russian with Trotsky's preface, which was in its turn published in French in *L'Humanité*.

master, the American Walt Whitman. While Rolland is all nerves, Whitman is flesh and blood. A muscular optimism breathes through his stanzas. He is not a socialist, nor a communist, contrary to what his bad Russian translator, Chukovsky, proclaims, and the reason for that is simple: by nature, because of his ideas, he is a pre-socialist.[19]

Trotsky quoted Martinet's review of Whitman in *L'Humanité* and concluded: "Whitman is not a socialist nor a communist, but his heir is not Harding or Hughes, it is the revolutionary proletarian." Ironically, Trotsky concurs with Chukovsky, whom he misread, or confused with Lunacharsky. Trotsky's comments might not be those of a "genial critic" as the newspaper wrote, but they reveal in what virulent ideological diatribes Whitman was sometimes involved.

In Germany, *Sozialistische Monatshefte* (Socialist Monthly) continued to publish Whitman's poems between 1918 and 1923, in Max Hayek's versions, with a peak in 1919. Whitman disappeared from 1924 to 1929, and came back in the late 1920s, with a different translator, the socialist Hermann Curth. But overall, the declining trend was representative of a loss of momentum. Interestingly, the poems published in the journal were not the typical socialist pieces, except for the eleventh section of "Salut au Monde!," which mentions Eastern Europe. A Lithuanian translation of "Beat! Beat! Drums!" was published in Latvia in 1928 by Antanas Venclova, a communist writer who later became a prominent intellectual and political figure in Soviet Lithuania.[20] A year later, more excerpts were published in the journal *Kūltura*. Most of them were translated by Kostas Korsakas, a Marxist activist (and later a scholar), while he was in jail. He mainly used Chukovsky's Russian translation.[21] As for Yugoslavia, Bojana Aćamović has thoroughly studied Whitman's reception between the two wars.[22] The poems published in the socialist press in 1919 and 1920 were mostly the same as in Soviet Russia ("Beat! Beat! Drums!" and "Pioneers! O Pioneers!").

---

19 *L'Humanité*, October 7, 1922, 1.
20 "Trimitai garsiau! Pilna burna būgnai!," in *Audra* [literary almanac; Riga], 1928, 22–23. A. Venclova also published translations of "Song of the Exposition" (in 1930, see below) and of Vladimir Friche's essay "Walt Whitman," *Kūltura*, 1929 (no. 12), 628–631.
21 About Whitman in Lithuania, see the essay by the foremost Lithuanian critic and political activist Vytautas Kubilius: "Pakeliui su Voltu Vitmenu," *Pergalė*, 1978 (no. 11), 116–128. Kubilius quotes a letter from Korsakas, in which he explains having Chukovsky's 168-page Whitman (therefore the 1923 edition) and also a few poems in German translation.
22 Bojana Aćamović, "Walt Whitman in the Yugoslav Interwar Periodicals: Serbo-Croatian Reception, 19–1940," *Walt Whitman Quarterly Review* 38, nos. 3–4: 139–168.

Aćamović also states that Russian and Soviet essays on Whitman were translated in the 1920s, and that the German *Sozialistische Monatshefte* was a source for Whitmanian material. These examples show increased communication between what one could call translators of the Comintern canon. They suggest a European socialist Whitman network whose center had moved eastward since the previous decades.

Turning "Salut au Monde!" into a parody

Whitman nonetheless gradually lost some of his aura. A revealing example is the rewriting of "Salut au Monde!" penned by Kurt Tucholsky in 1925. Earlier, I discussed his "freely inspired version" from 1913: at that time, Tucholsky had converted "Salut au Monde!" into a political pamphlet, denouncing exploiters and slavery, but emphatically concluding with Whitman's words: "Salut au monde! Each of us inevitable!" In 1925, under the pseudonym Theobald Tiger, he published another address to "Walt Wrobel" in the same journal. But after the war, the failure of German revolutions, and the death of *Weltbühne* contributor Gustav Landauer, Tucholsky's enthusiasm—or sense of "pathos"—was altered. His use of Whitman was parodic:

> Was siehst du, Walt Wrobel –?
> Ich sehe die entsetzliche obere Häuserfront der Berliner Straßen, unerbittlich, scharf liniiert, schwärzlich kasernenhaft;
> ich sehe neben dem unfreundlichen Mann am Schalter die kleine schmutzige Kaffeekanne, aus der er ab und zu einen Zivilschluck genehmigt;
> ich sehe das Skelett des Tauchers, ausgestreckt auf dem Meeresgrund, der Taucherhelm ist aufgeplatzt, und durch die Luken des untergegangenen Schiffs fliegt ein Schwarm Fische an die ehemalige Bar, sie rufen: "Sherry-Cobler –!";
> ich sehe den ehrenwerten Herrn Appleton aus Janesville (Wisconsin) auf der Terrasse des Boulevard-Cafés sitzen, lachende Kokotten bewerfen ihn mit Bällchen, er aber steckt seinen hölzernen Unterkiefer hart in die Luft;
> ich sehe das blonde Gesicht des jungen Diplomaten, der mit nachlässigem Monokel erzählt: "Seinerzeit, während dieser sojenannten Revolution...";
> ich sehe den kleinen Jungen vor der Obsthandlung stehen und sein Pipichen machen, nachher stippt er den Finger hinein

und malt Männerchen aufs Trottoir, das ist nicht hübsch von dem Kind –
Dies sieht mein Gesicht.²³

What do you see, Walt Wrobel—?
I see the dreadful upper facades of the Berlin streets, inexorable, sharply lined, blackish like barracks;
I see next to the unfriendly man at the counter the dirty little coffee pot, from which he now and then allows a civil sip;
I see the diver's skeleton stretched out on the seabed, the diving helmet has burst open, and through the hatches of the sunken ship a school of fish flies to the former bar, they call out: "Sherry-Cobbler—!"
I see the Honorable Mr. Appleton of Janesville, Wisconsin, sitting on the terrace of the Boulevard Café, laughing cocottes throwing balls at him, but he sticks his wooden jaw hard in the air;
I see the blond face of the young diplomat who, wearing a careless monocle, says: "At that time, during this so-called revolution...";
I see the little boy standing in front of the fruit shop and peeing, afterwards he sticks his finger in it and draws little men on the sidewalk, that's not pretty of the child—
That's what my face sees.

Each stanza enumerates what Walt Wrobel hears, tastes (the burnt crust of his aunt's fruit pie!), smells and feels. The satirical tone and the sense of humor that permeate the poem do not compensate for an overall grim mood: what the senses absorb is "mostly pain" (*Schmerz*). From one rewriting of "Salut au Monde!" to the other, Tucholsky moved from a confident relation to Whitman to a much more disillusioned one.

---

23 Theobald Tiger (pseud. of Kurt Tucholsky), "Die fünf Sinne," *Die Weltbühne* 21.2, no. 37 (September 15, 1925), 420.

2. In the US: Proletarian Whitman

Turning more partisan

Across the Atlantic, too, 1919 was—obviously—a year of Whitmanian celebrations. It was also the year when Horace Traubel died, after months of illness. He and his wife had moved to New York and stayed with their friends David and Rose Karsner.[24] Traubel wrote the poem "As I sit by Karsner's window" as a final address to Whitman: "I hear the noise of the vast city, Walt, just as you described it."[25] The 1919 celebrations did not have the same impact as in Europe, where they were the occasion of many translations and publications aimed at introducing the American poet, but they revealed how far Whitman had traveled to the Left. In May, there was a gathering on Fifth Avenue, with Horace Traubel and Helen Keller (Eugene Debs could not attend but sent a note). Written and visual materials featured in radical papers and magazines, such as the *Liberator*: in May 1919, Whitman's face appeared almost like a cameo between a review of John Reed's *Ten Days That Shook the World* and Bertrand Russell's *Proposed Roads to Freedom: Socialism, Anarchism and Syndicalism*.[26] More generally, annual dinners celebrating Whitman were occasions for socialist and communist speeches, as regularly reported in the *New York Times*: in 1920, a column read "Hail Walt Whitman as Red,"[27] while in 1923, a reader wrote an indignant letter, "Whitman Appropriated. The Poet Found to Be the 'Patron Saint' of Bolshevist Circles," in which he asked: "But why, pray tell me, is a Whitman dinner presumed to be the proper place for a Bolshevist demonstration?"[28] Whitman was indeed important for leftist unions and a number of radical intellectuals and poets throughout the 1920s and 1930s, in particular during the Great Depression. The contrast between critics' and academics' loss of interest in Whitman and his adulation by leftist writers is striking.[29]

---

24 Karsner was a disciple of Whitman, very close to Traubel (about whom he wrote the book *Horace Traubel: His Life and Work* [New York: Arens, 1919]); he named his daughter Walta Whitmana (the economist Walt Whitman Rostow, author of a "non-communist manifesto," was also named that way by his socialist parents).
25 Schmidgall, *Conserving Walt Whitman's Fame*, 386–388.
26 Woodcut by J. J. Lankes, *Liberator*, May 1919, 43; in 1920, for his birthday, Whitman was in full page. Lenin's birthday was celebrated in the same issue.
27 "Hail Walt Whitman as Red," *New York Times*, June 5, 1920.
28 Letter from A. M. Adams, *New York Times*, June 5, 1923, 20.
29 This contrast is articulated in Alan Golding's book on the formation of the American poetic canon *From Outlaw to Classic: Canons in American Poetry* (Madison: University of Wisconsin Press, 1995).

This Red Whitman prolonged the socialist Whitman of the early twentieth century and gathered further momentum from the Soviet reception, or more exactly what was known of it, often with some delay. In 1933, Albert Parry (who was Russian-born and had emigrated to the US in 1921) declared in his piece on Whitman in Russia: "Walt Whitman is now famous in Russia not as a mystic but as a revolutionary. He is now imitated by such class-conscious poets as Aleksey Gastev in his 'Poesy of the Working Blow,' and a host of other young Communists or Communist sympathizers."[30] In 1935, in the journal *International Literature* (a Soviet periodical published abroad in several languages), Leonard Spier also emphasized Whitman's popularity in Soviet Russia and observed that Whitman was the closest an American poet had come to formulating a "working-class ideology."[31] Mirsky's preface to the 1935 Soviet edition of *Leaves of Grass* was translated and published in the United States in 1937.[32] Yet Whitman was far from being a reference for the "bolshevists" alone, and he continued to be hailed by anarchists or socialists who were not aligned with Soviet positions.

Whitman for the workers

The Proletarian writer Meridel Le Sueur argues that, despite their puritanism, the American socialists knew and enjoyed Whitman in the 1920s because of his "passionate democracy, his love of Lincoln and poems about European revolutionists and for his love of the common people and occupations."[33] She adds that the Industrial Workers of the World liked Whitman even more because they "had a pagan streak" and believed in "free love," or at least in the freedom of love. Whitman was indeed popular among the Wobblies from the start. He was also quite often read in prison by political activists.[34]

Emma Goldman continued to spread Whitman's message to the masses. Her most extensive contribution on the poet was a lecture, the text of which was

---

30 Albert Parry, "Walt Whitman in Russia," *American Mercury*, September 1934, 107. Born Abraham Josipovich Paretsky, Parry left Russia in 1921; at the time of the article, he was a PhD student at the University of Chicago (he later became a professor of Russian studies at Colgate University). The article is remarkably well informed (it contains the first translations of early Russian reviews and mentions the Proletkult staging).
31 Leonard Spier, "Walt Whitman," *International Literature*, September 1935, 72–89.
32 D. S. Mirsky, "Walt Whitman: Poet of American Democracy," trans. Bernard Guilbert Guerney, *Dialectics*, no. 1 (1937), 11–29.
33 Meridel Le Sueur, "Jelly Roll" (1980), in Perlman, Folsom and Campion, *Walt Whitman: The Measure of His Song*, 421.
34 See M. Mendelson's discussions with American Communist Party leaders Elizabeth Gurley Flynn and Gus Hall in Maurice Mendelson, *Walt Whitman: A Soviet View*, trans. A. Bromfield (Moscow: Progress Publishers, 1976), 332; the book was first published in Russian in 1965.

kept in her manuscript notes.[35] The notes are not dated, but the fact that the lecture mentions the Soviet Tcheka is a clear indication that it was delivered after Goldman's return from her disastrous and disillusioning trip to the Soviet Union.[36] Goldman's Whitman was, obviously, an anarchist: his greatest contribution was the destruction of all hierarchies. Goldman also appreciated Whitman's "cry out for the liberation of sex." He was "the first to tear off the Puritanic rags which disfigured the bodies of men and women. Especially woman, who even more than man, was bound to the block of Puritanism." She quoted political poems such as "You Felons on Trial in Court," but also "A Woman Waits for Me." She also paid attention to Whitman's international fame and to the "universal" scope of his art:

> Old Walt lived to see himself proclaimed as the greatest poet of his time, not only in his own country, but nearly everywhere in Europe. In England, J. Addington Symonds and Edward Carpenter fell under the sway of the powerful originality of Whitman. In Germany it was the poet Freiligrath, a rebel to the very tips of his fingers, who rendered such a marvelous translation of *Leaves of Grass* that even the best critics, proclaimed it as great as the original. And of course France and Russia became enthused with the vigor, the beauty, of the clarion voice of Walt. . . .
>
> Horace Traubel is right when he says [that] Walt Whitman, as far as American [*sic*] is concerned, is very universal. He saw in America the free earth upon which a free strong humanity should dwell. But even America was to him only a part of the universe which he aimed to penetrate so passionately and poetically. One would do Whitman, the poet, a great injustice to see in him the apologist and sponsor of the democratic institutions. His art had absolutely nothing in common with the "national" art which reiterates the stale slogan of "My country 'tis of thee" or "Star Spangled Banner." He was as unlike the average democrat as the anarchist is unlike the typical bourgeois.

---

35 Emma Goldman, "Walt Whitman," *The Libertarian Labyrinth*, accessed September 30, 2023, https://www.libertarian-labyrinth.org/the-sex-question/emma-goldman-walt-whitman/.

36 "Democracy as conceived and sung by Walt Whitman, is still far from come. Whatever some of her admirers have once thought of democracy, they have recanted, sacrificed to the rule of dictatorship. Mr. George Bernard Shaw and many others have now become the pall-bearers of democracy, slain by the Tcheka and Fascism."

Whitman was read, discussed and also printed for the masses, like in the Haldeman-Julius edition. Based in Kansas, Emanuel Haldeman-Julius's publishing house had an especially wide audience in small towns and rural America. Their Little Blue Books series offered volumes small enough to fit in an overall pocket. Like Rhys's edition in England decades earlier, it was instrumental in popularizing Whitman. There were several versions of it, the first printed around 1919, the second one in 1924.[37] It was remembered by Meridel Le Sueur, and by Kenneth Patchen in a poem about strikes at Youngstown, Ohio, when he was still a child: "I went down through the woods / To the smelly crick with Whitman, / In the Haldeman-Julius edition."[38]

In addition, Whitman featured in socialist anthologies. In 1929, Marcus Graham's book of revolutionary poetry contained "Song of the Open Road" and called Whitman a precursor, along with Blake, Shelley and William Morris.[39] In the 1930s, the communist newspapers the *New Masses* (which replaced *Masses* and was much more in line with Soviet politics), *Comrades* and the *Daily Worker* contained a number of poems by Whitman, but also scores of musical settings, reviews of books on Whitman and short essays (such as Sam Roberts's 1938 pieces).

"Towards Proletarian Art": Whitman among leftist intellectuals

Waldo Frank was an avid reader of Romain Rolland, with whom he began a correspondence in 1914. His appreciation of Whitman as poet of the "multitudes" was infused with Rolland's conceptions and bears the mark of their transatlantic exchanges. In *Our America*, published in 1919, Frank sought to define his country by both delving into its historical roots (the Puritan legacy, the Transcendentalists) and painting the present. His diagnosis was that America had aged prematurely. The descriptions of life in New York mirror the portraits of degenerate city dwellers by Carpenter and Bazalgette. Franks asks: "Where are the Whitman multitudes today?"[40] They were crushed by spiritual emptiness, capitalist greed and Broadway simulacra. After the deaths of Lincoln

---

37 Dates of publication were not mentioned on the books. See Kenneth Price, "Walt Whitman in Selected Anthologies: The Politics of His Afterlife," *Virginia Quarterly Review* 81, no. 2 (Spring 2005): 147–162 and Jay Grossman, "Whitman in Your Pocket: The History of the Book and the History of Sexuality," in Cohen, *The New Walt Whitman Studies*, 101–120.
38 Kenneth Patchen, "The Orange Bears," in *Red Wine & Yellow Hair* (New York: New Directions, 1949), 31.
39 Marcus Graham, *An Anthology of Revolutionary Poetry* (New York: The Active Press, 1929).
40 Waldo Frank, *Our America* (New York: Boni and Liveright, 1919), 205.

and Whitman, "the storm of greed swirled higher. For forty years its black beat across our land was almost monotone. Unrivaled. The hearts and spirits of men and women flew before the blast of material aggrandizement like chaff of winnowed wheat. The grain was the gold." (222) Yet, "*Democratic Vistas* is quite as clearly our greatest book of social criticism as *Leaves of Grass* is our greatest poem." (205) American degeneration results from the loss of Whitmanian ideals, which must therefore be recovered, "because we cannot be so weak as to doubt that in this juncture of his spirit and our land is revelation." The end of the essay converts ideal into action, revelation into revolution:

> This then is our task. Whitman foresaw it and sang of it and warned us. We must go through a period of static suffering, of inner cultivation. We must break our impotent habit of constant issuance into petty deed. We must begin to generate within ourselves the energy which is love of life. For that energy, to whatever form the mind consigns it, is religion. Its act is creation. And in a dying world, creation is revolution. (231)

In the 1920s, Frank was a regular contributor to the French journal *Europe*, and then to the US magazine *New Masses*. He became a fellow traveler at the beginning of the 1930s and visited the USSR, before distancing himself from the American Communist Party in 1937.

Another prominent communist Whitmanian was the Jewish poet and novelist Mike Gold. I will later consider his "Ode to Whitman," but for now I will highlight his essay on Proletarian art. Born Itzok Isaac Granich, Gold was an ardent supporter of the Bolsheviks from the start. He worked for the *Masses* (edited by Floyd Dell and Max Eastman) and in 1922 became the executive director of Eastman's magazine the *Liberator* (with Claude McKay). His 1921 essay "Towards Proletarian Art"[41] offered one of the first American definitions of Proletarian culture. Rather than the Marxist lexicon, his language borrowed from the images of primitivism: the Masses "are never far from the heaven" and the "Social Revolution in the world to-day arises out of the deep need of the masses for the old primitive group life." (22) Whitman himself "dwelt among the masses, and from them he drew his strength." Of particular interest is the last part, "Walt Whitman's spawn": the poet was considered the sole example of

---

41 Irwin Granich, "Towards Proletarian Art," *Liberator* 4, no. 2 (February 1921), 20–22. Gold wrote under the pseudonym Irwin Granich, though in the same issue he is referred to as Michael Gold in a call for contributions to help his recovery after "a nervous breakdown."

(pre-)Proletarian art. His mistake was his belief in political democracy, but he revealed a path for Proletarian culture. Gold then associates Whitman with the Proletkult, in one of the first American reports on it:

> The Russian revolutionists have been aware with Walt that the spiritual cement of a literature and art is needed to bind together a society. They have begun creating the religion of the new order. The *"Prolet-Kult"* is their conscious effort towards this (23)....
>
> A great art will arise out of the new great life in Russia—and it will be an art that will sustain man, and give him equanimity, and not crucify him on his problems as did the old. The new artists feel the mass-sufficiency, and suffer no longer that morbid sense of inferiority before the universe that was the work of the solitaries. It is the resurrection.
>
> In America we have had attempts to carry on the work of old Walt, but they have failed, and must fail, while the propagandists still lack Walt's knowledge that a mighty national art cannot arise save out of the soil of the masses. (24)

Max Eastman was another radical journalist and writer for whom Whitman was significant. As one learns from Eastman's biography, his passion for Whitman was an early one, and did not only involve politics, but sexuality too.[42] His 1926 review of Emory Holloway's biography of Whitman was entitled "Menshevizing Whitman."[43] Drawing on Lenin's distinction between the "fighters" (the Bolsheviks) and the "reasoners" (the Mensheviks), he accused Holloway of taming Whitman. But what he meant was that Holloway failed to state "that Whitman was strongly homosexual." Granville Hicks, the communist activist and literary critic, had a chapter on Whitman in *The Great Tradition* (1933); like most Marxist critics of the time, he saw the limitations of his outdated political thought, but hailed him as "the founder of the new American literature, the literature of the industrial era."[44] In 1938, Newton Arvin, a professor of literature at Smith College and the author of several studies on American Renaissance literature, wrote a book whose main question was: "To what extent is Whitman a socialist poet?"[45] He broke new ground in US academia: at a time

---

42 Christoph Irmscher, *Max Eastman: A Life* (New Haven: Yale University Press, 2017).
43 Max Eastman, "Menshevizing Whitman," *New Masses* 2, no. 2 (December 1926), 12.
44 Granville Hicks, *The Great Tradition: An Interpretation of American Literature since the Civil War* (1933; Chicago: Quadrangle Books, 1969), 30.
45 Newton Arvin, *Whitman* (New York: Macmillan Co., 1938).

when Whitman was hardly studied, he not only suggested a radical and socialist reading, but openly addressed the question of homosexuality.[46]

Regarding poetry more specifically, Carl Sandburg and Vachel Lindsay have often been designated as Whitman's Proletarian heirs. While Sandburg did not address Whitman directly, he wrote the preface of the 1921 edition of *Leaves of Grass* for the Modern Library, presenting it as a book "to be owned, kept, loaned, fought over, and read till it is dog-eared and dirty all-over." (iv–v) Similarities between his poetry and Whitman's have often been pointed out.[47] While Vachel Lindsay considered Sandburg the only Whitmanian poet not to be overwhelmed by his master,[48] others, like the Russian critic Mirsky, labeled him an imitator and claimed he lacked originality. One of the most striking resemblances between them is the construct of a plastic poetic persona—in Sandburg's case, identifying with large groups: "I am the people—the mob—the crowd—the mass."[49]

John Reed, author of the famous account of the Russian Revolution *Ten Days That Shook the World*, also wrote poetry with strong Whitmanian overtones. The poem "America in 1918," written while Reed was in Russia, is particularly interesting from an internationalist perspective. It is an address to "his America," from the West of his youth to New York City, full of apostrophes and anaphora:

> Orchards forever endless, deep in blooming,
> Green-golden orange-groves and snow-peaks looming over . . .
> By raw audacious cities sprung from nothing,
> Brawling and bragging in their careless youth . . .
> I know thee, America!
> . . . .
> Keepers of dance-halls in construction-camps, bar-keeps, prostitutes,
> Bums riding the rods, wobblies singing their defiant songs, unafraid of death,

---

[46] Arvin was homosexual. In 1960, he was arrested and convicted for "pornography" after photographs of naked men were found during a search at his home, and he had to resign from Smith. See Barry Werth, *The Scarlet Professor: Newton Arvin; A Literary Life Shattered by Scandal* (New York: Doubleday, 2001).

[47] See for example Esther Lolita Holcomb, "Whitman and Sandburg," *English Journal* 17, no. 7 (September 1928): 549–555.

[48] Vachel Lindsay, "Walt Whitman," *New Republic*, December 5, 1923, "Views of American Poetry" supplement, 3–5.

[49] Carl Sandburg, "I am the People, the Mob," in *Chicago Poems* (New York: Henry Holt & Co., 1916), 172.

> Card-sharps and real-estate agents, timber-kings, wheat-kings,
>   cattle-kings...
> I know ye, Americans!
> ....
> The East Side, worlds within a world, chaos of nations,
> Sink of the nomad races, last and wretchedest
> Port of the westward Odyssey of mankind...
> At dawn vomiting colossal flood of machine-fodder,
> At evening sucking back with terrible harsh sound
> To beast-like tenements, garish nickelodeons, gin-mills.[50]

The longest part of the poem is devoted to the cosmopolitan East Side, with enumerations of characteristic details and places, from "Tomashevsky's Jewish coryphees" to "Armenian kitchens hung with Oriental carpets from New Jersey." Reed relocates Whitman's "Salut au Monde!" to America, more precisely to New York, as if the city alone could encapsulate the world: Whitman's original extension toward vast latitudes reverses into a centripetal vision, without losing its internationalist scope: "All professions, races, temperaments, philosophies, / All history, all possibilities, all romance, / America... the world...!" After Reed's death, Mike Gold wrote a tribute to his "Captain,"[51] inspired by Whitman's poem to Lincoln.

In Yiddish: "Salut au Monde!" as a marching hymn

From the start, with Bovshover's tribute, Whitman was hailed by American Yiddish poets as a socialist messiah. He was also important for the less political group Di Yunge poets, as shown by the translation of "Salut au Monde!" in 1912. These socialist and cosmopolitan receptions blended into internationalism in the 1920s and 1930s. The popularity of "Salut au Monde!" reached its climax, as the poem was imbued with political meaning.

One of the most striking instances is the rewriting of the poem by Reuben Ludwig. Born in the Ukrainian part of the Russian Empire, Ludwig emigrated to the US in the 1910s; he was briefly linked to the Inzikhistn (Introspectivists), before he settled in the Southwest. His poetry addressed Jewish life, social questions and expressed solidarity with African and Native Americans. His address

---

50 John Reed, "America 1918," *New Masses*, October 15, 1935, 17–19. The poem remained unpublished until 1935. According to the editor of *New Masses*, Reed began it in Russia and completed it in the US.
51 "John Reed's Body," *Liberator* 6, no. 10 (October, 1923), 21.

to Whitman in "Symposium," written in 1923, displayed the same mixture of alphabets and languages as the *Shriftn* translation of "Salut au Monde!" The title was in Latin script, and a direct quotation from "Salut au Monde!" read as a subtitle.

SYMPOSIUM
"What do you see, Walt Whitman?"

איך זע ברייטע וועגן פון ניו־ארלעאנס ביזן האדסאן.
איך זע געלע סאף־זומערדיקע גרעזלעך באפלעקן זייערע ברעגן.

FIGURE 6.2. First lines of Reuben Ludwig, "Symposium," *Gezalmete Lider* (New York: Aroysgegeben fun kolegn un fraynt mit der hilf fun Y. L. Perets shrayber-fareyn, 1927), 53.

But what the poet saw was no longer the world: it was the United States. A dysphoric vision revealed the betrayal of Whitman's and Lincoln's ideals:

> Ikh ze breyte vegn fun Nyu-Orleans bizn Hodson.
> Ikh ze gele sof-zumerdike grezlekh baflekn zeyere bregn.
> Ikh zukh umzist mayne shvere trit, vos hobn geakert zeyere veykhe, shtoybike rukns.
> Ikh zukh umzist di feste, grin-farbleterte shtamen fun mayne farzeyte kerner.
> Ikh ze di vent fun mayne oyfgeboyte shtet, tsefoylt un tsebreklt.
> Ikh ze, mayn folk, dem erd-arbeter fun ale shtatn,
> Tsugebundn tsu zayn aker-ayzn, on libe tsu der erd.
> Ikh ze dem freylekhn gold-zukher fun Kalifornye
> Mit geler opgekrokhener hoyt un tife ayngezunkene oygn,
> Sharndik mit tsiterndike finger fun a kargn – dem arts fun zayn grub.
> . . . .
> Ikh ze dem rizikn kholem—fun mir, dem gigant Volt Vhitman,
> Vi er vert oyf vayse vegn fun tsiterdike fis getrotn.
> Ikh ze dare bletlekh oyf der vayser Brodvey
> Fun milyonen bleykhe kinder getrotn.[52]

---

52 Reuben Ludwig, "Symposium," in *Gezalmete Lider* (New York: Aroysgegeben fun kolegn un fraynt mit der hilf fun Y. L. Perets shrayber-fareyn, 1927), 53–54. For a complete translation of the poem, see Julian Levinson, "Walt Whitman among the Yiddish Poets," *Tikkun* 18, no. 5 (2003): 59.

I see wide roads from New Orleans to the Hudson.
I see the yellow, end-of-summer blades of grass splattering their
  edges,
I seek in vain my heavy footprints, which plowed their soft dusty
  backs,
I seek in vain the firm, green-leaved stumps from the seeds I
  sowed.
I see the walls of the cities I built, crumbling and rotting.
I see my people, the farmers from all states,
Bound to their plows with no love for the earth.
I see the happy gold-miner from California
With yellow, peeling skin and deeply sunken eyes,
Scraping with the shaking fingers of a miser the ore of his mine.
. . . .
I see the enormous dream—that came out of me, the giant Walt
  Whitman,
Trampled by trembling feet on the white roads.
I see thin leaves on white Broadway,
Trampled by millions of pale children.

Whitman's poem underwent several major changes, as it was actualized in a different time and a different language. First, the salutation is to America and its states, in their Yiddish names. Whitman addressed the world in English, while Ludwig addresses America in Yiddish. Whitman is paradoxically renationalized in an internationalist language. Second, Whitman's enthusiastic vision turns into a dysphoric survey. All the components of his ravishing world are affected by a negative sign: Whitman seeks in vain, farmers have no love, verbs indicate decay instead of growth. The "pale children" (bleykhe kinder) are the poor and sad avatars of Whitman's "tan-faced children." In the second part of the poem, John Brown and Abraham Lincoln are summoned one after the other. The three great representatives of American democracy are thus able to hold a postmortem symposium in the space of the poem: "John Brown, what do you see?" "What do you see Abraham Lincoln?" Both give equally grim reports. The only symbol of unity is the large "sheaf" (garb) of the Mississippi, which binds everything together.

In 1929, an excerpt from "Salut au Monde!" featured in an elementary school textbook (chrestomathy);[53] it was given in I. J. Schwartz translation, except for

---

53 Yaakov Levin, ed., *Dos naye bukh literarishe un historishe khrestomatye: leyenbukh far dem eltern klas fun der elementarer shul: un dem ershtn klas fun mitlshul* (New York: Yidishe Shul, 1929), 339–340.

the title, which was no longer in French, but translated into Yiddish as "A grus der velt," and followed by the generic indication "ode." It comprised the stanza with references to the Slavs, Poles, Russians and Jews. In another transatlantic twist, the same extract can be heard in a propaganda film by Alexander Ford, *Mir Kumen on* (We are Coming), shot in 1936 and dedicated to the Vladimir Medem sanatorium for Jewish children in Poland (founded by the Jewish Labor Bund). At some point, the children begin their weekly entertainment with a recitation of the same section of the poem. It is heavily edited: the list of nationalities is considerably shortened, but references to Poland and Ukraine are added. It ends with wishes of peace sent not "from me and from America," but from "the children of the Medem Sanatorium." The film was censured in Poland, but shown in France and in the US in 1938.

Another Yiddish rewriting of "Salut au Monde!" with a communist agenda was Louis Miller's "I Hear Your Voice, Walt Whitman." Born Eliezer Meler in Volhynia, in 1889, Miller first translated a piece by Whitman in *Shriftn* in 1919. In the 1930s, he was a member of the Proletpen, a radical organization of Yiddish writers. His poem "I Hear Your Voice, Walt Whitman" was published in a 1939 collection, at a time when he was working on a quite extensive translation.[54] In "Salut au Monde!," Whitman also used "I hear" anaphorically, and in "Song of Myself" he was filled with "voices of the interminable generation of prisoners and slaves, / Voices of the diseas'd and despairing and of thieves and dwarfs." For "voice," Miller used the Hebrew word *kol* in the title, which turns into the main anaphora at the end of the poem (*koyles*). Miller addresses Whitman and asks: "Who are the thousands, Walt Whitman, / Who come with marching steps?" The answer follows in the enumeration of "mine-workers, farm-hands and peddlers," man and woman, the "brown-skinned" and the "white-skinned," Jew and Christian, all gathered under a red flag. The voices are those of prisoners, strikers, tortured people, whom Whitman joins in a chorus of millions "marching and fighting."

The idea that America had betrayed Whitman and that his true heirs were now in the Soviet Union was expressed by Isaac Isaacson, a writer from Podolia who emigrated to Argentina: "Lincoln's heirs have outlawed the only country that has strived to live up to [Whitman's] ideal" and "at the moment it is only the Russians, one hundred and fifty million, who walk with assured and rapid steps, just as he sang, with eyes and ears turned to him to hear his song."[55] The number alludes to Vladimir Mayakovsky's long poem *150. 000. 000*. It is the very idea

---

54 Louis Miler, "Ikh her dain kol, Volt Vitman," in *Do iz mayn heym* (New York: Farlag "Signal" beym "Proletpen," 1939), 58–60. The book of translations was published the following year (see Chapter 7).
55 Isaacson, *Eseyen un kritik vegn literatur un kunst*, 38.

that Pablo Neruda later converted into poetry in "Let the Rail Splitter Awake," yet another rewriting of "Salut au Monde!" (see Chapter 9).

In 1928, during a trip to Canada, Emma Goldman delivered her lecture on Whitman in Yiddish for a Montreal audience, "the Yiddish intelligentsia": "They were proud that I was one of their race, they reiterated. It was worth coming back to Montreal to reach their Yiddish hearts by the grace of the *goi* Walt Whitman."[56] A "goi" speaking Yiddish, in a conversation with Lincoln, in a sanatorium for Jewish children or in a Montreal home: this was yet another remarkable avatar of the internationalist Whitman during the interwar period.

Whitman and the Great Depression

In the wake of the Great Depression, Whitman loomed large in American public space, thanks to a program of murals in post offices, commissioned by the Treasury Department. The idea was to provide work and artwork, but also to boost the citizenry's morale by presenting a positive history of the country and valorizing its beloved figures. Quotes by Whitman were included on Mitchell Siporin's 1941 murals for the St. Louis (Missouri) Post Office:[57] "In the labor of engines and trades and the labor of fields, I find the developments. / And find the eternal meanings." More impressively, Whitman inspired the frescoes *Resources of America* of the US Post Office Bronx Central Annex (1939), by Ben Shahn and his wife Bernarda Bryson. Shahn was Jewish, born in Lithuania of a revolutionist father, and had emigrated at a young age to the US, where, among other things, he was Diego Rivera's assistant on the Rockefeller Center murals. On one of the panels, the poet is represented with a huge hand (the hand of "Salut au Monde!"?) pointing at his own lines, written on a blackboard (the last stanza of "As I walk, solitary, unattended…"), surrounded by workers.

The notion that Whitman's America had been betrayed by capitalist forces gained further force during the Great Depression. Stephen Vincent Benét (1898-1943) was a major literary figure of his time and the recipient of many prizes, including the Pulitzer for his long poem on the American Civil War *John Brown's Body*.[58] His "Ode to Walt Whitman" also reads as a dialogue with T. S. Eliot, from whom he borrowed many images and motifs to depict America's landscape during the Great Depression.

---

56 Emma Goldman, *Living My Life*, vol. 2 (1931; Dover: New York, 1970), 992.
57 On post office murals, and in particular on the St. Louis one, see Andrew Hemingway, *Artists on the Left: American Artists and the Communist Movement, 1926-1956* (New Haven: Yale University Press, 2002), 166–169.
58 Whitman features twice in this poem: as a nurse on the battlefield of Fredericksburg, and in a prose sequence where he imagines the Battle of Brooklyn Heights.

The reference to Eliot allows for a comparison with Hart Crane's tribute to Whitman in *The Bridge* (1930). While Whitman could appear in Crane as an antidote to Eliotian anxiety, nothing remained of his presence and legacy in Benét's world. Yet Benét did not despair either. By amending Whitman's message—rather than merely exhuming it—he outlined possible ways out. The ode comprises four parts, formally quite different. The first one is about Whitman's old age, agony and death; it bristles with images from Eliot and Whitman: "Now comes Fourth Month and the early buds on the tree."[59] Fourth month is April in Whitman's calendar, that is, the quintessential Eliotian month, the "cruellest month," "mixing / Memory and desire" (*The Waste Land*). The second part jumps from Whitman's death to the present time: "It is Fourth Month now and spring in another century." As the land of promise has been scarred by the ravages of the Depression, Whitman returns from the dead and asks his "comrades" about the state of the Union: "Is it well with these States?" (441) They answer:

> "We have made many, fine new toys.
> We—
> There is a rust on the land.
> A rust and a creeping blight and a scaled evil.
> For six years eating, yet deeper than those six years,
> Men labor to master it but it is not mastered.
> ....
> There is shadow in the bright sun, there is shadow upon the streets.
> They burn the grain in the furnace while men go hungry.
> They pile the cloth of the looms while men go ragged.
> We walk naked in our plenty." (442)

As Whitman asks where the gains have gone, the speech gears toward the denunciation of a system which disconnects work from gain. Men with hearts "like engines" robbed the workers: they are the brutal capitalist avatars of Eliot's weak and devitalized "hollow men." Rust turns into dust as the land is hit by dry tornadoes: "Over the great plains of the buffalo-land, / The dust-storm blows, the choking, sifting, small dust." The evocation of the economic crisis takes on powerful biblical overtones, with the American land struck by plagues such as drought and animal diseases. Again, Eliot's vision turns into a political stance, since the waste land results from the betrayal of the American pastoral ideal by

---

59 "Ode to Walt Whitman" (1935), in *Burning City* (1936), reprinted in *Selected Works of Stephen Benét*, 2 vols. (New York: Farrar and Rinehart Inc., 1942), 1:438.

capitalism: "And they have wasted the pasture and the fresh valley" in order to build "sham castles," slums, ugly factory towns, "but never Monticello, never again." (446) Monticello, Jefferson's estate in Virginia, stands by metonymy for a democratic-republican ideal that appears to be lost.

And yet, "Under dry winter / Arbutus grows." (444) The landscape from which human life has withdrawn is paradoxically the matrix of a rebirth. A man will come who will restore a connection to nature, and Whitmanian motifs will unfold again: "He grows through the earth and is part of it like the roots of new grass." (445) This line forecasts the prophetic tone of the last part:

> You're still the giant lode we quarry
> For gold, fools' gold and all the earthy metals,
> The matchless mine.
> Still the trail-breaker, still the rolling river.
>
> You and your land, your turbulent, seeking land
> Where anything can grow. (446)

The recovery of the pastoral will not be immediate, but, little by little, nature will retrieve its rights. The last stanzas turn to rivers as powerful agents of restoration. They come from all the states, which are enumerated, as in Whitman, and finally gather in the great Mississippi:

> Rivers from the high horse-plains and the deep, green Eastern pastures
> Sink into it and are lost and rejoice and shout with it, shout within it,
> They and their secret gifts,
> A fleck of gold from Montana, a sliver of steel from Pittsburgh,
> A wheat-grain from Minnesota, an apple-blossom from Tennessee,
> Roiled, mixed with the mud and earth and the changing bottoms
> In the vast, rending floods,
> But rolling, rolling from Arkansas, Kansas, Iowa,
> Rolling from Ohio, Wisconsin, Illinois,
> Rolling and shouting:
> Till, at last, it is Mississippi,
> The Father of Waters; the matchless; the great flood
> Dyed with earth of States, with the dust and the sun and the seed of half the States

> The huge heart-vein, pulsing and pulsing; gigantic; ever broader, ever mightier. (447)

Benét reverses many of the Whitmanian coordinates: the country is no longer charted by men opening roads from east to west, but by the movement of the waters from north to south. The abrasive power of the river wipes the slate clean. This is obviously quite different from the tabula rasa of the revolution, induced by men and social forces. The poem nonetheless makes powerful use of Whitman to denounce the consequences of capitalism. Though it is very unlikely that Benét had knowledge of Ludwig's Yiddish "Symposium," the coincidence between the two poems, with their final visions of the mighty Mississippi, is striking.

Regarding the state of the country in 1936, the poet Genevieve Taggard also addressed Whitman. Taggard embraced communist ideals at an early age—in November 1917, she gave a lecture at the Manhattan Opera House on Whitman and Mayakovsky. The poem "Night letter to Walt Whitman" opens the collection *Calling Western Union* (1936). It is in broken verse, with lots of spacings, which create a rugged landscape on the page—the formal work and originality of the layout are noteworthy, as they are quite rare in Proletarian poetry. Taggard evokes the earth "slowly to swamp to bad land returning"[60] or drying up into "dust riffled in dunes." Above all, she emphasizes an overwhelming sense of sterility and scarcity:

> Corn none   Cotton none   Hogs none   Cloth none

And while the poem expresses a wish for abundance, for the reconciliation of the machine and the garden (it mentions both the combine harvester and the lilacs), it ends on the "blah blah" of the radio and the triumph of the mean thistle:

> On the   bad land
> The thistle
> Scatters
> Wrong. (2)

Taggard's address to Whitman is much more arid than Benét's, but they share the same diagnosis: the Great Depression was the ultimate betrayal of Whitman's American ideal.

---

60 Genevieve Taggard, *Calling Western Union* (New York: Harper and Brothers, 1936), 1. The poem was first published in *New Frontier* 1, no. 3 (June 1936).

All these writers, from Traubel, Reed and Sandburg to Gold and Taggard, enjoyed a certain fame in the USSR, where they were translated and included in anthologies of Western or revolutionary poetry. They were often paired with Whitman, thus consolidating the Proletarian genealogy they had established (as in Ivan Kulyk's 1928 anthology[61] or Mikhail Zenkevich's in 1946). John Reed's "America 1918" was translated into Russian by Ivan Kashkin in his 1960 anthology of American literature, which also included Whitman, Sandburg and Taggard. These poets were studied by Soviet critics, often in more detail than in the West, and considered as Whitman's true heirs.[62]

3. Supplementing Whitman's America

Between the national and the international, another space was essential to the reception of Whitman's poetry: the continental. In the late nineteenth and early twentieth centuries, Whitman was the model of "continental" poetry, namely, of a poetry freed from European models, able to encompass the immensity of America's expanses and the richness of its geography.[63] But in time, the continental scale became an intermediary towards the international. In addition, inside the US, other Whitmanian voices emerged, the voices of minorities, especially of African Americans. They added yet other impulses towards internationalism.[64]

"The other America"

Between the end of the nineteenth century and World War II, Whitman's reception in South America evolved from admiration and emulation to a more critical position. In the introduction, I mentioned Armando Vasseur's translation into Spanish (1912). The prologue of *Poemas* insisted that Whitman would bring fresh air to Hispanic American literature, which had been spoiled by European

---

61 In the preface to his anthology in Ukrainian, Kulyk emphasized that contemporary American poetry, which he called the "Democratic Renaissance" (Demokratychnyi Renesans) was infused with Whitman's spirit. He saluted the beginnings of "proletarian poetry" in the US (Sandburg was a genius, Claude McKay and Mike Gold provided "yeast" and were eating away at imperialism). He sent his anthology to Taggard.
62 See Libman, *Amerikanskaia literatura v russkikh perevodakh i kritike. Bibliografiia 1776–1975*.
63 I develop this point in *Fortunes de Walt Whitman*, 230–264.
64 On US minorities and internationalism in the first half of the twentieth century, see Steven S. Lee, *The Ethnic Avant-Garde: Minority Cultures and World Revolution* (New York: Columbia University Press, 2015).

(especially French) "emanations."[65] By breaking the mold of medieval metrics, Whitman gave the American intellect "freedom of creation and expression." This continental claim was somewhat paradoxical since Vasseur used the Italian translation by Gamberale at length, as well as the French translation by Bazalgette. Translating Whitman seems to have been the ultimate achievement of a poet whose own work epitomizes the concept of nuevomundismo (New Worldism).

As time went by, however, poets wanted to be more than Whitman's counterparts: they aimed at supplementing or even correcting his work. The unmixed enthusiasm of Martí or Vasseur was followed by more ambiguous readings. For Spanish-speaking America, two main differences with Whitman's poetry were stressed, to various degrees: on the one hand, its "Spanishness" or "Latinity," and on the other hand, its strong native components, its "Indianness." In the poetry of Leopoldo Lugones or José Santos Chocano, America was not only a "New World," but also a land of history. Rubén Darío considered that South America was able to preserve not only the Spanish past, but Native American civilization: "If there is poetry in our America, it lies in old things: in Palenke and Utatlán, in the legendary Indian and the thin and sensual Inca, in the great Moctezuma in his golden chair. The rest is yours, Whitman the democrat."[66] South American poets also shifted from an aesthetic interest in Whitman—father of modernity, liberator of American verse—to a more political one, as they began to denounce the betrayal of the poet's legacy. This was already visible with Rubén Darío, who went from unequivocal praise in his 1890 sonnet to castigating Yankee imperialism in the poem "To Roosevelt" (1905): "It is with the voice of the Bible, or the verse of Walt Whitman, / That we should get to you, Hunter!"[67] The poem opposes North America, turned toward the future, power and money, and "our" America, valuing its past, religion and love.

Most Brazilian poets discovered Whitman in the 1920s; by then, he was no longer the model of a continental vision, but rather the catalyst of Latin American differentiation from the US. An example is Jorge de Lima, who presented his work as a necessary update of Whitman's vision. The title of the poem "My America" (1927) points to *another* America. It surveys several countries of Latin America, like a reduced version of "Salut au Monde!" The United States is presented as a system of racial segregation, far removed from Brazilian intermixing, with "the blacks lynched by the whites / the accused electrocuted

---

65 Walt Whitman, *Poemas: Versión de Armando Vasseur* (Valencia: F. Sempere y compañía, Editores, 1912), xii.
66 Rubén Darío, *Prosas profanas y otros poemas* (1896; Madrid: Editorial Castalia, 1983), 87.
67 "¡Es con voz de la Biblia o verso de Walt Whitman / Que habría que llegar hasta ti, Cazador" (Darío, *Azul...*, 201).

at Sing-Sing."[68] Whitman, the poet who claimed to see everything, is charged with blindness: he invented the "new world," but did not see "the other America breaking through." The last stanza contrasts the Yankee "over there" with the Brazilian "here," as de Lima embraces the national myth of *miscigenação*:

> Aqui os mulatos
> substituíram os negros gigantes de Vachel Lindsay.
> Aqui não há os selvagens felizes de Mary Austin
> Negros,
> Selvagens,
> Amarelos,
> —o arco-íris de todas as raças canta pela boca
> de minha nova América do Sul,
> uma escala diferente da vossa escala,
> Alfred Kreymborg,
> Whitman!
>
> Here the mulattoes
> have replaced Vachel Lindsay's giant negroes.
> Here we don't find the good savages of Mary Austin.
> The Negroes,
> The Savages,
> The Yellows,
> —the rainbow of all races sings through the mouth
> of my new South America,
> a different scale than your scale,
> Alfred Kreymborg,
> Whitman!

This poem is indicative of a shift in Whitman's Latin American reception, from the nuevomundista claim at the turn of the century, to political appropriation and critical uses.

Black Whitman, Red Whitman

The tendency to extend, supplement or correct Whitman began at the same time in the United States. His significance for the Harlem Renaissance has been

---

68 "negros linchados pelos brancos / réus electrocutados em Sing-Sing"—Jorge de Lima, "A minha América," in *Poesia completa*, vol. 1 (Rio de Janeiro: Nova Fronteira, 1980), 78.

studied in detail,[69] but it is illuminating to read the emerging African American Whitman in a larger transnational context—which is why I refer to a "Black Whitman," belonging to several connected cultural spheres: Atlantic, continental and internationalist.

"I, Too, Sing America"

Like many Europeans at the time, Alain Locke, the pioneering intellectual of the Harlem Renaissance, linked Whitman to Verhaeren: in 1917, he wrote an essay on the Flemish poet, in which he praised Whitman at length. In the *New Negro* (1925), he contended that it was up to African Americans to realize Whitman's ideal. Langston Hughes, the main figure in Whitman's Black reception, was close to a number of people involved in Soviet art and politics, and he visited the USSR in 1932. However, he read Whitman a long time before he was drawn toward communism: he discovered his poetry as a high school student in Cleveland and read him assiduously in the early 1920s when he moved to Harlem. Hughes took a box of books with him on a trip to Nigeria, which he eventually threw overboard, except for *Leaves of Grass*: Whitman was the only poet he had with him in Africa.[70]

Throughout his life, Hughes paid tribute to Whitman in various articles and edited anthologies. He planned a volume for children and one containing Whitman's poems about African and Native Americans to be called "Walt Whitman's Darker Brothers"; while neither found a publisher, he did place an anthology of Black poetry with Marxist International Publishers in 1946. Hughes included a section of "tributary poems by non-negroes" in *The Poetry of the Negro, 1746-1949: An Anthology*, which he edited with Arna Bontemps: Whitman opened it with four poems (the order was not chronological since he was followed by Blake and Wordsworth).[71] In 1953, when Lorenzo Dow Turner pointed out racist remarks in Whitman's prose, Hughes argued that one must separate the man (the prose) from his work (the poetry), and keep only the best of the latter—he wrote the poem "Old Walt" at that time.

What made Whitman so central to Hughes? Firstly, Whitman invented a fictional and plastic persona. In "The Negro Speaks of Rivers," Hughes makes a

---

69 See George B. Hutchinson, "The Whitman Legacy and the Harlem Renaissance," in Folsom, ed., *Walt Whitman: The Centennial Essays*, 201–216.
70 See Arnold Rampersad, *The Life of Langston Hughes*, vol. 1 (Oxford: Oxford University Press, 1986), 72.
71 Arna Bontemps and Langston Hughes, ed., *The Poetry of the Negro, 1746–1949: An Anthology* (Garden City, NY: Doubleday, 1949).

similar use of the first person, combining it with patterns from a traditional blues song: "I bathed in the Euphrates when dawns were young," "I heard the singing of the Mississippi when Abe Lincoln went down to New Orleans, and I've seen its muddy bosom turn all golden in the sunset."[72] Contrary to Whitman, the "I" does not project itself on the horizons of the future, but sinks into the depths of time: "My soul has grown deep like the rivers." This is yet another rewriting of "Salut au Monde!," this time adjusted for African American history. Another poem, "America," questions the possibility of embodying an entire nation. The "I" reiterates Whitman's combination of "one's self" with a plurality of selves: "Who am I? / I am the ghetto child, / I am the dark baby, / I am you." (53) *The Weary Blues* also contained an "epilogue," which became Hughes's most famous poem, "I, Too." First published in 1925 in *Survey Graphic*, reprinted the same year in the *New Negro*, it was written during another transatlantic episode in Hughes's life. After his trip to Africa, Hughes spent a long time in Europe, especially in Paris; while in Genoa, his money and passport were stolen and he could not get back to France as planned. He tried to return to the United States, but had great difficulty finding a ship that would accept him. He eventually got a job as a ship's cook—one of the few positions available for Black people. From the first line, "I, too, sing America," to the last, "I, too, am America," the "darker brother" emulates Whitman (46).

In time, other aspects of Whitman's poetry drew Hughes's attention, especially its negotiation between ideals and reality. As Ed Folsom argues, Whitman taught him "the art of longing."[73] The anthology of his own poetry, in 1959, began with the words "So Long," and the last section opened with "I, Too"; the very last poem, "Freedom's Plow," tied together traditional song, blues and Whitmanian reminiscences: "America! / Land created in common, / Dream nourished in common, / Keep your hand on the plow! Hold on!"[74] Whitman's "so long" was thus ultimately transformed into "hold on."

Hughes's poetry does not essentialize Black identity: it is not contained within racial, national or linguistic boundaries. In *The Poetry of the Negro*, African American poets were numerous, but there were also French-speaking Black poets (Césaire, Damas, Jacques Roumain and his poem "Langston Hughes"),

---

72 Langston Hughes, *The Collected Poems*, ed. A. Rampersad (New York: Knopf, 1997), 23. Published in *The Crisis* in 1921, it later became part of his first collection *The Weary Blues* (1926).
73 This aspect has been thoroughly analyzed by Ed Folsom in "So Long! So Long! Walt Whitman, Langston Hughes and the Art of Longing," in Blake and Robertson, ed., *Walt Whitman: Where the Future Becomes Present*, 127–143.
74 Hughes, *The Collected Poems*, 267.

Spanish-speaking poets (Nicolás Guillén, whom Hughes translated extensively) and "non-Negro" poets. Hughes had a particular interest in García Lorca: he translated *Blood Wedding* and planned to translate *Poet in New York*. African Americans were well represented in the latter collection; in Lorca's ode to Whitman, a Black child announces the possible restoration of the Whitmanian dream. By including Nicolás Guillén's long suite on García Lorca in his anthology, Hughes invited the Andalusian poet into his wider Black world, alongside Whitman, albeit not with quite the same status. Hughes's Whitmanian bridge was transatlantic and transcontinental.

"Yo también"

Hughes's reception comforted both his Whitmanian genealogy and internationalist scope. Vera Kutzinski has shown that "I, Too" "circulated in the Hispanic Americas in no fewer than fifteen different translations, with four additional versions published in Spain," and appeared in nine anthologies and fifteen periodicals.[75] African American poetry was translated and published in the USSR, where several poets were invited.[76] As early as 1924, Claude McKay was paired with Whitman in an anthology of revolutionary poetry. As McKay's fortunes changed in the 1930s (he was too close to Trotsky and Eastman), Langston Hughes became the most prominent African American poet, and "I, Too," often featured in Soviet periodicals and anthologies. When "The Negro speaks of rivers" and "I, Too" were translated into Lithuanian in the communist journal *Trečias Frontas* (Third Front), they followed Whitman's "Song of the Exposition."[77] Other issues featured Mayakovsky and Sandburg.

Of particular interest are Hughes's translations by the Spanish poet Rafael Alberti. In 1933, he translated "I, Too" for the communist magazine *Octubre*, and in 1937, four other poems by Hughes (who was in Madrid at the time) for the republican journal *El mono azul*.[78] In 1936, Alberti wrote "Yo también canto a América," with Hughes's line, in English, as an epigraph. It seems to

---

[75] Vera Kutzinski, *The Worlds of Langston Hughes: Modernism and Translations in the Americas* (Ithaca, London: Cornell University Press, 2012), 62. See 62–84 for a detailed analysis.
[76] See Olga Panova's work, in particular, "African-American Literature in the Soviet Union, 1917–1930s: Contacts, Translations, Criticism and Editorial Policy," in David Featherstone and Christian Høgsbjerg, eds., *The Red and the Black: The Russian Revolution and the Black Atlantic* (Manchester: Manchester University Press, 2021), 97–120.
[77] *Trečias Frontas*, no. 2, April 1930. The poems were not integral; for "I, Too," the end was kept, with the title "Amerikos Negro poezija" (American Negro poetry). Antanas Venclova translated Whitman and Bronys Raila translated Hughes.
[78] *Octubre*, August–September 1933, 10; *El mono azul*, August 19, 1937.

continue Hughes's poem: "I too sing America, traveling / with the blue pain of the Caribbean Sea"[79] and ends with a typical Whitmanian opening on the future: "Yo también canto a América futura." "I too," writes Alberti, but to whom does he refer? To Hughes or to Whitman himself, whose imagination flew over the continent? Some ten years later, Pablo Neruda wrote a very controversial poem, "Let the Rail Splitter Awake," which resurrected Whitman to vilify the US and praise the Soviet Union. I will return to this work but, for now, I want to emphasize that when the poetic voice leaves America for the USSR, where it will join Whitman, it claims: "Yo también más allá de tus tierras, América"[80] (I, too, beyond your lands, America). "Yo también," like Alberti, whom Neruda came to know well during his long stay in Spain, where he was a consul (and an avid reader of *El mono azul*)? Or, through Alberti, like Hughes? Or, through Hughes, like Whitman, the main subject of this poem?

Another (later) instance is "Imagem noturna de Copacabana," by the Afro-Brazilian poet Abdias do Nascimento, which begins with a question: "Deverei tambén cantar o Brasil?"[81] (Shall I, too, sing Brazil?). The poet overcomes his doubts and finally expresses a form of Whitmanian cosmic wonder. The interlinguistic and intercontinental circulation of this line makes the palimpsest particularly dense and draws a map of poets linked by their Whitmanian claim and their common refusal of borders.

Coda: Three American intermedial "Salut au Monde!"

The poem "Salut au Monde!" was one of the most quoted, translated and rewritten during the interwar period, especially in the US. In addition to the various occurrences analyzed in this chapter, I want to highlight three versions or adaptations, which involve other media than text and point to intermediality as a complement to linguistic strategies.

First of all, the internationalist reception permeated the American reception in general, even when it was not as highly partisan as the Proletarian appropriations. The poem was thus published separately in 1930 by the then recently founded Random House press. It contained illustrations by Vojtěch Preissig, the Czech painter and illustrator, who later fought in the resistance against the

---

79 "Yo también canto a América, viajando / con el dolor azul del mar Caribe," *Repertorio Americano*, September 26, 1936, 6–7 (published in San José, Costa Rica). The poem was included as in the collection *De un momento a otro (Poesía e historia), 1932–1937*.
80 Neruda, *Obras completas*, 1:688.
81 Abdias do Nascimento, *Axés do sangue e da esperança* (Rio de Janeiro: Achiamé/Rioarte, 1983), 64.

Nazis. Visual art was indeed a very apt medium to translate the poem into an international message. The image even precedes the text, with a Modernist version of Michelangelo's Adam flying over the wonders of the world.

FIGURE 6.3. Linoleum cut by Vojtěch Preissig, in Walt Whitman, *Salut au Monde!* (New York: Random House, 1930), 9. Berlin State Library.

The book was printed in Prague. With 390 copies, it was certainly not an object for the masses and was more in line with the cosmopolitan Modernist reception of the poem. It is nonetheless a perfect example of the transatlantic and transnational Whitman.

Two other versions were much more political. They were not illustrations but adaptations for the stage. The first one was performed at the Neighborhood Playhouse in New York in 1922. The idea came from the director of the theater, Irene Lewisohn, and the music was composed by Charles T. Griffes and Edmond W. Rickett. One of the most thorough reviews, by Léon Bazalgette appeared in the French communist newspaper *L'Humanité*; it included a letter by Anne Traubel (Horace's widow), who had attended the show. Bazalgette compared it to a medieval mystery play infused with longing for the modern world and noted: "The staging evokes similar attempts seen last year in Germany and in Russia."[82]

---

82 Léon Bazalgette and Anne Traubel, "Une fête de poésie en Amérique. Salut au Monde," *L'Humanité*, July, 16, 1922, 4.

Was Bazalgette aware of the Proletkult staging? Was Irene Lewisohn aware of it? The description that followed was indeed very reminiscent of it. The setting was quite simple: the poet stood on brown rocks and a huge blue disk surrounded with moving clouds represented the world. The show contained three parts, with a prologue in which "cosmic forces united with the poet," who was joined by dancers and a choir (another coincidence with the Proletkult). The first part showed the dawn of humanity, the second various religions, and the third one—which was very "colorful"—was devoted to the enumeration of all the nationalities ("You, Spaniard from Spain," "Russ from Russia," etc.) As the enumeration unfolded, a "splendid red banner" appeared. In the end, all the characters merged, "bound by Human fraternity" and sang: "Each of us inevitable, / Each of us limitless . . ." Again, the eleventh section of the poem was highlighted in red.

Sixteen years later, in the context of the Great Depression and as a result of the New Deal's cultural policy, "Salut au Monde!" was staged again, this time at the New York City Federal Dance Theatre. The choreographer was Helen Tamiris, whose aim was to bring dance to the masses. She had already conceived *Whitman Suite* in 1934, and "Salut au Monde!" was her first commission for the FDT. Tamiris was not a member of the Communist Party, but the FDT was closed in 1939 after it was attacked by the House Un-American Activities Committee.

FIGURE 6.4. Richard Halls, *Federal Dance Theatre presents Salut au monde adapted from a poem of that name by Walt Whitman*. 1936. New York City: Federal Art Project. Library of Congress.

The program stated: "the theme is particularly fitting, and expresses the attitudes of America, in these days of social distrust." Racial and social issues entwined: the program bore a pseudo-quote from "Salut au Monde!" with an added apostrophe to "the working man and working woman."[83] It ended with, again, words from section 11, the same that the children of *Mir Kumen On* recited in Yiddish that very year. After a solo by Tamiris (a greeting to Whitman), a group of dancers showed "the struggle and disharmony among the races, and the efforts of a few brave souls to create understanding." In the final episode, Tamiris called on "the struggling toilers of all nationalities, represented by the group, to unite in peace and work together on a common earth." (30)

"Salut au Monde!," then, underwent a profound transformation through the 1920s and 1930s: from a song of cosmopolitan wonder, it became a call for racial and internationalist solidarity. The FDT poster encapsulates interwar Red and Black Whitman. Whitman belonged to "Comintern aesthetics."[84]

---

[83] Quoted in Elizabeth Cooper, "Tamiris and the Federal Dance Theatre 1936-1939: Socially Relevant Dance Amidst the Policies and Politics of the New Deal Era," *Dance Research Journal* 29, no. 2 (Autumn, 1997): 29.

[84] Amelia Glaser and Steven Lee, eds., *Comintern Aesthetics* (Toronto: Toronto University Press, 2020). As Glaser and Lee note in their coda to the book, it was at its most sectarian (the hardline period of 1928–1933) that the Comintern had "the most sustained appeal among anti-imperialist and anti-racist activities around the world" (530).

Chapter 7

Pioneers and Pionery: political transfers (1886–1944)

While "Salut au Monde!" is the common thread of Whitman's internationalist reception, "Pioneers! O Pioneers!" was quoted and used during a more specific period, between the end of the nineteenth century and World War II, and with a stricter socialist agenda. It provides not only a case study but a coda to the three preceding chapters.

Written at the end of the civil war in 1865, the poem first belonged to *Drum-Taps*, before changing section twice and finally finding its place in "Birds of Passage." It is a Reconstruction poem, in the spirit of the late war or immediate postwar poems. Its rhetorical and metrical constraints are strong, with quatrains and trochees, unusual prosody for Whitman. The trochees were meant to capture the "Western movement beat," but the marching rhythm and strophic regularity boosted the broader political reception of the poem: it was easier to remember than a poem in free verse, and it was galvanizing. The anaphora of the first person plural, also quite rare in Whitman, was another asset. Thematically, however, "Pioneers" was not completely suitable for socialist and internationalist purposes. Indeed, with a great democratic impulse, the poem called for a rally and a redirection of energies towards the American West, in order to complete the process of national reunification. The pioneers are referred to as "Western youths" and are specifically associated with the states of Colorado, Nebraska, Arkansas and Missouri. Weapons are now used to conquer territory and exploit it: the mention of the "sharp-edged axes" at the very beginning evokes "Song of the Broad-Axe," a hymn to agrarian work. Whitman's pioneers essentially clear the soil and toil the land. The title of Willa Cather's novel *O Pioneers*, published in 1913, is an allusion to that aspect of the poem. Yet, again, Whitman's poem brings together "the machine and the garden," and, though not prevailing, references to industrial work provide material for socialist uses:

> We primeval forests felling,
> We the rivers stemming, vexing us and piercing deep the mines within,
> We the surface broad surveying, we the virgin soil upheaving,
>   Pioneers! O Pioneers! (stanza 7, LG 192)

The mines were particularly evocative for workers in Northern England, the home of British Whitmanism. Similarly, the nationalist dimension of the poem could be overcome and blended into a universalist sentiment. Coming after "Song of the Universal," "Pioneers" could be read as an American example valid for the whole world. And, indeed, some stanzas, like the fifth, devoid of national references, sound like internationalist rallying cries:

> All the past we leave behind,
> We debouch upon a newer mightier world, varied world,
> Fresh and strong the world we seize, world of labor and the march,
>   Pioneers! O Pioneers! (LG 192)

According to John Spargo, Marx himself knew these lines by heart.[1] This call for a clean slate, for global momentum, used enough key words ("seize," "labor," "march") to create a socialist anthem. Kirsten Harris notes that when the passage was reprinted in English socialist newspapers, the spelling was systematically changed to the standard British "labour." This involved a cultural transfer, toward the industrial and political semantic web of "labour." The meaning of "march" could also be reworked: instead of the pioneering nationalist advance, it could designate a protest march, as in William Morris and Edward Carpenter's poems.

Socialist uses of "Pioneers! O Pioneers!" are a remarkable illustration of Whitman's political journey over fifty years, from Britain's Labour Church to Proletarian literature in the United States, via Soviet propaganda.[2] Indeed, while

---

1 John Spargo, *Karl Marx: His Life and Work* (New York: Huebsch, 1910), 276.
2 There were certainly other uses of the poem in other places. Vanessa Steinroetter showed that the German reception was quite different: the poem did draw some attention on the Left but was given particular significance by the nationalist Wilhelm Schölermann in his 1904

the poem featured in other languages and areas (it was included in the 1909 Czech anthology[3] and in Armando Vasseur's 1912 *Poemas*, for instance),[4] it is within this triangle that it was most conspicuously appropriated for political aims.

1. Preamble: the British marches of the "Pioneers"

For his 1886 edition of *Leaves of Grass*, intended for a wider, more popular audience than Rossetti's edition, the socialist Ernest Rhys chose as the epigraph to his introduction the fourth stanza of the poem:

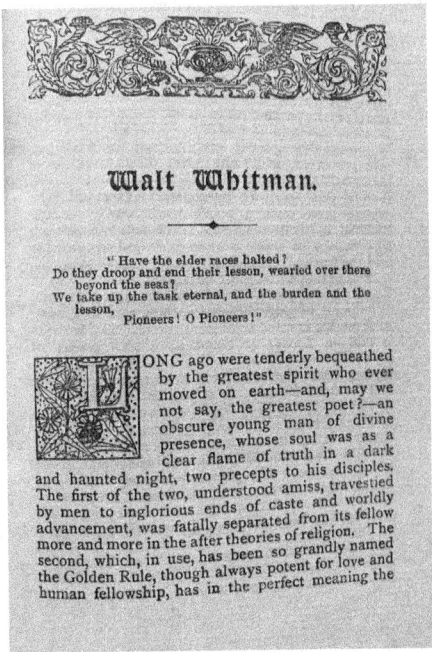

FIGURE 7.1. Introduction to *The Poems of Walt Whitman*, by Ernst Rhys (London: Walter Scott, 1886), ix.

---

translation (Vanessa Steinroetter, "'Pioneers! O Pioneers!' and Whitman's Early German Translators," *Interdisciplinary Studies in the Long Nineteenth Century*, no. 9 [November 2009], doi: https://doi.org/10.16995/ntn.520).

3   Walt Whitman, *Básník zítřku*, trans. Emanuel Lešehrad (Prague: n.p., 1909).
4   Vasseur translated the title as "¡Pioners! ¡Oh pioners!" (*pioner* is a neologism in Spanish); his version emphasized the colonial side of the poem, transforming the "pioneers" into "conquistadores." "Conquering, holding, daring, venturing, as we go, the unknown ways" thus became: "Conquistadores, nos apropiamos todo, osando, si arriesgándonos a medida que hollamos las rutas desconocidas" (Vasseur, *Poemas*, 58).

Detached from the rest, the phrase "elder races" may refer beyond Europeans and acquire broader meaning. Indeed, Rhys identified with the "younger races," and wrote: "We, who are young, may well respond to him, too, and advance fearlessly in the lines of his unique initiative." (xxviii), The British reception of the poem paved the way for other socialist appropriations. It was so rich that Kirsten Harris has devoted a whole chapter of her book to the topic.[5] I will very briefly present her conclusions, as a necessary preamble to discussing the Russian, Soviet and Proletarian American pioneers.

The poem was popular both within the Eagle Street College and the Labour Church. James William Wallace concluded two of his Bolton speeches with it: he contended that the war of which Whitman spoke prefigured a larger war that awaited all humanity.[6] The Labour Church Pioneers was an organization that sought to extend the Labour Church's influence. As Harris writes, they published a handbill to recruit new "pioneers" with a selection of eleven stanzas from Whitman's poem, essentially taken from the beginning and the end, leaving aside the more nationalistic core. The poem featured in the socialist press too. As he reported in the *Labour Leader* on demonstrations in Sileby, Leicestershire, in April 1895, the politician Sam Hobson quoted stanzas from "Pioneers."[7] In the same newspaper, twenty years later, the obituary for one of Britain's most famous socialists, Keir Hardie, quoted the poem again and ended with the statement that "Hardie was a pioneer."[8]

Harris goes on to draw a parallel between Whitman's poem and William Morris's "The March of the Workers," a favorite of socialist demonstrations, whose terms, syntax and rhythm are strangely reminiscent of "Pioneers."[9] I will also add that by 1921 Whitman's poem and its socialist uses were famous enough to be parodied in a *Nation and Athenaeum* article about the railway industry:

---

5   Kirsten Harris, "'Have the Elder Races Halted?' Uses of Whitman's 'Pioneers! O Pioneers!,'" in *Whitman and British Socialism*, 169–191.
6   Harris, *Whitman and British Socialism*, 174–177.
7   Sam Hobson, "The Boot War," *Labour Leader*, April 13, 1895.
8   W. C. Anderson, "The Life and Ideals of Hardie," *Labour Leader*, October, 7, 1915, 7. The selection includes the fourth stanza ("All the past we leave behind . . .") and the last one ("Till with sound of trumpet . . .").
9   "On we march then, we the workers, and the rumour that ye hear / Is the blended sound of battle and deliv'rance drawing near; / For the hope of every creature is the banner that we bear, / And the world is marching on." This song is in Edward Carpenter's collection, *Chants of Labour*, which also contains excerpts from Whitman.

Come! (as the poet inspiredly sang)—
Come, my Hard Faced children!
Swift! Spring to your places!
Swift! to the head of your army!
Profiteers, O profiteers![10]

2. Russian and Soviet Pionery

Fake Pioneers

As mentioned in Chapter 4, the initial poem that Chukovsky "translated" was "Pioneers! O Pioneers!," which featured in the first issue of the satirical journal *Signal*, in 1905. This text led to his arrest and trial. Yet, even if he later presented the whole poem as a translation, Chukovsky only inserted a single line from Whitman, the third one, as a footnote clearly indicated in 1905. In fact, the poem bore more resemblance with another fake translation, the poem "From Walt Whitman," published a few years before by Tan-Bogoraz.

> Загорелою толпою
> Подымайтесь, собирайтесь для потехи, для игры,
> В барабаны застучите, наточите топоры!
> Оставайся кто захочет,
>
> Мы должны идти, родные, нас удары ждут в бою!
> Всё для нас, от нас и с нами – в новом радостном краю.
> Что за дело до дрожащих, до трусливо уходящих
> И до всех старух шипящих, отзывающих назад.
>
> Мы пируем, мы ликуем на развалинах горящих,
> Миллионы исступленных к нам на оргию спешат.
> Оставайся кто захочет . . .
> Мы бросаемся по скалам,
>
> Мы вздымаем новь степную, мы взрываем рудники,
> Мы несемся по теченью обезумевшей реки.

---

10 S. O., "The Great Railway Ramp," *The Nation and the Athenaeum*, February 19, 1921, reprinted in Henry S. Saunders, ed., *Parodies on Walt Whitman* (New York: American Library Service, 1923), 160.

Мир почившим и усталым.
    Завтра милые могилы мы цветами уберем,

    А сегодня по могилам с ликованием пойдем!
По неведомым тропинам,
По долинам, по равнинам, чрез пучины чуждых вод,
    Побеждая и хватая, мы смеясь идем вперед.

    Дальше сжатыми рядами!
К бою, к смерти, к неудаче – только, только не назад!
Если мертвыми падете, вас живые заместят.
    Оставайся кто захочет . . .[11]

    You, tanned crowd
Rise, gather for amusement, for play,
Beat your drums, sharpen your axes!
    Stay if you want to,

    We must go, my kinsmen, the blows await us in battle!
All is for us, from us, and with us, in the new land of joy.
Who cares for those who tremble, for those who cowardly go away
    And for all the old women hissing and calling back.

    We rejoice, we exult in burning ruins,
Millions of enthusiasts rush to our orgy.
Stay if you want to,
    We rush over the rocks,

    We rise up to the new steppe, we blow up the mines,
We rush down the stream of the mad river.
Peace to the deceased and the weary.
    Tomorrow we'll adorn the dear graves with flowers,

    But today we will walk through the graves and rejoice!
Along unknown paths,

---

11 *Signal*, November 13 [26], 1905, 2.

> Through valleys, through plains, through deep strange waters,
> Conquering and grasping, we go forward and laugh.
>
> Onward in tight rows!
> To battle, to death, to failure, but never backward!
> If you fall dead, the living will replace you.
> Stay if you want to...

In his 1906 essay on Whitman, Chukovsky continued to quote this 1905 version, as if his own poem really were a translation. And in the 1907 chapbook, which gathered for the first time all of his translations from Whitman, he included the poem at the end of the collection, under the title "Zachinateli" (Beginners). He made a few changes to it, such as replacing "we must go" with "we must bring fire" and introducing an apostrophe to sailors. Such changes were by no means efforts to go back to the original, but minor rewritings of his own text to enhance its revolutionary stance. Whitman's pioneers thus made a very strange debut in Russia: as Tan had done years earlier, Chukovsky hid behind Whitman's name and offered a piece loosely inspired by the American poet as a translation. The poem was reprinted in several collections of revolutionary poetry in the 1920s as a poem by Whitman.[12] Paradoxically, "Pioneers" was well known in Russia, and yet it remained untranslated in Russian until 1918. A full translation was published earlier in the Russian Empire, but in Latvian: though the author of the 1908 anthology was not a political activist, his selection included "Pioneers! O Pioneers!"[13]

Chukovsky confessed that he was quite ashamed of his first translations, especially his efforts to restore rhymes and tame Whitman. In 1913, he wrote in his diary how eager he was to correct the flaws of his previous work and do Whitman justice. However, he did not include "Pioneers! O Pioneers!" in his 1914 edition, nor in the large circulation editions of 1918 and 1919. Was he so ashamed that he wanted the poem to be forgotten altogether? One can only speculate, but this absence was quite odd, since he included all the other classic revolutionary pieces.

---

12 The 1905 version was reprinted in *Pervoe Maia: Sbornik stikhotvorenii* (Nizhny Novgorod: Kul'tura, 1923) and the 1907 version, "Zachinateli," in *Sbornik revoliutsionnykh stikhov dlia deklamatsii* (Moscow: Gosizdat, 1921).
13 Vitmens, *Zāļu stiebri*, trans. K. Jēkabsons, 8–12.

Avant-garde *Pionery*

Precisely at the time when "Pioneers" remained absent from Chukovsky's editions, it was translated and published alone in a remarkable format by the Cooperative Segodnia (Today), founded in February 1918 in Petrograd. The idea was to provide readers with cheap but artistically illustrated books, especially children's books. It gathered several artists, among whom Nikolai Lapshin (a founder of the Russian school of illustration), Vera Ermolaeva and Nathan Altman. *Pionery* by Whitman stands out among the thirteen books that the Cooperative published. The translator was anonymous, or rather, was only mentioned by the initials "M. S."[14] They could stand for "Semion Mstislavskii," one of the pseudonyms of Simon Dubnov,[15] a famous (and pioneering) historian of Jewish literature and culture, as well as a political activist: he co-founded the Yiddish Folkspartei (Jewish People's Party) after the 1905 pogroms and in 1917 he became a professor of Jewish history at Petrograd University. What suggests his work is that his daughter, Sofia Dubnova, worked at the Segodnia Cooperative, where she published *Mat'* (Mother). However, he is not known to have practiced translation. Another hypothesis would be Samuil Marshak, who became one of the finest Soviet translators from English. Even though I cannot connect him to Segodnia, he is a more likely candidate, since he knew English and translated many poems in 1917, at a time when he lived in Petrograd.[16]

---

14 In his 1942 bibliographical notes on "Whitman in the USSR," Chukovsky mentions this edition for the first time, only referring to "M. S," and insisting on its "errors" (*Internatsional'naia Literatura*, 1942 [nos. 1–2], 204). His example was the translation of the lines: "Raise the mighty mother mistress, / Waving high the delicate mistress, over all the starry mistress, (bend your heads all)." "M. S." translated "Elevate the mother-mistress / Raise her high, higher than other firmaments." Chukovsky was appalled that M. S. did not understand that the "starry" mistress was the American flag with its stars and stripes and found his translation absurd. But neither had Chukovsky considered the intriguing expression "mother mistress," and he had translated the lines directly as: "With us the flag [znamia], our flag / Raise higher our starry flag, it is our native mother" (in his 1923 version as well as in 1935).

15 According to Ivan Masanov's dictionary of Russian writers' pseudonyms: *Slovar' psevdonimov russkikh pisatelei, uchënykh i obshchestvennykh deiatelei*, vol. 2 (Moscow: Knizhnaia palata, 1957), 202.

16 Like Chukovsky, Marshak lived in England for a couple of years (1912–1914). His biographer Matvei Geiser notes that in 1917, Marshak did not write a single poem of his own, but translated a lot of English verse (especially Blake, Wordsworth and Shelley's *The Wandering Jew*). He was in Petrozavodsk in 1918, but still sent his work to Petrograd. In *Samuil Marshak* (Moscow: Molodaia Gvardiia, 2006), 133.

FIGURE 7.2. Cover of Uot Uitman, *Pionery*, trans. M. S. (Petrograd: Segodnia, 1918). Illustration by Vera Ermolaeva. *Public Domain Review.*

The poem was illustrated by Vera Ermolaeva. She was an avant-garde artist, a member of the Bloodless Murder Futurist circle, and she attended Viachestlav Ivanov's Wednesdays (artistic meetings held in his apartment, at the so-called Tower in Saint Petersburg), where she was invited by Chukovsky. Ermolaeva was a major artist. Segodnia was closed after she was sent in 1919 by the Narkompros to teach at the People's Art School in Vitebsk. Like so many avant-garde artists, she became suspect in the 1930s and was a victim of the Terror (she was shot in 1937). The cover of *Pionery* takes its cue from Futurist aesthetics: the lines are simple and dynamic, the colors solid. The arms of one of the pioneers seem to draw a sickle, the other one holds a large pick; in addition to the stars, they adorn the name "Walt Whitman" with all the symbols of communism. The illustrations were made using engravings on linoleum and were painted by hand. Sergei Yesenin, whose *Baby Jesus* was published by Segodnia, owned a copy of *Pionery*. The quality of the work and the scarcity of the painted copies (125 out of one thousand) make this edition a bibliophile's dream.

Figure 7.3. Inside of Uot Uitman, *Pionery*, trans. M. S. (Petrograd: Segodnia, 1918). Illustration by Vera Ermolaeva. National Library of France.

From "frontline fighters" to pionery

In 1923, as if to make up for his neglect of the poem, first disfigured and then omitted, Chukovsky published his first real translation, twice, under the title "Peredovye boitsy" (Frontline fighters).[17] It was included in his new anthology of Whitman's poetry, with some editing and rearrangements: "Pioneers! O Pioneers!" was sometimes translated as "You are the frontline fighters," sometimes as "We are the frontline fighters," and sometimes as "O frontline fighters," while the "daughters of the West" became "daughters and wives." In the critical study that followed the translations, Chukovsky again lambasted Balmont's work, and pointed out that his predecessor had never translated "Pioneers"—but

---

17 Uot Uitmèn, *Peredovye boitsy* (Petrograd: Gosudarstvennoe Izdatel'stvo, 1923). Three thousand copies of this four-page leaflet were printed.

neither had he until then! The same year, he also published the poem separately, in a large format, on May Day. The two versions, though contemporary, differed substantially. The First of May one was more propagandistic: the stanzas with national references (the names of the American states) were edited out. In the stanza about "the elder races," the word *my* (we) was in bold letters—it is hard to say if this resulted from a clear intention or from a print defect, but the fact remains that it is the only instance in the whole poem (except for the initial letter of each line, systematically in bold).

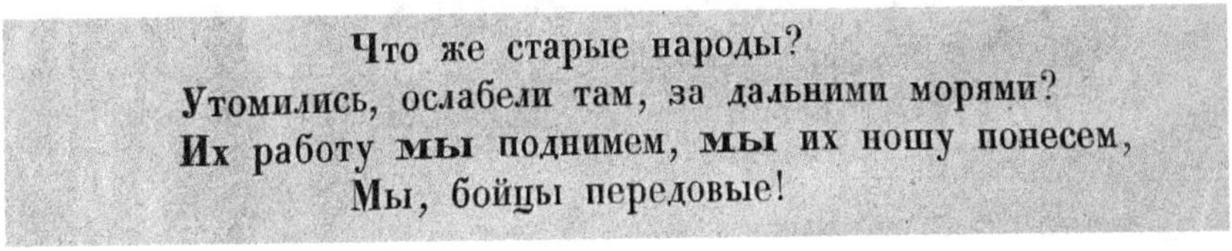

> Что же старые народы?
> Утомились, ослабели там, за дальними морями?
> Их работу **мы** поднимем, **мы** их ношу понесем,
> Мы, бойцы передовые!

FIGURE 7.4. Detail from Uot Uitmèn, *Peredovye boitsy*, trans. K. Chukovskii (Petrograd: Gosudarstvennoe Izdatel'stvo, May 1, 1923). Russian State Library.

In 1931, Chukovsky translated the poem again, with drastic changes, and included this version in his new selection from Whitman. The preface to this book was published separately for the journal *Ogonëk*, on the seventy-fifth anniversary of *Leaves of Grass*.[18] At that time, Chukovsky was not in a comfortable position (his famous tale "Crocodile" had been disparaged by Lenin's widow) and his piece contained more conformist ideas than usual: Whitman was presented as the "precursor of revolutionary poets." Again, Chukovsky insisted that he was sued for his first 1905 "translation." He concluded with his new version of "Pioneers," using for the first time the term *pionery* to translate the title and the refrain. The poem was considerably changed and abridged, with only twelve stanzas (out of twenty-six). It looked like a translation of Ernst Rhys's "Pioneers" rather than of the agrarian poem Chukovsky had praised in 1906. While the Russian lines had been considerably longer than the English ones in 1923, they were much closer in length in this new version. All the stanzas containing national references were deleted, whereas the one with internationalist potential was padded out (the term *mir*, which means both "world" and "peace" in Russian, was used over and over again). Above all, Chukovsky really made this poem a *pioneer* song, especially in the first stanza: "stroino, chagom" (in order, step) was a familiar refrain for a Komsomol pioneer. The versions in the article and in the book differ slightly: the latter is longer (fourteen stanzas

---

18 Kornei Chukovskii, "Predtecha revolutsionnykh poètov," *Ogonëk*, 1931 (no. 7).

instead of twelve) but, because of the very small format of the book, the lines were presented differently and broken into several pieces. The quatrains, which are a hallmark of the poem, were lost and converted into six-line stanzas.

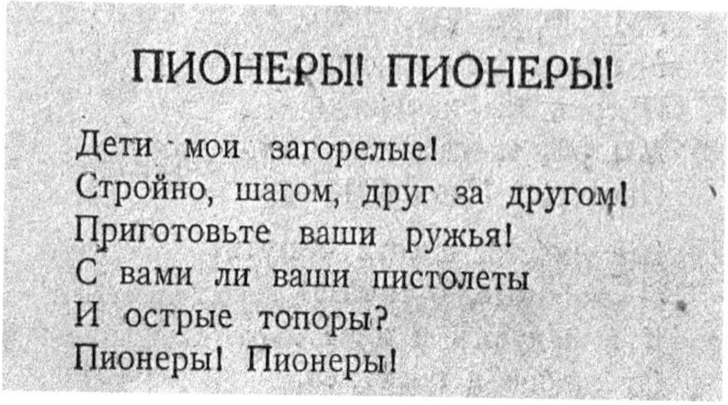

> ПИОНЕРЫ! ПИОНЕРЫ!
>
> Дети мои загорелые!
> Стройно, шагом, друг за другом!
> Приготовьте ваши ружья!
> С вами ли ваши пистолеты
> И острые топоры?
> Пионеры! Пионеры!

FIGURE 7.5. Detail from Uot Uitmèn, *List'ia Travy*, trans. K. Chukovskii (Moscow: Ogonëk, 1931), 9. Russian State Library.

In 1932, in the following edition, the quatrains were restored, but there were still only fourteen of them. Three years later, in 1935, the translation of the poem was almost complete, with twenty-four stanzas out of twenty-six.[19] In a short 1939 text entitled "Prose and Verse of Walt Whitman,"[20] Chukovsky quoted an abbreviated version once more: he added the stanza left out in 1931 ("Have the elder races halted?") but deleted the one referring to tilling and clearing the land: internationalism took precedence over American agrarianism. Finally, when the poem was reprinted in the 1944 edition, it contained twenty-five stanzas. The omission of just one stanza is difficult to explain, especially as it did not contain any US domestic references. I have focused on cuts and the dispositions of the lines, but a close examination of the words and rhythms reveals constant experimentations as well.

Apart from the 1918 Segodnia edition, there was another complete translation of the poem, but not by Chukovsky. In 1935, Dmitri Maizels, who was eager to publish his work on Whitman, but was starkly rebuked by Chukovsky (see Chapter 5), had two pieces accepted by the monthly *Molodaia Gvardiia*: an extract from "Song of Myself," and "Pioneers" in its entirety.[21] Both versions appeared to supplement or correct Chukovsky.

---

19 In the copy held at the Moscow State Library, it is one of the three poems ticked by a reader in the table of contents.
20 Kornei Chukovskii, "Proza i stikhi Uolta Uitmana," *Literaturnaia Gazeta*, May 30, 1939, 2.
21 Uot Uitmèn, "Pionery," trans. D. Maizels, *Molodaia Gvardiia*, 1935 (no. 7), 32–33.

"Pioneers" was also used for left-wing propaganda in Eastern Europe. Bojana Aćamović writes about a Serbian translation of the poem by Svetislav Stefanović in the journal *Republika* (an organ of the Republican Democratic Party of Yugoslavia) in April 1920. The poem, "placed prominently in the middle of the spread," was presented as a "'powerful dithyramb,' which today should be addressed to the children of the East, not the West."[22] It was also quoted in Polish in Antonina Sokolicz's 1921 pamphlet. The name of the translator was not given, and the source was the journal *Towarzysz* (Comrade). Interestingly, the poem was, once again, heavily edited, with only half of the stanzas featured, and the refrain was changed to: "Hej, pionierzy, w górę czoła, równym szykiem idźcie w świat!" (raise your heads and walk in line into the world). However, "Pioneers" was not the most popular political poem by Whitman in interwar Western Europe—a conclusion admittedly based on the partial corpus of texts I can read or decipher. By contrast, it reappeared at the vanguard of social poetry in the US.

3. In the US: "O New Pioneers"

Pionern: a velt fun marsh un arbet

A resurgence of interest in the poem can be found in a Yiddish poem by Abraham Liessin written in 1922, and entitled "Di Pionern" (The Pioneers). Liessin was a major figure of Jewish socialism: born in Minsk, in 1872, he was an active member of the Bund. Threatened with arrest, he left for the US in 1897. The poem is not a translation from Whitman, nor does it contain any explicit reference to his work, apart from the title. Since *pioner* was not an uncommon word in Yiddish, one could find the link weak. However, two elements point to Whitman. The first is precedent: Liessin was well aware of Whitman and translated "O Captain! My Captain!" as early as 1913.[23] The second is poetic and stylistic: the poem is a series of quatrains and relies on questions and exclamations. It is an optimistic vision of the triumph of the people, of the "hopeful march of the world,"[24] filled with radiant light. The poem opened the section "Di Ershte Trit" (The First

---

22 Aćamović, "Walt Whitman in the Yugoslav Interwar Periodicals," 147–148.
23 Abraham Liessin, *Lider un poemen, 1888–1938*, vol. 3 (New York: Forverts Asosyeyshon, 1938), 322–323.
24 Liessin, *Lider un poemen*, 1:109–110.

Step) of Liessin's collected works, illustrated by Marc Chagall—the text stood opposite the beautiful drawing of a demonstration.

In 1940, Louis Miller published the longest Yiddish selection of poems from *Leaves of Grass*. Miller's Whitman was a socialist poet: as explained in the bio-bibliographical note that followed the anthology, Whitman wrote "the song of the average working men" and delivered "a message of socialist poetry."[25] It is no surprise that the selection contained all the classic Whitmanian socialist pieces: "To a Foil'd European Revolutionaire," "To a Common Prostitute." Miller insisted that "Whitman's faith in the masses gave him the illusion that America was already the country of his future democracy." (205) In order to make the dream come true, union and action were necessary: "it must be remembered that in Whitman's time, the working-class was not organized." With organization in place, the future would fulfil Whitman's ideal. Significantly, the poem ending the selection was "Pionern! O Pionern!" Each stanza was marked with a number, as in Rhys's British edition: this made the poem look almost like a plan for action, and extended its length to seven pages. This final poem, with its rallying cries, showed the way to convert the vision of the first one ("Democratic Songs") into a reality. Moreover, as an epigraph to his essay at the end of the book, Miller selected the fifth stanza, which, separated from the rest, reads as a variation on "The Internationale," announcing a tabula rasa and the "world of marching and labor": "a velt fun marsh un arbet".

The pioneers during the Great Depression

Whitman's pioneers were the focus of two contemporary odes by Stephen Vincent Benét and Michael Gold (1935-1937). Both odes must be read, once again, in the context of the Great Depression. Let me first return to Benét's poem, discussed in the previous chapter as a political rewriting of both Whitman and Eliot. Just after the "comrades" admit how much they suffer, Whitman asks, in a short, isolated line, "My tan-faced children?" These are of course the pioneers he addressed in his poem: "Come, my tan-faced children!" The response is a grim picture:

> "These are your tan-faced children.
> These skilled men, idle, with the holes in their shoes.
> These drifters from State to State, these wolvish, bewildered boys
> Who ride the blinds and the box-cars from jail to jail,

---

25 Volt Vitman, *Lider: Fun Bukh: Bletlekh Groz*, trans. L. Miller (New York: Yiddish Cooperative Book League, 1940), 203.

> Burnt in their youth like cinders of hot smokestacks,
> Learning the thief's crouch and the cadger's whine,
> Dishonored, abandoned, disinherited.
> These, dying in the bright sunlight they cannot eat,
> Or the strong men, sitting at home, their hands clasping nothing,
> Looking at their lost hands.
> These are your tan-faced children, the parched young
> ....
> The women with dry breasts and phantom eyes.
> The walkers upon nothing, the four million.
> These are your tan-faced children."[26]

The sun no longer glows, but burns and consumes; the pioneers do not march, but drift or sit aimlessly at home. The insistent allusions add the bitterness of the broken dream to the harshness of reality.

Even more focused on Whitman's pioneers was Michael Gold's "Ode to Walt Whitman," published in 1935 in the *New Masses*. The title announces a eulogy in the tradition of the many odes to Whitman, but the first two-thirds of the poem express desolation. Whitman is still there, his presence still visible or palpable, but his legacy is betrayed:

> Walt Whitman loafed under the trees
> Leaned on his cane and observed
> In a slow and sunburned Manhattan—
> But now they've killed his God
> His love and horsecars and old trees—
> ....
> God is hate dollars chromium speed—
> And no lilacs bloom, Walt Whitman—
> No hope no grass no quiet
> Nothing to love but Coney Island
> Your ocean now a garbage dump
> Where millions of young greenbaums sport[27]

Now means *no*: hope has resorbed into negation. The Jewish proletariat, the millions of young "greenbaums," are the miserable avatars of Whitman's dreamed-of

---

26 Stephen Benét, "Ode to Walt Whitman," 442–443.
27 Michael Gold, "Ode to Walt Whitman," *New Masses*, November 5, 1935, 21.

"Americanoes." The next stanza is an acidic rewriting of "Song of Myself" ("Walt Whitman, a kosmos, of Manhattan the son"):

> And me a son of Walt Whitman
> A son of Manhattan the bitch
> Born on Rat and Louse street
> Near Tuberculosis avenue—
> . . . .
> And me a son of Walt Whitman
> Kicked into a basement to die—
> Eddie Greenbaum, skinny shipping clerk—
> Americano at twelve a week—

Whitman's great expanses shrink and sink underground. Gold's subterranean world is the antithesis of the high road in *Leaves of Grass*. The poet denounces the utopia, the dream that Whitman led him to believe in: "Doped by a priest named Walt Whitman— / Why did I mistake you for the sun?" At that climax of disillusionment, the pioneers enter:

> O Pioneers, our foreman was a nervous little rat—
> And all day like a third degree
> Down in the basement hell with democracy
> Commercial madhouse from 8 to 6
> I knew the clatter speedup and gangrened air
> Electric bulb sweat and coffin fears—
> Above us the macy gimbel millionaires
> Plotted bargains in young greenbaums and kelleys—
> Hell hell hell and low wages
> And little salesgirls puked among the rayon—
> Such was our life, O Pioneers—

All of a sudden, the poetic dream comes true: through the miracle of strikes and protests, Whitman's words regain value. They are endorsed by Lenin, who advised to "not scorn the dream." Whitman's prophetic vision unfolds again and forecasts the reconciliation of the pastoral ideal and the communist city:

> See, see new skyscrapers for Manhattan
> Communist factories for human love—
> A pure ocean, and sunlit homes not tenements—
> Streets for sun and friendship

And no more Tuberculosis avenues—
And no more hell in a basement—
Son of Walt Whitman, to strike is to dream!

The dialectical process is completed: Whitman's dream was initially thwarted, but negativity will be overcome in the communist future.

The last stanza brings together all the apostrophes and motifs of the poem into a synthetic and symphonic momentum:

O Pioneers we build your dream America—
O Walt Whitman, they buried you in the filth
The clatter speedup of a department store basement
But you rose from the grave to march with us
On the picket line of democracy—
Sing sing O new pioneers with Father Walt
Of a strong and beautiful America
Of the thrushes and oceans we shall win
Of sun, of moon, of Communism and joy in the wind
Of the free mountain boys and girls—
It will come! It will come! The strikes foretell it!
The Lenin dreams of the kelleys and greenbaums
Deep in the gangrened basements
Where Walt Whitman's America
Aches, to be born—

The oscillation between the first person singular and the third person plural has stabilized, allowing for the assumption of the communist "we," with strong Mayakovskian overtones. But for all its propagandistic rhetoric and for all its insistent repetitions ("see, see," "sing sing," "It will come! It will come!"), the poem does not altogether erase the images of misery, which ultimately resurface. The ode displays an unorthodox Marxist reading of *Leaves of Grass* and history, with Lenin as the midwife of Whitman's America, bringing about the communist pastoral. "Ode to Walt Whitman" was reviewed in the Soviet *Literaturnaia Gazeta* in 1938.[28]

Another mention of Whitman's "Pioneers" is in a poem by Langston Hughes, published in 1936, "Let America be America Again." From the very title, one recognizes the restoration scenario so often at play in the evocation of Whitman's lost America: "Let it be the dream it used to be. / Let it be the pioneer on the

---

28 "Maikl Gold ob Uote Uitmene," *Literaturnaia Gazeta*, August, 26, 1938, 1.

plain / Seeking a home where he himself is free."[29] Hughes's encompassing and fluid persona is typically Whitmanian (and Hughesan, as discussed in the previous chapter): "I am the farmer, bondsman to the soil. / I am the worker sold to the machine." And, again, the apostrophe to the Pioneers is loaded with political meaning: "Beaten yet today—O, Pioneers! / I am the man who never got ahead, / The poorest worker bartered through the years." (190)

In 1937, Archibald MacLeish wrote a poem to complement photographs of the Great Depression—*Land of the Free* was published the following year. Text and images contrast sharply: the dream of "the land of the free" is negated by the actual conditions of the jobless and homeless shown in the photographs. In one of the poems, the assertion "We told ourselves we were free because we were free"[30] is sustained by a stanza from "Pioneers," the same that E. Rhys had chosen as an epigraph to his edition of *Leaves of Grass* ("Have the elder races halted? . . ."). Opposite the text is a photograph by Dorothea Lange of a Mississippi plantation owner, by his car, with a Coca-Cola ad. But what most deeply contradicts the American principles as enunciated by Whitman is the photograph on the next page, the famous portrait *Migrant mother*, also by Dorothea Lange, with the simple line "Now we don't know." At the end of dozens of images of the pea-pickers on the road, MacLeish introduced more hopeful photographs of demonstrations, giving a possible new meaning to the concept of liberty. Though the last pages remain filled with doubt ("We wonder. / We don't know. / We're asking?"), political action appears as a means to restore meaning to Whitman's words, to turn the wishful exhortation into a reality.

"Pioneers" did not disappear altogether from socialist and communist references after the 1930s, but it was much less present and was no longer an international hymn of the revolution. Just as a communist government was instituted in Poland by the Soviet Union, right after World War II, a translation was published in the local journal *Odra* (Oder) and dedicated to "Polish pioneers, going to the West, toward the Nysa, toward the Oder and the Baltic." However, the journal was more focused on local and regional culture than on politics (it was actually liquidated in 1952):[31] this version was hardly internationalist. "Pionery" was not included in postwar Soviet editions of Whitman between 1954 and 1970. After World War II, "Pioneers! O Pioneers!" was definitely replaced in Europe and in the Americas by "Salut au Monde!"

---

29 Hughes, *The Collected Poems*, 189. The poem was first published in *Esquire* (July 1936).
30 Archibald MacLeish, *Land of the Free* (San Diego: Harcourt, Brace and Company, 1938), unpaged.
31 Walt Whitman, "Pionierzy, o pionierzy!," trans. Stanisław Helsztyński, *Odra: Tygodnik literacko-społeczny* (Katowice, Wrocław, Szczecin), May 26, 1946, 3. S. Helsztyński was a writer and a professor of English literature.

Chapter 8

Anti-fascist Whitman (1936–1945)

There is a strong continuity between the anti-fascist Whitman of the late 1930s and the wartime Whitman who stood on the side of the Allies, especially the US and the Soviet Union. Once again, Whitman was the champion of "Democracy," a word that functioned as a unifying mantra, in spite of its different meanings. Léon Felipe's 1941 translation of "Song of Myself" also bridged the reception of Whitman between the Spanish Civil War and World War II, from the defeat of the republicans to the hope of a global fight against fascism. In the US, however, Whitman was hailed as the poet of democracy not only by left-wing writers and intellectuals, but also, more generally, in the context of the country's affirmation as a superpower—including on a cultural level.

1. "Against war and fascism"

I will introduce this part with the beautiful 1936 edition of *Leaves of Grass* illustrated by Rockwell Kent. Though it was not commissioned by a politically committed publisher (on the contrary, George Macy, who ran Heritage Press, was quite conservative) and placed no particular emphasis on the political poems, it was illustrated by a left-wing activist. Rockwell Kent co-founded the American Artists Congress in 1936, an association of graphic artists supported by the Communist Party USA as part of a "popular front," a broader alliance against fascism. Their original motto was: "Against war and fascism." Kent later became a major figure in Soviet and American cultural exchanges: his work was promoted in the Soviet Union, with exhibitions at the Pushkin Museum, and he received the Lenin prize in 1967. At the time of that edition, the focus of the international Left was the coup against the Second Spanish Republic and the war that ensued: more than a civil war, it was a military exercise for fascist powers, especially Italy and Nazi Germany.

"Spain 1873–74," Spain 1936–1939

Whitman wrote the poem "Spain 1873–74" to celebrate the short-lived First Republic of Spain. It later joined the "Autumn Rivulets" cluster in *Leaves of Grass*. It is thematically quite reminiscent of "Europe" and "Years of the Modern." During the Spanish War, it was quoted in various publications. The *New Masses* used it in October 1936 next to a report on the republican counteroffensive. The illustration by Rockwell Kent updated Whitman's allegory: the Second Spanish Republic was drawn crushing the *fascio* and the swastika.

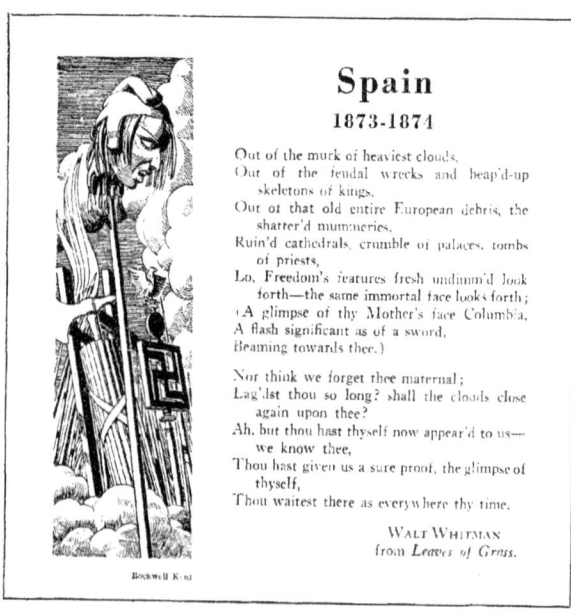

FIGURE 8.1. "Spain 1873–74" by Walt Whitman, illustrated by Rockwell Kent. *New Masses*, October 20, 1936, 11. Rights courtesy of Plattsburgh State Art Museum, State University of New York, USA, Rockwell Kent Collection, Bequest of Sally Kent Gorton. All rights reserved.

In 1938, the poem was published in *La Nouvelle Revue Française*.[1] It was translated into French by Fernand Auberjonois, a Swiss writer and journalist, who became an American citizen during World War II so that he could join the army and fight. It was also quoted in Russian by Chukovsky, who wrote an essay on Whitman in June 1939, shortly before the Ribbentrop-Molotov pact (after which Whitman mostly disappeared from Soviet discourse, together with any direct attack on fascism). Chukovsky wrote: "when particularly disturbing news came from heroic republican Spain, the *Daily Worker* printed Whitman's poem 'Spain, 1873–74,' and readers forgot that these stirring lines were written sixty-five years ago and perceived them as written today."[2]

The poem also served as an epigraph in Raúl González Tuñón's *La Muerte en Madrid* (1939). González Tuñón was an Argentinian communist poet who witnessed the Spanish Civil War firsthand as a war correspondent. Like Pablo Neruda, to whom he was close, he was deeply affected by the war and published testimonial poems. In the first edition of *La Muerte en Madrid*, he quoted as an epigraph a poem by Miguel Hernández, but in the second one, it was replaced by Whitman's poem "Spain" (in Spanish).

León Felipe: from "Song of Myself" to "Salut au Monde!"

The most powerful use of Whitman in the wake of the Spanish Civil War—rather than during the war itself—was León Felipe's 1941 "translation" of "Song of Myself." León Felipe was Spanish, but he left for Mexico in 1922, and then again for the United States, where he taught Spanish at Cornell University. He returned to Spain in 1931, only to set off again for Latin America, as a cultural attaché of the Second Spanish Republic in Panama. The civil war brought him back briefly to his homeland, but in 1938 he emigrated permanently to Mexico. His translation of "Song of Myself" was, so to speak, his poetic visa to America. It was also a profoundly political gesture, directed against fascism.

Entitled *Canto a mí mismo*, the translation was preceded by a long "Prologue," comprised of several poems, asking: "Is this song inappropriate?"[3] Of what use could the translation be to confront "the helmet and the miter," namely the army and the Church? This obviously referred to Franco's Spain, but further allusions to Chamberlain and Roosevelt indicated the wider context of World War II. Felipe answered that the song was more relevant than ever. But then again, why Whitman, "when the thunder suppresses and pulverizes the word freedom?" (14)

---

1 Walt Whitman, "Espagne. 1873-1874," *Nouvelle Revue Française*, no. 301 (October 1938), 689.
2 Kornei Chukovskii, "Uolt Uitman," *Literaturnaia Gazeta*, June 6, 1939, 2.
3 "¿Es inoportuna esta canción?" León Felipe, *Canto a mí mismo* (1941; Madrid: Visor, 2008), 11.

Firstly, because Whitman was a democratic poet: he had no family, no genealogy, he was "the son of the land [tierra], like any legitimate American. Here lies the difference with the European. Here lies the difference between the pioneer and the conquistador." (14) He was as Adamic as Isaiah, as evidenced in "Song of Myself": "My tongue, every atom of my blood form'd from this soil, this air, / Born here of parents born here from parents the same, and their parents the same." Yet, the quote is not an obvious illustration of Felipe's point, since Whitman did present his genealogy in it. To debunk the idea of American rootedness, Felipe translated "soil" as *tierra*, whose meaning is broader, and "air" as *vientos* (winds), one of his favorite motifs, which he developed in most of his works and associated with poetry.

Second, Whitman was heroic: "And more than a poet of democracy / he is a mystical and heroic poet." (20) But it was not so much the victors that Whitman celebrated, as the vanquished, the weak and the dead. At the very beginning of the prologue, Felipe inserted a long quote from section 18 of "Song of Myself," with its "Vivas to those who have fail'd" becoming "¡Hurra por los muertos!" (Vivas to the dead!). It features twice in the book, since it is repeated a few pages after, in the translation itself. Another example of emphasis on the vanquished is the rendering of the line "Embody all presences outlaw'd or suffering," detailed as: "Encarno todas las tragedias / la del forajido / la del poseso / la del convicto / la del leproso, / la del mendigo…" (118)[4] The poem is not, however, a requiem for the dead nor an assent to defeat, but a call to action and revolt: "Song of Myself is, no more and no less, an invitation to heroism addressed to the *average man*, to the man in the street." (20) The translation therefore enhances the injunctions in Whitman's poems, adding words like *mirad* (look) and *oíd* (listen). In section 44, the imperative "let us stand up" unfolds over three redundant lines: "levantémonos / arriba / de pie todos." (138) In the prologue, Felipe insists that along with "instructions," Whitman brought a "signal," emphasized by the italics:

> Y ésta es la señal: "*Salut au monde.*"
> "La mano alta y perpendicular
> (no el brazo oblicuo ni el puño cerrado)
> la mano alta y perpendicular." (23)

> And the signal is: "*Salut au monde.*"
> The hand high and perpendicular

---

4 Literally: "I embody all tragedies: that of the fugitive, that of the possessed, that of the condemned, that of the leper, that of the beggar."

(not the arm raised at an angle, not the clenched fist)
the hand high and perpendicular.

The "quote" paraphrases a single line from Whitman: "I raise high the perpendicular hand, I make the signal." The parenthesis introduces Felipe's own comments and, again, updates Whitman's gesture by explicitly differentiating it from Nazi or fascist gestures. The following quote also changes Whitman's words significantly: "All islands to which birds wing their way I wing my way myself" becomes "en todas las islas donde canten los pájaros, canta mi canción" (I sing my song). And then the signal is reiterated and emphasized with exclamations:

> Porque después que yo me vaya, quede la luz encendida en todos
>   los albergues y en todos los hogares de los hombres,
> hago la señal: "*Salut au monde.*"
> Antes que los signos infamantes que ha enseñado el odio a la
>   mano del hombre, levantó este poeta la suya, alta y perpendicular, para saludar al mundo en nombre del amor: "*¡Salut
>   au monde!*" (23)

> Because after I leave, let light remain in all the inns and all the
>   homes where men live,
> I give the signal: "*Salut au monde.*"
> Rather than the infamous signs taught by hatred to the hand of
>   man, this poet raised his hand, high and perpendicular, to
>   celebrate the world in the name of love: "*¡Salut au monde!*"

The end of the poem condemns Chamberlain, Churchill and Roosevelt for not picking up Whitman's signal. The English and Americans, "fathers of Democracy," are eventually summoned to "bet on Whitman the hero today." (24) To denounce the betrayal of Whitman's legacy was a common stance in the 1930s, which Felipe updated in the context of World War II.

The immediate political implications of the translation are therefore made explicit. Yet it harbors political meaning on other levels as well. Firstly, the very act of translating is significant, as shown by the intertwined metaphorical networks in the prologue:

> Ésta es la hora de trasbordar las consignas poéticas eternas;
> de trasvasar de un cuenco a otro cuenco las genuinas esencias de
>   los pueblos;

> con vinos de otras cepas y de otros lagares,
> con vinos del norte y del sur ... (12)

> It's time to transship the eternal poetic instructions;
> to transfer from one vessel to another the authentic essences of
>   the people;
> with wines from other grape varieties and other presses,
> with wines from the north and the south ...

What Felipe means, in short, is that the point of arrival is more important that the point of departure. Translation shows the solidarity of peoples, their ability to communicate. The prefix *tras-* is the first tool of the activist poet-translator: more than internationalism, translation promotes transnationalism.

More importantly yet, Felipe's conception of translation, as the (re)actualization of a text belonging to everyone, as a challenge to the idea of authorship, is deeply political. *Canto a mi mismo* comprises two parts, distinct but almost continuous. The authorship is unclear, from the very epigraph, a quote from Whitman, introduced by the words "The prologue speaks." The whole prologue, in free verse, uses all the characteristic devices of Whitman's poetry: dots, interpellations, interrogative and negative structures. The insertion of English words, untranslated, is a hybridization process borrowed from the American poet. Felipe integrates Whitman's quotations in all sorts of ways, with and without quotation marks, with and without italics, in the original language or in translation. This prologue corresponds to what is said about "Song of Myself"— that it is a symphony for all instruments, voices and landscapes. Prologue and "paraphrase" follow each other smoothly.

While the prologue "whitmanizes" Felipe's voice, the translation "felipizes" Whitman's. One of the major changes is the spacing and arrangement of the lines and poems. The sections of "Song of Myself" are clearly distinguished, with a page break for each, and Whitman's long lines are often broken into several lines, which verticalize the poem. Felipe also makes numerous omissions and rearrangements. The beginning of section 4 is a representative example:

> Whitman:
>   Trippers and askers surround me,
>   People I meet, the effect upon me of my early life or the
>   ward and city I live in, or the nation,
>   The latest dates, discoveries, inventions, societies, authors
>   old and new,
>   My dinner, dress, associates, looks, compliments, dues

Felipe:
> Me rodean gentes nuevas,
> gentes que me acosan a preguntas...
> Me llegan recuerdos de mi infancia,
> de mi barrio,
> de la ciudad,
> de la nación;
> pienso en las grandes fechas,
> en los grandes sucesos,
> en los grandes inventos;
> en las nuevas empresas;
> en los autores (en los antiguos y modernos);
> me requieren la comida,
> los amigos,
> los vestidos;
> me preocupan los ademanes,
> las atenciones,
> las deudas. (39)

Context also justifies alterations. Felipe explains that he translated "happiness" as *alegría* (joy) rather than *felicidad*, because there is no happiness in this world, only the joy that effort can provide (20). Of course, Felipe does not refer to *Canto a mi mismo* as a translation, but as a "paraphrase": a commentary of Whitman's text in his own words and structures. Nevertheless, this text became the most famous version of Whitman in the Spanish-speaking world.

It sparked quite a controversy. The most ferocious criticism came from Jorge Luis Borges, whose review stated that Felipe's version was "erroneous and periphrastic," mocked the use of onomatopoeia and deplored that "the ample voice of the psalms had turned into the short and bland cries of the *Cante jondo*."[5] Felipe, though never mentioning Borges explicitly, replied to him in *Ganarás la luz* (You will earn the light), arguing that Whitman's poetics was very close to his own. He develops his conception of text as a commons to be used by all and blends his words with Whitman's: "What I do with the book of Jonah and with the book of Job, I also do with Whitman, if such is the will of the Wind. I change the verses and make them mine because I am on public ground, on a common meadow, on the green grass of the world, *upon leaves of grass*. And

---

5 Jorge Luis Borges, "Walt Whitman: Canto a mi mismo: Traducido por León Felipe," *Sur* 12, no. 88 (January 1942), 69.

what is the grass?"⁶ At this point, he inserts, without quotation marks, section 6 of "Song of Myself," on the meanings of the grass, and then resumes: "I stand on God's handkerchief. I stand on the green steep hill where the Wind blows. I am at home. And I, who would never allow myself to change sentences in the smallest newspaper or punctuation in a historical chronicle, have no embarrassment here, now, to change Whitman's words and Jehovah's words in my own way." (119) Felipe goes against the grain: while in the "chronicle," each sign matters and takes precedence over the content, in the poem, the "spirit" takes precedence. The form, usually considered as intrinsic to the poem, can be changed or altered without damage. Poetic art and the art of translation are one and the same: the idea of plagiarism makes as little sense for a creator as the idea of betrayal for a translator. Both the poet and the translator can retrieve as much as they like from the great universal poem that belongs to all and "transfer" it into their own words:

> Sections 44 and 45 of *Song of Myself* are contained in Chapter VIII of the Book of Proverbs. I don't know if Whitman knew that. Scholars will say it is almost a paraphrase. (Let them debate it and get it straight, it is their job.) I set out to translate these two songs so freely that even today, when I reread them, I don't know if they are from the Bible, from Whitman, or if they are mine. (120)

What changes the meaning of this one single preexisting text is historical context. One might argue that this is a way to justify plagiarism, lack of originality and a tendency toward repetition (a visible trend indeed in Felipe's work). On the other hand, this approach to translation serves a political statement: it challenges the idea of authorship, but instead of valorizing the text as an autonomous entity, as the structuralists later did, it promotes collective property of ideas and poetry. Felipe's "paraphrase" played a key role in the transmission of Whitman's "signal" in the Spanish-speaking world and the next chapter will show the internationalist acme of "Salut au Monde!" during the Cold War.

Extending the commons (Max Aub)

Let me break with chronology and briefly fast-forward before going back to World War II. I would like to draw attention to an extension of Felipe's

---

6 León Felipe, *Ganarás la luz* (1943; Madrid: Cátedra, 2006), 110.

"paraphrase" of Whitman, a small poem entitled "Orgullo" and attributed to "Josef Waskiewitz." The poem featured in the "translated anthology" (Antología traducida), published in 1963 in Mexico by the Spanish exile Max Aub. This anthology was in fact a great fictional game, since Max Aub himself was the author of the poems. For each fictitious author, Aub provided an equally fictitious short biography. Behind all the invented names and lives, one usually recognizes a real poet, whose work was pastiched. In the case of Waskiewitz, it was obviously Whitman. "Orgullo" rephrased in Spanish section 6 of "Song of Myself," in which a child asks about the meaning of the grass:

¿Qué creéis? ¿Ser alguien? ¿Quién es alguien? No lo sabéis.
Ninguno de vosotros sabe quién es alguien: Ése que le habla la hierba y que la hierba entiende, curvándose como la cintura de mi amada.
¡Hablad a la hierba, habladle y reventad de pena, que no os entiende! Ni la hierba, ni las piedras... Sólo sabéis hablar quedo al oído de vuestro ombligo.[7]

What do you think? That you are someone? Who is someone? You don't know.
None of you know who is someone: The one to whom the grass speaks and that the grass understands, wrapping itself like the belt of my beloved.
Speak to the grass, speak to it and burst with pain, because it does not understand you! Neither the grass, nor the stones... You only know how to speak in a low voice, to the ear of your navel.

Waskiewitz was presented as a Polish poet, who was born in 1857 and died in 1907: he stood as a bridge between Whitman and Aub (who was born in 1903 and whose full name was Aub Mohrenwitz). By presenting his own creation as a translation from an invented poet, Aub too challenged the idea of authorship. But there might be yet another name contained in Waskiewitz. Indeed, Max Aub and León Felipe knew each other well: they were both Spanish emigrants to Mexico, and they read and critiqued each other. With all its interpellations, exclamations and questions, Waskiewitz's style resembles that of Felipe's

---

7   Max Aub, *Antología traducida*, 1st expanded ed. (Barcelona: Editorial Seix Barral, 1972), 110. Previous edition: Mexico City, Editorial Universidad Nacional Autónoma de México, 1963.

Whitman. *Canto a mí mismo* was not the only translation known to Aub, who owned the 1922 French edition of the Mercure de France,[8] and who was close to Díez Canedo, another translator of Whitman. It is therefore a choice to present a very Felipean Whitman. Put another way, Whitman + Felipe + Aub = Waskiewitz. This poem thus implements Felipe's poetic art, whereby any poem is a draft "open to any luminous collaboration."

2. World War II: The Whitman pact

During World War II, and significantly after 1941, Whitman's poetry became a more frequent and global anti-fascist reference, including in China.[9] I will focus on the Allies, especially the US and the Soviet Union, where Whitman, after almost two years of absence (during the pact of nonaggression with Germany), was summoned again. For reasons different than in the early 1920s, Whitman was an agent of poetic propaganda in the two countries, now fighting on the same side.

A "wartime Whitman" in the US

As mentioned in the previous chapter, Louis Miller published the large selection from Whitman *Lider* in 1940. The emphasis on the word "Democracy" was particularly striking: it began with "Chants Democratic" (in the 1860 version) and ended with excerpts from *Democratic Vistas*. Just before "Pioneers! O Pioneers!," the final poem, Miller included "Captain, my Captain." The book contained several images of Whitman, but also of the house where he was born in Long Island. There is something deeply poignant about this first extensive translation published at the time when Yiddish speakers were being slaughtered in Europe.[10]

After the US entered the conflict, emphasis was quite predictably put on Whitman's war poems. In 1942, Kurt Weill composed his three "Whitman Songs," for voice and piano: "O Captain! My Captain!," "Beat! Beat! Drums!,"

---

8 See the online inventory of Max Aub's library, accessed June 15, 2022, http://maxaub.org/biblioteca/.
9 "Despite the adverse circumstances, . . . the Chinese interest in Whitman, far from being dampened, reached a peak around 1942 when the war entered the most critical phase. . . . The most noteworthy [translator] was Chu. Under the pen name of Gao Han, he started translating Whitman while in jail in the early 1930s 'in order to oppose the Fascist reign of terror.'" Xilao Li, "Walt Whitman in China," 4.
10 On the translation itself, see Albert Waldinger, "Stopping by the Woods: Classic American Poems in Yiddish," *TTR*, 16, no. 2 (2003): 155–174.

and "Dirge for Two Veterans." In 1943, a Yiddish anthology of war poems contained "O Captain! My Captain!," "Beat! Beat! Drums!" and "America," next to Langston Hughes's "I Too Sing America."[11] A particularly interesting edition was *A Wartime Whitman*, edited by Major William A. Aiken. As Andrew Jewel and Kenneth Price write, the Armed Service Editions came about in 1942.[12] They printed very large runs (one hundred thousand copies)—small, light books with soft covers.

FIGURE 8.2. Cover of William Aiken, ed., *A Wartime Whitman* (New York: Armed Services Editions, 1945). Author's collection.

The selection from Whitman (1945) included "Pioneers! O Pioneers!" and of course many civil war poems, regrouped in a section simply entitled "War." The order of the sections was meaningful, beginning with "America Singing" and ending with "Toward the Future." Major Aiken staged his Whitmanian revelation in the foreword, in an interesting combination of defamiliarization and homeliness, of grandeur and prosaicness:

> It was early Christmas morning, 1943. I had to admit that I was homesick. It was cold comfort to realize that I shared this moment of loneliness with many thousands of other American soldiers scattered throughout the world. Suddenly I caught my breath. Above the stillness of the sleeping city, a tenor voice rose fresh and clear:

---

11 I. Kissin, ed., *Lider fun der milkhome: Antologye* (New York: Bibliotek fun poezie un esayen, 1943).
12 Andrew Jewell and Kenneth Price, "Twentieth-Century Mass Media Appearances," in *A Companion to Walt Whitman*, ed. Donald Kummings (Oxford: Wiley-Blackwell, 2009), 354.

> As I walked out in Laredo one morning,
> As I walked out in Laredo one day,
> I saw a poor cowboy wrapped up in a blanket,
> Wrapped up in a blanket and cold as the clay.
>
> It was strange to hear such words at this time in a land of Muslims, minarets and muezzins,—strange, but comforting. Apparently I was not so far from home after all. A feeling of contentment spread about me. I had heard America singing. That was all I needed. I closed my eyes and was soon asleep....
>
> How could I hold fast to this fresh revelation of America, which had been spread out before me in the snatches of song last night and in a church service this morning? One voice I knew could do it. It was to be heard in Walt Whitman's *Leaves of Grass*. So I began my search. I went to the English and French bookshops, and even to the native bookstalls. Whitman? Who was he?[13]

Whitman was the voice of America, which "held fast" to a cowboy song, but also mingled with the calls of the "muezzins." Aiken further explained that "there is a natural bond between Whitman and the American serviceman" and that he made his selection of poems thinking of "Stephe," a soldier who wanted to carry the best of *Leaves* in his pocket or his knapsack. The Armed Services Edition also published a biography of Whitman.[14]

Another important wartime anthology had a different political agenda. It was the work of the communist critic Samuel Sillen, and was published in 1944 by International Publishers (founded in 1924 by Alexander Trachtenberg, a socialist and then communist activist). The poems were introduced by a substantial presentation and a foreword: "This volume has a definite purpose. It aims to present Walt Whitman as a living force in the war against fascist barbarism as well as in the peace which America and the other United Nations seek to achieve through unconditional victory."[15] In his presentation, Sillen insisted on the conciliation of the "national" and the "international," with arguments quite typical of Soviet rhetoric since the 1930s: "The struggle for nationalism

---

13 William Aiken, ed., *A Wartime Whitman* (New York: Armed Services Editions, 1945), 7.
14 Henry Seidel Canby, *Walt Whitman, an American: A Study in Biography* (New York: Armed Services Edition, 1944).
15 Sillen, *Walt Whitman*, 9.

had to be combined with the struggle for internationalism." (16) Sillen used the standard Stalinist lexicon:

> His internationalism, to be sure, has nothing in common with a rootless cosmopolitanism. Scorning self-willed expatriates, the poet would have agreed with his early contemporary, the Russian critic, Vissarion Belinsky, that "whoever does not belong to his land of birth does not belong to humanity in general." Yet he emphasized, in turn, that the true patriot rejects a narrow chauvinism. (43)

The poems were regrouped under several sections, among which, as one would expect, a copious selection from the civil war poems. But the rest of the anthology was very different from Major Aiken's *Wartime Whitman*: "Pioneers! O Pioneers!" was included in its entirety; the section "The Laboring Masses" contained "A Song for Occupations" and "Song of the Broad-Axe," while, under the heading "Salute to the World," all the communist favorites were to be found: "France, the 18th Year of these States," "Europe, the 72nd and 73rd years of these States," "Spain 1873–74," "To a Foil'd European Revolutionaire" and "O Star of France," a poem "which expressed for his time the feelings of our own generation when the Nazis marched into Paris by traitors sold" (44). All these poems were presented as "calls for action."

Critical work also gained momentum. Of course, some publications were not the immediate consequence of the war and had been a long time coming. This was the case with F. O. Matthiessen's seminal book *American Renaissance*, which reestablished and settled the canon for decades. Matthiessen, a professor at Harvard University, was not the first academic to dedicate a book to Whitman (I mentioned Newton Arvin's 1938 work), but the prestige of his position and of his publisher made this contribution quite different from previous ones.

Matthiessen's insistence on democracy as a theme and on originality as a characteristic resonated strongly in the context of the country's positioning on the international stage. Other titles published the same year, such as Frances Winwar's *American Giant Walt Whitman and his Times* and Babette Deutsch's *Walt Whitman Builder for America*,[16] indicate the same emphasis. One of Deutsch's main ideas was that Whitman was a great poet for children

---

16 Frances Winwar, *American Giant Walt Whitman and His Times* (New York, London: Harpers & Brothers, 1941); *Walt Whitman Builder for America* (New York: Julian Messner, 1941).

and a large part of the book was a selection of poems considered particularly suited to them. During these years, Sculley Bradley, who became an important Whitman scholar, published his first articles, whose titles show how much the current context shaped his interpretations: "Walt Whitman, Poet of the Present War," "Walt Whitman and the Postwar World."[17] Bradley argued that Whitman had foreseen the future ordeals of democracy and provided the ideal for which the US was now fighting. Max Eastman reconciled the national and the international in "Walt Whitman: Poet of Democracy": Whitman belonged to the canon of world poetry, could stand next to Shakespeare, Goethe, Pushkin, Dante, Hugo and Li Po, and his "democracy" transcended nation.[18] This emphasis was also visible on a larger continental scale, where Whitman was generally an ambassador of the "Good Neighbor policy" that had been implemented by Franklin Delano Roosevelt since 1933. One of the first book-length studies in Spanish was published in Uruguay in 1944—it was entitled "Walt Whitman, the Democratic Voice of America."[19]

Looking for Whitman on the White Sea

In the USSR, Whitman had largely disappeared from reviews and journals as of 1936. He made a brief comeback in 1939, as an "anti-fascist" poet, before the Ribbentrop-Molotov pact put on hold any attack on fascist powers. In June 1939 (two months before the pact), Chukovsky published an article which, as mentioned earlier, quoted "Spain. 1873–74." He explained that never before "had the masses of America shown such an affinity for Walt Whitman."

> To a large extent, this happened because the "good gray-haired poet" turned out to be their reliable ally in the fight against the impending threat of fascism. For although Walt Whitman died about half a century ago (in 1892), he is perceived today by the broad masses as one of the most active anti-fascist writers.
>
> Recently, curious cases have been observed in progressive journalism: as soon as reactionaries undertake a campaign

---

17 Sculley Bradley, "Walt Whitman, Poet of the Present War," *General Magazine and Historical Chronicle*, no. 45 (October 1942): 7–14; "Walt Whitman and the Postwar World," *South Atlantic Quarterly*, no. 42 (July 1943): 220–224.
18 Max Eastman, "Walt Whitman: Poet of Democracy," *Reader's Digest*, no. 42 (June 1943), 29–33.
19 José Gabriel, *Walt Whitman, la voz democrática de América* (Montevideo: Ediciones Ceibo, 1944).

against the working masses, the working-class newspapers print one or another poem by Whitman, and millions of readers perceive it as a burning response to the events that are taking place today.

In the spring of last year, when the conquest plans of the German-Italian aggressors were carried out, the newspaper of the French Communist Party, *L'Humanité*, published an old poem by Whitman, "To a Foil'd European Revolutionaire," and it sounded as if it had been written in the midst of current events.[20]

This was certainly the most directly political comment Chukovsky had ever made on Whitman. But in a fast-changing political context, it was already untimely. Just a couple of months later, the Axis powers were no longer the archenemies of the USSR. Only after Germany breached the pact and launched the Operation Barbarossa did the anti-fascist discourse resume and intensify.

In 1941 and 1942, several poems by Whitman were published in *Internatsional'naia Literatura*.[21] These were the last years of the journal, which had been founded in 1931 and was a major channel for foreign literature: once the Soviet Union entered the Great Patriotic War and the Comintern was dissolved, there was no place for it. In 1941, even before the German invasion, a long article on Whitman by Chukovsky was published, including poems in new translations (starting with "For You, Democracy" and ending with "When Lilacs Last . . .") and illustrations (with a picture of "Negro children at Whitman's house"). In the first issue of 1942, Dimitri Gorbov translated excerpts from *Democratic Vistas*. In the last issue of the year, war poems were translated by Mikhail Zenkevich, an important poet, who later specialized in translating American poetry, especially Robert Frost.

---

20 K. Chukovskii, "Uolt Uitman," *Literaturnaia Gazeta*, June 10, 1939, 2. On April 22, 1939, *L'Humanité* did indeed publish a piece entitled "For You O Democracy," with two excerpts, from the poem bearing that title, and from "To a Foiled European Revolutionaire." The introductory text, by Georges Chennevière, asked: "Does not the poem sound as if written after one of the multiple aggressions and annexations by the gang of the Axis powers?" (8).

21 On the history of the journal, see Aleksei Mikheev, "Mezhdu dvumia ottepeliami" and Arlen Blium, "Internatsional'naia literatura: podtsenzurnoe proshloe," *Inostrannaia literatura*, 2005 (no. 10). Called the journal of the "World Revolution" in 1931, it became "International Literature" in 1933. Although its agenda changed through a decade of political turmoil, it kept until the end the internationalist motto: "Proletarians of all countries, unite!" It was published in several languages (English, Spanish, German and French).

A tenth edition of Chukovsky's translation, announced in 1939,[22] was finally published in 1944, in a print run of ten thousand copies, even though paper was in short supply. At that point, Whitman had become a champion of the American-Soviet alliance against fascism. The echo with US discourse at the time is striking: there was the same emphasis on "Democracy."[23] The concept was obviously quite different in the two countries, but its pervasive use during the war tended to blur all nuances. *Internatsional'naia Literatura* reported the opening of a monument to Whitman at Bear Mountain Park, commenting on the sculpture by Jo Davidson and on the inscription from "Song of the Open Road" on the pedestal. In 1942, the young composer Alexander Zhivtsov set "O Captain! My Captain!" to music.[24] The poem did not belong to the Whitmanian Soviet repertoire and its introduction was clearly due to the wartime context.

New critics and scholars emerged. Maurice Mendelson, who later became Chukovsky's main successor as a Whitman scholar, published an article in *Novyi Mir* in 1945.[25] Twenty years later, he began his study on Whitman with an anecdote: in 1942, he happened to be in Arkhangelsk, where American and British sailors, who were bringing matériel to the USSR, were stranded after German submarines had attacked their ships. Mendelson described the sailors as they were wandering through the streets of the Soviet Far North, taking a stunned look at this unknown country. "They behaved in various ways. Some of them approached life in the land of the Soviets, the land of socialism, with curiosity, anxiously picking up news from the fronts."[26] Mendelson was drawn to one of them, who was a little bit older and had "a certain comfortable carelessness about his baggy clothing, big work-worn hands, bright-blue eyes with an open expression." That man remained a stranger, fascinating yet impenetrable, until he asked Mendelson how to get a copy of a book that he "greatly treasured," had always carried with him for "dozens of years," and that he had just lost after German bombings:

---

22 Excerpts were published in *Literaturnaia Gazeta*, May 30, 1939 and the tenth edition was announced as the most comprehensive so far. But when it was printed in 1944, it was still only a selection.
23 Dmitri Gorbov, "Velikii poet demokratii" (Great poet of Democracy), *Internatsional'naia Literatura*, 1942 (nos. 1-2), 201–202. In the same issue, Chukovskii published a bibliography on Walt Whitman in the USSR (204–206).
24 Aleksandr Zhivtsov, *Moi Kapitan. Dlia Golosa*, 1942.
25 Morris Mendel'son, "Uolt Uitmen," *Novyi mir*, 1945 (nos. 5-6), 183–188.
26 Mendelson, *Walt Whitman. A Soviet View*, 9.

> The American was asking about a book, but he seemed to be speaking about a living human being, someone very close and dear to him.
>
> The book which the foreign sailor sought—and found—in Arkhangelsk, was a collection of poems. On its title page were the words *Leaves of Grass*. The author of the book was a nineteenth-century American poet—Walt Whitman.
>
> This was not the first time that I had met people for whom Whitman was a kind friend who showed them the beauty of the human soul. But this American sailor, who during the bloodiest of wars related with such sadness his loss to a chance Soviet acquaintance, helped me feel more fully the magnetic attraction of Whitman's poetic word, the beauty of his verse and the strength of his democratic spirit.[27]

The story is reminiscent of Major Aiken's search for Whitman, except that minarets were replaced by "the fresh delicate greenery of the short northern summer" and the sailor found the book! The story can be read as a parable on the power of Whitman's poetry to bring people—and peoples—together. One can relate it to Chukovsky's discovery of Whitman in 1901, in the port of Odesa, thanks to an American sailor who sold him his copy: from the South of the Russian Empire to the Far North of the Soviet Union, Whitman was a poet of ports and sailors, entering sometimes as a smuggler, sometimes as the ambassador of an Allied country.

The honor of poets (the French Resistance)

Though Whitman was not a major reference for the French Resistance, his name, largely absent in the 1930s, reappeared during the war. In 1943, the last two stanzas of "O Star of France," in Jules Laforgue's translation, were published on the front page of the clandestine paper *Les Lettres françaises* (an organ of the National Front resistance movement, founded by Jacques Decour and Jean Paulhan). The poem was presented as "a tribute to our country, momentarily vanquished, and of which Whitman did not want to despair."[28] Sometimes, he was featured in papers that were not literary at all. As an example, *Rouge midi*, a regional organ of the Communist Party, published in Marseille, cited several

---

27 Ibid., 10.
28 "Étoiles de France" (sic), *Les Lettres françaises*, no. 12 (December 1943), 1.

poems and presented Whitman as the one who "foresaw, announced and praised the great American Democracy, and beyond, the fully accomplished great fraternal Democracy of the world, toward which all men are now walking on every road, on every ladder."[29] Whitman was also quoted in *L'Éternelle revue*, another clandestine publication, founded by Paul Éluard.[30] One of the most striking references is precisely to be found in Éluard's preface to the anthology of civil poetry *L'Honneur des poètes*, in 1943. Éluard, like all the French surrealists, had never shown any interest for the American poet before. Yet he opened his preface with Whitman's name, and associated it with other prestigious poets:

> Whitman animated by his people, Hugo calling to arms, Rimbaud seized by the Commune, Mayakovsky, exalted and exalting: it is towards action that poets with immense sight are, one day or the other, drawn. Their power over words being absolute, their poetry can never be diminished by the more or less rough contact of the outside world. Struggle can only give them back their strength.[31]

On a very different note, Whitman inspired a poem by Benjamin Fondane. A native of Moldavia, Fondane emigrated to France and became a French citizen just before World War II. He was a prisoner of war but managed to escape and lived in hiding. While he had been highly critical of Marxism and communism, his anti-fascist commitment drew him to the circle of the Resistance poets— Éluard published some of his poems (under the name Isaac Laquedem). In May 1944, Fondane was arrested by the French police and deported to Auschwitz, where he was murdered. His last poems were gathered, according to his will, in the collection *Le Mal des fantômes* (The Ache of ghosts). One poem bears the epigraph "after Walt Whitman." The connection with Whitman is not, however, obvious. As the poet is sitting at a gala and listening to music, his thoughts suddenly go to a shipwreck, to the mystery of the *Lusitania*, to the *Titanic*, to women swept from the deck and drowned. The theme of shipwrecks belongs

---

29 Suzanne Engelson, "Un grand poète américain: Walt Whitman," *Rouge midi. Organe régional du Parti communiste*, September, 3, 1944, 4.
30 January 1, 1944 (on the last page: "Pour toi, tout mon effort à moi, ô Démocratie, pour te servir, *ma femme*.")
31 Pierre Seghers, *La Résistance et ses poètes: Récit* (Paris: Pierre Seghers, 2022), 334. The preface was not signed when the collection was first published (on July 14, Bastille Day).

indeed to Whitman's poetry,[32] but it is rarely picked up by his readers. Fondane, who was obsessed with the "abyss" (gouffre), paid attention to the darker side of Whitman's poetry, to its fascination with death. The poem ends with a pessimistic question, in contrast with Éluard's call to action: "Is there only the victory of / brutal power?" (N'est-il victoire que de la / force brutale?).[33] Fondane's rewriting bears a tragic and prophetic mark, which sets it apart from common uses of Whitman during the war.

1945: Singing the spring

In the US, the war had confirmed Whitman as a national poet; this was the time of Paul Hindemith's famous adaptation of Whitman's poems for Lincoln as an oratorio.[34] Partisan uses were put on hold. By contrast, Whitman regained strength as a political poet in Europe and in Latin America. In 1945, the communist poet Johannes Becher, who had been in exile in the USSR for ten years, published a sonnet to Whitman in the new journal *Aufbau*. It presented Whitman's poetry as an "enraptured hymn of Freedom" (der Freiheit hymnisches Entzücken) and its rhythms as "high-flung bridges." Lifted by human freedom (*Menschenfreiheit*), Whitman was, once again, a prophet:

> Er sah DIE Zukunft vor sich aufgeschlagen.
> Das Sternenbanner war sein Firmament.
> O welch ein Glanz lag auf Amerika![35]

> He saw THE future wide open before him.
> The star-spangled banner was his firmament.
> Oh what a brightness shone on America!

---

32 "I look where the ship helplessly heads end on, I hear the burst as she strikes, I hear the howls of dismay, they grow fainter and fainter" ("The Sleepers," LG 359). Also see "Patroling Barnegat" in the "Sea-Drift" cluster.
33 Benjamin Fondane, *Le Mal des fantômes* (Paris: Verdier, 2006), 51.
34 Paul Hindemith, *When Lilacs Last in the Dooryard Bloom'd, a Requiem for Those We Love* (commissioned in 1945, after the death of F. D. Roosevelt, by the conductor Robert Shaw, it was first performed in 1946). See Kowalke, "For Those We Love: Hindemith, Whitman, and 'An American Requiem.'"
35 Johannes Becher, "Walt Whitman," *Aufbau*, no. 1 (November 1945), 286, reproduced in Allen and Folsom, *Walt Whitman and the World*, 217–218. W. Grünzweig thinks the poem was written in the early 1940s, during Becher's years of Soviet exile (ibid., 171).

This sonnet sealed the poetic alliance of the star-spangled banner and the red flag.

In 1945, several new meaningful translations were published in Europe. Pavel Eisner, one of the most prominent Czech translators, prepared an anthology entitled "Democracy, my Wife! Selected Poems from Leaves of Grass". Eisner concluded his preface with the idea that Whitman "decreed for us all the motto of all sacred Revolutions: Allons! The road is before us!"[36] The Romanian artist Margareta Sterian also translated poems, which she illustrated.[37] Both were Jewish and had survived years of hardship and fear (Eisner narrowly escaped deportation). In 1945 again, Concha Zardoya published an anthology *Cantando a la primavera* in Madrid.[38] Born in Chile, Zardoya moved to Spain when she was eighteen and is thus another instance of a transatlantic translator. She was much involved with the republicans, contributing to the Cultura Popular efforts. She left Spain for the US in 1948, when the hopes for change she had (briefly) entertained at the end of World War II were crushed. She translated Whitman precisely at that time of hope—the title of her anthology sounds indeed more like Pablo Neruda than Walt Whitman—and wrote her first collection of poems at that time: *Pájaros del Nuevo Mundo* (Birds of the New World). Zardoya became one of Whitman's main translators in Spanish and later published more comprehensive versions. It was also in 1945 that Czesław Miłosz translated Whitman for the first time; his choice of "Dirge for Two Veterans"[39] was not as optimistic as Eisner's or Zardoya's. Miłosz's relationship with Whitman is complex and beyond the scope of the present study.[40]

The end of the war was also the beginning of Whitman's communist deployment in Latin America. In 1945, Raúl González Tuñón, mentioned at the start of this chapter, published *Primer canto argentino*.[41] While its title recalls the nuevomundista Whitmanian tradition, the volume was in fact very radical. It opened with two epigraphs: a telegram from Moscow, assuring the author of the interest taken in his war poems and of the support of the USSR, followed by a quotation from Whitman, "And mine a word of the modern, the

---

36 Walt Whitman, *Demokracie, ženo má! Vyber ze Stébel trávy*, trans. Pavel Eisner (Prague: Jaroslav Podroužek, 1945), 14. The selection was not, however, narrowly political: "Song of Myself" was entirely translated, while "Pioneers! O Pioneers!" was not included. "Salut au Monde!" was prominently featured.
37 Walt Whitman, *Poeme*, trans. Margareta Sterian (Bucarest: Pro Pace, 1945).
38 Walt Whitman, *Cantando a la primavera*, trans. Concha Zardoya (Madrid: Ed. Hispánica, Adonais, 1945).
39 Walt Whitman, "Pieśń dla poległych," trans. Czesław Miłosz, *Przekrój*, no. 30 (1945), 7.
40 It has been largely documented. See Skwara, *Polski Whitman*, 229–251.
41 Raúl González Tuñón, *Primer canto argentino* (Buenos Aires: author's edition, 1945).

word En-Masse"—En-Masse was translated as "MULTITUD." Whitman was therefore not just the voice of the great continental expanses, but of Moscow as well. The first poem was addressed to Argentina and the last to the Soviet Union. As the next chapter will show, Pablo Neruda wrote a piece along a similar pattern just a few years later. The links between González Tuñón and Neruda were many: Tuñón published his poem "Madrid" in a magazine edited by Neruda and Nancy Cunard,[42] wrote his *Canto argentino* in Chile, and published it in Argentina when Neruda lived there in exile: one can assume that the two poets responded to each other in these transatlantic poems, bridges of words between America and the USSR, which González Tuñón sketched out and Neruda completed at the beginning of the Cold War.

---

42 *Los poetas del mundo defienden al pueblo español*, Paris, no. 5 (1937); the famous poem "Spain" by W. H. Auden was published in the same issue.

Chapter 9

"Salut au Monde!" across the Iron Curtain (1946–1956)

Whitman's fortunes took different turns in the decade that followed World War II. As the Soviet Union extended its influence in Europe, so did Whitman. While his presence was particularly conspicuous in the satellites of the USSR, it also grew stronger in parts of Western Europe, especially France, where interest in his poetry was renewed after three decades of relative indifference. In the US during this period, at a time when American literature became established as a field of study, Whitman truly entered the national canon. This may a be a reason why he lost appeal as a voice of radical protest. However, this political decline was counterbalanced by the spectacular arrival of *camarada* Whitman in Latin America. The poet became part of what Rossen Djagalov called "Second-to-Third World"[1] culture: a reference, even a "solidarity trope," shared by Soviet culture and the Third World. South America and the Caribbean became the new hot spots of the internationalist Whitman. Whitman's reception also increased in China, and the 1955 celebrations for the anniversary of *Leaves of Grass* were the climax of this extended partisan Whitmania.

---

1 Djagalov, *From Internationalism to Postcolonialism*. As Djagalov explains, the expression "Third World" was prohibited in the Soviet Union until the 1970s, but it was indeed the space targeted by a more global internationalism.

1. "Salut au Monde!": a French comeback

In the immediate postwar years Whitman's reception regained momentum in Europe, on both sides of the Iron curtain. In 1946, Reisinger's German translation was reprinted in separate chapbooks—one of them was entitled "Salut au Monde."[2] Tin Ujević published a collection of Whitman in Croatian in 1951.[3] In Western Europe, Whitman's revival was particularly strong where communist parties were influential. In 1950, a new complete Italian translation by Enzo Giachino was published.[4] Caterina Bernardini has shown that Sibilla Aleramo, who had written about Whitman before, started emulating his "bardic voice" in her own poetry after she joined the Communist Party and travelled to Moscow.[5] I will focus on Whitman's revival in cultural spheres fostered by the French Communist Party, which has garnered little attention until now.

In the first years after the war, Whitman often featured in *Les Lettres françaises*, the former Resistance journal, which had become an important literary publication. In February 1946, the travel writer Marc Chadourne published an account of a long trek in the American West, during which he read Whitman, whose presence he felt like "a hand on his shoulder."[6] Chadourne argued that his poems were more needed than ever as "something to prove this puzzle the New World" (a quote from "To Foreign Lands"), especially after the first "atomic explosion." While Chadourne's text is a classic narrative of camping in the American West, it introduces the idea of a "new New World," a world changed by the Bomb, in which Whitman is summoned again as a guide. From Pablo Neruda's *Let the Rail Splitter Awake* to Allen Ginsberg's "Plutonian Ode," this would be a constant usage of Whitman after World War II.

The following year, Whitman was repurposed to denounce the French colonial system. On the front page, a piece entitled "Walt Whitman's reach" stated that "the equality of people should not be rhetorical," that France should be ashamed of "Algerian and Tunisian people wearing rags" and that an end should be brought to the Indochina War. These political statements were framed by a

---

2   Walt Whitman, *Salut au monde* (Berlin: Suhrkamp Verlag, 1946).
3   Walt Whitman, *Vlati Trave*, trans. Tin Ujević (Zagreb: Zora, 1951). Ujević was condemned by the Communist Party for his support of an independent state of Croatia after the war and could only resume his work in 1950.
4   Walt Whitman, *Foglie d'erba* (Turin: Einaudi, 1950).
5   Bernardini, *Transnational Modernity*, 140–143. Bernardini quotes a poem entitled "Mia Italia un dì" from *Luci della mia sera* (1956), whose catalogs and anaphora are reminiscent of "Salut au Monde!"
6   Marc Chadourne, "L'énigme du Nouveau monde," *Les Lettres françaises*, no. 95 (February 15, 1946), 3.

quote from "For You O Democracy," and the declaration that "only Democracy will save us, provided we feel it as strongly as Whitman did."⁷ This was one of the few instances of an anticolonial Whitman. In 1947, a new anthology was published by Guy Lévis Mano (who had published Lorca's "Ode to Walt Whitman" in 1938); the poems were translated by Hélène Bokanowski (who had translated Langston Hughes the year before).

In 1948, Paul Jamati published his book on Whitman in Pierre Seghers's series Poètes d'aujourd'hui. A large part was biographical, as Jamati tried to see beyond the "legend" of Whitman (Whitman the nurse, Whitman the saint, Whitman the prophet). Meanwhile, he contributed to another legend, which was part of the communist narrative: how Whitman was despised and even harassed by his contemporaries, with much insistence on his dismissal from the Bureau of Indian Affairs by the newly appointed secretary of interior, James Harlan, in 1865. Jamati discussed Whitman's *engagement*, the new watchword of the French intellectual Left: "his sense of human solidarity, of popular fraternity, makes him the poet of *engagement*; among his contemporaries, he is the only *poète engagé*."⁸ Jamati was also a poet. In 1950, he published a collection entitled *Poèmes datés* (Dated poems), which gathered pieces written in 1948 and 1949. While the prologue is an address to the "comrade, friend, brother,"⁹ the poem "Message" addresses the "smug Yankees," unworthy of their fathers, when they should be the heirs of Lincoln and Whitman:

> N'aurez-vous conjugué vos efforts et votre puissance
> Aux efforts et à la puissance de vos frères
> Que pour en venir à renier vos frères ?
> . . . .
> Mais vous, vrais Américains,
> Neveux de Lincoln et de Whitman,
> Qui vous dressez courageusement comme des combattants de
>   l'humanité,
> Recevez ce salut de France,
> Le salut des peuples de la terre,
> Notre salut le plus tendre et le plus confiant
> Et nos clameurs d'allégresse.¹⁰

---

7   Claude Morgan, "Le souffle de Walt Whitman," *Les Lettres françaises*, no. 154 (May 2, 1947), 1.
8   Paul Jamati, *Walt Whitman* (Paris: Seghers, 1948), 129.
9   Paul Jamati, *Poèmes datés* (Paris: Seghers, 1950), 9.
10 Ibid., 13–14. Poem "written on April 12, 1948."

Have you combined your efforts and power
With the efforts and power of your brothers
Only to end up denying your brothers?
. . . .
But you, true Americans,
Nephews of Lincoln and Whitman,
Who bravely stand up as fighters for humanity,
Receive this salutation from France,
The salutation of the peoples of the Earth,
Our tenderest and most trusting salutation
And our clamors of joy.

The salutation is reversed: while Whitman greeted the world from America, America is now greeted from France and from the "peoples of the Earth." The poem "1848-1958" ends with a familiar rallying cry, in capital letters: "PROLÉTAIRES DU MONDE ENTIER, UNISSEZ-VOUS" (Proletarians of the world, unite).

Les Lettres françaises emphasized Jamati's political assessments of Whitman, one of those who "decided to change the world."[11] In September, they published a piece entitled "The great fellow is still alive and Walt Whitman speaks louder than the petty man." The author, Jacques Gaucheron, resurrects Whitman as a civil servant whose superior (the "petty man") has received complaints, and imagines their dialogue (this was an update of the Bureau of Indian Affairs episode). To each accusation, Whitman replies with quotes from his poems, such as "I speak the password primeval, I give the sign of Democracy." Gaucheron concludes:

> Poems are not mere answers prepared for an interrogation by the House Committee on Anti-American Activities. But they are what stands out today. . . .
>
> The titanic fraternity of men, across nations (see "Salut au monde"), of which Whitman dreamt, is a rebuttal of all the restrictions that America is currently trying to enforce on other countries.
>
> Walt Whitman's Hail to World is not the same as Mr Truman's.[12]

---

11 *Les Lettres françaises*, no. 201 (March, 25, 1948), 3.
12 Jacques Gaucheron, "Le grand bonhomme vit encore et Walt Whitman parle plus haut que le petit monsieur," *Les Lettres françaises*, no. 223 (September 2, 1948), 3.

Gaucheron's use of "Salut au Monde!" as an antidote to the Marshall Plan and a response to intensifying American anticommunism anticipates Pablo Neruda's major manipulation of the poem, which I will later examine in detail.

In 1951, a new communist magazine was founded by the politician Pierre Cot, a Parti Radical minister before the war who had supervised the overhaul of French military aviation, now a member of the Society of the Friends of the USSR and a witness for *Les Lettres françaises* at the landmark Kravchenko trial.[13] However, while remaining pro-Soviet, he increasingly advocated "neutrality" and collaboration between East and West. *Défense de la Paix* answered the need for a "true international journal," with editions in several countries and languages, with contributors "professing diverse ideas," but "all resolved to make a joint effort of communication and to defend peace."[14] This opening program was followed by the integral translation of "Salut au Monde!"

FIGURE 9.1. "Salut au monde par Walt Whitman," *Défense de la Paix*, no. 1 (1951), 6. Bibliothèque Nationale de France.

---

13 *Les Lettres françaises* defamed Victor Kravchenko, the Soviet defector and author of the memoir *I Chose Freedom*; Kravchenko sued the review for libel, which led to a celebrated trial in 1949.

14 *Défense de la Paix*, no. 1 (June 1951), 1. Claude Morgan, who contributed to *Les Lettres françaises*, was editor in chief.

A subsequent essay explained the choice of the poem as a manifesto for the journal:

> "Salut au monde" is truly the poem of peaceful coexistence among all peoples.
> Walt Whitman identified with the whole world; he felt himself to be of all countries and races.
> No one had more of a sense of, and reverence for, human dignity than he. "HOW," he wrote, "DARE YOU PLACE ANYTHING BEFORE A MAN?"
> In the aftermath of the United Nations' victory over Nazism, it seemed that all the Allied leaders were animated by a Whitmanian spirit. (11)

This commentary introduced the joint resolution of the Yalta conference, quotes by President Truman and Stalin, as well as a speech from the renowned communist scientist Pierre Joliot-Curie. The magazine targeted the general public: it also contained chess problems, sports features and recipes from all over the world (in this issue, "paella a la Valenciana!"). It is not that often that Whitman's poetry stood "amid the kitchenware," like the Muse in "Song of the Exposition." Another example of this Whitman "defending Peace" is the premiere in Paris of Joris Ivens's documentary *Peace will prevail* (about the Congress for Peace in Warsaw): the Salle Pleyel was covered in flags from the People's Republic of China, the USSR, Britain and France, and poems by Whitman, Mayakovsky and Mao Zedong were read before the show.[15]

2. *Saludo al mundo*: from Neruda to Mir

The militant Whitman, especially the communist one, continued to become more global after World War II. In Iran, Ehsan Tabari, a Marxist philosopher, poet and co-founder of the Tudeh Party of Iran published a translation of "Out of the Cradle Endlessly Rocking" in 1946[16]—a couple of years later, he went into exile to the Soviet Union, where he stayed for nine years, before leaving for East Germany. But nowhere was the upsurge of interest in Whitman more visible

---

15 Henry Magnan, "La Paix filme à Varsovie," *Le Monde*, July 12, 1951. Magnan believed that the prettiest poem was the one by Mao Zedong.
16 See Fomeshi, "Political Reception of Whitman," *The Persian Whitman*, 115–130.

than in Latin America. In Brazil, this was particularly the case during the years immediately following World War II. As Maria Clara Bonetti Paro observes, there was a hiatus between Whitman's reception in the 1920s, which focused on aesthetics, and the 1940s reception, which focused on politics and ideology. Already in 1944, a selection of Whitman's poetry was entitled "Saudação ao Mundo."[17] In 1945, the anthropologist Luís da Câmara Cascudo translated three poems (among them "For You O Democracy") for a newspaper in the city of Natal, Rio Grande do Norte, a very poor region that was far from the Modernist center, São Paulo, where Whitman had been discussed in the 1920s. This was unusual, as Cascudo was conservative and anticommunist.[18] The following year, the socialist Oswaldino Marques published his first collection of poems as well as a substantial translation from Whitman. In 1947, the poet Jorge de Lima summoned the American bard in the poem "Democracia." That same year, the sociologist Gilberto Freyre delivered an important lecture on "Comrade Whitman." He insisted on the political, social and economic dimensions of the poetry: for Whitman, the enemy was not so much the monarchy as the plutocracy. However, his reading was not political in the partisan sense of the term. Freyre considered both "Soviet democracy" and "Western democracies" as incomplete. Whitman's socialism was valued as "pan-human," and Freyre's reading was permeated with Christian doctrine rather than Marxism.[19] His lecture was published and later translated into English. This political turn can also be felt in other parts of Latin America. Miguel Mendoza's essay on Whitman the "singer of Democracy," published in Mexico in 1946,[20] is another example of this new political emphasis.

Pablo Neruda's *Let the Rail Splitter Awake*

The most striking example of this shift is undoubtedly the evolution of Pablo Neruda's relation to Whitman: in the 1930s, he translated section 2 from "Song

---

17 Walt Whitman, *Saudação ao Mundo e Outros Poemas*, trans. Mario D. Ferreira Santos (Sao Paulo: Flama, 1944).
18 While Cascudo favored the Allies during World War II, he joined the nationalist right-wing movement *Integralismo* in the 1930s and continued to support them. The translations were reprinted as a chapbook to launch the Publishing House of Recife (in the Rio Grande too) in 1957.
19 Gilberto Freyre, *O camarada Whitman: conferência lida na Sociedade dos Amigos da América do Rio de Janeiro, em 22 de Maio de 1947, precedida de uma saudação a Gilberto Freyre* (Rio de Janeiro: J. Olympio, 1948).
20 Walt Whitman, *Walt Whitman, Cantor de la Democracia: Ensayo biográfico y breve antología*, trans. Miguel R. Mendoza (Mexico City: Secretaría de Educación Pública, 1946).

of Myself," a call to enjoy the "atmosphere," but in 1948, it was in the fiercely partisan poem *Que despierte el leñador*[21] that he invoked Whitman. In 1950, it was included in *Canto General*, Neruda's grand epic, as the ninth canto.

As an introduction to this poem, I would like to emphasize that Neruda regularly presented Mayakovsky as Whitman's counterpart—"Mayakovsky is the Whitman of the Russian Revolution, he is what Whitman was for the industrial revolution, for American growth"[22]—or successor: "After Walt Whitman, what expectations! All the leaves of grass were planted and one could no longer walk on the lawn. Yet Mayakovsky came along and poetry sounded like a roundhouse: whistles, sighs, sobs, sounds of trains and armored carriages."[23] Neruda hung the portraits of Rimbaud and Mayakovsky side by side in his Santiago home, but he saw a difference between Rimbaud, "the grand defeated," and Mayakovsky, "sonorous and sensitive element of one of Man's great victory," a poet belonging to his country and his time, like... Whitman: "Both are part of the struggle and the space of great epochs. Whitman is not a decorative element in Lincoln's War of Emancipation: his poetry unfolds with the lights and shadows of battles."[24] Neruda wished to involve Mayakovsky and Whitman in a dialogue that history had not allowed: "Strength, tenderness and fury make Mayakovsky the greatest example so far of our poetic age. Whitman would have loved him. Whitman would have heard his cry across the steppes, as an answer, through time and for the first time, to his grand civil rogations."[25] Indeed, in Neruda's poetry, the cries of Whitman and Mayakovsky cross steppes, oceans and time to celebrate the communist man.

In 1945, after he joined the Chilean Communist Party, Neruda was elected deputy in the northern mining provinces of Chile. The following year, he supported the candidacy of Gabriel González Videla to the presidency of the republic. Once elected, González Videla turned against his former allies and declared the Communist Party illegal. In February 1948, Neruda delivered a resounding speech to the Senate—"I accuse"—before being placed under arrest. This was the beginning of a period in hiding and then exile, which

---

21 The poem is probably better known today as "Let the Woodcutter Awaken" (in Jack Schmitt's translation of *Canto General*). However, I will refer to it with the title of the coeval translation by Waldeen, which was influential in US communist circles (see below) and which I will use.
22 Pablo Neruda, "Interview with Rita Guibert in 1970," in *Obras completas*, 5:1164.
23 Pablo Neruda, "Contestando una encuesta," *Ercilla*, July 17, 1968, in ibid., 5:173.
24 Pablo Neruda, "Dos retratos de un rostro," *Ercilla*, September 25, 1968, in ibid., 5:183.
25 Pablo Neruda, "Sobre Maiakovski," *Boletín de la Sociedad de Amigos de la URSS*, México, July 15, 1943, in ibid., 4:481.

lasted until 1952.[26] During these years, Neruda wrote many of the poems that would make up *Canto General*, especially the most forcefully militant ones. *Let the Rail Splitter Awake* was finished in May 1948 and first published in July by Ediciones de la Resistencia, the Chilean Communist Party's publishing house, and in Cuba, by Neruda's friends.[27] That same year, the *Antología Popular de la Resistencia* was also published, which brought together texts by Neruda, Nicolás Guillén, Julio Moncada and an apocryphal collection by "popular poets" (in fact, Neruda as well). What *Let the Rail Splitter Awake* shared with these texts against González Videla was an extreme virulence. A difference, however, is that the battle shifted from domestic to foreign politics. Whitman's resurrection in a Soviet uniform should be read in a Cold War context.

The first section opens with an evocation of the nineteenth-century United States, a land of peace, harmony and mineral beauty:

>Al oeste de Colorado River
>hay un sitio que yo amo.
>Acudo allí con todo lo que palpitando
>transcurre en mí, con todo
>lo que fui, lo que soy, lo que sostengo.
>.............................
>América extendida como la piel del búfalo,
>aérea y clara noche del galope,
>allí hacia las alturas estrelladas,
>bebo tu copa de verde rocío.

>West of the Colorado River is a place I love.
>I turn towards it, with everything that lives in me,
>with all that I was, and am, and believe.
>.............................
>America, stretched like a buffalo hide,
>aerial, clear night of gallop,

---

26 Paul Jamati in his 1948 collection attacks those who go after all the "Pablo Nerudas of this earth." ("Émulation," in *Poèmes datés*, 11).

27 In Cuba, one thousand copies were printed in the "Yagruma" series (no. 2), thanks to Juan Marinello (the secretary of the Cuban Communist Party), Nicolás Guillén and Ángel Augier. The poem was also published in December in the Costa Rican magazine *Repertorio Americano*, with a portrait of Lincoln, one of Whitman (after Pearsall's photograph again) and a drawing of Neruda sitting on a cloud.

> there, toward the starred summits,
> I drink your cup of green dew.[28]

Its writers are mentioned: Melville, a "spruce tree," Whitman "innumerable as grain," Poe and his "mathematical darkness." The style is also extraordinarily close to Whitman's, since the lines are unusually long and the "I" conspicuous. The dilation of the poetic body is similar to Whitman's cosmic extension of the self: "There, from within my central rock of being / I could extend my eyes, ears, hands, on the air." The enumeration of what the poet sees and hears condenses images from *Leaves of Grass*: the locomotive,[29] the moon on the ship from Manhattan (an allusion to "Crossing Brooklyn Ferry"), the song of the machines (evocative of "I Hear America Singing"). Further on, Neruda uses other Whitmanian devices, such as the insertion of a foreign word: "I love the *farmer*'s little house." The American landscape is a Whitmanian palimpsest rather than a firsthand depiction. However, a few metaphors and personal motifs are grafted onto this almost translated text: the condor, the cup, the bell, or, in the fourth stanza, alfalfa and poppies. In other words, two poems overlap, as if they were superimposed: they are entwined rather than merged. The Nerudean inlays are like the signature of this homage to Whitman. But they can also be interpreted as the first signs of an appropriation that becomes more radical with each stanza.

In contrast with the first, the second section depicts contemporary America and shows how the ideals of the past were betrayed: the tone is fierce and the harmonious vision of the landscape gives way to a brutal denunciation of politicians. American soldiers return from the war only to watch anti-Nazi principles mocked by aggressive imperialism, "Marshall cocktails," and criminal racism, symbolized by the Ku Klux Klan's cross of flames. In the third section, however, the text settles back into eulogy: the poet shifts from America to the USSR, the current refuge of past American values, the place where the hopes that once belonged to the US can now be fulfilled.

> Yo también más allá de tus tierras, América,
> ando y hago mi casa errante, vuelo, paso,

---

28 Pablo Neruda, *Canto general*, in *Obras completas*, 1:682; *Let the Rail Splitter Awake and Other Poems*, trans. Waldeen (New York: Masses and Mainstream, 1950), 19.

29 In his garden at Isla Negra, Neruda kept an old locomotive, which he described as follows: "It is so powerful, loaded with grain, so fertile, piercing, roaring, rumbling! It has sorted grain, spat sawdust, felled forests, sawed planks, cut boards, emitted smoke, grease, sparks, fire, whistled until the prairies shook. If I love it so much, it is because it looks like Walt Whitman" (Pablo Neruda, "El locomóvil," in *Una casa en la arena*, in *Obras completas*, 3:133).

canto y converso a través de los días.
Y en el Asia, en la URSS, en los Urales me detengo
y extiendo el alma empapada de soledades y resina. (688)

I also go beyond your lands, America,
there I make my wandering home, flying, traveling, singing
and conversing throughout the days.
And in Asia, in the USSR, in the Urals I pause
and expand my soul permeated with solitude and resin. (26)

An informed reader can recognize all the layers of references in "Yo también," "I, Too" (Whitman, Hughes and Alberti—see Chapter 6). As in Whitman, travel is imaginary, since Neruda visited the USSR for the first time only in 1949. Interestingly, in the Resistencia press version, which probably corresponds to a draft, this stanza was absent: it was added to the poem in a late phase of its writing. The third section mirrors the opening one, with the same words carrying the same impression of homeliness, peace and prosperity:

Amo cuanto en las extensiones
a golpe de amor y lucha el hombre ha creado.
Aún rodea mi casa en los Urales
la antigua noche de los pinos
y el silencio como una alta columna.
Trigo y acero aquí han nacido
de la mano del hombre, de su pecho. (688)

I love whatever man has created in space
by blow of struggle and love.
My house in the Urals is still surrounded
by the ancient night of pines
and silence like a tall beehive.
    Here, wheat and steel
were born from the hand of man, from his breast. (26)

The construction of the poem updates the idea of *translatio imperii* and combines it with Hegelian-Marxist dialectics. Whitman invited the Muse to leave for America, where a "new empire, grander than any before"[30] awaited her,

---

30 Whitman, "A Broadway Pageant," LG 168.

and Neruda now beckons the reader to new territories, whose principles are bound to extend to the whole world. This part of the poem is written again in a Whitmanian manner, until the imitation becomes outright quotation:

> Walt Whitman, levanta tu barba de hierba,
> mira conmigo desde el bosque,
> desde estas magnitudes perfumadas.
> **Qué ves allí, Walt Whitman?**
> **Veo, me dice mi hermano profundo,**
> **veo cómo trabajan las usinas,**
> **en la ciudad que los muertos recuerdan,**
> **en la capital pura,**
> **en la resplandeciente Stalingrado.**
> **Veo desde la planicie combatida,**
> **desde el padecimiento y el incendio,**
> **nacer en la humedad de la mañana**
> **un tractor rechinante hacia las llanuras.**
> Dame tu voz y el peso de tu pecho enterrado,
> Walt Whitman, y las graves
> raíces de tu rostro
> para cantar estas reconstrucciones!
> Cantemos juntos lo que se levanta
> de todos los dolores, lo que surge
> del gran silencio, de la grave
> victoria:
>   Stalingrado, surge tu voz de acero,
> renace piso a piso la esperanza
> como una casa colectiva,
> y hay un temblor de nuevo en marcha
> enseñando,
> cantando
> y construyendo. (689-690)

> Walt Whitman, lift up your grassy beard,
> look with me from this wood,
> from these fragrant heights,
> **what do you see, Walt Whitman?**
> **I see, my wise brother tells me,**
> **how factories are working in that city**

> **remembered by the dead,**
> **in pure resplendent Stalingrad.**
> **I see how from the embattled plains,**
> **from the suffering and the flames,**
> **in the humid morning there is born**
> **a tractor which clanks toward the fields.**
> Give me your voice and the strength of your buried breast,
> Walt Whitman, and the solemn roots that are your face
> so as to sing these reconstructions!
> Together we will pay homage to what arises
> from all the grief, to what surges up
> from the deep silence, from the somber
> victory. (28)

"Que ves allí, Walt Whitman?" is a direct translation from "Salut au Monde!": "What do you see, Walt Whitman?" The sequence is built on the same anaphoric model and unfolds through a series of lines introduced by "I see." Interestingly, the passage in bold, which corresponds to the Whitman prosopopoeia, was also absent from the Resistencia edition. And the whole passage came later: moving it to the third section (from the fifth) put Whitman in a pivotal position and consolidated the dialectic movement of the poem (section 1: Democracy in America; section 2: its negation; section 3: Soviet synthesis). Neruda's overview of the USSR, interspersed with American scenes denouncing capitalism, is also quite reminiscent of Dziga Vertov's *A Sixth of the World*, which was itself very Whitmanian (see Chapter 5). Even though it is difficult to know whether Neruda had seen the film, the coincidence is striking: all three, Whitman, Vertov and Neruda, use the anaphora "I see" to introduce the inventory; the tractor that stands out in Neruda was one of the few words underlined in Vertov's intertitles. Whitman is thus resurrected so that he may intone, through Neruda, the song of Stalingrad. The two voices finally merge into a "common song" (Cantemos juntos). The following section has prophetic overtones: "Que venga Abraham," "Let Abraham come": "Abraham" obviously refers to both the biblical figure and to Lincoln (in Waldeen's translation: "Let Abe come"). Just as Whitman is resurrected as a Soviet bard, Lincoln is awakened to lead the anti-fascist forces inside and outside the United States: he must lift up his axe "against the new slaveholders, / against the slave-lash." As Harris Feinsod contends, this is a prime example of the way "Latin American poets of the early Cold War disclose an integrationist tendency by transforming iconic figures of US racial amelioration such as Abraham Lincoln into poetic figures of hemispheric unity."[31] The last section is a surprising combination of sheer militant discourse, with a series of nominal verses hammering the word *paz* (peace), and a declaration of humility: "I have not come to resolve anything" (Yo no vengo a resolver nada). This line sounds like a last-minute retraction, as if, having turned the *canto* into slogans and pushed it to the edge of tautology, the poetic voice needed to tone down its inflammatory rhetoric.

Neruda's poem was translated almost immediately into English, by American-born Waldeen Falkenstein, better known as Waldeen. In the 1930s, Waldeen emigrated to Mexico, where she became a famous choreographer and dancer, and where she met Neruda.[32] As early as October 1948, part of the poem was translated under the title *Let the Rail Splitter Awake*, for the new Communist Party journal *Masses and Mainstream*. The following year, it was adapted for a staged and danced version at the American Continental Congress for World Peace in Mexico City: there were songs from Peru, Ecuador and Mexico, a ballet conceived by Waldeen, and a recorded reading of her translation (Neruda himself also read). In 1950, it was entirely translated as a chapbook, with a few other poems, Neruda's Mexico speech and a foreword by a familiar name, Samuel Sillen.[33] The presentation opened with Whitman: "Walt Whitman once wrote that the great poet enlisted in a people's cause 'can make every word he speaks draw blood.' This is true of Pablo Neruda. He is a poet-in-arms." (5) He insisted that Neruda's poem addressed a US audience: "Neruda speaks directly to the people of the United States. . . . This is a cry born of love for all that is good on this continent, love for the heritage of Lincoln and Whitman." (6) He summarized Neruda's poetry with Whitman's words: "whoever touches this poetry touches a man." (8)

As I will argue in the next chapter, *Let the Rail Splitter Awake* contributed to re-introducing a partisan Whitman in the US. The poem was largely distributed and translated into several languages, especially after it earned the International Peace Prize in Warsaw in 1950. It was translated into Polish and Romanian as

---

31 Harris Feinsod, *The Poetry of the Americas: From Good Neighbors to Counterculture* (Oxford: Oxford University Press, 2017), 17.
32 See Jonathan Cohen, "Waldeen and the Americas: The Dance Has Many Faces," accessed Novembre 15, 2022, https://www.jonathancohenweb.com/waldeen.html.
33 Neruda's speech was extremely vehement, and, building on Alexander Fadeyev's anathemas, it attacked T. S. Eliot as well as Jean-Paul Sartre for their "obscene religion of annihilation and disgusting vices" (Neruda, *Let the Rail Splitter Awake*, 14.)

early as 1949 (by the Romanian Workers' Party), into Russian,[34] into Czech and into Chinese (printed in Shanghai) in 1950, into German (Austria), Hungarian, Polish (again) in 1951, and again into German (GDR) in 1955. Waldeen's English translation was printed by the All-India Peace Committee, on the occasion of Neruda's visit to India, with a foreword by Ilya Ehrenburg, which insisted on the reference to Whitman.[35] In other words, Whitman found in Neruda a potent megaphone that carried his voice far into the communist world.

Rendering unto Whitman what belongs to Whitman

In 1949, León Felipe also gave a lecture in Mexico City entitled "España y yo" (Spain and I), which can be read as a response to the end of *Let the Rail Splitter Awake*:

> No vengo a enseñar nada...
> Ni a repartir catecismos... ni consignas...
> ....
> Y no me envía nadie: Ni el demócrata... ni el Tirano... ni el
>   Vaticano... ni el Kremlin.
> No pertenezco a ninguna cofradía...
> y no soy súbdito de ninguna nación...[36]
>
> I am not here to teach anything...
> Nor to hand out catechisms... or instructions...
> ....
> And nobody sends me: Not the Democrat, not the Tyrant...
>   not the Vatican... not the Kremlin.
> I don't belong to any brotherhood...
> and am not the subject of any nation...

Felipe rewrote Neruda's "No vengo a resolver nada" as "No vengo a enseñar nada." In spite of its final turnaround, *Let the Rail Splitter Awake* was in fact Stalinist propaganda, an explicit celebration of the Kremlin and a

---

34 Pablo Neruda, *Da probuditsia lesorub! Stikhi i poèmy* (Moscow: Pravda, "Ogonëk," 1950), 150,000 copies.
35 It bore the title *Peace for Twilights to Come*, from a line at the end of the poem (Mumbai, 1950).
36 León Felipe, *España y el viento* (Madrid: Libertarias/Prodhufi, 1993), 29.

political exposé complete with instructions and orders for action. Felipe implicitly criticized the way Neruda hijacked Whitman's transnationalism for a pseudo-internationalism at the service of the Soviet state; he, on the contrary, was "not the subject of any nation," and was therefore faithful to Whitman's "Salut au Monde!"

That same year, the Chilean Gregorio Gasman published a separate translation of the poem, entitled *Saludo al mundo*, and illustrated by Ernesto Barreda. Gasman was the author of literary columns in the weekly *El Siglo*, the organ of the Chilean Communist Party. In 1943, he referred to Whitman in a contribution on the "responsibility of the poet." It was a wartime essay, in line with the imperative of the period: the poet's responsibility was to "reflect his time, from a human, real, anti-fascist point of view";[37] the same year, he wrote a tribute to Neruda, "the voice of democracy."[38] In his preface to *Saludo al mundo*, Gasman emphasized again the function of the democratic bard. He detailed eight reasons why *Leaves of Grass* was the most important work of American literature: its style, its fame, its personality, its in-progress structure, its international prestige, its influence, its Americanism, and, finally, the fact that it was "the active voice of democracy."[39]

In 1948, the term "democracy" gained yet additional layers of meaning. Videla's government passed the Law of Permanent Defense of Democracy, which banned the Communist Party; the newspaper *El Siglo* was shut down and, from September 1949, published clandestinely, under the name . . . *Democracia*. Although Gasman's preface was not openly Marxist, and used the vocabulary of the Enlightenment, showing that Whitman embodied the ideals of "liberty, equality and fraternity," there could be no misapprehension: Gasman's use of such a lexicon was primarily meant to avoid censorship, and his translation was indeed a pro-communist gesture. Gasman took over from Neruda as translator and advocate of "Salut au Monde!," using it for domestic rather than foreign affairs.

---

37 Gregorio Gasman, "Responsabilidad del poeta," *El Siglo*, April 11, 1943.
38 Gregorio Gasman, "Sobre Pablo Neruda," *El Siglo*, October 10, 1943.
39 Walt Whitman, *Saludo al mundo*, trans. G. Gasman (Santiago de Chile: Ediciones de Librería Neira, 1949), 10.

FIGURE 9.2. Cover of Walt Whitman, *Saludo al mundo*, trans. G. Gasman (Santiago de Chile: Ediciones de Librería Neira, 1949). Illustration Ernesto Barreda. Author's collection.

In 1955, Neruda himself "retranslated" the poem. On the occasion of the hundredth anniversary of *Leaves of Grass*, it was precisely "Salut au Monde!" that he published in *La Gaceta de Chile*. Except that a new appropriation replaced the previous one: Neruda signed in his own hand a translation that was not his at all, since he copied, word for word, with only a few cuts, the first translation of the poem by Armando Vasseur in 1912. One wonders about this choice: Why did Neruda use Vasseur's translation rather than Gasman's? Did Neruda want to return to Vasseur's nuevomundista Whitman and strip him of the combat clothes of the years 1948-1949?[40] But then why did he present himself as the translator? One can only conjecture.

Pedro Mir's *Countersong to Walt Whitman*

Pedro Mir was a Dominican poet with Cuban and Puerto Rican heritage. Like Neruda, Mir went into exile, in 1947, while his country was under the

---

40 The "Ley de Defensa Permanente de la Democracia" was still in force (it was abolished in 1958), even though Neruda had returned from exile and González Videla was no longer in power.

dictatorship of Rafael Trujillo. From then on, Mir's ideological commitments consolidated and he participated in writers' congresses in the early 1950s. At the same time, his poetry became more and more permeated with Whitman. In 1949, he wrote his first long poem, *Hay un país en el mundo* (*There Is a Country in This World*), which was published in Cuba. Its central enumerative sequence was introduced by the verb *miro* (I look) and punctuated by the anaphora *y* (and), a structure, once again, very reminiscent of the catalogues in "Salut au Monde!" However, the enumeration goes off its Whitmanian course, shifting from a survey of natural beauties to an outraging list of exactions. This structure is reminiscent of Neruda's *Que despierte el leñador*, and I would argue that Mir's negotiation with Whitman is also part of an ongoing debate with Neruda, as became more obvious in *Contracanto a Walt Whitman*.

This long poem, published in Guatemala in 1952,[41] takes up the tradition of denouncing the betrayal of Whitman's legacy. It shows how the Whitmanian democratic subject, a representative "I," has been perverted into a conquering and avid "I," how the verb "to have" has replaced the verb "to be." The subtitle of the poem is "Canto a nosotros mismos": song to ourselves. The poem underwent revisions between its first edition and later ones. In 1952, it was dedicated "A LOS PARTIDARIOS DE LA PAZ" (To those who support peace). "Peace" was then the watchword of communist organizations—incidentally, the name of the poet, "Mir" means "peace" (and "world") in Russian. It contained a portrait of Whitman and three epigraphs. The first is from *Miracles of Our Lady*, by Gonzalo de Berceo, the second is loosely translated from Whitman: "Yo, Walt Whitman, un cosmos, / un hijo de Manhattan," and the third is translated from Nikolay Ostrovsky's *How the Steel was Tempered*, a Soviet favorite: "Swept along by the maelstrom of battle Pavel lost all sense of self these days. His individuality merged with the mass and for him, as for every fighting man, the word 'I' was forgotten; only the word 'we' remained: our regiment, our squadron, our brigade."[42] Whitman appears as a stage between religious medieval poetry and the archetype of socialist realism, his "I" in transition from mystical to collectivist. The quote from Ostrovsky is an excellent example of how Soviet literature could be "creatively misinterpreted to fit emancipatory struggles."[43] In subsequent

---

41 By the group Saker-Ti and the Guatemalan committee of Solidarity with the Dominican People.
42 Nikolai Ostrovsky, *How the Steel Was Tempered*, trans. R. Prokofieva, vol. 1 (Moscow: Foreign Languages Publishing House, 1952), 288. Mir gave the quote in Spanish. The English translation of the novel was published the same year as the *Countersong* and could have been the source of the epigraph.
43 Djagalov, *From Internationalism to Postcolonialism*, 16.

(and much later) editions, it was edited out, as an unwelcome trace of Stalinist commitment. It was replaced with the following: "Countersong to a famous poem by Walt Whitman published in 1855 with the title "Song of Myself" and which begins as follows: 'I, Walt Whitman, a cosmos, of Manhattan the son.'" This line, however, was located in the middle of Whitman's poem. To pretend that it was at the beginning is a way to present the opening of *Countersong* as its exact counterpoint: "I, / a son of the Caribbean, / West Indian to be precise," "raw product of a simple / Puerto Rican girl / and a Cuban worker."[44] At first, the subject faithfully reiterates Whitman's process of identification, through enumerations and anaphora: "and I the pioneer and I the gold digger / and I the pioneer and I the gold digger."[45] The sequence ends with a direct quote from "Song of Myself," the same line as in the epigraph, only presented differently:

> y yo
> 　　　¡Walt Whitman,
> 　　　　　　un cosmos,
> 　　un hijo de Manhattan . . . ! (89)

With section 10, the tone changes, as Whitman's democratic ideal appears to have been lost. Mir brings Whitman's harsh diagnosis from *Democratic Vistas* into the poem and updates it:[46] individualism and greed have triumphed on Wall Street, while imperialism is spreading (this is the classic Leninist view of the evolution of capitalism). The "I" becomes imperial in its turn: "Bring me Central America," "Bring me South America." But with section 15, the third phase of *Countersong* is launched: after the initial homage to Whitman and the denunciation of his betrayal, the restoration of his spirit can begin. What makes it possible is the replacement of the first singular person by the plural. *Nosotros* is the new watchword of hope and change:

---

44 "Yo, / un hijo del Caribe, / precisamente antillano." "Producto primitivo de una ingenua criatura borinqueña / y un obrero cubano." Pedro Mir, *Contracanto a Walt Whitman*, in *Poemas* (Madrid: Ediciones de la Discreta, 2009), 81. Translated by Jonathan Cohen in Pedro Mir, *Countersong to Walt Whitman and Other Poems* (Leeds: Peepal Tree Press Limited, 2017), 65.
45 Original: "yo el cowboy yo el aventurero / y yo el pioneer y yo el lavador de oro" (88).
46 José Manuel Batista reads *Contracanto* as a critical response to *Democratic Vistas*, in "Ni cósmico ni democrático: El Contracanto a Walt Whitman de Pedro Mir," *Symposium* 62, no. 4 (Winter 2009): 235–257. On the contrary, Rafael Bernabe has (convincingly) argued that "Mir's *Countersong* tended to save Whitman from some of his ambiguities." In *Walt Whitman and His Caribbean Interlocutors: José Martí, C. L. R. James, and Pedro Mir. Song and Countersong* (Leiden: Brill, 2021), 266.

> Y ahora
> ya no es la palabra
> > yo
> la palabra cumplida
> la palabra de toque para empezar el mundo.
> Y ahora
> ahora es la palabra
> > nosotros. (101)
>
> And now
> it is no longer the word
> > I
> the accomplished word
> the password to begin the world
> And now
> now it is the word
> > we (107)

Mir again adopts Whitman's enumerative technique, prompting the sequences with the anaphora *nosotros* (nosotros los ferroviaros, nosotros los mineros, nosotros los campesinos), which resonates in strategic places.

The poem ends with prophetic stanzas, which conjugate the plural subject in the future tense: the Latin American people and their poets will stand together against cynicism and oppression. Mir restores the spirit of the Whitmanian message, by extending it to the entire continent and substituting the "we" for the "I." As Jonathan Cohen argues, "the section embodies Mir's radical hemispheric vision."[47] It also resonates as an internationalist call, in the context of the defense of "peace," as Mir establishes a distinction between those who make a wrongful use of Whitman and the true "poets to come:"

> Los que no quieren a Walt Whitman el demócrata,
> sino a un tal Whitman atómico y salvaje.
> . . . .
> ¡No, Walt Whitman, aquí están los poetas de hoy
> levantados para justificarte!

---

[47] Jonathan Cohen, "'Countersong to Walt Whitman': Pedro Mir's Radical Dialogue with the Bard," *TIES*, no. 7 (2023), accessed April 10, 2023, http://revueties.org/document/1154-document-sans-titre.

> —¡*Poetas venideros, levantaos, porque vosotros debéis justificarme!*
> Aquí estamos, Walt Whitman, para justificarte.
> Aquí estamos
> > por ti
> > > pidiendo paz.
>
> La paz que requerías
> para empujar el mundo con tu canto. (105)

> Those of you who do not want Walt Whitman, the democrat,
> but another Whitman, atomic and savage.
> . . . .
> No, Walt Whitman, here are the poets of today
> aroused to justify you!
> *Poets to come! . . . Arouse! for you must justify me.*
> Here we are, Walt Whitman, to justify you.
> Here we are
> > for your sake
> > > demanding peace.
>
> The peace you needed
> to drive the world with your song. (115, 117)

Yet, as is often the case with responses to Whitman, the layers of conversation are multiple: the countersong is also addressed to León Felipe, as Pedro Mir much later explained. He said of Felipe's prologue to *Canto a mí mismo*: "These are verses by León Felipe himself, in the style of Whitman, but he expresses in them a position that seems to me to contradict Whitman's vision of democracy, since León Felipe says he prefers the heroic to the democratic, and I feel that the heroic is always the product of war, so I decided to respond."[48] Mir preferred democracy to heroism, peace to war. In *Countersong*, the word "Democracy" shines in all its glory— "resplandeció la palabra / Democracia" (86). The beard is a motif that reappears regularly in the *Countersong*,[49] like a relic from the prophetic Whitman, and a pointer to other intertexts: García Lorca's "Ode to

---

[48] Interview with Coromoto Galvis, accessed January 18, 2023, http://www.cielonaranja.com/mir-galvis.htm. Mir claimed that he could not publish and read his poem as planned in Mexico because of Felipe's opposition. Felipe happened to be the president of the "Amigos de la Paz" association (Friends of Peace), while Mir was attacking him for being bellicose! The poem was published in Guatemala rather than Mexico.

[49] Translation: "your sensitive bard," "your luminous bard," "your unsuspected bard."

Walt Whitman," with the beard "full of butterflies," as well as Neruda's *Let the Rail Splitter Awake*, where Whitman was summoned to "raise his beard of grass."

Indeed, in its logic and structure, *Countersong* resembles Neruda's poem: the evocation of Whitman's ideal democracy in the nineteenth century,[50] followed by a charge against its betrayal—Mir insisting on the capitalist hijacking, Neruda on imperialism—and finally the reinstatement of Whitman as a tutelary figure. Neruda's model was indeed decisive for Mir, who wrote his first great poem in 1949, in Cuba, precisely where Neruda had published *Let the Rail Splitter Awake* a year earlier. José Manuel Batista suggests a Bloomian reading of *There Is a Country in This World*: Mir intended to measure himself against Neruda and to rewrite *Let the Rail Splitter Awake* on a smaller, more local scale.[51] It would argue that this cure for "anxiety of influence" continued in *Contracanto a Walt Whitman*, this time via the master of masters, Whitman. Enrico Mario Santí convincingly shows that "contest or conquest of wills over the most accurate and powerful appropriation of the American bard's legacy" raged between Octavio Paz, Pablo Neruda and Jorge Luis Borges.[52] A parallel and more political discussion also unfolded between Neruda, Felipe and Mir.[53]

León Felipe turned out to be right when he wrote that Whitman brought a signal with "Salut au Monde!": the poem functioned as a baton in a relay of rescripts and partisan uses. These appropriations also raise questions of authorship: poets sometimes explicitly borrow from Whitman, but sometimes directly graft quotes onto their own poems. The series of "Salut au Monde!" also reveal that debates with Whitman were seldom one-on-one dialogues, but rather polyphonic conversations.

---

50 Christopher Conway has suggested that Mir subverted the rhetoric of Manifest Destiny, proposing the restoration of a "Western Arcadia" in the US South. This process implied the idealization of Whitman's America, in particular the avoidance of racial tensions. Christopher Conway, "Of Subjects and Cowboys: Frontier and History in Pedro Mir's '*Countersong to Walt Whitman*,'" *Walt Whitman Quarterly Review* 15, no. 4 (1998): 162. I would argue that the same is true of Neruda.
51 José Manuel Batista has shown that *There Is a Country in the World* reproduces the rhetorical structure of *Let the Rail Splitter Awake*: evocatio, indignatio, admonitio, convertio, conciliatio (humilitas). "In the Shadow of a Giant: Mir's Struggle Against Neruda," *SECOLAS Annals* 38 (2006): 79–92.
52 Enrico Mario Santí, *Ciphers of History: Latin American Readings for a Cultural Age* (New York: Palgrave Macmillan, 2005), 69.
53 On a smaller scale, Whitman was also a reference for the communist Haitian poet René Depestre. He cited the lines "Camerado this is no book / Who touches this touches a man" as an epigraph to his 1952 collection *Traduit du grand large. Poèmes de ma patrie enchaînée* (Translated from the open sea. Poems of my enchained homeland).

3. The centennial of *Leaves of Grass* in 1955

Anniversaries are significant dates for reception studies, especially in terms of official, national and political commemorations. The communist celebrations for the centennial of the first edition of *Leaves of Grass* in 1955 were particularly abundant and marked the apotheosis of Whitman as poet of "world peace."

New Soviet translations, critics and responses

After the war, Chukovsky's versions were still authoritative, but they were increasingly supplemented. New translators, sometimes quite prestigious, contributed to the 1954 and 1955 editions. Samuil Marshak, the likely translator of "Pioneers! O Pioneers!" in 1918, had become very famous as an author for children as well as for his translations of Shakespeare's sonnets and many British Romantic poets. Ivan Kashkin was an acclaimed translator, who had brought on new practices in the 1930s, with the magazine *Internatsional'naia Literatura*; he translated Hemingway, with whom he was in close contact (a character in *For Whom the Bell Tolls* was named after him). Vilgem Levik was also well known: he translated many poets, from Heine to Ronsard. Other names include M. Zenkevich—and, for once, a woman, V. Limanovskaia (whose translation of "Memories of President Lincoln" had been published previously in *Ogonëk* in 1952).

Chukovsky also began to lose his monopoly as "Whitman's propagandist"[54] and critic, as he was joined by Maurice Mendelson, another interesting transatlantic figure. Born in Russia in 1904, he left in 1922 for the US and joined the US Communist Party. He returned to the Soviet Union in 1931; contrary to D. S. Mirsky, he survived the years of Terror and held various teaching positions. After World War II, he taught at the Moscow State Pedagogical Institute of Foreign Languages, where he gave lectures on Twain and Whitman, mostly in English, which was unusual at the time. In 1954, he published an essay[55] on Whitman which was quite influential in the Soviet Union and in some of its satellites—according to Marta Skwara, Mendelson's essay (along with Paul Jamati's) was the main work of criticism about Whitman in Poland after World War II.[56] He also wrote the introduction to the 1954 new edition of *Leaves of Grass*; for the 1955 reprint, he shared that honor with Chukovsky, whose preface contained new ideas. Indeed, for the first time, Chukovsky emphasized Whitman's empathy

---

54 As Chukovsky was called in *Literaturnaia Gazeta*, May 30, 1939, 2.
55 Morris Mendel'son, *Uolt Uitmen: kritiko-biograficheskii ocherk* (Moscow: Gosudarstvennoe izd-vo khudozhestvennoi literatury, 1954).
56 Skwara, *Polski Whitman*, 74.

with the oppressed and his ability to make the reader empathetic too. Chukovsky recognized this "live combination of aesthetics and ethics" in Russian literature. That was the reason why Whitman was appreciated in Russia earlier than in the US. Chukovsky also refuted that Whitman was a mystic and replaced the idea of "cosmic consciousness" with "astronomical knowledge": Whitman translated positive science into sensations. In 1955, there was a flurry of essays in journals and in the press, by Chukovsky and Mendelson, but also Yassen Zassoursky, who later became dean of the School of Journalism at Moscow State University. The journal *Inostrannaia Literatura* (Foreign Literature) was launched that year, in the context of the Thaw: it was the successor of *Internatsional'naia Literatura*, closed down in 1943, and remains the foremost foreign literature journal in Russia. Its first issue contained a presentation and a selection from Whitman: a choice of poems and of prose extracts by new translators, all quite different from the classic Whitman pieces of the past decades. Whitman and Romain Rolland were the only two authors featuring in the section "Classics" (Literaturnoe Nasledie).[57]

The World Peace Council and the 1955 celebrations

In 1954, the WPC (World Peace Council, an organization founded in 1949, considered by the United States to be a communist Trojan horse),[58] listed the authors to be celebrated during the following year in order to build "friendly links" across borders: Schiller, Mickiewicz, Montesquieu, Andersen, Cervantes and Whitman.

In the US, one of the rare homages to a communist and internationalist Whitman was written in . . . Yiddish, a language that could probably evade the Red Hunt of the 1950s more easily than English. Its author was Aaron Kurtz, a poet who already had a long record of leftist collections. In a piece for "the 100th year of the first edition of Leaves of Grass,"[59] Kurtz gathers most stock phrases of Whitman's Yiddish reception: even though America has not lived up to his dream, Whitman is a giant, a "novi" whose voice ("kol") still resonates loud and free. Whitman is once again resurrected, but with Soviet and Maoist twists: he will meet Mao Zedong, Zhou Enlai, and Ho Chi Minh, and listen to

---

57 "Uolt Uitmen," *Inostrannaia Literatura*, July 1955 (no. 1), 160–164.
58 For detailed information on the WPC, see Walter Grünzweig, "Whitman and the Cold War. The Centenary Celebration of *Leaves of Grass* in Eastern Europe," in *Walt Whitman: The Sesquicentennial Essays*, ed. Susan Belasco, Ed Folsom and Kenneth Price (Lincoln: University of Nebraska Press, 2007), 343–360.
59 Aaron Kurtz, "Volt Vitman," *Lider* (New York: Aaron Kurtz Book Committee, 1966), 210–215.

the echo of his songs in Moscow, Prague, Budapest and Warsaw. A selection from Whitman's poetry and prose was put together by "International Publishers," with a reprint of Samuel Sillen's essay on Whitman "poet of Democracy," that is, poet of the masses and spokesman of international ideals. An abridged version was published in the USSR.[60] Sillen, together with Mendelson, provided the standard communist reading for the celebrations. His contribution was also translated into French by Paul Jamati.[61]

Sillen and Jamati were indeed the two authorities on Whitman in France. In 1955, the journal *Horizons. La Revue de la paix*, which had succeeded *Défense de la Paix*, had a special section for the six anniversaries selected by the WPC. Whitman, "the good gray poet," was presented by Jamati again, who focused again on one episode of Whitman's life: how James Harlan investigated accusations against Whitman and fired him from the Bureau of Indian Affairs. Whitman, like Dante, Shakespeare and Cervantes, had not been recognized by his smug contemporaries, but, like them, he could rely on his future audience.[62] Another interesting contribution was the journal *Europe*. In accordance with its guideline (two authors per issue), Whitman was "paired" with the French communist novelist Henri Barbusse, a name that loomed large in the Soviet canon (Barbusse died in Moscow in 1935 while he was writing Stalin's biography). The main presentation was written by the communist Renaud de Jouvenel, who borrowed, he admitted, most of his remarks from Sillen, especially about Whitman's passion for Russia.[63] The issue also contained some poems, and, while "Salut au Monde!" was not part of the anthology, "Years of the Modern" featured twice, in Jamati's and in de Jouvenel's translations (as "Âge moderne" and "Temps modernes"), with its internationalist call: "Are all nations communing? is there going to be but one heart to the globe?"[64] Jamati also wrote an homage to Léon Bazalgette, who introduced Whitman to France: even though Bazalgette overused the words "prophet" and "Gospel," he revealed to other nations, and maybe to the US, that Whitman was a "social poet." Finally, an essay by Maurice Herra, entitled "*Leaves of Grass* in Europe and in Latin America," addresses a global

---

60 Samiuèl Sillen, "Zametki ob Uitemene," *Literaturnaia Gazeta*, June 14, 1955, 4.
61 Samuel Sillen, "Walt Whitman, Poète de la démocratie américaine." *La Pensée, Revue du rationalisme moderne*, no. 69 (September 1956), 77–91; no. 70 (November 1956), 69–82. Jamati explained in his presentation that the threat to American democracy had changed from an external one in 1944 to an internal one in 1956.
62 *Horizons. La Revue de la paix*, nos. 50–51 (July–August, 1955), 156–164.
63 Renaud de Jouvenel, "Walt Whitman," *Europe* 33, no. 119 (November 1955), 91–107.
64 "Temps modernes" is the French translation of Chaplin's movie *Modern Times*, but also evokes *Les Temps modernes*, Jean-Paul Sartre's, Simone de Beauvoir's and Maurice Merleau-Ponty's journal.

Whitman,[65] covering the British, German, French, Italian and even Danish receptions. It noticed how popular Whitman was in France before World War I, while his "naïve enthusiasm" discredited him afterwards. It contrasted the lack of interest for Whitman in Spain with his success in Latin America, and provided a translation of Darío's sonnet to Whitman. Above all, it reaffirmed that Whitman's success was most spectacular in Russia and reiterated the Soviet narrative: while Balmont was "unfaithful" (his English was so bad that he replaced Whitman's "lilacs" with "lilies"),[66] Chukovsky's work was impeccable; Whitman had a strong influence on several Soviet poets (Khlebnikov, Larionov, Oredezh, Mayakovsky), whom he helped find themselves. Herra even quoted the Soviet literary encyclopedia to find a cause for this success: Whitman's sense of "collectivism."

In the Soviet Union, a brochure detailed all "the bibliographical and methodical material to help large libraries," following the recommendations of the WPC. The presentation of the poetry, inspired by Mendelson's 1954 essay, insisted that the bourgeois literati were doing all they could to prevent access to Whitman's legacy, and did not hesitate to distort and falsify the contents of his poetry. Conversely, Stalin held the life-oriented spirit and optimism of Whitman's poetry in very high regard, and contrasted it with the "global philosophy of despair." It contained a list of eighteen poems to be read, mostly the classic political pieces, "Europe," "Spain 1873–74," "The Mystic Trumpeter," "To a Foiled European Revolutionaire," "For you O Democracy." It outlined the program of a Whitman evening, including the specific pages to read from the poems listed, as well as prose extracts (like Whitman's "letter to the Russian people"). It also included material for exhibits: quotes from Lenin (about the revolutionary tradition of the American people) and from Whitman (about the people and love for freedom). It even specified which illustration to use: once again, Pearsall's portrait. According to a report on the Whitman evening at the Moscow Conservatory, the presentation by Mendelson and the reading by Chukovsky were followed by a concert.[67]

Walter Grünzweig has demonstrated the similar role of the WPC in Eastern Germany, Poland and Czechoslovakia. Whitman's life, work and reception were presented in the same fashion. Grünzweig also emphasizes the role of exiled communists, the American Abraham Chapman in Czechoslovakia (under the name Abe Capek) and the British George Bidwell in Poland, author of an essay translated by his Polish wife. Regarding Eastern Germany, he mentions

---

65 Maurice Herra, "'Feuilles d'herbe' en Europe et en Amérique latine," 137–145.
66 The remark actually came directly from Chukovsky, who liked to point out Balmont's mistakes.
67 *Literaturnaia Gazeta*, June 14, 1955, 1.

the airing of music and poems by Whitman on July 3, and provides details of a lecture and recitation at Leipzig University in December. With respect to Poland, Grünzweig describes a celebration on December 30, with "enactments" of Whitman's poetry, set to Native American and African music. Marta Skwara, for her part, notes the composition of some thirty articles on Whitman in Poland, across a broad range of publications, and remarks that they always contained the same pictures and the same biographical information, mostly originating from Mendelson. All this was, therefore, very much in line with the Soviet celebrations.

The Czech reception, however, seems to have been less homogeneous. What stands out is a new translation by the poet and future dissident Jiří Kolář, in collaboration with Zdeněk Urbánek. At the time, Kolář was in a difficult position, since he had been labeled as "reactionary" in 1948 and had spent a year in jail in 1953 after the manuscript of *Prometheus's liver* was found. To be more precise, there were two translations, for two different publishing houses, which present some revisions. Ivá Malková's research in the archive of the Publishing House Československý spisovatel reveals that the idea of translating Whitman came from Kolář himself (as early as 1952), and that the work was ready by 1954 (it is possible that Kolář worked on it while imprisoned).[68] In other words, it was not a state command for the particular occasion of the anniversary. In his preface, Kolář underscored, like all the communist Whitmanians of his time, the fact that Whitman suffered from being harshly criticized: in this case, it is hard not to see an analogy between the poet's fate and his translator's.

I would also like to draw attention to the remarkable Hungarian edition of Whitman, published in 1955. It was based on the same principle as the 1954 Soviet one: it reprinted existing translations (by Árpád Pásztor, Zoltán Jékely) and added new ones by many different translators. Several of them stand out, as they became quite famous in the history of Hungarian literature, such as Magda Szábo and László Lator. György Faludy translated "A Prayer for Columbus." Faludy was a Jewish poet who had fled Hungary in 1938 and served in the US army. He was arrested after his return in 1946 and confessed to the communist state security forces that he was a spy—which was not true, as his interrogators could have guessed from the names of the Western contacts that he gave: Captain Edgar Allan Poe and . . . Major Walt Whitman.[69] In 1949, he was sent to Recsk camp (known as the "Hungarian Gulag"), with many other intellectuals. When he returned three years later, he threw himself into translation, and in 1956, he was able to leave Hungary for London.

---

68 Ivá Malková, "Kolář – Whitman," *Literární Archiv*, no. 46 (2014): 177–194.
69 György Faludy, *My Happy Days in Hell* (New York: William Morrow & Co., 1963), 288.

The WPC script was also followed in China, as Xilao Li and Guiyou Huang discuss.[70] A conference was organized in November 1955, with invitations sent to Paul Robeson and Samuel Sillen. Zhou Yang made a speech about Whitman's revolutionary character and the betrayal of his ideals in contemporary America. Essays by Maurice Mendelson and Abe Capek were translated into Chinese. At that point, Moscow really was the site where the communist world literature canon was built. The selection of Whitman's poems, translated by Chu Tunan, which had been published only a few months before the Proclamation of the People's Republic of China in 1949, was reprinted by the People's Literature Press, with a new preface emphasizing the political Whitman. This revival did not last, since even before the Cultural Revolution, in 1959, an influential poet, He Qifang, criticized Guo Moruo for adopting all the dangerous aspects of Whitman's poetry. This put an end to Whitman's reception in China for twenty years.[71] In any case, 1955 marked a remarkable moment of global communist synchronization, before the Sino-Soviet split.

Yevtushenko and Neruda: watermelons and strawberries

The centennial had less official repercussions. Two contemporary poems were written in its wake, by poets who would later meet and write about each other: Yevgeny Yevtushenko and Pablo Neruda. In 1955, Yevtushenko mentioned Whitman in a poem that appears to be the first instance of creative reception in Russian since Mayakovsky. In "Prologue," he declares that he feels close to Yesenin and Whitman ("Mne blizki i Esenin, i Uitmen"). Yevtushenko embraces the American's persona, his claims to universal dilation, his embrace of self-contradiction ("I'm overworked, and idle too [ia natruzhennyi i prazdnyi]" and his wish to dissolve into the grass to grow from it again:

> Пою и пью,
>   не думая о смерти,
> раскинув руки,
>   падаю в траву,
> и если я умру на белом свете,
> то я умру от счастья, что живу.

---

70 Xilao Li, "Walt Whitman in China," *Walt Whitman Quarterly Review* 5, no. 3 (Spring 1986): 1–8; Guiyou Huang, "Whitman in China," *Whitman and the World*, 412–413.
71 See Xilao Li's bibliography in *Walt Whitman Quarterly Review* 5, no. 3 (Spring 1986): 43–47.

>   I sing and drink,
>   giving no thought to death;
>   with arms outspread
>   I fall upon the grass,
>   and if, in this wide world, I come to die,
>   then it's certain to be
>   from sheer joy that I live.⁷²

The poet also loves to crunch "cool scarlet slices of watermelon." The watermelon is a recurring motif in Whitman's reception. It probably originates in an anecdote from Peter Doyle, Whitman's intimate friend. Doyle told Richard Maurice Bucke about a time in 1865 when he and Walt bought a watermelon in Washington, DC, cut it in pieces and ate it on the sidewalk. When some people snickered at them, Whitman said: "They can have the laugh, we have the melon."⁷³ In his April Fool's Day account of Whitman's funeral (1913), Guillaume Apollinaire imagined heaps of watermelons. Ezra Pound used that motif in a parody of Whitman: "Lo, behold, I eat water melons. When I eat water melons the world eats water melons through me. When the world eats water melons, // I partake of the world's water melons."⁷⁴ In 1955, Allen Ginsberg pictured Federico García Lorca "down by the watermelons" in "A Supermarket in California." Ginsberg's poem was published in English in 1956 and translated into Russian in 1961 (in *Inostrannaia Literatura*). It is not very likely that Yevtushenko knew Ginsberg's poem when he wrote "Prologue," but the coincidence is intriguing.

Neruda's "Ode to Walt Whitman" was published as a conclusion to the collection *New Elementary Odes* in 1956, but was written in the course of 1955. The odes are a watershed in Neruda's poetry, with a new focus on the everyday, on nature, matter and objects. The poem to Whitman, however, shows that political struggle was still on the poetic agenda. The beginning is a tribute to Whitman's role as a poet of nature and great American expanses. Neruda explains how, in the wet Chilean South, he touched Walt Whitman's hand and walked barefoot on his "firm dew" (firme rocío).⁷⁵ Whitman taught Neruda to see and grasp his surroundings firsthand, "to be American." He is represented "gallivanting through the alfalfa / gathering the poppies," and rushing into

---

72 Yevgeny Yevtushenko, *The Poetry of Yevgeny Yevtushenko, 1952–1963*, trans. and ed. George Reavey, bilingual ed. (New York: October House, 1965), 4–7. Revised translation in Yevgeny Yevtushenko, *The Collected Poems, 1952–1990* (New York: Henry Holt and Company, 1991), 21–22.
73 Richard Maurice Bucke, *Calamus* (Boston: Maynard, 1897), 41.
74 Ezra Pound, *The Spirit of Romance* (London: J. M. Dent & sons, 1910), 179.
75 Pablo Neruda, *Nuevas odas elementales*, in *Obras Completas*, 2:428.

the kitchens at nightfall. This bucolic scene resuscitates the nuevomundista Whitman. However, its content and form belong to Neruda and owe nothing to his predecessor. The landscape is typically Chilean: the alfalfa and the poppies are recurring motifs throughout Neruda's verse and they are always strongly associated with Chile. The style, patently metaphorical, as well as the very short lines, are distinctively Nerudean. In other words, Neruda demonstrates that he understood Whitman's lesson: "He most honors my style who learns under it to destroy the teacher." (LG 73). This was indeed a regular point in his comments about Whitman: "'Nothing exterior shall ever take command of me,' said Walt Whitman. And the paraphernalia of literature, with all its merits, should never be a substitute for creation."[76] And again: "Walt Whitman was a great comrade (*compañero*) for me. I have not been very Whitmanian in my style, but I am profoundly Whitmanian in receiving his vital lesson."[77]

However, just like in *Let the Rail Splitter Awake*, the beginning of the poem functions as a benign preamble that paves the way for a radical use of Whitman in the second half. Indeed, it was "not only" the land that Whitman was looking for: he also dug up "man," "the humiliated slave," and he sent a small basket of strawberries to the miner buried underground. From the slave to the miner, from the nineteenth century to 1956, men have been supported and galvanized by Whitman, who is enlisted again for communist struggles. He is called a "good baker" (*buen panadero*), a metaphor that Neruda regularly used for civil poets, who provide essential food to the people—one thinks of the poem "Artes poética (I)" (in *Fin de mundo*) or his Nobel Prize acceptance speech. Whitman's message resisted the assaults of McCarthyism and imperialism: current persecutions have not crushed yet the grass of his book, "the vital source of its freshness." (431) The people, black as well as white, will convene and rebel again:

>   tu pueblo
>   blanco
>   y negro,
>   pueblo
>   de pobres,
>   pueblo simple
>   como
>   todos
>   los pueblos,

---

76 Neruda, *Obras completas*, 5:772. The quote is from Neruda's memoirs. He also wrote down this line on the front page of his copy of the first edition of *Leaves of Grass*.

77 Pablo Neruda, "Interview with Rita Guilbert (1970)," in *Obras Completas*, 5:1154.

no olvida
tu campana:
se congrega cantando
bajo
la magnitud
de tu espaciosa vida:
entre los pueblos con tu amor camina
acariciando
el desarrollo puro
de la fraternidad sobre la tierra. (432–433)

your people
white
and black
poor
people
simple people
as
all
the people,
do not forget
your bell:
they meet
under the vastness
of your spacious life
among the peoples with your love they advance
caressing
the pure development
of brotherhood on earth.

Neruda transforms the *Liberty Bell*, a symbol of American independence taken up by the abolitionists, into a communist bell updating a biblical message: "Proclaim liberty through all the land unto all the inhabitants thereof" (Leviticus 25:10). The last lines weave together all the watchwords of his political poetry: *pueblo, amor, caminar, tierra*. The ode thus encapsulates his changing attitudes toward Whitman, from following a geographical and continental model to "unburying" the bard for partisan uses.

In 1941, León Felipe had referred to "Salut au Monde!" as a "signal." That signal was picked up and transformed into a communist motto, a rallying cry for "peace" in the decade that followed the war. Latin America became the center of the Whitmanian Left, with a combination of internationalism and pan-Americanism. Yet Whitman was seldom a reference for anticolonial struggles outside Latin America, whose resources were often spoiled by US and multinational companies and whose politics suffered outside interference, but which was not strictly speaking in a colonial situation. A more thorough research should be done for Asia and Africa, but, at least in African texts written in European languages, Whitman does not seem to have had much appeal for anti-imperialist voices. Even with such limitations, Whitmanian internationalism extended its reach during this period, as the 1955 celebrations revealed. While Whitman's presence would later recede from that global space, especially after Maoist China's isolation, it would wax stronger again in the United States. The year 1955 was also a watershed in that regard: it was when Allen Ginsberg wrote and read aloud in Berkeley his poem "A Supermarket in California." Even though Ginsberg did not have a communist agenda, the poem picked up the tradition of opposing the Whitmanian pastoral to the current ills of society. By placing Whitman next to García Lorca, the poem also initiated a reconciliation between the political and the gay Whitman. In the following years, Whitman was a shared reference for the Latin American Left and the Beat Generation.

Chapter 10

Back from the USSR (1955–1980s)

After the climax of 1955, Whitman's presence was less conspicuous in the Eastern bloc, but he remained a classic of Soviet literature, with a flurry of translations in the various languages of the Union. In the 1960s and 1970s, Whitman was again a leftist reference in the US, in the context of the Vietnam War and the emergence of the counterculture. Whitman was back from the USSR, but this was not a direct trip. In most cases, the immediate link with the Soviet Whitman was indeed weakened, especially in comparison with the "Red Whitman" of the 1930s. However, the domestic political Whitman remained strongly transnational, mostly through a Latin American detour, and, again, the mediation of Pablo Neruda. The connection between American and Russian poets through Whitman continued to exist, but changed direction: Allen Ginsberg, who contributed to the resurrection of the political Whitman, introduced a liberal, almost dissident Whitman in the USSR. More generally, a major characteristic of this period is the reconciliation of the political poet with the poet of the body.

1. A Soviet classic

In the USSR, Whitman remained a classic. After 1955, both Chukovsky's translations and the collective one were regularly reprinted. The 1970 revised edition added translations by Boris Slutsky, who was then a major name of Soviet poetry—he was also an acclaimed translator from Yiddish. This edition was supplemented in 1982: for the first time, Whitman's poetry was entirely translated into Russian.[1] Whitman was also translated into several other languages of the union—as were many foreign authors of the Soviet canon, from Jack London to Victor Hugo. The 1969 issue of *Soviet Life* (a Soviet magazine published in the US) stated that Whitman was available in 320,000 copies and six languages in the USSR. In 1982, at a conference in Camden, Yassen Zassoursky mentioned a dozen languages. However, no detail was provided in either case. The translators in charge were usually poets or recognized writers: such was the case for Antanas Miškinis in Lithuania (1959),[2] Mirdza Ķempe and Rihards Rudzītis in Latvia (1960),[3] Boris Kabur in Estonia (1962),[4] Vitaly Korotich in Ukraine (1969),[5] Mukagali Mukataev in Kazakhstan (1969), Suyunbai Eraliev in Kyrgyzstan (1970),[6] Yanka Sipakov in Belorussia (1978).[7] The Georgian translation, published in 1966, was the result of a collaboration: among the translators was Lana Gogoberidze, who had written her dissertation on Whitman at Tbilisi University in 1954,[8] and later became a famous film director and politician. "Song of Myself" was entirely translated into Ukrainian in 1977 by Les' Herasymchuk:[9] while it was followed by a classic Soviet presentation (Whitman exemplified Marx's idea that all aspects of life had to be taken into account, he was close to exiled socialists in the US, who might have influenced his views, and he paid a lot of attention to the Commune de Paris), it was in itself an interesting choice and a move from the usual selections. Herasymchuk explained that he had to compromise with the journal editor: the presentation was a concession. He translated a more substantial collection in 1984.[10]

---

1 Uolt Uitmen, *List'ia travy* (Moscow: Khudozhestvennaia literatura, 1982).
2 Uoltas Vitmenas, *Žolės lapai* (Vilnius: Grožinė literatūra, 1959).
3 Volts Vitmens, *Zāļu stiebri* (Riga: LVI, 1960).
4 Walt Whitman, *Rohulehed* (Tallinn: Eesti Riiklik Kirjastus, 1962; preface Rein Sepp).
5 Uolt Uitmen, *Lystia travy: Poeziï* (Kyiv: Dnipro, 1969; preface V. Koptilov); Vitaly Korotich later became the popular editor in chief of the journal *Ogonëk* in the late 1980s.
6 Uolt Uitmen, *Jalbıraktar: Irlar* (Frunze: n.p., 1970). Suyunbai Eraliev was National Poet of Kyrgyz SSR in 1974 and was awarded many prizes.
7 Uolt Uitmien, *Listsie travy* (Minsk: Mastats. lit., 1978). The translation was advertised in *Soviet Life* (no. 269 [February 1979], 62). The cover of the book was, again, illustrated with Pearsall's photograph.
8 Its title was "Criticism of American reality in the work of Walt Whitman." In 1966, she published a book that was drawn from it.
9 Uolt Uitmen, "Pisnia pro samogo sebe," *Vsesvit*, 1977 (no. 2), 136–182.
10 Uolt Uitmen, *Poeziï* (Kyiv: Dnipro, 1984).

The Baltic translators suffered from the harsh repressive policies of Soviet occupation after World War II. Boris Kabur, an author of children's books and a translator (he also translated Longfellow) was arrested in 1947 and sent to Siberia, where he had to stay until 1954. Antanas Miškinis, a professor, poet and translator (from English and Russian), was arrested in 1948 and sent to a labor camp. Upon his return in 1956, he worked intensely on his own poetry and on translations. Two translators contributed to the Latvian edition. Mirdza Ķempe, a known poet and translator, was a member of the Writers' Union. Her position was very different from that of Rihards Rudzītis, head of the Latvian Roerich Society and author of a book about N. Roerich, arrested as an "enemy of the people" in 1948, held in a Komi camp and sent to a gulag in Kazakhstan. He was liberated after Stalin's death but his works remained banned. Contrary to Miškinis and Kabur, who "repented" and became members of the Union of Writers, Rudzītis died an outcast in 1960, the same year as the new Latvian Whitman was published. As in the case of the Hungarian poet György Faludy, it is difficult to make sense of the grim contrast between Whitman's poetry and the hardships most of the translators were going through or were just coming back from.

As for critical discourse, Maurice Mendelson became the main authority on Whitman in the 1960s and 1970s. His influential 1954 essay was followed by a book,[11] which, again, emphasized Whitman's socialist awareness, and paid attention to the evolutions of his political thought. His studies were circulated in the West by Soviet networks (the monograph was translated into English and published by Progress Press in 1976). Chukovsky seems to have been quite annoyed at the competition and wrote rancorous comments in his diary.[12] The title of his last important contribution, *My Whitman* (1966), probably bears witness to his mood. However, one can also understand the title as an attempt to distance himself from the official Whitman and document a more personal relationship—in the same way that Marina Tsvetaeva's *My Pushkin* resisted "Our Pushkin." One of the last Soviet contributions on Whitman was Tatiana Venediktova's dissertation in 1982. After that, Whitman seems to have withered away in what is sometimes referred to as the "bezvozdushnoie prostranstvo" (airless space) of the early 1980s.

---

11 Maurice Mendel'son, *Zhizn' i tvorchestvo Uitmena* (Moscow: Nauka, 1965).
12 "The reader is not as interested in young Whitman's political convictions as M-son imagines, and in general, political convictions are the superficial part of Whitman, not the deep one. Think of the idiot who would characterize Fet's poetry by his political convictions." (Chukovskii, *Dnevnik*, 2:227, on April 1, 1955).

Maurice Mendelson opened the English version of his Whitman study with an evocation of the 1955 and 1969 anniversaries: "Both these dates left an indelible mark on the minds of the thousands—many, many thousands—of men and women in the land where I live, the Union of Soviet Socialist Republics."[13] It is difficult to assess the veracity of this statement, but one can say that, while Whitman was less and less referred to by poets and artists, he remained a figure in "popular culture."[14] As an example, he was mentioned in a 1975 musical film entitled *Smok i malysh* (Smoke and the kid), an adaptation of Jack London's *Smoke Bellew*[15]—Jack London was by far the most prominent American prose writer of the Soviet canon and the film was part of the celebrations scheduled for his centennial. It was shot in the Murmansk region (as an equivalent of London's Klondike). At some point, the main character, played by the popular actor Beniamin Smekhov, reads quite a long section from "Song of the Open Road" to his fellow traveler, who thrills to his words, and only interrupts to exclaim: "Let's go, then."

Though Whitman was not during these years a major reference for poets, a few instances of creative reception are noteworthy, especially in languages other than Russian. In 1961, the Lithuanian Justinas Marcinkevičius started his "Publicist poem" with an epigraph from Whitman, "Žodžiai yra mūsų kunai": "Words are our bodies." It reverses Whitman's declaration: "Human bodies are words." It is a poem about the poet's mother, about mourning, and about language, quite far from the usual political uses of Whitman. Another Lithuanian instance is a poem by Eduardas Mieželaitis, who won the Lenin Prize in 1962 for his work *Žmogus* (Man), and was able to travel to many countries, including the US. He wrote "Niagara Falls or a Walk with Walt Whitman," a long poem addressing Whitman. It contains two lines in English, after one of Whitman's "inscriptions": "And mind the word of the modern, / the word En-Masse." "Mind" instead of "mine" could be a simple typo, but it was never corrected and Mieželaitis's translators kept the alteration. Indeed, it updates Whitman's democratic message: "the great sun of democracy which Whitman sang / is setting on this continent. Today it rises / over the Old World from the continent

---

13 Mendelson, *Walt Whitman*, 7.
14 The distinction between highbrow and popular culture makes little sense in a system controlled by the state. By "popular culture," I refer to the Soviet entertainment industry, which produced comedies, Westerns and Easterns.
15 The film was in Russian but the production and the director, Raimondas Vabalas, were Lithuanian.

of socialism."¹⁶ This is the classic communist scenario: Whitman and his democracy are resurrected in the USSR, and then disseminated to other countries. Yet the poem is mostly an ars poetica, more concerned with the words themselves, "words en masse," a "waterfall of words" that can "no longer can be squeezed / into the confines of iambics, dactyls and the rest." The poem goes back to the emphasis on free verse and on the chaotic, torrential eloquence that characterized Whitman's reception before the revolution.¹⁷ Both Marcinkevičius's and Mieželaitis's poems were translated into Russian. Mieželaitis was presented as an heir to Whitman.¹⁸

In a posthumous 1967 collection, a piece by the Ukrainian poet Oleksii Bulyga was entitled "Legend of Walt Whitman."¹⁹ The collection was called "Resurrection" and dealt mainly with themes of nature and immortality. Whitman was indeed resurrected and given voice in the poem. But it is above all the insistence on vegetation cycles, on the leaves that fall in order to sate the earth and grow again that makes it distinct from the typical Whitman Soviet version. The regularity of the six rhyming quatrains adds to its cyclical sense.

In 1980, Andrii Chuzhyi published his first collection of poems. As discussed in Chapter 2, Chuzhyi was the co-founder of the Uman "Walt Whitman Boundless" in 1921. He was arrested in the 1930s and spent some twenty years (until Stalin's death) in the Gulag system and in exile. Upon his return, he wrote poetry again, although almost none of it was published. Whitman remained a model for him throughout the years. Between 1951 and 1965, he wrote the long poem "A young grand-father on Whitmanian roads":

> Останнім часом
> я постійно спілкуюся з Уолтом Уїтменом,
> бо в дорогах без нього ніяк не можна!
> І його настрої, вкладені в «Листя трави»,
> стали моїми, й це мені не заважає
> бути самим собою,

---

16 Eduardas Mieželaitis, "Niagaros Krioklys, arba pasivaikščiojimas su Voltu Vitmenu," in *Barokinė Lyra* (Vilnius: Lietuvos rašytojų sąjungos leidykla, 2009), 142; trans. D. Rottenberg, *All poetry*, accessed September 24, 2023, https://allpoetry.com/Niagara-Falls,-Or-A-Walk-With-Walt-Whitman.
17 See Elena Baliutytė-Riliškienė, *Eduardas Mieželaitis tarp Rytų ir Vakarų: pasivaikščiojimas su Waltu Whitmanu ir staugsmas su Allenu Ginsbergu* (Eduardas Mieželaitis between East and West: a walk with Walt Whitman and a ride with Allen Ginsberg) (Vilnius: Lietuvių literatūros ir tautosakos institutas, 2019).
18 Boris Gilenson, "Poet of the World. Poet of Time and Space," *Soviet Life*, no. 6 (June 1969), 47.
19 Oleksii Bulyha, "Legenda Uitmena," in *Skresinnia* (Kyiv: Molod', 1967), 59–60.

оскільки може претендувати
на самостійність той,
хто всесвіт своєї душі
будує зі всесвітів великих поетів,
мислителів минулого й сучасного.[20]

Lately
I've been in constant contact with Walt Whitman,
because one can't do without him on the road!
And his moods, which he put into *Leaves of Grass*,
have become mine, and that doesn't stop me
from being myself,
because the only one who can claim
to be independent,
is he who builds the universe of his soul
from the universes of great poets,
thinkers of the past and the present.

Again, Whitman is not evoked for political purposes, but as a model of autonomy, of the compatibility of outside influences with truth to one's self. Between 1968 and 1973, Chuzhyi wrote the poem "I am wearing the Wandering Jew's raincoat (Dream)." In a dream, the poet contemplates himself, his face the face of "Whitman from Uman," his shirt open, before taking to the road with a few books in a bundle (among them, *Leaves of Grass* and Grigori Skovoroda's *Garden of Songs*). In 1980, Whitman still represented for Chuzhyi originality, authentic experience and poetry:

Я знаю
як важко після Уїтмена
бути своєрідним
Він же все своєрідне
побачив
понюхав
прослухав
покуштував
до всього доткнувся

---

20 Andrii Chuzhyi, "Molodyi didus' na uitmenivs'kykh dorohakh," in *Poezii*, 63. *Didus'* is a diminutive.

> очима
> руками
> душею
> і розповів про це.²¹

> I know
> how hard it is to be unique
> after Whitman.
> For everything that is unique
> he saw
> he smelled
> he listened to
> he tasted
> he touched everything
> with his eyes
> hands
> soul
> and told about it.

Whitman also remained a reference in the Soviet satellites, especially in Eastern Germany. As an example, Walter Grünzweig mentions a poem by Gabriele Eckart, which embraces the tradition of talking back to Whitman. Were he still alive, Whitman would sing in "endless wonder" of crowds, of millions of faces, of children in the shade of lilac trees. Instead of the usual prosopopoeia, the poem suggests a relay, as Eckart will substitute for Whitman in the present time:

> doch du bist tot, Walt Whitman,
> deshalb sei mein Lehrer; lehr mich deine Rhythmen!
> ich singe statt deiner!²²

> but you're dead, Walt Whitman,
> so be my teacher; teach me your rhythms!
> I will sing in your place!

---

21 "Ia znaiu," in ibid., 42.
22 Gabriele Eckart, "An Walt Whitman," in Bernd Jentzsch, ed., *Ich nenn euch mein Problem. Gedichte der Nachgeborenen* (Wuppertal: Peter Hammer, 1971), reproduced in Allen and Folsom, *Walt Whitman and the World*, 218–219.

Grünzweig observes that Whitman "not only received official support but was read by young people; official and popular interest coincided in a strange way." Indeed, Whitman was used by many young readers "in order to undertake a literary voyage to a country that had so many mythical connotations."[23] Yet the coincidence was not perfect, since the Whitman who was officially supported might not have been exactly the same as the one who was privately appreciated.

2. Pablo Neruda as Whitmanian go-between

Nerudean repercussions

Neruda's role was quite central in the communication of Whitman's political uses. In France, Whitman was among the poets celebrated by Louis Aragon in his collection *The Poets* (1960). Aragon was very close to Neruda, for whom he wrote several poems. Even though, in this case, the connection was not explicit, I would argue that Aragon's Whitman bears resemblance with the poet who was walking on the Chilean shores at the beginning of Neruda's ode. He is the poet of incarnation, the one who "bequeathed himself to grow from the grass."

> À toi géant triste et superbe
> D'où la manne des mots émane
> Poète vert des *Feuilles d'herbe*
> Ciel ou prairie ô Walt Whitman
> Vieil homme en blanc Chair faite verbe[24]

> To you, sad and superb giant
> From whom the manna of words emanates
> Green poet of *Leaves of Grass*
> Sky or prairie O Walt Whitman
> Old man in white Flesh made into word.

With Erich Arendt's new German translation of Whitman in 1966, it was, rather, Neruda's partisan Whitman who was put to the fore. Arendt was a writer and translator with many links to Spanish-language Whitmania: he fled Nazism

---

23 Grünzweig, *Constructing the German Whitman*, 160.
24 Louis Aragon, "Prologue," in *Les Poètes* (1960), in *Œuvres poétiques complètes*, vol. 2 (Paris: Gallimard, "Pléiade," 2007), 353.

in 1933, joined the International Brigades in Spain, and went into exile in Colombia from 1941 to 1950, before returning to the newly established GDR. He translated many Spanish poets, especially those of the Spanish Civil War (Vicente Alexandre, Miguel Hernández), and several collections by Neruda, starting with *Canto general* in 1953. In 1955, his translation of *Let the Rail Splitter Awake* was published separately, with the more directly rousing title *Holzfäller, wach auf!* (Woodcutter, wake up!) and the addition of a subtitle "Hymn to Peace."[25] Whitman was the only poet whom Arendt translated from English, for *Volk und Welt*, a publishing house founded in 1947 and dedicated to Soviet and anti-fascist texts.[26] It was likely Neruda who introduced Whitman to Arendt, and this East German Whitman appeared to be very Nerudean indeed. The cover of the book resembled an illustration of *Let the Rail Splitter Awake* in which a bat-flown American Capitol was trying the crush the allegory of Peace.

FIGURE 10.1. Cover of Walt Whitman, *Lyrik und Prosa* (Berlin: Volk und Welt, 1966). Author's collection.

---

25 Pablo Neruda, *Holzfäller, wach auf! Hymnus auf den Frieden* (Leipzig: Insel, 1955).
26 Walt Whitman, *Lyrik und Prosa* (Berlin: Volk und Welt, 1966). Arendt translated the poetry and Helmut Heinrich the prose.

A final companion

Neruda himself returned to Whitman a few years after his "Ode," in a different context, although still from a Cold War perspective. In the 1969 collection *Fin de Mundo* (End of the World), he lamented once again the loss of past America ("What has this nation turned into / What have Lincoln and Whitman turned into?"),[27] before unleashing invectives against the "Estados Escupidos" (Covetous States). While acknowledging that Whitman did not belong to the present because "his name is nineteenth century,"[28] Neruda insisted that Whitman was still accompanying him and his contemporaries, because there was "no one else."

Indeed, Whitman accompanied Neruda in his last political activities and last poems. In 1970, Salvador Allende was elected president of the Chilean Republic and his government, the Unidad Popular, a left-wing alliance, proceeded to nationalize the huge copper mines of the Northern provinces. As this was against the interests of American companies, the United States financed the destabilization of the country. Neruda, who actively supported Allende's campaign, was appointed Chilean ambassador to France during his term. This context is essential to understand his last references to Whitman.

In 1972, Neruda delivered a speech at the Pen Club in New York City: "I have come to renegotiate my debt with Walt Whitman."[29] He had just taken part in a meeting about Chile's public debt, and his entire speech mixed reports on it with declarations of admiration for Whitman, establishing a parallel between financial debt and intellectual or artistic debt. Whitman was his greatest "creditor," the first "totalizing" poet, and his qualities were those of a "leader."[30] In other words, his most important debt came from culture and literature, and it was a debt that could be paid back in many ways. The speech then shifted to foreign policy, drawing a parallel between Whitman's postcolonial situation and that of newly independent countries, before returning to the Chilean context. At that point, Neruda did not refer to Whitman, but to Coleridge: he mentioned the end of *The Rime of the Ancient Mariner* and the punishment hanging over the murderer of the albatross—the dense and enigmatic symbol in Coleridge becoming an allegory for the predicament of Chile.

---

27 Pablo Neruda, "Y aquella nación qué se hizó? / Lincoln y Whitman qué se hicieron?" Neruda, *Obras completas*, 3:422.
28 Pablo Neruda, "Se llama Siglo Diecinueve," in ibid., 3:438.
29 It is also known in English as "We Live in a Whitmanesque Age" (*New York Times*, April 14, 1972).
30 "Vengo a renegociar mi deuda con Walt Whitman." Neruda, *Obras completas*, 5:358-359.

A few months later, Neruda enlisted Whitman again, in a more explicit fashion, and with even more vehemence than in *Let the Rail Splitter Awake*. Between December 1972 and January 1973, he wrote the provocative and radical collection *Incitement to Nixonicide and Eulogy of the Chilean Revolution*. The preface, entitled "peremptory explanation," presented the poem as the execution post (*paredón*) of the tyrant, in this case Nixon, and the poet as the executioner: "Now get ready, I'm going to shoot."[31] In the very first poem, Whitman is called upon to shoot with him:

> Es por acción de amor a mi país
> que te reclamo, hermano necesario,
> viejo Walt Whitman de la mano gris,
>
> para que con tu apoyo extraordinario
> verso a verso matemos de raíz
> a Nixon, presidente sanguinario. (709)
>
> It is out of love for my country
> that I summon you, my necessary brother,
> old Walt Whitman with a grey hand,
>
> so that with your extraordinary help
> verse by verse, we kill at the root,
> Nixon, the bloodthirsty president.

These circumstantial poems aim at effective slogans rather than subtle rhythms and images. Neruda uses the *terceto encuardenado*, a Spanish adaptation of Dante's terza rima from the Baroque tradition. It was the tercet used by Quevedo in his satirical sonnets, and already adapted by Neruda during the Spanish Civil War. And while Whitman "old brother / of the ancient America, splendor" opens the whole collection, Alonso de Ercilla, "the imperishable," is called at his side to end it. In his epic *La Araucana*, the Spanish soldier and poet praised the Mapuche and their resistance. Neruda blends his own voice with that of Ercilla in the following poem, "We speak together" (Juntos hablamos)—a variation on "Let's sing together" (Cantemos juntos) in *Let the Rail Splitter Awake*. The last words, in capital letters, are Ercilla's: Chile will not be defeated, "NI A EXTRANJERO DOMINIO SOMETIDA" (nor subject to foreign power [741]). The date of

---

31 "Ahora, firmes, que voy a disparar!"—*Incitación al nixonicidio y alabanza de la revolución chilena*, in Neruda, *Obras completas*, 3:707 (first ed. editorial Quimantú, 1973).

1973, mentioned at the very end, gives them new significance. The process recalls León Felipe's idea: to quote in a different context excerpts from past poets, from "the great preexisting poem," is a way to update them and to change their meanings. Anachronistic reading is an interpretative stance, an ars poetica as well as a political strategy.

3. Whitman and the counterculture

Whitman made a major comeback in the US literary landscape with the counterculture and the Beat poets. This is an aspect of Whitman's reception that has been well documented and that I will not cover comprehensively. What interests me here is to show the importance of the (Sovietized) Latin American detour, through Pablo Neruda, in the return of Whitman as a political poet in the US. This return implied many changes, however, in particular a new elegiac mood.

Walter Lowenfels: American and Soviet dialogs

An important figure in the reinstatement of a partisan Whitman in the US was Walter Lowenfels. A communist poet and journalist, he was tried in 1954 for "conspiracy to overthrow the government." In 1960, he put together *Walt Whitman's Civil War*, which gathered all of Whitman's writings related to the war.[32] In the preface, Lowenfels explained that this was not a new book about Whitman, but a new book by Whitman. Shortly afterward, he campaigned against the Vietnam War and published an anthology of veterans' poems and pacifist poems.[33] In 1969, Whitman featured prominently in his anthology *The Writing against the Wall: 108 American Poets of Protest*, with the epigraph: "My call is the call of battle, I nourish active rebellion." The poem "Respondez!" (rejected from later editions of *Leaves of Grass*) came just before "Let America Be America Again" by Langston Hughes (a poem discussed in Chapter 7). In 1969, for Whitman's 150th birthday, the communist magazine *American Dialog* put together a special issue, with contributions from familiar leftist Whitmanians: Langston Hughes, Rockwell Kent, Abe Capek, but also Walter Lowenfels and ... Korney Chukovsky. A few years later, this issue was debated in the magazine *Inostrannaia Literatura*. In an essay entitled "Camerado, I give you my hand," I. Popov provided a large survey of American contemporary protest

---

32 Walter Lowenfels, ed., *Walt Whitman's Civil War* (New York: Knopf, 1960).
33 Walter Lowenfels, ed., *Where Is Vietnam? American Poets Respond* (New York: Double Day Anchor, 1967).

poetry (especially about the Vietnam War) and emphasized Lowenfels's role in coordinating and disseminating it. Popov considered the "relation with the Whitmanian tradition as a barometer of the state of American poetry."[34] Walter Lowenfels also ensured the continuity of the Whitman/Neruda connection. After the coup in Chile, he gathered multiple homages for Neruda and Allende in *For Neruda. For Chile. An International Anthology*, and introduced them with a long quote about liberty from Whitman's 1855 preface. But Lowenfels's Whitman was not only a militant poet, as the 1970 anthology *The Tenderest Lover* indicates. *Leaves of Grass* is presented as "the song of sex and amativeness,"[35] between men and women as well as between men, even though "the only evidence of consummated homosexuality is in [the] poems." (xviii) It reflected contemporary problems such as "the social revolution, the sexual revolution, friendship between all nations": the sexual revolution made its way between the other two aspects that were usually picked up by communist Whitmanians.

Walter Lowenfels died in 1976. A couple of years later, Thomas McGrath, another communist poet who participated in the book *For Neruda*,[36] published a tribute entitled "Revolutionary Frescoes—the Ascension," "in memory of Walter Lowenfels." He listed all the comrades whom Lowenfels would join in his afterlife. After Marx, Engels, Lenin, but also Ezekiel, Woody (Guthrie) and Cisco (Houston), Whitman is mentioned as essential:

> And now, in the pause that follows, I remember walking with you
> And your other comrade, Walt Whitman, beside the Jersey shore
> While he talked of news of these states and foiled revolutionaires
> Out of an earlier time; and we run to keep up with his stride.
> Himself with his beard full of butterflies, you with the moon on
>   your forehead!
> Midnight ramblers and railers! By the cradle endlessly rocking,
> Of a fouled contaminant sea you both saw clean and young . . .
> Father of the dream, you said he was; father of poets.
> I see you now in the Shades, old Double Walt, dear outlaws.[37]

---

34 I. Popov, "Kamerado, ia daiu tebe ruku," *Inostrannaia Literatura*, 1973 (no. 5), 201–207.
35 Walter Lowenfels, ed. and J. K. Lambert, illustrations, *The Tenderest Lover: The Erotic Poetry of Walt Whitman*, 4th ed. (New York: Dell Publishing, 1978), vii.
36 McGrath had already written a poem in 1948 entitled "A Warrant for Pablo Neruda," published in the *Voice of Scotland*, at the time when the Chilean poet was being hunted down by President González Videla's police.
37 Thomas McGrath, "Revolutionary Frescoes—the Ascension," *Praxis*, no. 2 (1978), reprinted in Perlman, Folsom and Campion, *Walt Whitman: The Measure of His Song*, 400–401.

This is again Neruda's Whitman, the comrade, but also Lorca's Whitman, with his beard full of butterflies. The land is wasted, and the sea is contaminated: it is now uncertain that the "dream" can come true and that Whitman and his double can come back from the "Shades."

Lawrence Ferlinghetti: Goodbye, comrade?

When Neruda told Ferlinghetti that he enjoyed his "wide-open poetry," Ferlinghetti answered that Neruda had paved the way for him and his fellow American poets.[38] I would argue that Neruda also paved the way for Whitman's return. Ferlinghetti and Neruda first met in Cuba, in 1960, at a time of enthusiasm for the revolution. In January 1961, in the context of heightened tensions between Cuba and the US, Ferlinghetti wrote an odd elegy for Fidel Castro, "One thousand Fearful Words for Fidel Castro," as if he had already died: "Fidel ... Fidel ... your coffin passes by / thru lanes and lanes and streets you never knew."[39] The poem compares Castro with "old honest Abe," who also had a "little Civil War" and rewrites Whitman's tribute to Lincoln: "While lilacs last in the dooryard bloom, Fidel / your futile trip is done / yet is not done." It was published in *Starting from San Francisco*, whose title is a Californian variant of Whitman's "Starting from Paumanok." The first part of the collection is mainly an elegiac inventory of the American landscape. Against a backdrop of "mining towns, once roaring," "now shrunk to the railhead," a question arises: "Who stole America?" (13) In other words, this Whitmanian collection is infused with what Enzo Traverso calls, after Walter Benjamin, "left-wing melancholia."[40] An elegiac mood also permeated Louis Simpson's addresses to Whitman in *At the End of the Open Road* (1963) or Jack Kerouac's mentions.[41]

Ferlinghetti resurrected a more combative Whitman in "Populist Manifesto" (1976), an injunction to poets to "come down" from their closed worlds, an address to all the "self-occulting supersurrealists," "bedroom visionaries, "closet agitpropagators," "Groucho Marxist poets," and "leisure-class Comrades."[42] This

---

38 On the relationship between the Beat poets and Latin America, see Deborah N. Cohn, *The Latin American Literary Boom and U. S. Nationalism during the Cold War* (Nashville: Vanderbilt University Press, 2012), particularly the sections on Ferlinghetti's and Ginsberg's stay in Chile and about the success of Neruda's reading at Berkeley.
39 Lawrence Ferlinghetti, *Starting from San Francisco* (New York: New Directions, 1961), 79.
40 Enzo Traverso, *Left-Wing Melancholia: Marxism, History and Memory* (New York: Columbia University Press, 2017).
41 See Rumeau, *Fortunes de Walt Whitman*, 362–374.
42 Lawrence Ferlinghetti, *Who Are We Now?* (New York: New Directions, 1976), 62–63. The epigraph of the book is a quote from Edward Carpenter's *Days with Walt Whitman*:

truculent diatribe is reminiscent of Pablo Neruda's "Celestial poets" in *Canto general*, an attack on "intellectualists," "Rilkists," "surrealists butterflies burning in a tomb."[43] Ferlinghetti asks: "Where are Whitman's wild children" and urges poets: "Of your own sweet Self still sing / yet utter 'the word en-masse.'" However, just a couple of years later, Whitman was mentioned again, in a depressing end-of-the-open-road vision: at Seattle's market, a "big bearded man" looking like Walt Whitman stands still in the cold rain with a cardboard sign on him that reads: "I AM OVER 70 / MY DOG HAS THREE LEGS / NOBODY / WANTS US." Elegiac feelings have taken over.[44]

Allen Ginsberg: Hello again, *camerado*!

The weakening of the partisan Whitman accompanied, and even somehow anticipated, a waning faith in communism. However, this decline was counterbalanced by the return of a more liberal Whitman, the Whitman who sang the Body Electric and its multiple appetites. The case of Allen Ginsberg is especially interesting, since it is related to the Russian and Soviet developments of Whitman's legacy. Indeed, Ginsberg's intermediaries with Whitman included Russian poets. Ginsberg's mother was Russian and he liked to emphasize his Russian "parentage," which, poetically speaking, translated into multiple references to Mayakovsky. The epigraph of *Howl* in the original 1955 edition consisted of two almost Mayakovskyan lines from Whitman: "Unscrew the locks from the doors! / Unscrew the doors themselves from their jambs!" Like Neruda, Ginsberg often paired Whitman and Mayakovsky. Ginsberg also knew Neruda's poetry well, and he too wrote a tribute to the Chilean poet when he died.[45] However, though he was drawn toward revolutions, Ginsberg never adhered to institutional communism, let alone Stalinism, and remained critical of all totalitarian ideologies. His Mayakovsky was very different from Neruda's: he was an iconoclast who smashed traditions as well as a victim of a system that crushed him. Neruda's Mayakovsky was all optimism and heroism, Ginsberg's was about negativity and suffering.

"Underneath all art and social life, sex and fraternity."
43 Pablo Neruda, *Canto general*, trans. Jack Schmitt (1991; Berkeley: University of California Press, 2000), 166–167.
44 From the title of Gregory Corso's tribute to Kerouac and requiem for America, in which Corso exclaims: "How a Whitman we were always wanting." *Elegiac Feelings American* (New York: New Directions, 1970), 6–8.
45 Allen Ginsberg, "On Neruda's Death," in *Mind Breaths all over the Place*, in *Collected Poems, 1947–1997* (New York, Harper Collins, 2006), 615. However, Ginsberg's admiration for Neruda was not reciprocated and the latter preferred not to meet him at a poetry festival that could have brought them together in 1965.

With Ginsberg, the homoerotic side of Whitman's poetry resurfaced, after remaining in the closet for decades. To be more exact, Federico García Lorca's "Ode to Walt Whitman" (written in the late 1930s and published posthumously) had already emphasized a gay Whitman, but in quite an ambivalent way. In "Love Poem on Theme by Whitman" (1954), Ginsberg undertook a sexual exploration that was directly inspired by from "The Sleepers": "I'll go into the bedroom silently and lie down between the bridegroom and the bride."[46] "A Supermarket in California," written a year later, did not focus on sexuality, but suggested homoeroticism as it paired a "childless" Whitman with Lorca. Though childless, Whitman was addressed as a "father," as if poetic filiation could be a substitute for biological.[47] In "Death to Van Gogh's Ear!" (1957), Ginsberg brought the political and the gay Whitman together: "Franco has murdered Lorca the fairy son of Whitman / just as Mayakovsky committed suicide to avoid Russia."[48] Ginsberg, Lorca: Whitman did have sons after all. The murder of Lorca was a major theme of communist poetry, from Aragon to Neruda. By comparing it with Mayakovsky's suicide, Ginsberg undermined a tenet of anti-fascist discourse: Russia too killed its poets.

"A Supermarket in California" was translated into Russian in 1961 in the journal *Inostrannaia Literatura*. As Gregory Dandeles points out, "supermarket" was translated as "market" (*rynok*), which, at the time, designated a place where one could find a number of products missing from the state stores: the criticism of consumerism was thus repurposed as a criticism of the black market.[49] This was true of other works by Ginsberg. As Dandeles writes: "Soviet censors published *Howl* simply as anti-American propaganda." (39) The irony is that many readers found in Ginsberg what the censors failed to see and received the poems as models of resistance against oppressive governments.

Ginsberg became central for the Estradny poets, especially Voznesensky and Yevtushenko. They met when Ginsberg traveled to the USSR in 1965 (after he had been expelled from Cuba and sent to Prague). The collection *The Fall of America. Poems of These States, 1965-1971* was written after that trip to the USSR and, according to Gregory Dandeles, it bears the mark of the Estradny poets, for whom poems were meant for the ear, based on rhythm and declaimed to large audiences. The first part is a journey "through the vortex," from west to east, and the second a "zig-zag through the states," back west: everywhere, like

---

46 Ginsberg, *Collected Poems*, 123.
47 On Ginsberg and filiation, see Catherine A. Davies, *Whitman's Queer Children: America's Homosexual Epics* (London: Continuum, 2012).
48 Ginsberg, *Collected Poems*, 175.
49 Gregory Dandeles, "Avant-Gardes at the Iron Curtains: A Transnational Reading of Allen Ginsberg and the Soviet Estradny Movement" (PhD diss., University of Michigan, 2017), 46.

in Ferlinghetti's *Starting from San Francisco*, the lost prairie has been replaced by works and cars, already in a dilapidated state. The epigraph of the first edition was a page-length quote from *Democratic Vistas*.[50]

Ginsberg returned to Whitman in 1978, with "Plutonian Ode." This epic of a new world, ruled by atomic power, opens with a question: "What new element before us unborn in nature?" and an answer: "At last inquisitive Whitman a modern epic, denotative, Scientific theme" (710). The second stanza amplifies the address and introduces a sense of doom: "Father Whitman I celebrate a matter that renders Self oblivion!" At the end of an apocalyptic sequence, the poet addresses a large audience, from past, present and future: "This ode to you O Poets and Orators to come, you father Whitman as I join your side, you Congress and American people." (713) This poem about atomic angst was written at the very time when Ginsberg translated the stanzas that Neruda had devoted to the topic in … *Let the Rail Splitter Awake*. Better yet, he published the translation from Neruda in the same collection as "Plutonian Ode" and called it an "adaptation."[51] Ginsberg selected only the last two stanzas but, otherwise, his translation was rather literal, more so than Waldeen's version (which he knew, and whose title he kept). Ginsberg really only changed one word, as he replaced the first occurrence of "Abraham" with "Lincoln," erasing the ambiguity in Neruda, who had superimposed the biblical patriarch with the American president (Waldeen had done the same, but in a more colloquial way, with "Abe"). Had Ginsberg translated the stanzas where Neruda quoted Whitman in Spanish, he would have produced an interesting reverse translation. But he was obviously more interested in the end of *Let the Rail Splitter Awake*, which puts aside partisanship and propaganda and expresses the desire to simply "sing."

This pessimistic inclination was even more conspicuous in "Ode to failure" (1980). Once again, Ginsberg paid homage to Whitman, who had hailed "those who had failed" and who, as a prophet, had failed too: "Walt Whitman viva'd local losers—courage to Fat Ladies in the Freak Show!" while "Mayakovsky cried, Then die! my verse, die like the workers' rank & file fusilladed in Petersburg!" (745) Again, Ginsberg associated Whitman and Mayakovsky as poets of failure, just like himself, who had remained impotent against "Intellectual Unions of KGB & CIA in turtlenecks & underpants, their woolen suits & tweed." In 1984, for the collection *Cosmopolitan Greetings* (a title which announces a variation on "Salut au Monde!"), Ginsberg wrote a preface entitled "Improvisation in Beijing." This corresponded to the reopening of China and to the beginning

---

50 "Intense and loving comradeship…"
51 "Adapted from Neruda's "'Que dispierte el leñador'" [sic], in Ginsberg, *Collected Poems*, 704–706.

of a third phase in Whitman's Chinese reception.⁵² In this preface, he praised Whitman as the one who "gave world permission to speak with candor," and who "opened poetry's verse-line for unobstructed breath," thus giving him reasons to write poetry. Again, the celebration of Whitman came with the denunciation of all forms of totalitarianism, in particular Stalinist repression and Soviet anti-semitism: other reasons to write are the fact that "Russian poets Mayakovsky and Yesenin committed suicide," and that "Moscow said Stalin exiled 20 million Jews and intellectuals to Siberia." (938–939)

A final example of a transnational mention of Whitman lies in "Salutations to Fernando Pessoa" (1988). Ginsberg hails Pessoa as a reader of Whitman, of the "inestimable comerado Walt" and establishes sexual and poetic connections: "He entered Whitman so I enter Pessoa" (976). The end of the poem casts a very Pessoan doubt on the efficacy of words, with a reference to "Pessoa Schmessoa." Ginsberg's Pessoa is a Whitmanian camerado with a Jewish American twist. In the end, Ginsberg replaced the Whitman/Mayakovsky connection (to which he had already given a pessimistic inflexion) with a Whitman/Pessoa axis on his global map of dissenting poets.

4. From transatlantic to transmediterranean: new paths

This last section will take us to areas less visited so far, the Mediterranean, and the francophone and Arabic-speaking worlds. These areas became more connected with the transatlantic sphere in the course of the 1960s and 1970s. A central figure here is Jean Sénac, who, like Ginsberg, whom he admired, put the "body electric" to the fore. Sénac was a Francophone poet who from very early on supported Algerian independence. He wrote calls for struggle glorifying the heroes of the War of Liberation, and, in 1966, he was part of the Algerian delegation to the USSR, where he met Yevtushenko. However, his positions were complex and difficult to hold in a context of partisan struggle: Sénac advocated, like Kateb Yacine, a multicultural Algeria that would not promote nationalism and impose Arabic on other local languages. His homosexuality made him even more marginal and vulnerable, and he remained a *gaouri* (a European), someone who did not belong. He was murdered in 1973 in circumstances that remain unclear.

In 1959, in Peñiscola (Spain), Sénac wrote "Words with Walt Whitman," which was published in 1962, the year of Algerian independence, in *Les Cahiers*

---

52 See Huang, "Whitman in China," 415–420.

du Sud, reprinted in *La Rose et l'Ortie* (The Rose and the Nettle) in 1964, in a deluxe edition with plates by the engraver Mohammed Khadda, and again in *Citoyens de beauté* (Citizens of beauty) in 1967. The poem belonged to a pivotal period, both in the history of Algeria and in Sénac's poetry, which evolved from a celebration of political struggle to a broader, more cosmic and erotic vision of the world. The partisan collections *Matinale de mon peuple* (1961) and *Aux héros purs* (1962) were followed by *Citoyens de beauté*, in which homoeroticism loomed large. However, as early as 1959, in this poem *with* Whitman (rather than *to*), Sénac presented the body as an interface between oneself and others, oneself and the world. It is significant that the poem was included in two different collections, as a link between them. More specifically, the reference to Whitman has several functions.[53] First of all, Whitman is the poet of democracy, as the first stanza makes clear, with a quote from "Song of the Open Road":

> Walt Whitman, à l'heure où autour de nous la liberté
>   s'effondre comme un hôtel abandonné,
> et que de toutes parts les maquignons gagnent les hauteurs à
>   l'affût
>   de notre dernière parole,
> rends-nous le souffle et cet "ardent mal de contact"
>   dont nos yeux ont gardé l'orage.[54]
>
> Walt Whitman, at a time when freedom around us
>   is crumbling like an abandoned hotel,
> and on all sides the tricksters gain the heights in search
>   of our last word,
> give us back our breath and this "longing ache of contact"
>   from which our eyes have retained the storm.

Sénac presents himself as one of the "poets to come" and Whitman is resurrected to consider the discrepancies between his dreams and the current state of the world:

---

53 Katia Sainson has listed the parallels between Sénac and Whitman in "'L'ardent mal de contact:' les 'Paroles avec Walt Whitman' de Jean Sénac," *Algérie Littérature / Action*, Spécial Sénac, nos. 133–136 (September–December 2009): 85–100.

54 Jean Sénac, *Œuvres poétiques* (Arles: Actes Sud, 1999), 344. This is the version in *La Rose et l'Ortie*. In *Citoyens de Beauté*, the poem is dedicated to Jacques Miel and presents typographical variations.

> Je chante avec toi, Walt Whitman.
> Le compagnon que tu attendais est venu,
> et dans ta grande barbe déjà pousse une inquiétude de seigle
> "Je n'attendais pas cette tristesse ni le consentement à la phrase
>   des autres.
> Je n'attendais pas cette nostalgie de lunes.
> Ce que j'attendais, camarade, c'est l'athlète au salut vital,
> et la parole nue, auréolée de sa liqueur.
> Ce que j'attendais, lèvres à lèvres,
> c'est le soleil dans un mot cru."
> Oh, Walt Whitman,
> et tu repousses mes chardons! (345)

> I am singing with you, Walt Whitman.
> The companion you were waiting for has come,
> and in your large beard, a disquiet of rye is growing already,
> "I wasn't expecting these melancholy moons.
> What I was waiting for, comrade, was the athlete with his vital
>   salutation
> and the naked word, haloed by its liquor.
> What I expected, lip to lip,
> was the sun in a coarse word."
> Oh, Walt Whitman,
> and you push my thistles away!

The companion has turned up, but the comrade faces discouragement, as the melancholy moons seem to have triumphed over the energetic sun. However, all hope is not lost, and the poem unfolds the classic scenario of *deploratio/restoratio*. Sénac urges his readers to take to the road again, in search for the lost sun: "So we have to get back on the road, / walk towards the heart of summer." (345) What follows is a classic piece of political poetry, full of hope, "free men" and "good men." However, the poem does not end there, but with the epiphany of Whitman's body. Sénac, who had read André Gide extensively, knew that Whitman's name was a password and a discreet form of coming out. The depiction of Whitman's august body plunging into the sea functions as a sesame of recognition and can be read as one of Sénac's first hints at his own homosexuality:

> Et Walt Whitman, encore une fois, derrière les remparts de l'Espagne,
> secouant comme une cendre ses cuisses de colombe,
> entra dans la mer jusqu'aux épaules
> et il nagea,
> et les jeunes gens le regardèrent, oubliant pour une seconde les Françaises en bikini. (346)

> And Walt Whitman, once again, behind the walls of Spain,
> shaking like ashes his dove-like thighs,
> went into the sea up to his shoulders
> and he swam,
> and the young men looked at him, forgetting for a second the French women in bikinis.

The passage is reminiscent of the twelfth section of "Song of Myself," in which twenty-eight swimmers with splendid bodies are caressed by the invisible hand of a woman gazing longingly at them from the shore. Years later, Ginsberg, with whom Sénac had many affinities, also remembered Whitman's "swimmers huffing naked on the wave."[55] The poem ends in suspense: "And I took a pebble, / and for a long time I ran it against my lips / before I said the first word."[56] This first word to Whitman could also be interpreted as the beginning of a new creative phase, more intimate and less militant. Sénac's evolution was obviously not determined by the sole reading of Whitman, but it is quite remarkable that this poem was the first to combine erotic and political writing, the first instance of what Sénac later called the "corpoem" (a portmanteau combining the words "body" and "poem").

Another interesting feature of the poem is that it suggests not only dialogue, but also polyphonic conversation. In addition to Whitman, Sénac sees four other poets, who, "like a cloud of ship," all came from "from the working-class areas, from the fields" to celebrate Whitman. They are all Spanish poets: Federico García Lorca, Miguel Hernández, Ramón Sijé (for whom Hernández wrote an elegy), and Blas de Otero. Sénac, who had Spanish origins, later wrote a *Spanish Diwân*: the Mediterranean seems to be a connecting space between the country of his ancestry and the country where he was born and chose to stay, Algeria. Two

---

[55] Allen Ginsberg, "I Love Old Walt Whitman So," in *White Shroud Poems*, in *Collected Poems*, 900.

[56] "Et j'ai pris un galet, / et longtemps je l'ai promené sur mes lèvres / avant de dire le premier mot." Sénac, *Œuvres poétiques*, 436.

of these poets actually wrote about Whitman: Lorca of course, but also Blas de Otero, whose poem, entitled "Posición," focuses, once again, on Whitman's beard:

> Amo a Walt Whitman por su barba enorme
> y por su hermoso verso dilatado.
> Estoy de acuerdo con su voz, conforme
> con su gran corazón desparramado.[57]

> I love Whitman for his huge beard
> and for the beauty of his dilated verse.
> I agree with his voice, consistent
> with his vast, outspread heart.

This poem belongs to Blas de Otero's pivotal collection *Pido la paz y la palabra (1951–1954)* (I ask for peace and speech), which broke with metaphysics and engaged in activist poetry;[58] Sénac too found himself in a watershed "position."

I would also like to mention, to further extend the possibilities of this discussion, a poem that also echoes Lorca and Neruda, albeit implicitly. In 1970, the Syrian poet Adonis wrote "A Grave for New York," which contained a very long address to Whitman, at first invisible: "Whitman, // I did not see you in Manhattan, and yet I saw everything." But the reiteration of a line ("The clock indicates the moment" from "Song of Myself," in Arabic) finally brings him back. As the bell called the people together in Neruda, the clock signals the time for union and struggle:

> Whitman, let it be our turn now. I make a ladder of my gaze. I weave my steps into a pillow, and we shall wait. Man dies, but he is more eternal than the grave. the grave. Let it be our turn now. I wait for the Volga to flow between Manhattan and Queens. I wait for the Hwang Ho to empty where the Hudson empties. . . . There is a little red book rising, not the stage

---

57 Blas de Otero, *Pido la paz y la palabra*, in *Obra completa*, ed. Sabina de la Cruz (Barcelona: Galaxia Gutenberg, 2013), 238.
58 In an interview with Hubert Juin, Blas de Otero stated: "my writing has undergone a great change: the social concerns appear to me to be the only object of preoccupation." Otero explained that his language was both close to that of the people and nourished by that of the writers he most admired: Fray Luis de León and Machado in Spanish, as well as Nâzim Hikmet and . . . Whitman (Blas de Otero, *Obra completa*, 1113). Otero also met Neruda and paid homage to him in "El espectro de Neruda."

crumbling to pieces beneath the words but this one that expands and grows, a stage of wise madness and rain that clears so that it can inherit the sun. Let it be our turn now. New York is a rock that rolls on the forehead of the world.[59]

The apocalyptic tone of García Lorca and the political fierceness of Neruda combine in this address, which metabolizes Whitman's poetic energy. I should add that Whitman and Lorca are two important figures for Modernist and contemporary Arab-speaking poets, such as the Iraqi Saadi Youssef, who translated Whitman,[60] and they continue to be paired in poems.[61] This could obviously be a whole new chapter, but it is important at least to mention it at the end of this journey into Whitman's internationalist expanses.

Despite certain lines of continuity, notably with Neruda, the 1960s and 1970s saw significant developments in the political reception of Whitman, which correlated with the emergence of the counterculture and major reshapings of politics in the West: new ideas about community and the relationship between the individual and society—the notion that the private and intimate are thoroughly political. The lead blanket of the Brezhnev years allowed some of these redefinitions to filter through Eastward, and the Second World was not completely impervious to the liberal and anti-ideological Whitman that was emerging. The movement globally reverted: it was no longer Moscow that shaped the dominant reception of the militant Whitman, but rather the United States. However, this permeability had limits, and the Whitman increasingly claimed by gay communities in the US in the 1980s had no place in the Soviet Union. The end of the 1970s and the 1980s marked the loss of Whitman's momentum in the Second World. This decline, however, was somehow compensated for by the return of Whitman in China and by the dissemination of his poetry in various languages, such as Arabic.

---

59 Adonis, "A Grave for New York," in *A Time Between Ashes and Roses: Poems*, trans. Shawkat M. Toorawa (New York: Syracuse University Press, 2004), 169–171. The translator identifies the French translation by Roger Asselineau as the source of the quotes from Whitman. For an analysis of the poem, see Roger Asselineau and Ed Folsom, "Whitman and Lebanon's Adonis," *Walt Whitman Quarterly Review* 15 (Spring 1998): 180–184.
60 In his 1995 poem "America, America," Saadi Youssef claims: "Whitman and his beard full of butterflies" (*Qasai'd Sadhijah* [Damascus: al-Mada, 1996]; *Without an Alphabet, Without a Face*, trans. Khaled Mattawa [Saint Paul: Graywolf Press, 2002]).
61 In "The Burial of Walt Whitman" (2012), the Iraqi poet Abdel Muneim Ramadan imagines several encounters between Lorca and Whitman. See the English translation of the poem in Adnan Haydar and Michael Beard, "A Translation of Abdel-Muneim Ramadan's 'Walt Whitman's Funeral,' and Some Notes on Whitman in the Arab World," *Walt Whitman Quarterly Review* 35, no. 1 (2017): 127–136.

Coda

The decline of Whitman's popularity in the Soviet Union accelerated in the second half of the 1980s and in the 1990s. Because he had been so conspicuous in the Soviet canon, he looked, perhaps, like a worn-out, unconvincing poet of Democracy both during glasnost and after the collapse of the Soviet Union. According to Stephan Stepanchev, "by 1990 visitors to Russia could not find a single copy of Chukovsky's translations in any bookstore in Leningrad."[1] During the long interval from the mid-1980s to the mid-2010s, the Russian and Western receptions seem to bear very little, if any, relation to each other, and indeed may even appear to be antithetical: while in Russia, Whitman went dark, he regained visibility and political significance in the West, especially as a gay symbol.

Quite recently, his poetry was reprinted in Russia, especially in 2019, the year of the bicentennial (the translations are not new, however). This availability comes with a restriction: the collections are labeled only suitable for people over sixteen.[2] Whitman as monument and icon has also reappeared in Russian

---

1 Allen and Folsom, *Walt Whitman and the World*, 312.
2 If anything, Whitman could have fallen under the category "denying family values" (+18), since none of the reasons listed for the +16 category applies (depiction of violence or drug abuse, use of swearwords).

public space. Once again, these instances are fraught with politics, and more or less conscious misunderstandings. In 2009, a monument to Whitman by the sculptor Alexander Burganov was set up on the campus of the State University of Moscow (Lomonosov), in front of the Department of Philology. While Moscow boasts innumerable monuments to national writers, those to foreign writers are less common. The Whitman one is part of a transatlantic diptych: it is the counterpart of a monument to Pushkin, by the same sculptor, erected in 2000 on the campus of George Washington University (Moscow offered the monument to Pushkin and Washington the monument to Whitman). Burganov was awarded "national artist of the Russian Federation" and several of his works were installed in Moscow. Some of them bear a connection with American history, particularly insofar as it interacts with Russia's.[3] The Pushkin/Whitman duo is part of this bilateral monumental project.

FIGURE 11.1. Alexander Burganov, *Monument to Alexander Pushkin*, 2000, bronze, Washington University Campus. Photograph Julia Mendova.

---

3 Burganov sculpted four statues of Americans in Moscow: in addition to Whitman, John Quincy Adams (first American ambassador to Russia), Abraham Lincoln, shaking hands with Alexander II to commemorate the 150th anniversary of the abolition of serfdom in 2011, and Ronald Reagan, shaking hands with Gorbachev.

FIGURE 11.2. Alexander Burganov, *Monument to Walt Whitman*, 2009, bronze, Moscow State University Campus. Photograph Anna Shvets.

Both poets stand in front of a Corinthian column, a neoclassical setting which is quite strange for Whitman, but which seems to be one of Burganov's favorite devices (a similar column stands on the monument to Lincoln and Alexander II). It is hard to say whether the column and Pegasus are personal hallmarks or if they were really conceived as significant ornaments for both Pushkin and Whitman. It is a coincidence, of which Burganov might not have been aware, that Pegasus was also used as the colophon of the World Literature publishing house in the 1920s. However, the effect here is one of symmetry between two poets celebrated as national bards. Maurice Mendelson had ended his study with a parallel between Pushkin and Whitman, comparing the famous lines of the "Monument" ("Ia pomiatnik sebe . . .") with those of "By Blue Ontario's Shore," thus defining world literature as a sum of national masterpieces.[4] Such a conception, far from the emphasis on interconnectedness prevalent in the 1920s, seems magnified in the bronze of the two monuments. The Whitman monument in Moscow was unveiled by Yuri Luzhkov, then mayor of Moscow, Russian Foreign Minister Sergei Lavrov and US Secretary

---

4   Mendelson, *Walt Whitman: A Soviet View*, 334–335.

of State Hillary Clinton.⁵ Lavrov reiterated the idea that Whitman had had an exceptional fortune in Russia and emphasized the parallels between Pushkin and Whitman:

> If [Alexander Pushkin] is our everything, then [Walt Whitman] is America, as his contemporaries described him. Like Alexander Pushkin, who had the "gift of universal compassion" [sposobnost' vsemirnoi otzyvchivost'] American poetry reformer Whitman combined an outstanding creative talent with a deep philosophical vision of history and understanding of the unity of human civilization. It is no accident his poetry was almost immediately translated into Russian and received significant response in our country. What contributed to the recognition of Whitman's work in Russia, I think, was the interest and respect that the US poet had for our cultural and historic heritage. He penned a successful and powerful comparison of our peoples, which develops the idea of Alexis de Tocqueville about the commonality of destinies of America and Russia, which is displayed on the pedestal of this remarkable monument: "You Russians and we Americans!"⁶

Lavrov's Pushkin was defined by Dostoevsky's, as the embodiment of Russia's soul and its "fraternal aspiration to reunite mankind"—it was precisely on the occasion of the unveiling of Pushkin's monument in Moscow, in 1880 that Dostoevsky wrote his famous speech on the poet. For her part, Hillary Clinton declared: "I agree with Minister Lavrov that just as Pushkin and Whitman reset poetry, we are resetting our relationship for the 21st century." She also quoted Whitman's words on the pedestal⁷ and concluded: "We need to continue to work to make sure we find common ground on behalf of the Russian and American people, and that our two great nations help to lead the world in the twenty-first

---

5 "Amerika delitsia s Rossiei svoim poètom" [America shares its poet with Russia], *Moskovskii Gosudarstvennyi Universitet*, accessed March 15, 2023, https://www.msu.ru/news/amerika_delitsya_s_rossiey_svoim_poetom.html.

6 "Lavrov uveren, chto vera v vozmozhnosti sblizheniia Rossii i SShA seichas 'kak nikogda vostrebovana'" [Lavrov is certain that faith in the possibility of rapprochement between Russia and the US is now "in demand as never before"], *Newsru.com*, accessed March 15, 2023, https://www.newsru.com/russia/14oct2009/lavrov_hill.html.

7 "You Russians and we Americans, so far apart from each other, so seemingly different, and yet in ways that are most important, our countries are so alike."

century for greater peace, prosperity, and progress."⁸ Korney Chukovsky, who was very aware of his role in cultural exchanges, might have appreciated the ceremony as it echoed his own quote from the American poet: "Did not Walt Whitman say that poetry was capable of forging stronger links than the ablest of diplomats could?"⁹ However, behind the apparently consensual speeches (albeit they were not devoid of points of divergence, even then), lay a vexed issue, which Clinton avoided: Luzhkov was notoriously homophobic and had repeatedly banned the Gay Pride parade in Moscow. Nikolay Alekseyev and Nikolay Bayev, two LGBT rights activists, expressed their frustration that Clinton would not mention the topic.¹⁰ Obviously, Burganov's works and official speeches do not sum up Whitman's reception in contemporary Russia.¹¹ But both the monument and its unveiling ceremony bear witness to how political it has remained. They reveal a double process constantly at play in the history of reception. The first is inertia: the same quotes are repeated over and over (in this case, Whitman's words of address) and the same commonplaces are reiterated (Whitman's fortune in Russia was exceptional). The second is plasticity: the poet can be put to different uses depending on the domestic and geopolitical priorities of the day. However contradictory, the two dynamics interact constantly. The monument and the speeches also reveal how national and international issues—or rather global ones at this point—continue to frame the reception of poets and lay bare the ambiguities of discourses about a particular nation's world-historical mission.

Thirteen years later, Russia launched a brutal war on Ukraine. Oddly, in the context of heightened tensions with the US, Whitman's portrait reappeared, larger than ever, as an eerie replica of Grigoriev's portrait for the Petrograd revolutionary festival in 1918 (Fig. 3.2). Grigoriev's painting is kept at Pskov Museum of Arts, in the north of Russia. In the fall of 2022, the city implemented a program of murals to promote the collections of the museum. Two paintings

---

8   Hillary Rodham Clinton, "Remarks at Unveiling of Walt Whitman Monument," US Department of State, accessed March 15, 2023, https://2009-2017.state.gov/secretary/20092013clinton/rm/2009a/10/130544.htm.
9   Korney Chukovsky, "Thoughts on Receiving an Honorary Degree at Oxford," *Oxford Magazine*, May, 31, 1962, 341.
10 "Walt Whitman's statue welcomed by anti gay Moscow mayor Yuri Luzhkov," *Sunday Times*, October 15, 2009, https://www.thetimes.co.uk/article/walt-whitman-statue-welcomed-by-anti-gay-moscow-mayor-yuri-luzhkov-v0ng08hpm22. The article calls Whitman "American poet and gay icon."
11 A symposium at Moscow State University in October 2019, organized by Tatiana Venediktova (held in a room overlooking Burganov's monument and containing a portrait of . . . Pushkin) covered various topics, including Whitman's recent creative reception in Russia. Kirill Korchagin's presentation illuminated connections with a number of contemporary poets (I. Golanskoi, T. Zul'fikarov, S. Timofeev, N. Azarova).

by Grigoriev were chosen: *An Old Man from Olenets* (*Olenetskii Dëd*) and *Walt Whitman*. The icon-like painting, representing Whitman's prophetic face with a pink and blue halo, was reproduced on the facade of a very tall building in the central district.

FIGURE 11.3. Mural with Boris Grigoriev's *Walt Whitman*, Kiselev Street 11, Pskov. *Pskovskaia Lenta Novostei*, October 29, 2022.

A resident complained to the city administration that the mural was inappropriate, some disparaged the choice on social media, on the grounds that it went against the anti-"gay-propaganda" Russian legislation, while others defended it. The Pskov authorities replied that the choice was fine.[12] But to what extent were

---

12 "Pskovichka poschitala neumestnym mural s izobrazheniem amerikanskogo poèta Uolta Uitmena i poprosila gubernatora pomeniat' ego" [A woman residing in Pskov considered the mural depicting the American poet Walt Whitman inappropriate and asked the governor to change it], *Pskovskaia Guberniia*, October 24, 2022, https://gubernia.media/news/pskovichka-poschitala-neumestnym-mural-s-izobrazheniem-amerikanskogo-poeta-uolta/; "Boris Ëlkin otvetil na pros'bu pskovichki ubrat' mural s izobrazheniem amerikanskogo poèta s fasada doma v Pskove" [Boris Yolkin responded to a Pskov resident's request to remove a mural depicting an American poet from the facade of a house in Pskov], *Pskovskaia Guberniia*, November 1, 2022, https://gubernia.media/news/boris-elkin-otvetil-na-prosbu-pskovichki-ubrat-mural-s-izobrazheniem-amerikans.

they aware of all the implications of Whitman's portrait? Grigoriev's image has a long story of being misinterpreted. It was an intriguing choice for a banner at the Petrograd festival. Then, as the banner was lost, the painting was mislabeled: the inscription on the back of the portrait read "Karl Kautsky," thus mistaking the poet for the Marxist philosopher who severely criticized the Bolsheviks and was called a renegade by Lenin.[13] Until it was correctly identified again, the painting remained hidden. At the bottom of the Pskov mural, there is a caption with a reference to Whitman. But how familiar is his name exactly? What is the effect of the portrait on passers-by? It seems that many mistake him for Tolstoy. In a way, Whitman's appropriation by Grigoriev, his conversion of Pearsall's photograph into an "iconic" painting of a poet-prophet, has proven successful beyond all expectations: Whitman has become indeed one of the "Faces of Russia," as Grigoriev called one of his cycles of paintings.

One might argue that, like Grigoriev's portrait, Whitman's poetry has been much misinterpreted, a word I have carefully avoided while tracing how it was transferred and used in Russian, Soviet and internationalist contexts. I must admit that these last examples make it difficult not to wonder at what point Whitman's poetry was forgotten altogether, and the alliance of "the man and the book" was reduced to a mere trademark. Whitman's example clearly reveals how complex chains of reception, combining selection, translation and transmediality, sometimes amount to oversimplified constructs, at best disappointing, if one considers them as interpretations of the poem, at worst dangerous, as they can become—and have become— tools of propaganda. Yet the very existence of such chains bears witness to the ongoing power of poets to generate thoughts and images, to spark debate and controversy. Whitman remains an icon, hardly in the religious sense, but in the semiotic sense: he lost much of his sacred and prophetic attributes, but his image continues to spread and to aggregate new meanings, like the everlasting "signal" raised at the end of "Salut au Monde!"

Also see the local media *PLN* (*Pskovskaia Lenta Novostei*)— https://m.pln24.ru/culture/465176.html and https://m.pln24.ru/culture/465432.html, especially for the reader's forums.

13 Rimma Nikandrovna, presentation at the Pskov Museum, quoted in Aleksei Semënov, "Russkii alfavit," *Pskovskaia Guberniia*, November, 25, 2015, https://gubernia.media/number_767/07.php.

Appendix

A Whitman socialist and internationalist *vade mecum*

These are some of the most quoted poems (or sections of poems) by socialist and internationalist readers of Whitman. "Pioneers! O Pioneers!" is not included because it is partly cited in Chapter 7. The poems are given in the order in which they appear in the so-called "deathbed" edition (1891–1892), even though they were often used and quoted from earlier versions (especially from William Michael Rossetti's anthology *Poems by Walt Whitman*, based on the 1867 US edition). For comprehensive versions, see *The Walt Whitman Archive*.[1]

For You O Democracy.

Come, I will make the continent indissoluble,
I will make the most splendid race the sun ever shone upon,
I will make divine magnetic lands,
    With the love of comrades,
        With the life-long love of comrades.

---

1 The Walt Whitman Archive, accessed November 2, 2023, https://whitmanarchive.org/biography/correspondence/tei/yal.00254.html#yal.00254_n1.

I will plant companionship thick as trees along all the rivers of America, and
    along the shores of the great lakes, and all over the prairies,
I will make inseparable cities with their arms about each other's necks,
    By the love of comrades,
      By the manly love of comrades.

For you these from me, O Democracy, to serve you ma femme!
For you, for you I am trilling these songs.

[1860 (as part of a longer poem in "Calamus"); 1867 (in its present form, with the title "A Song"; 1881 with current title.]

Salut au Monde!

1

O take my hand Walt Whitman!
Such gliding wonders! such sights and sounds!
Such join'd unended links, each hook'd to the next,
Each answering all, each sharing the earth with all.

What widens within you Walt Whitman?
What waves and soils exuding?
What climes? what persons and cities are here?
Who are the infants, some playing, some slumbering?
Who are the girls? who are the married women?
Who are the groups of old men going slowly with their arms about each other's necks?
What rivers are these? what forests and fruits are these?
What are the mountains call'd that rise so high in the mists?
What myriads of dwellings are they fill'd with dwellers?

2

Within me latitude widens, longitude lengthens,
Asia, Africa, Europe, are to the east—America is provided for in the west,
Banding the bulge of the earth winds the hot equator,

Curiously north and south turn the axis-ends;
Within me is the longest day—the sun wheels in slanting rings—it does not set for months,
Stretched in due time within me the midnight sun just rises above the horizon, and sinks again,
Within me zones, seas, cataracts, plains, volcanoes, groups,
Oceanica, Australasia, Polynesia, and the great West Indian islands.

3

What do you hear Walt Whitman?

I hear the workman singing and the farmer's wife singing,
I hear in the distance the sounds of children and of animals early in the day,
I hear emulous shouts of Australians pursuing the wild horse,
I hear the Spanish dance with castanets in the chestnut shade, to the rebeck and guitar,
I hear continual echoes from the Thames,
I hear fierce French liberty songs,
I hear of the Italian boat-sculler the musical recitative of old poems,
I hear the locusts in Syria as they strike the grain and grass with the showers of their terrible clouds,
I hear the Coptic refrain toward sundown, pensively falling on the breast of the black venerable vast mother the Nile,
I hear the chirp of the Mexican muleteer, and the bells of the mule,
I hear the Arab muezzin calling from the top of the mosque,
I hear the Christian priests at the altars of their churches, I hear the responsive base and soprano,
I hear the cry of the Cossack, and the sailor's voice putting to sea at Okotsk,
I hear the wheeze of the slave-coffle as the slaves march on, as the husky gangs pass on by twos and threes, fasten'd together with wrist-chains and ankle-chains,
I hear the Hebrew reading his records and psalms,
I hear the rhythmic myths of the Greeks, and the strong legends of the Romans,
I hear the tale of the divine life and bloody death of the beautiful God the Christ,
I hear the Hindoo teaching his favorite pupil the loves, wars, adages, transmitted safely to this day from poets who wrote three thousand years ago.

4

What do you see Walt Whitman?
Who are they you salute, and that one after another salute you?

I see a great round wonder rolling through space,
I see diminute farms, hamlets, ruins, graveyards, jails, factories, palaces, hovels, huts of barbarians, tents of nomads upon the surface,
I see the shaded part on one side where the sleepers are sleeping, and the sunlit part on the other side,
I see the curious rapid change of the light and shade,
I see distant lands, as real and near to the inhabitants of them as my land is to me.

I see plenteous waters,
I see mountain peaks, I see the sierras of Andes where they range,
I see plainly the Himalayas, Chian Shahs, Altays, Ghauts,
I see the giant pinnacles of Elbruz, Kazbek, Bazardjusi,
I see the Styrian Alps, and the Karnac Alps,
I see the Pyrenees, Balks, Carpathians, and to the north the Dofrafields, and off at sea mount Hecla,
I see Vesuvius and Etna, the mountains of the Moon, and the Red mountains of Madagascar,
I see the Lybian, Arabian, and Asiatic deserts,
I see huge dreadful Arctic and Antarctic icebergs,
I see the superior oceans and the inferior ones, the Atlantic and Pacific, the sea of Mexico, the Brazilian sea, and the sea of Peru,
The waters of Hindustan, the China sea, and the gulf of Guinea,
The Japan waters, the beautiful bay of Nagasaki land-lock'd in its mountains,
The spread of the Baltic, Caspian, Bothnia, the British shores, and the bay of Biscay,
The clear-sunn'd Mediterranean, and from one to another of its islands,
The White sea, and the sea around Greenland.

11

You whoever you are!
You daughter or son of England!

You of the mighty Slavic tribes and empires! you Russ in Russia!
You dim-descended, black, divine-soul'd African, large, fine-headed, nobly-form'd, superbly destin'd, on equal terms with me!
You Norwegian! Swede! Dane! Icelander! you Prussian!
You Spaniard of Spain! you Portuguese!
You Frenchwoman and Frenchman of France!
You Belge! you liberty-lover of the Netherlands! (you stock whence I myself have descended;)
You sturdy Austrian! you Lombard! Hun! Bohemian! farmer of Styria!
You neighbor of the Danube!
You working-man of the Rhine, the Elbe, or the Weser! you working-woman too!
You Sardinian! you Bavarian! Swabian! Saxon! Wallachian! Bulgarian!
You Roman! Neapolitan! you Greek!
You lithe matador in the arena at Seville!
You mountaineer living lawlessly on the Taurus or Caucasus!
You Bokh horse-herd watching your mares and stallions feeding!
You beautiful-bodied Persian at full speed in the saddle shooting arrows to the mark!
You Chinaman and Chinawoman of China! You Tartar of Tartary!
You women of the earth subordinated at your tasks!
You Jew journeying in your old age through every risk to stand once on Syrian ground!
You other Jews waiting in all lands for your Messiah!
You thoughtful Armenian pondering by some stream of the Euphrates! you peering amid the ruins of Nineveh! you ascending mount Ararat!
You foot-worn pilgrim welcoming the far-away sparkle of the minarets of Mecca!
You sheiks along the stretch from Suez to Bab-el-mandeb ruling your families and tribes!
You olive-grower tending your fruit on fields of Nazareth, Damascus, or lake Tiberias!
You Thibet trader on the wide inland or bargaining in the shops of Lassa!
You Japanese man or woman! you liver in Madagascar, Ceylon, Sumatra, Borneo!
All you continentals of Asia, Africa, Europe, Australia, indifferent of place!
All you on the numberless islands of the archipelagoes of the sea!
And you of centuries hence when you listen to me!
And you each and everywhere whom I specify not, but include just the same!

Health to you! good will to you all, from me and America sent!

Each of us inevitable,
Each of us limitless—each of us with his or her right upon the earth,
Each of us allow'd the eternal purports of the earth,
Each of us here as divinely as any is here.

13

My spirit has pass'd in compassion and determination around the whole earth,
I have look'd for equals and lovers and found them ready for me in all lands,
I think some divine rapport has equalized me with them.

You vapors, I think I have risen with you, moved away to distant continents, and fallen down there, for reasons,
I think I have blown with you you winds;
You waters I have finger'd every shore with you,
I have run through what any river or strait of the globe has run through,
I have taken my stand on the bases of peninsulas and on the high embedded rocks, to cry thence:

Salut au monde!
What cities the light or warmth penetrates I penetrate those cities myself,
All islands to which birds wing their way I wing my way myself.

Toward you all, in America's name,
I raise high the perpendicular hand, I make the signal,
To remain after me in sight forever,
For all the haunts and homes of men.

[1856 ("Poem of Salutation"); 1860 with current title; 1881.]

Europe, The 72d and 73d Years of These States.

Suddenly out of its stale and drowsy lair, the lair of slaves,
Like lightning it le'pt forth half startled at itself,

Its feet upon the ashes and the rags, its hands tight to the throats of kings.

O hope and faith!
O aching close of exiled patriots' lives!
O many a sicken'd heart!
Turn back unto this day and make yourselves afresh.

And you, paid to defile the People—you liars, mark!
Not for numberless agonies, murders, lusts,
For court thieving in its manifold mean forms, worming from his simplicity the poor man's wages,
For many a promise sworn by royal lips and broken and laugh'd at in the breaking,

Then in their power not for all these did the blows strike revenge, or the heads of the nobles fall;
The People scorn'd the ferocity of kings.

But the sweetness of mercy brew'd bitter destruction, and the frighten'd monarchs come back,
Each comes in state with his train, hangman, priest, tax-gatherer,
Soldier, lawyer, lord, jailer, and sycophant.

Yet behind all lowering stealing, lo, a shape,
Vague as the night, draped interminably, head, front and form, in scarlet folds,
Whose face and eyes none may see,
Out of its robes only this, the red robes lifted by the arm,
One finger crook'd pointed high over the top, like the head of a snake appears.

Meanwhile corpses lie in new-made graves, bloody corpses of young men,
The rope of the gibbet hangs heavily, the bullets of princes are flying, the creatures of power laugh aloud,
And all these things bear fruits, and they are good.

Those corpses of young men,
Those martyrs that hang from the gibbets, those hearts pierc'd by the gray lead,
Cold and motionless as they seem live elsewhere with unslaughter'd vitality.

They live in other young men O kings!
They live in brothers again ready to defy you,
They were purified by death, they were taught and exalted.

Not a grave of the murder'd for freedom but grows seed for freedom, in its turn to bear seed,
Which the winds carry afar and re-sow, and the rains and the snows nourish.

Not a disembodied spirit can the weapons of tyrants let loose,
But it stalks invisibly over the earth, whispering, counseling, cautioning.

Liberty, let others despair of you—I never despair of you.

Is the house shut? is the master away?
Nevertheless, be ready, be not weary of watching,
He will soon return, his messengers come anon.

[1850 ("Resurgemus") in the New York *Daily Tribune*; 1855 (no title); 1856 ("Poem of the Dead Young Men of Europe, the 72nd and 73rd Years of These States"); 1860 with current title.]

To a Foil'd European Revolutionaire.

Courage yet, my brother or my sister!
Keep on—Liberty is to be subserv'd whatever occurs;
That is nothing that is quell'd by one or two failures, or any number of failures,
Or by the indifference or ingratitude of the people, or by any unfaithfulness,
Or the show of the tushes of power, soldiers, cannon, penal statutes.

What we believe in waits latent forever through all the continents,
Invites no one, promises nothing, sits in calmness and light, is positive and composed, knows no discouragement,
Waiting patiently, waiting its time.

(Not songs of loyalty alone are these,
But songs of insurrection also,

For I am the sworn poet of every dauntless rebel the world over,
And he going with me leaves peace and routine behind him,
And stakes his life to be lost at any moment.)

The battle rages with many a loud alarm and frequent advance and retreat,
The infidel triumphs, or supposes he triumphs,
The prison, scaffold, garroté, handcuffs, iron necklace and lead-balls do their work,
The named and unnamed heroes pass to other spheres,
The great speakers and writers are exiled, they lie sick in distant lands,
The cause is asleep, the strongest throats are choked with their own blood,
The young men droop their eyelashes toward the ground when they meet;
But for all this Liberty has not gone out of the place, nor the infidel enter'd into full possession.

When liberty goes out of a place it is not the first to go, nor the second or third to go,
It waits for all the rest to go, it is the last.

When there are no more memories of heroes and martyrs,
And when all life and all the souls of men and women are discharged from any part of the earth,
Then only shall liberty or the idea of liberty be discharged from that part of the earth,
And the infidel come into full possession.

Then courage European revolter, revoltress!
For till all ceases neither must you cease.

I do not know what you are for, (I do not know what I am for myself, nor what any thing is for,)
But I will search carefully for it even in being foil'd,
In defeat, poverty, misconception, imprisonment—for they too are great.

Did we think victory great?
So it is—but now it seems to me, when it cannot be help'd, that defeat is great,
And that death and dismay are great.

[1856 ("Liberty Poem for Asia, Africa, Europe, America, Australia, Cuba, and The Archipelagoes of the Sea."); 1860, 1867 ("To a Foiled Revolter or Revoltress"); 1881 with current title.]

Years of the Modern.

Years of the modern! years of the unperform'd!
Your horizon rises, I see it parting away for more august dramas,
I see not America only, not only Liberty's nation but other nations preparing,
I see tremendous entrances and exits, new combinations, the solidarity of races,
I see that force advancing with irresistible power on the world's stage,
(Have the old forces, the old wars, played their parts? are the acts suitable to them closed?)
I see Freedom, completely arm'd and victorious and very haughty, with Law on one side and Peace on the other,
A stupendous trio all issuing forth against the idea of caste;
What historic denouements are these we so rapidly approach?
I see men marching and countermarching by swift millions,
I see the frontiers and boundaries of the old aristocracies broken,
I see the landmarks of European kings removed,
I see this day the People beginning their landmarks, (all others give way;)
Never were such sharp questions ask'd as this day,
Never was average man, his soul, more energetic, more like a God,
Lo, how he urges and urges, leaving the masses no rest!
His daring foot is on land and sea everywhere, he colonizes the Pacific, the archipelagoes,
With the steamship, the electric telegraph, the newspaper, the wholesale engines of war,
With these and the world-spreading factories he interlinks all geography, all lands;
What whispers are these O lands, running ahead of you, passing under the seas?
Are all nations communing? is there going to be but one heart to the globe?
Is humanity forming en-masse? for lo, tyrants tremble, crowns grow dim,
The earth, restive, confronts a new era, perhaps a general divine war,
No one knows what will happen next, such portents fill the days and nights;
Years prophetical! the space ahead as I walk, as I vainly try to pierce it, is full of phantoms,

Unborn deeds, things soon to be, project their shapes around me,
This incredible rush and heat, this strange ecstatic fever of dreams O years!
Your dreams O years, how they penetrate through me! (I know not whether I sleep or wake;)
The perform'd America and Europe grow dim, retiring in shadow behind me,
The unperform'd, more gigantic than ever, advance, advance upon me.

[1865 ("Years of the Unperform'd"); 1872, 1881 with current title.]

Bibliography

1. Editions, translations of Whitman

Whitman, Walt. *Poems: Selected. With an Introduction by William Michael Rossetti.* London: John Camden Hotten, 1868.

Whitman, Walt. *The Poems of Walt Whitman: Selected.* With an Introduction by Ernest Rhys. London: Walter Scott, 1886.

Whitman, Walt. *Canti scelti.* Translated into Italian by Luigi Gamberale. Milan: Sonzogno, 1887.

Whitman, Walt. *Grashalme. Gedichte.* Translated into German by Karl Knortz and Thomas Rolleston. Zürich: Verlag-Magazin, 1889.

Whitman, Walt. *Grashalme.* Translated into German by Wilhelm Schölermann. Leipzig: Diederichs, 1904.

Whitman, Walt. *Grashalme: Eine Auswahl.* Translated into German by Karl Federn. Minden: Bruns, 1904.

Whitman, Walt. *Stébla trávy: vybor.* Translated into Czech by Jaroslav Vrchlický. Prague: Nakladatel B. Koči, 1906.

Whitman, Walt. *Grashalme.* Translated into German by Johannes Schlaf. Leipzig: Reclam, 1907.

Uitman, Uot. *Poèt-anarkhist Uot Uitman: Perevod v stikhakh i kharakteristika.* Translated into Russian by Kornei Chukovskii. Saint Petersburg: Kruzhok molodykh, 1907.

Vitmens, Volts. *Zāļu stiebri.* Translated into Latvian by Robert Skargas, pseud. of Kārlis Jēkabsons. Riga: Imantas apgāds, 1908.

Whitman, Walt. *Básník zítřku.* Translated into Czech by Emanuel Lešehrad. Prague: 1909.

Whitman, Walt. *Feuilles d'herbe: Traduction intégrale d'après l'édition définitive.* Translated into French by Léon Bazalgette. Paris: Mercure de France, 1909.

Whitman, Walt. *Fulles d'herba.* Translated into Catalan by Cebrià Montoliu. Barcelona: Biblioteca popular de "L'Avenç," 1909.

Vitmens, Volts. *Brīvā teka.* Anonymous translation. Riga: ģeralkomisija pee A. Golta, 1911.

Uitman, Uol't. *Pobegi travy.* Translated into Russian by Konstantin Bal'mont. Moscow: Skorpion, 1911.

Whitman, Walt. *Poemas: Versión de Armando Vasseur.* Translated into Spanish. Valencia: F. Sempere y compañía, Editores, 1912.

Uitmèn, Uot. *Poèziia griadushchei demokratii.* Translated into Russian by Kornei Chukovskii. Moscow: Sytin, 1914.

Whitman, Walt. *Le Panseur de plaies: Poèmes, lettres et fragments de Walt Whitman sur la guerre.* Translated into French by Léon Bazalgette. Paris: Édition de la Revue Littéraire des Primaires, 1917.

Whitman, Walt. *Ode à la France.* Translated into French by Léon Bazalgette, with eleven woodcuts by Paul Combet-Descombes. Paris: À la Belle Édition, 1917.

Whitman, Walt. *Œuvres choisies: Poèmes et proses.* Translated into French by Jules Laforgue, Louis Fabulet, André Gide, Valery Larbaud, Jean Schlumberger, Francis Vielé-Griffin. Introduction by Valery Larbaud. Paris: La Nouvelle Revue française, 1918.

Uitmèn, Uot. *Poèziia griadushchei demokratii.* Translated into Russian by Kornei Chukovskii. Petrograd: Parus, 1918.

Uitman, Uot. *Pionery.* Translated into Russian by S. M. Illustrations by Vera Ermolaeva. Petrograd: Artel' Khudozhnikov Segodnia, 1918.

Whitman, Walt. "A un rivoluzionario vinto d'Europa." Translated into Italian by Palmiro Togliatti. *L'Ordine nuovo,* July 12, 1919, 68.

Whitman, Walt. *Calamus.* Translated into French by Léon Bazalgette, with ten woodcuts by Frans Masereel. Geneva: Éditions du Sablier, 1919.

Whitman, Walt. *Der Wundarzt. Briefe, Aufzeichnungen und Gedichte aus dem amerikanischen Sezessionskrieg.* Translated into German by Gustav Landauer and Ivan Goll. Zürich: Max Rascher Verlag, 1919.

Whitman, Walt. "Europa." Translated into Italian by Palmiro Togliatti. *L'Ordine nuovo*, no. 29 (December 6–13, 1919), 226.

Whitman, Walt. *Les Dormeurs.* Translated into French by Léon Bazalgette. With sixteen woodcuts by Marcel Gaillard. Paris: François Bernouard, 1919.

Uitmèn, Uot. *Poèziia griadushchei demokratii.* Translated into Russian by Kornei Chukovskii. Petrograd: Izdanie petrogradskogo soveta rabochikh i krasnykh deputatov, 1919.

Whitman, Walt. *Six poèmes.* Translated into French by Léon Bazalgette. Ornamental compositions by Jean Lurçat. Paris: A.-G. Gonon, 1919.

Semper, Johannes. *Walt Whitman.* Talinn: Varrak, 1920.

Uot-Uitmèn. *Evropa: Instsenirovannoe stikhotvorenie s prologom.* Arkhangelsk: Izdanie Prosvet. Otdela Polit-Prosvet. Upravleniia Belomorskogo Voennogo Okruga, 1920.

Whitman, Walt. *Grashalme. Neue Auswahl.* Translated into German by Hans Reisinger. Berlin: S. Fischer Verlag, 1920.

Whitman, Walt. *Walt Whitman's Poems.* Edited by Emanuel Haldeman-Julius. Girard, Kansas: People's Pocket Series, 1919. New edition: *Poems of Walt Whitman.* Edited by Nelson Antrim Crawford. Girard, Kansas: Haldeman-Julius Co., 1924.

Whitman, Walt. *Leaves of Grass.* Introduction by Carl Sandburg. New York: Modern Library, 1921.

Uitmèn, Uot. *List'ia travy, Proza.* Translated into Russian by Kornei Chukovskii. Petrograd: Gosudarstvennoe izdatel'stvo, "Vsemirnaia Literatura," 1922.

Uitman, Uol't. *Revoliutsionnaia poèziia Evropy i Ameriki. Uitman.* Translated into Russian by Konstantin Bal'mont. Moscow: Gosudarstvennoe izdatel'stvo, 1922.

Whitman, Walt. *Walt Whitmans Werk.* Translated into German by Hans Reisinger. Berlin: S. Fischer Verlag, 1922. Multiple reprints.

Uitmèn, Uot. *Peredovye boitsy.* Translated into Russian by Kornei Chukovskii. Petrograd: Gosudarstvennoe izdatel'stvo, 1923.

Uitmèn, Uot. *Poèziia griadushchei demokratii.* Translated into Russian by Kornei Chukovskii. Moscow: Gosudarstvennoe izdatel'stvo, 1923.

Oytmēn, Owōt. Translated into Armenian by Gurgen Haykuni. Moscow: Hammer and Sickle, 1923.

Uot Uitmen, "Lystia travy." Translated into Ukrainian by Ivan Kulyk. *Chervonyi shliakh*, June 1924, 84–89; August–September 1924, 99–106; October 1924, 54–59.

Whitman, Walt. "Trimitai garsiau! Pilna burna būgnai!" Translated into Lithuanian by Antanas Venclova. *Audra* [literary almanac] 22–23. Riga: n.p., 1928.

Whitman, Walt. *Salut au Monde!* Illustrated by Vojtéch Preissig. New York: Random House, 1930.

Uitmèn, Uot. *List'ia travy*. Translated into Russian by Kornei Chukovskii. Moscow: Ogonëk, 1931.

Uitmèn, Uot. *Izbrannye stikhotvoreniia*. Translated into Russian by Kornei Chukovskii. Leningrad: Moscow: Khudozhestvennaia Literatura, 1932.

Vitman, Valt. *Finf un tsvantsig lider*. Translated into Yiddish by Abraham Asen. New York: Idish lebn, 1934.

Uitman, Uolt. *List'ia travy*. Translated into Russian by Kornei Chukovskii. Leningrad; Moscow: Khudozhestvennaia Literatura, 1935.

Uitmèn, Uot. "Pionery." Translated into Russian by Dmitri Maizels. *Molodaia Gvardiia*, 1935 (no. 7), 32–33.

Whitman, Walt. *Leaves of Grass*. Illustrated by Rockwell Kent. New York: Heritage Press, 1936.

Whitman, Walt. "Espagne. 1873–1874." *Nouvelle Revue Française*, no. 301 (October 1938), 689.

Vitman, Volt. *Lider: Fun Bukh: Bletlekh Groz*. Translated into Yiddish by Louis Miller. New York: Yiddish Cooperative Book League, 1940.

Uitman, Uolt. *Izbrannye stikhotvoreniia i proza*. Translated into Russian by Kornei Chukovskii. Moscow: OGIZ, 1944.

Whitman, Walt. *Saudação ao Mundo e Outros Poemas*. Translated into Portuguese by Mario D. Ferreira Santos. Sao Paulo: Flama, 1944.

Whitman, Walt. *A Wartime Whitman*. Edited by William Aiken. New York: Armed Services Editions, 1945.

Whitman, Walt. *Cantando a la primavera*. Translated into Spanish by Concha Zardoya. Madrid: Ed. Hispanica, Adonais, 1945.

Whitman, Walt. *Demokracie, zeno má! Vyber ze Stebel trávy*. Translated into Czech by Pavel Eisner. Prague: Jaroslav Podroužek, 1945.

Whitman, Walt. *Poeme*. Translated into Romanian by Margareta Sterian. Bucarest: Pro Pace, 1945.

Whitman, Walt. "Pieśń dla poległych." Translated into Polish by Czesław Miłosz. *Przekrój*, no. 30 (1945), 7.

Whitman, Walt. *Cantos de Walt Whitman*. Translated into Portuguese by Oswaldino Marques. Rio de Janeiro, José Olímpio, 1946.

Whitman, Walt. *I Hear the People Singing: Selected Poems*. Introduction by Langston Hughes. New York: International Publishers, 1946.

Whitman, Walt. "Pionierzy, o pionierzy!" Translated into Polish by Stanisław Helsztyński. *Odra: Tygodnik literacko-społeczny* [Katowice, Wrocław, Szczecin], May 26, 1946, 3.

Whitman, Walt. *Saludo al mundo*. Translated into Spanish by Gregorio Gasman. Santiago de Chile: Ediciones de Librería Neira, 1949.

Whitman, Walt. *Foglie d'erba*. Translated into Italian by Enzo Giachino. Turin: Einaudi, 1950.

Whitman, Walt. *Vlati Trave*. Translated into Croatian by Tin Ujević. Zagreb: Zora, 1951.

Uitmen, Uolt. *Izbrannoe*. Various translators. Moscow: Gosudarstvennoe izdatel'stvo khudozhestvennoi literatury, 1954; reprint *List'ia travy*. Moscow: Gosudarstvennoe izdatel'stvo khudozhestvennoi literatury, 1955.

Uitmen, Uolt. Choice of poems [in Russian]. *Inostrannaia Literatura*, 1955 (no. 1), 160–164.

Whitman, Walt. "Saludo al mundo," Translated into Spanish by Pablo Neruda. *La Gaceta de Chile*, October 1955.

Uitmen, Uolt. *Stikhotvoreniia i proza*. Translated into Russian by Kornei Chukovskii. Moscow: Pravda, 1955.

Vitmenas, Uoltas. *Žolės lapai*. Translated into Lithuanian by Antanas Miškinis. Vilnius: Grožinė literatūra, 1959.

Vitmens, Volts. *Zāļu stiebri*. Translated into Latvian by Mirdza Ķempe and Rihards Rudzītis. Riga: LVI, 1960.

Whitman, Walt. *Rohulehed*. Translated into Estonian by Boris Kabur. Tallinn: Eesti Riiklik Kirjastus, 1962.

Whitman, Walt. *Lyrik und Prosa*. Translated by Erich Arendt and Helmut Heinrich. Berlin: Volk und Welt, 1966.

Uitmen, Uolt. *Lystia travy: Poezii*. Translated into Ukrainian by Vitaly Korotich. Kyiv: Dnipro, 1969.

Uitmen, Uolt. *Izbrannye proizvedeniia*. Various translators. Moscow: Khudozhestvennaia literatura, 1970.

Uitmen, Uolt. *Jalbıraktar: Irlar*. Translated into Kyrgyz by Suyunbai Eraliev. Frunze: 1970.

Whitman, Walt. *The Tenderest Lover: The Erotic Poetry of Walt Whitman*. Edited by Walter Lowenfels and illustrated by J. K. Lambert. New York: Delacorte press, 1970.

Uitmen, Uolt. "Pisnia pro sebe." Translated into Ukrainian by Les' Herasymchuk. *Vsesvit*, 1977 (no. 2), 136–182.

Uitmien, Uolt. *Listsie travy*. Translated into Belorussian by Yanka Sipakov. Minsk: Mastats. lit., 1978.

Uitmen, Uolt. *List'ia travy*. Translated into Russian. Moscow: Khudozhestvennaia literatura, 1982.

Uitmen, Uolt. *Poezii*. Translated into Ukrainian by Les' Herasymchuk. Kyiv: Dnipro, 1984.

Whitman, Walt. *Poetry and Prose*. New York: Library of America, 1996.

Whitman, Walt. *Leaves of Grass*. Edited by Michael Moon. New York: Norton, 2007.

2. Sources

Abieva N. A. "Nachalo znakomstva s Uoltom Uitmenom v Rossii." *Russkaia Literatura* 1986 (no. 4): 185–195

Aćamović, Bojana. "Walt Whitman in the Yugoslav Interwar Periodicals: Serbo-Croatian Reception, 1918-1940." *Walt Whitman Quarterly Review* 38, no. 3–4 (2021): 139–168.

Adams, A. M. "Whitman Appropriated. The Poet Found to Be the 'Patron Saint' of Bolshevist Circles." *New York Times*, June 6, 1923.

Adonis. *A Time Between Ashes and Roses: Poems*. Translated from Arabic by Shawkat M. Toorawa. New York: Syracuse University Press, 2004.

Alegría, Fernando. *Walt Whitman en Hispanoamérica*. Mexico City: Studium, 1954.

Allen, Gay Wilson. "A Backward Glance. History of My Whitman Studies." *Walt Whitman Quarterly Review* 9, no. 2 (1991): 91-100.

———. *Walt Whitman Handbook*. Chicago: Packard & Co., 1946.

Allen, Gay Wilson, and Ed Folsom, eds. *Walt Whitman and the World*. Iowa City: University of Iowa Press, 1995.

Alpers, Boris. *Teatral'nye ocherki*. Moscow: Iskusstvo, 1977.

Alston, Charlotte. *Tolstoy and His Disciples: The History of a Radical International Movement*. London: I. B. Tauris, 2014.

Anderson, W. C. "The Life and Ideals of Hardie." *Labour Leader*, October, 7, 1915.
Anonymous. "Hail Walt Whitman as Red." *New York Times*, June 6, 1920.
———. "Maikl Gold ob Uote Uitmene." *Literaturnaia Gazeta*, August, 26, 1938, 1.
Aragon, Louis. *Œuvres poétiques complètes*. Paris: Gallimard, "Pléiade," 2007.
Arvin, Newton. *Whitman*. New York: Macmillan Co., 1938.
Athenot, Éric. "1886, année vers-libriste: Laforgue, traducteur de Walt Whitman." In *L'Appel de l'étranger. Traduire en langue française en 1886*, edited by Sylvie Humbert-Mougin, Lucile Arnoux-Farnoux, Yves Chevrel, 107–123. Tours: Presses Universitaires François-Rabelais, 2015.
Aub, Max. *Antología traducida*. Mexico City: Editorial Universidad Nacional Autónoma de México, 1963; Barcelona: Editorial Seix Barral, 1972.
Bahr, Hermann. "Barbaren." *Die Neue Rundschau* 19, no. 12 (1908), 1774–1781.
———. "Walt Whitman." *Die Neue Rundschau* 30, no. 1 (1919), 555–564.
Bain, Mildred. *Horace Traubel*. New York: Albert and Charles Boni, 1913.
Baliutytė-Riliškienė, Elena. *Eduardas Mieželaitis tarp Rytų ir Vakarų: pasivaikščiojimas su Waltu Whitmanu ir staugsmas su Allenu Ginsbergu*. Vilnius: Lietuvių literatūros ir tautosakos institutas, 2019.
Bal'mont, Konstantin. *Iz mirovoi poèzii*. Berlin: Knigoizdatel'stvo Slovo, 1921.
———. "Pevets lichnosti i zhizni" (1904). In *Belye Zarnitsy*, 59–84. Saint Petersburg: Izd. Pirozhkova, 1908.
———. "Poèziia bor'by (Idealizovannaia Demokratiia)" (1907). In *Belye Zarnitsy*, 85–134.
———. "Poliarnost'" (1908); repr. as introduction to Uolt' Uitman. *Pobegi travy*, 5–8. Moscow: Skorpion, 1911.
Basterra, Ramón de. "Inquilino de Bilbao. Oda a la Villa." *Hermes*, no. 16, April 1918.
Batista, José Manuel. "In the Shadow of a Giant: Mir's Struggle against Neruda." *SECOLAS Annals* 38 (2006): 79–92.
———. "Ni cósmico ni democrático: El Contracanto a Walt Whitman de Pedro Mir," *Symposium* 62, no. 4 (Winter 2009): 235–257.
Bazalgette, Léon. *Émile Verhaeren*. Paris: E. Sansot, 1907.
———. *Le "Poème-Évangile" de Walt Whitman*. Paris: Mercure de France, 1921.
———. *Walt Whitman. L'Homme et son oeuvre*. Paris: Mercure de France, 1908.
Bazalgette, Léon, and Anne Traubel. "Une fête de poésie en Amérique. Salut au Monde." *L'Humanité*, July, 16, 1922, 4.

Beasley, Rebecca. *Russomania: Russian Culture and the Creation of British Modernism, 1881–1922.* Oxford: Oxford University Press, 2020.

Becher, Johannes. "Walt Whitman." *Aufbau*, no. 1 (November 1945), 286.

Benét, Stephen. *Selected Works.* New York: Farrar and Rinchart Inc., 1942.

Benjamin, Walter. "The Path to Success in Thirteen Theses." In *Selected Writings*, vol. 2, translated by Rodney Livingstone, 144–147. Cambridge, MA: Harvard University Press, 1999.

Berliand, Iryna, ed. *Ekzekutsiia: Zbirnyk umans'kykh bezmezhnykiv.* Kyiv: Dukh i Litera, 2003.

Bernabe, Rafael. *Walt Whitman and His Caribbean Interlocutors: José Martí, C.L.R. James, and Pedro Mir. Song and Countersong.* Leiden: Brill, 2021.

Berman, Antoine. *La Traduction et la Lettre ou l'Auberge du lointain.* Paris: Seuil, 1999.

Bernardini, Caterina. *Transnational Modernity and the Italian Reinvention of Walt Whitman: 1870-1945.* Iowa City: University of Iowa Press, 2022.

Bidney, Martin. "Leviathan, Yggdrasil, Earth-Titan, Eagle: Bal'mont's Reimagining of Walt Whitman." *Slavic and East European Journal* 34 (Summer 1990): 176–191.

Binns, Henry Bryan. *The Great Companions.* London: A. C. Fifield, 1908.

———. *The Life of Walt Whitman.* London: Methuen & Co., 1905.

Blok, Aleksandr. "O sovremennoi kritike." In *Sobranie sochinenii*, vol. 5, edited by V. Orlov, A. Surkov, K. Chukovskii. 203–208. Moscow: Khudozhestvennaia Literatura, 1962.

Bloom, Harold. "Near the Quick. Lawrence and Whitman." In *The Anatomy of Influence*, 255–265. New Haven: Yale University Press, 2011.

———, ed. *Walt Whitman.* New York: Infobase Publishing, 2009.

Bloor, Reeve Ella. *We Are Many.* New York: International Publishers, 1940.

Blum, Eliezer (B. Alkvit). *Vegn tsvey un andere.* New York: Farlag Inzikh, 1931.

Bontemps, Arna, and Langston Hughes, eds. *The Poetry of the Negro, 1746-1949: An Anthology.* Garden City, NY: Doubleday, 1949.

Borges, Jorge Luis. *El otro, el mismo.* Buenos Aires: Emecé, 1964.

———. "Walt Whitman: Canto a mi mismo. Traducido por León Felipe." *Sur* 12, no. 88 (January 1942), 68–70.

Borodin, A. *Uot Uitmèn.* Baku: Rubiny, 1922.

Bovshover, Joseph. *Gezamelte shriften poezye un proza.* New York: Fraye arbayter shtite, 1911.

Bradley, Sculley. "Walt Whitman and the Postwar World." *South Atlantic Quarterly*, no. 42 (July 1943): 220–224.

———. "Walt Whitman, Poet of the Present War." *General Magazine and Historical Chronicle*, October 1942, 7–14.

Bulyha, Oleksii. *Skresinnia*. Kyiv: Molod', 1967.

Bucke, Richard Maurice. *Calamus*. Boston: Maynard, 1897.

———. *Cosmic Consciousness: A Study in the Evolution of the Human Mind*. New York: Dutton & Co., 1901.

———. *Walt Whitman*. Philadelphia: David McKay, 1883.

———. Thomas B. Harned, and Horace Traubel, eds. *In Re Walt Whitman*. Philadelphia: David McKay, 1893.

Biok, Richard Moris. *Kosmicheskoe soznanie*. Petrograd: Novyi chelovek, 1915.

Buell, Lawrence. "American Literary Emergence as a Postcolonial Phenomenon." *American Literary History* 4, no. 3 (Fall 1992): 411–442.

Burns Fern, Elizabeth. "The Democracy of Whitman." *Mother Earth* 1, no. 11 (January 1907): 23–30; no. 12 (February 1907): 15–21.

Buzzi, Paolo. *Poema dei quarantanni*. Milan: Edizioni futuriste di "poesia," 1922.

C. S. "Maxim Gorky on the Russian Revolution." *New York Times*, April, 15, 1906, magazine section, 31–33.

Canby, Henry Seidel. *Walt Whitman, an American: A Study in Biography*. New York: Armed Services Edition, 1944.

Carpenter, Edward. *Chants of Labour*. London: Swan Sonnenschein & Co., 1892.

———. *Civilisation: Its Cause and Its Cure and Other Essays*. London: Swan Sonnenschein & Co., 1891.

———. *The Intermediate Sex: A Study of Some Transitional Types of Men and Women*. London: George Allen & Unwin Ltd., 1908.

———. *Towards Democracy*. 1905. New York: Kenneley 1912.

Casanova, Pascale. *La République des lettres*. Paris: Seuil, 2008.

Casseres, Benjamin de. "The Renaissance of the Irrational." *Camera Work*, June 1913, 22–24.

Cavanagh, Clare. "Whitman, Mayakovsky, and the Body Politic." In *Rereading Russian Poetry*, 202–222. New Haven: Yale University Press, 1999.

Cestre, Charles. "Walt Whitman, poète de l'Amérique en guerre." *Revue des Nations latines*, October 1918, 168–183.

Chadourne, Marc. "L'énigme du Nouveau monde." *Les Lettres françaises*, no. 95 (February 15, 1946), 3.

Chennevière, Georges. "'Les Fêtes du Peuple.' Commémoration du centenaire de Walt Whitman." *L'Humanité*, June 2, 1919, 2.

Chesterton, G. K. "Is Humanism a Religion." In *The Thing: Why I Am a Catholic*, Collected Works, vol. 3, 137–148. San Francisco: Ignatius Press, 1986.

Chistova I. "Turgenev i Whitman." *Russkaia literatura*, 1966 (no. 2): 196–199; trans. *Walt Whitman Quarterly Review* 13, no. 1–2 (1995): 68–72.

Chukovskaia, Lidiia. *Zapiski ob Anne Akhmatovoi*. Moscow: Soglasie, 1997.

Chukovskii, Kornei. "Anekdot." *Rech'*, February 22 [March 7], 1914.

———. *Dnevnik*. 2 vols. Moscow: Sovetskii Pisatel', 1991.

———. "Ego-futuristy i Kubo-futuristy." In *Almanakh izdatelstva "Shipovnik,"* vol. 22, 95–125. Saint Petersburg: Shipovnik, 1914.

———. "L. Tolstoi ob Uolte Uitmane." *Literaturnaia Gazeta*, August 25, 1940, 4.

———. "Maiakovskii i Uitman." *Leningrad*, 1941 (no. 2), 18–19.

———. "Mirovoi vostorg." *Rech'*, July 18 [31], 1909.

———. *Moi Uitmen*. Moscow: Progress, 1966.

———. "O puti k primireniiu." *Odesskie Novosti*, November 26, 1904.

———. "Pervyi futurist." *Russkoe Slovo*, June 4 [17], 1913.

———. "Poèziia budushchego." *Russkoe Slovo*, July 5 [18], 1913.

———. "Predtecha revolutsionnykh poetov." *Ogonëk*, 1931 (no. 7), 14.

———. "Proza i stikhi Uolta Uitmana." *Literaturnaia Gazeta*, May 30, 1939, 2.

———. "Uolt Uitman." *Literaturnaia Gazeta*, June 10, 1939, 2.

———. "Uolt Uitmen v SSSR: Bibliograficheskie zametki." *Internatsional'naia Literatura*, 1942 (nos. 1–2), 204–206.

———. "Uoltu Uitmenu, Blagodarnost' i slava." *Literaturnaia Gazeta*, May 28, 1969, 8.

———. "Uot Uitmen: Lichnost' i demokratiia ego poèzii." *Maiak. Literaturno-publitsisticheskii sbornik*, 1906 (no. 1), 240–256.

———. "Revoliutsiia i literatura. Poèt-anarkhist Uot Uitman." *Svoboda i zhizn'*, September 24 [October 7], 1906.

———. "Slushaite Uitmena!" *Literaturnaia Gazeta*, May 20, 1955, 6.

———. *Sobranie Sochinenii v piatnatsati tomakh*. Moscow: Agentstvo FTM, Ltg, 2013.

Chuzhyi, Andrii. *Poeziï: Virshi ta poemy*. Kyiv: Radians'kyi pys'mennyk, Kyiv, 1980.

———. *Tvory*, ed. V. T. Polishchuk. Cherkasy: Siiach, 1997.

Clark, Katerina. *Eurasia without Borders: The Dream of a Leftist Literary Commons, 1919–1943*. Cambridge, MA: Harvard University Press, 2021.

———. *Moscow, the Fourth Rome: Stalinism, Cosmopolitanism, and the Evolution of Soviet Culture, 1931–1941*. Cambridge, MA: Harvard University Press, 2011.

Claudel, Paul. "Richard Wagner. Rêverie d'un poète français." *La Revue de Paris*, July 15, 1934, 269–292.

Cohen, Jonathan. "'Countersong to Walt Whitman': Pedro Mir's Radical Dialogue with the Bard." *TIES*, no. 7 (2023), accessed April 10, 2023, http://revueties.org/document/1154-document-sans-titre.

Cohen, Matt. *Whitman's Drift: Imagining Literary Distribution*. Iowa City: University of Iowa Press, 2017.

Cohn, Deborah N. *The Latin American Literary Boom and U. S. Nationalism during the Cold War*. Nashville: Vanderbilt University Press, 2012.

Conway, Christopher. "Of Subjects and Cowboys: Frontier and History in Pedro Mir's '*Countersong to Walt Whitman*.'" *Walt Whitman Quarterly Review* 15, no. 4 (1998): 161–171.

Cooley, Broche. *Uzorn*. Los Angeles: Aroysgegebn fun a grupe fraynt, 1931.

Cooper, Elizabeth. "Tamiris and the Federal Dance Theatre 1936-1939: Socially Relevant Dance Amidst the Policies and Politics of the New Deal Era." *Dance Research Journal* 29, no. 2 (Autumn 1997): 23–48.

Corso, Gregory. *Elegiac Feelings American*. New York: New Directions, 1970.

Cravan, Arthur. "Sifflet." *Soil* 1, no. 1 (December 1916), 36.

Dagen, Philippe. *Le Primitivisme: Une invention moderne*. Paris: Gallimard, 2019.

Dandeles, Gregory. "Avant-Gardes at the Iron Curtains: A Transnational Reading of Allen Ginsberg and the Soviet Estradny Movement." PhD diss., University of Michigan, 2017.

Darío, Rubén. *Azul . . . Cantos de vida y esperanza*. Madrid: Espasa Calpe, 1994 [1888, 1890].

———. *Prosas profanas y otros poemas*. Madrid: Editorial Castalia, 1983 [1896].

David, Jérôme. *Spectres de Goethe: Les Métamorphoses de la littérature mondiale*. Paris: Les Prairies ordinaires, 2011.

Davies, Catherine A. *Whitman's Queer Children: America's Homosexual Epics*. London: Continuum, 2012.

Debs, Eugene. "About Walt Whitman." *Conservator* 18, no. 5 (July 1907), 73.

Deitch, Mattes. *Tsum noentstn shtern*. Tel Aviv: Peretz Publications, 1959.

Djagalov, Rossen. *From Internationalism to Postcolonialism: Literature and Cinema between the Second and Third Worlds*. Montreal: McGill-Queen's University Press, 2020.

Drey, Arthur. "Walt Whitman." *Die Aktion*, no. 24 (September 4, 1911), 907.

Duhamel, George. "Rubrique Les Poèmes." *Mercure de France*, April 13, 1913, 576.

Eastman, Max. "Menshevizing Whitman." *New Masses* 2, no. 2 (December 1926), 12.

———. "Walt Whitman: Poet of Democracy." *Reader's Digest*, no. 42 (June 1943), 29–33.

Eckel, Leslie. *Atlantic Citizens: Nineteenth-Century Writers at Work in the World.* Edinburgh: Edinburgh University Press, 2013.

Edwards, Michael. *Le Bonheur d'être ici.* Paris: Fayard, 2011.

Einboden, Jeffrey. *Nineteenth-Century U. S. Literature in Middle Eastern Languages.* Edinburgh: Edinburgh University Press, 2013.

Èizenshtein, Sergei. *Izbrannye proizvedeniia v 6 tomakh.* Moscow: Iskusstvo, 1964.

———. *Neravnodushnaia priroda.* Moscow: Muzei Kino, Èizenshtein Tsentr, 2006.

Engelson, Suzanne. "Un grand poète américain: Walt Whitman." *Rouge midi. Organe régional du Parti communiste,* September, 3, 1944, 4.

Erkkilä, Betsy. "'To Paris with my Love:' Walt Whitman among the French Revisited." *Revue d'Études Françaises Américaines,* 108, no. 2 (2006): 7–22.

———. *Walt Whitman among the French.* Princeton: Princeton University Press, 1980.

Espagne, Michel. "Comparison and Transfer: A Question of Method." In *Transnational challenges to national history writing,* edited by Matthias Middel and Lluis Roura, 36–53. New York: Palgrave MacMillan, 2013.

Estraikh, Gennady. "Utopias and cities of Kalman Zingman, an uprooted Yiddishist dreamer." *East European Jewish Affairs* 36, no. 1 (June 2006): 31–42.

Ètkind, Efim. *Poèziia i perevod.* Moscow: Sovetskii Pisatel', 1963.

Etherington, Ben. *Literary Primitivism.* Stanford: Stanford University Press, 2017.

Eventon, I. S., ed. *Poeziia v bol'shevistskikh izdaniiakh: 1901–1917.* Leningrad: Sovetskii pisatel', 1967.

Faludy, György. *My Happy Days in Hell.* New York: William Morrow & Co., 1963.

Feinsod, Harris. *The Poetry of the Americas: From Good Neighbors to Counterculture.* Oxford: Oxford University Press, 2017.

Felipe, León. *Canto a mí mismo.* 1941. Madrid: Visor, 2008.

———. *España y el viento.* Madrid: Libertarias/Prodhufi, 1993.

———. *Ganarás la luz.* 1943. Madrid: Cátedra, 2006.

Ferlinghetti, Lawrence. *Starting from San Francisco.* New York: New Directions, 1961.

---. *Who Are We Now?* New York: New Directions, 1976.
Ferreira, Carla Sofia. "Seeing through French Eyes: 'Vers Libre' in Whitman, Laforgue, and Eliot." *Cambridge Quarterly* 45, no. 1 (2016): 20–41.
Folsom, Ed. "Impact on the World." In *The New Walt Whitman Studies*, edited by Matt Cohen, 231–247. Cambridge: Cambridge University Press, 2019.
---. "So Long! So Long! Walt Whitman, Langston Hughes and the Art of Longing." In *Walt Whitman: Where the Future Becomes Present*, edited by David Haven Blake and Michael Robertson, 127–143. Iowa City: University of Iowa Press, 2008.
---, ed. *Whitman East and West: New Contexts for Reading Walt Whitman*. Iowa City: University of Iowa Press, 2002.
Fomeshi, Benham M. *The Persian Whitman: Beyond a Literary Reception*. Leiden: Leiden University Press, 2019.
Frank, Waldo. *Our America*. New York: Boni and Liveright, 1919.
Franklin, Kelly Scott. "A Translation of Whitman discovered in the 1912 Spanish Periodical *Prometeo*." *Walt Whitman Quarterly Review* 35, no. 1 (2017): 115–126.
Freiligrath, Ferdinand. "Walt Whitman." *Augsburger Allgemeine Zeitung*, April 24; June 10; June 19, 1868, 257–259; 369–371; 385.
Freyre, Gilberto. *O camarada Whitman: conferência lida na Sociedade dos Amigos da América do Rio de Janeiro, em 22 de Maio de 1947, precedida de uma saudação a Gilberto Freyre*. Rio de Janeiro: J. Olympio: 1948.
Friche, Vladimir. "Uot Uitmèn." *Vestnik zhizni*, 1919 (no. 3–4), 67–70.
Gabriel, José. *Walt Whitman: La voz democrática de América*. Montevideo: Ediciones Ceibo, 1944.
Gasman, Gregorio. "Responsabilidad del poeta." *El Siglo*, April 11, 1943.
---. "Sobre Pablo Neruda." *El Siglo*, October 10, 1943.
Gasquet, Joachim. *L'Art vainqueur*. Paris: Nouvelle librairie nationale, 1919.
Gaucheron, Jacques. "Le grand bonhomme vit encore et Walt Whitman parle plus haut que le petit monsieur." *Les Lettres françaises*, no. 223 (September 2, 1948), 3.
Geiser, Matvei. *Samuil Marshak*. Moscow: Molodaia Gvardiia, 2006.
Ghéon, Henri. "Les Poèmes : le whitmanisme." *Nouvelle Revue Française*, no. 17 (June 1912), 1053–1071.
Gilenson, Boris. "Poet of the World. Poet of Time and Space." *Soviet Life*, June 1969, 47.
Ginsberg, Allen. *Collected Poems, 1947–1997*. New York, Harper Collins, 2006.

Glaser, Amelia, and Steven Lee, ed. *Comintern Aesthetics*. Toronto: Toronto University Press, 2020.

Gold, Mike. "John Reed's Body." *Liberator* 6, no. 10 (October 1923), 21.

———. (Granich, Irwin). "Towards Proletarian Art." *Liberator* 4, no. 2 (February 1921), 20–22.

Gold, Mike (Michael). "Ode to Walt Whitman." *New Masses*, November 5, 1935, 21.

Golding, Alan. *From Outlaw to Classic: Canons in American Poetry*. Madison: University of Wisconsin Press, 1995.

Goldman, Emma. *Living My Life*. Vol 2. Dover: New York, 1970.

Gombrich, Ernst. *The Preference for the Primitive: Episodes in the History of Western Taste and Art*. New York: Phaidon, 2002.

González Tuñón, Raúl. *Primer canto argentino*. Buenos Aires: author's edition, 1945.

Gorelik, Sch. *Groyse neshomes*. Dresden: Wostok, 1921.

Gosse, Sir Edmund. "A Note on Walt Whitman." *New Review* 10 (April 1894), 447–57, reprinted in *Critical Kit-Kats*. New York: Dodd, Mead, 1896.

Graham, Marcus. *An Anthology of Revolutionary Poetry*. New York: The Active Press, 1929.

Greenberg, Uri Zvi. *Kelape Tish'im Ve-tish'ah*. Tel Aviv: Sadan, 1928.

Gribova, Zinaida. *Khudozhniki "Amaravelly:" sud'by i tvorchestvo*. Moscow: MBA, 2009.

Grillaert, Ned. *What the God-Seekers Found in Nietzsche: The Reception of Nietzsche's Übermensch by the Philosophers of the Russian Religious Renaissance*. Amsterdam: Rodopi, 2008.

Grossman, Joan Delaney, and Ruth Rischin, eds. *William James in Russian Culture*. Landham: Lexington Books, 2003.

Grünzweig, Walter. *Constructing the German Walt Whitman*. Iowa City: University of Iowa Press, 1994.

———. "'For America—For All the Earth.' Walt Whitman as an International(ist) Poet." In *Breaking Bounds*, edited by Betsy Erkkilä and Jay Grossman, 238–249. Oxford: Oxford University Press, 1996.

———. "'Salut au Monde!': Walt Whitmans weltliterarische Programmatik und sein globales Netzwerk." In *Vergleichende Weltliteraturen / Comparative World Literatures*, edited by Dieter Lamping and Galin Tihanov, 163–182. Berlin: Metzler, 2019.

———. "Whitman and the Cold War. The Centenary Celebrations of Leaves of Grass in Eastern Europe." In *Walt Whitman: The Sesquicentennial Essays*, edited by Susan Belasco, Ed Folsom and Kenneth Price, 343–360. Lincoln: University of Nebraska Press, 2007.

Gerasimov, Mikhail. "O vechere Petrogradskogo Proletkul'ta." *Gorn*, 1918 (no. 1), 56–57.

Grossman, Jay. "Whitman in Your Pocket: The History of the Book and the History of Sexuality." In *The New Walt Whitman Studies*, edited by Matt Cohen, 101–120. Cambridge: Cambridge University Press, 2020.

Guilbeaux, Henri. "Walt Whitman." *L'Effort libre*, May–June 1912, 576–577.

———. *Walt Whitman: Portraits d'hier*. Paris: H. Fabre, 1910.

Hamsun, Knut. *Fret det moderne Amerikas aandsliv*. Copenhagen: Philipsens Forlag, 1889.

Harris, Kirsten. *Whitman and British Socialism: "The Love of Comrades."* London: Routledge, 2016.

Harshav, Barbara, and Benjamin Harshav, eds. *American Yiddish Poetry: A Bilingual Anthology*. 2nd ed. Stanford: Stanford University Press, 2007.

Hartmann, Sadakichi. *Conversations with Walt Whitman*. New York: E. P. Coby & Co., 1895.

Haydar, Adnan, and Michael Beard. "A Translation of Abdel-Muneim Ramadan's 'Walt Whitman's Funeral,' and Some Notes on Whitman in the Arab World." *Walt Whitman Quarterly Review* 35, no. 1 (2017): 127–136.

Hemingway, Andrew. *Artists on the Left: American Artists and the Communist Movement, 1926–1956*. New Haven: Yale University Press, 2002.

Herasymchuk, Les'. *Amerykans'kyi bard v Ukraini*. Kyiv: IVNVKP Ukreliotekh, 2009.

Herra, Maurice. "'Feuilles d'herbe' en Europe et en Amérique latine." *Europe* 33, no. 119 (November 1955), 137–145.

Hicks, Granville. *The Great Tradition: An Interpretation of American Literature since the Civil War*. 1933. Chicago: Quadrangle Books, 1969.

Hobson, Sam. "The Boot War." *Labour Leader*, April 13, 1895.

Holcomb, Esther Lolita. "Whitman and Sandburg." *English Journal* 17, no. 7 (September 1928): 549–555.

Hoover, J. Edgar. *Masters of Deceit: The Story of Communism in America and How to Fight It*. New York: Henry Holt and Company, 1958.

Hughes, Langston. *The Collected Poems*. Edited by A. Rampersad. New York: Knopf, 1997.

Hutchinson, George B. "The Whitman Legacy and the Harlem Renaissance." In *Walt Whitman: The Centennial Essays*, edited by Ed Folsom, 201–216. Iowa City: University of Iowa Press, 1994.

Irmscher, Christoph. *Max Eastman: A Life*. New Haven: Yale University Press, 2017.

Isaacson, Isaac. *Eseyen un kritik vegn literatur un kunst*. Buenos Aires: Visn, 1933.

Ivanov, Viacheslav. *Sobranie sochinenii*. Brussels: Foyer Oriental Chrétien, 1987.

Jamati, Paul. *Poèmes datés*. Paris: Seghers, 1950.

———. *Walt Whitman*. Paris: Seghers, 1948.

James, William. "Pragmatism and Religion." In *Pragmatism*, 131–144. Cambridge, MA: Harvard University Press, 1975.

———. *The Varieties of Religious Experience*. 1905. New York: The Modern Library, 1936.

Jangfeldt, Bengt. *Mayakovsky: A Biography*. Translated by Harry D. Watson. Chicago: University of Chicago Press, 2014.

Jannacone, Pasquale. *La poesia di Walt Whitman e l'evoluzione delle forme ritmiche*. Turin: Roux Frassati & Co., 1898.

Jewell, Andrew, and Kenneth Price. "Twentieth-Century Mass Media Appearances." In *A Companion to Walt Whitman*, edited by Donald D. Kummings. 341–359. Oxford: Wiley-Blackwell, 2009.

Jouvenel, Renaud de. "Walt Whitman." *Europe* 33, no. 119 (November 1955), 91–107.

Karsner, David. *Horace Traubel: His Life and Work*. New York: Arens, 1919.

Kaufman, Naum. "Chelovek s apparatom." *Sovetskii èkran*, 1929 (no. 5), 5.

Khlebnikov, Velimir. *Collected Works*. Translated by Paul Schmidt. Vol. 1 edited by C. Douglas; vol. 3 edited by R. Vroon. Cambridge, MA: Harvard University Press, 1987.

———. *Sobranie sochinenii*. 6 vols. Moscow: Nasledie, IMLI RAN, 2000–2006.

Khotimsky, Maria. "World Literature, Soviet Style." *Ab Imperio* 3 (2013): 119–154.

Kin, Ostap, ed. *New York Elegies: Ukrainian Poems on the City*. Boston: Academic Studies Press, 2019.

Kirby-Smith, H. T. *The Origins of Free Verse*. Ann Harbor: The University of Michigan Press, 1996.

K[irillov], V. "Uot Uitmen i proletarskii teatr." *Griadushchee*, July 1918 (no. 5), 12.

Kissin, I., ed. *Lider fun der milkhome: antologye*. New York: Bibliotek fun poezie un esayen, 1943.

Kubilius, Vytautas. "Pakeliui su Voltu Vitmenu." *Pergalė*, 1978 (no. 11), 116–128.

Kugel', Alexander. (Homo novus). "Zametki." *Teatr i iskusstvo*, nos. 26–27 (August 14, 1918).

Kowalke, Kim H. "For Those We Love: Hindemith, Whitman, and 'An American Requiem.'" *Journal of the American Musicological Society* 50, no. 1 (Spring 1997): 133–174.

Kulyk, Ivan, ed. *Antolohiia amerykans'koï poeziï, 1855–1925*. Kharkiv: Derzhavne vydavnytstvo Ukrainy, 1928.

Kunichika, Michael. "'The ecstasy of breadth': The Odic and the Whitmanesque Style in Dziga Vertov's *One Sixth of the World* (1926)." *Studies in Russian and Soviet Cinema* 6, no. 1 (2012): 53–74.

Kurtz, Aaron. *Lider*. New York: Aaron Kurtz Book Committee, 1966.

Kuzmin, Mikhail. "K. D. Bal'mont." *Zhizn' iskusstva*, no. 399 (March 16, 1920), 1–2.

Kutzinski, Vera. *The Worlds of Langston Hughes: Modernism and Translations in the Americas*. Ithaca: Cornell University Press, 2012.

Laforgue, Jules. *Œuvres complètes*. Lausanne: L'Âge d'homme, 1995.

Landau, Zisha. *Antologye: di Idishe dikhtung in Amerike biz yohr 1919*. New York: Farlag Idish, 1919.

Landauer, Gustav. "Walt Whitman." *Vossische Zeitung* 47, no. 143 (1907), 2.

Larbaud, Valery. *Ce vice impuni, la lecture: Domaine anglais*. Paris: Gallimard, 1936.

———. *Œuvres*. Paris: Gallimard, "Bibliothèque de la Pléiade," 1957.

Larionov, Mikhail. "Luchistaia zhivopis'." In *Oslinyi khvost' i michen.'* Moscow: Izd. Ts. A. Miunster, 1913.

Lasserre, Pierre. "Walt Whitman." *L'Action française*, April 27, 1909.

Lawrence, D. H. *The Complete Poems*. Harmondsworth: Penguin Books, 1993.

———. *Studies in Classic American Literature*. Edited by E. Greenspan, L. Vasey and J. Worthen. Cambridge: Cambridge University Press, 2003.

Lebesgue, Philéas. "De Whitman à Verhaeren et au-delà." *Les Visages de la Vie*, no. 6 (1909).

———. "Walt Whitman et la poésie contemporaine." In Philéas Lebesgue, Alphonse Marius Gosser and Henri Strentz, *Essai d'expansion d'une esthétique*. Le Havre: Éditions de la Province, 1911.

Lecomte, Joseph. "Un poète américain: Walt Whitman." *La Vie intellectuelle* (Brussels), no. 1 (1908), 17–28.

Lee, Steven S. *The Ethnic Avant-Garde: Minority Cultures and World Revolution*. New York: Columbia University Press, 2015.

Leighton, Lauren. *Two Worlds, One Art: Literary Translation in Russia and America*. De Kalb: Northern Illinois University Press, 1991.

Leftwich, Joseph, ed. *The Golden Peacock: A Worldwide Treasury of Yiddish Poetry*. 2nd ed. New York: T. Yoseloff, 1961.

Le Sueur, Meridel. "Jelly Roll." 1980. In *Walt Whitman: The Measure of His Song*, edited by Jim Perlman, Ed Folsom and Dan Campion, 421–424. Duluth : Holy Cow! Press, 1998.

Levet, Henry Jean-Marie. *Cartes postales et autres textes, précédés d'une conversation de Léon-Paul Fargue et Valery Larbaud*. Paris: Poésie/Gallimard, 2001.

Levin, Yaakov, ed. *Dos naye bukh literarishe un historishe khrestomatye: leyenbukh far dem eltern klas fun der elementarer shul: un dem ershtn klas fun mitlshul*. New York: Yidishe Shul, 1929.

Levinson, Julian. "Walt Whitman among the Yiddish Poets." *Tikkun* 18, no. 5 (2003): 57–69.

Levinson, Julian. *Exiles on Main Street: Jewish American Writers and American Literary Culture*. Bloomington: Indiana University Press, 2008.

Leivick, H. *A blat oyf an eplboym*. Buenos Aires: Kium, 1955.

Li, Xilao. "Walt Whitman in China." *Walt Whitman Quarterly Review* 5, no. 3 (Spring 1986): 1–8.

Libman, Valentina. *Amerikanskaia literatura v russkikh perevodakh i kritike: Bibliografiia 1776–1975*. Moscow: Nauka, 1977.

Liessin, Abraham. *Lider un poemen (1888–1938)*. New York: Forverts Asosyeyshon, 1938.

Lima, Jorge de. *Poesia completa*. Rio de Janeiro: Nova Fronteira, 1980.

Lindsay, Vachel. "Walt Whitman." *New Republic* 37, December 5, 1923, "Views of American Poetry" supplement, 3–5.

Lista, Giovanni. *Le Futurisme: Textes et manifestes (1909–1944)*. Ceyzérieu: Champ Vallon, 2015.

Lourenço, Eduardo. *Fernando, Rei da Nossa Baviera*. Lisboa: Imprensa Nacional-Casa da Moeda, 1986.

———. *Pessoa revisitado*. Porto: Editorial Inova, 1973.

Lovejoy, Arthur, and George Boas. *Primitivism and Related Ideas in Antiquity*. Baltimore: Johns Hopkins Press, 1935.

Lowenfels, Walter, ed. *Walt Whitman's Civil War*. New York: Knopf, 1960.

———, ed. *Where Is Vietnam? American Poets Respond*. New York: Double Day Anchor, 1967.

———, ed. *The Writing against the Wall: 108 American Poets of Protest*. New York: Double Day & Co., 1969.

Lucini, Gian Pietro. *Ragion poetica e programma del verso libero: Grammatica ricordi e confidenze per servire alla storia delle lettere contemporanee*. Milan: Edizione di Poesia, 1908.

Ludwig, Reuben. *Gezalmete Lider*. New York: Aroysgegeben fun kolegn un fraynt mit der hilf fun Y. L. Perets shrayber-fareyn, 1927.

Lukash, Ivan. *Tsvety iadovitye* [1910]. N.p.: Salamandra PVV, 2018.

Luk'ianova, Irina. *Kornei Chukovskii*. Moscow: Molodaia Gvardiia, 2006.

Lundkvist, Artur. *Naket Liv*. Stockholm: Bonniers, 1929.

Lunn, Eugen. *Prophet of Community: The Romantic Socialism of Gustav Landauer*. Berkeley: University of California Press, 1973.

MacLeish, Archibald. *Land of the Free*. San Diego: Harcourt, Brace and Company, 1938.

Maeterlinck, Maurice. *Le Cahier bleu*. Edited by Joanne Wieland Burston. Ghent: Éditions de la Fondation Maurice Maeterlinck, 1977.

Maiakovskii, Vladimir. *Polnoe sobranie sochinenii v 13 tomakh*. Moscow: Khudozhestvennaia literatura, 1955–1961.

Malková, Ivá. "Kolář – Whitman." *Literární Archiv*, no. 46 (2014): 177–194.

Mally, Lynn. *Culture of the Future: The Proletkult Movement in Revolutionary Russia*. Berkeley: University of California Press, 1990.

Maliuchenko, G. S. "Pervye teatral'nye sezony novoi epokhi." In *U istokov: Sbornik statii*, edited by Dmitri Shchlegov, 242–331. Moscow: VTO, 1960.

Mandel'shtam, Osip. *Sobranie sochinenii*. Moscow: Art-Biznes-Tsentr, 1993.

Maples Arce, Manuel. *Super-poema bolchevique en 5 cantos*. Mexico City: Editorial Andrés Botas e Hijo, SUCR, 1924; *City. Bolshevik Super-Poem in 5 Cantos*. Translated by K. M. Cascia in *Stridentist Poems*. Storrs: World Poetry Books, 2023.

Martí, José, "El poeta Walt Whitman." *La Nación* [Buenos Aires], June 26, 1887.

Martin, Robert K., ed. *The Continuing Presence of Walt Whitman: The Life after the Life*. Iowa City: University of Iowa Press, 1992.

Masson, Elsie. "Walt Whitman, ouvrier et poète." *Mercure de France*, August 1, 1907, 385–390.

Mayzel, Nayman, ed. *Amerike in Yidishn vort antologye*. New York: Ikuf, 1955.

McGrath, Thomas. "Revolutionary Frescoes—the Ascension." *Praxis*, no. 2, 1978.

Mendelson, Maurice. *Life and Work of Walt Whitman: A Soviet View.* Translated by A. Bromfield. Moscow: Progress Publishers, 1976.

Mendel'son, Morris. "Uolt Uitmen." *Novyi mir,* March 1945, 183–188.

———. *Walt Whitman: Kritiko-biograficheskii ocherk.* Moscow: Goslitizdat, 1954.

Mendoza, Miguel R. *Walt Whitman, Cantor de la Democracia: Ensayo biográfico y breve antología.* Mexico: Secretaría de Educación Pública, 1946.

Merrill, Stuart. *Une voix dans la foule.* Paris: Mercure de France, 1909.

Meschonnic, Henri. *Poétique du traduire.* Lagrasse: Verdier, 1999.

Mgebrov, Aleksandr. *Zhizn' v teatre.* Moscow, Leningrad: Academia, 1932.

Michaud, Régis. *Mystiques et réalistes anglo-saxons, d'Emerson à Bernard Shaw.* Paris: Armand Colin, 1918.

Mieželaitis, Eduardas. *Barokinė Lyra.* Vilnius: Lietuvos rašytojų sąjungos leidykla, 2009.

Miler, Louis. *Do iz mayn heym.* New York: Farlag "Signal" beym "Proletpen," 1939.

Mir, Pedro. *Contracanto a Walt Whitman: Canto a nosotros mismos.* Guatemala: Ediciones Saker-Ti, 1952.

———. *Poemas.* Madrid: Ediciones de la Discreta, 2009.

———. *Countersong to Walt Whitman and Other Poems.* Translated by Jonathan Cohen and Donald Walsh. Leeds: Peepal Tree Press Limited, 2017.

Mirskii, D. S. "Poèt amerikanskoi demokratii." Preface to *List'ia travy,* 1935, 9–30. Translated by Stephen Stepanchev, in *Walt Whitman and the World,* edited by Gay Wilson Allen and Ed Folsom, 300–338. Iowa City: University of Iowa Press, 1995.

Mirsky, D. S. *A History of Russian Literature: From Its Beginnings to 1900.* London: Routledge, 1926–1927.

———. "Walt Whitman: Poet of American Democracy." Translated by Bernard Guilbert Guerney. *Dialectics,* 1937 (no. 1), 11–29.

Montes, Eugenio. "En el centenario de Walt Whitman." *Cervantes,* May 1919, 70–76.

Montoliu, Cebrià. *Walt Whitman, l'home i sa tasca.* Barcelona: Societat Catalana d'Edicions, 1913.

Morgan, Claude. "Le souffle de Walt Whitman." *Les Lettres françaises,* no. 154 (May 2, 1947), 1.

Murray, Natalia. *Art for the Workers: Proletarian Art and Festive Decorations of Petrograd, 1917–1920.* Leyden: Brill, 2018.

Murray, Nina. "Walt Whitman in Russia. Three Love Affairs." *Public Domain Review*, May 29, 2019. https://publicdomainreview.org/essay/walt-whitman-in-russia-three-love-affairs/

Nascimento, Abdias do. *Axés do sangue e da esperança*. Rio de Janeiro: Achiamé/Rioarte, 1983.

Negri, Ada. "Il gigante della libera America." *Il figurinaio* 5, no. 8 (February 19, 1893), 2–3.

Nel'dikhen, Sergei. "Puti Russkoi Poèzii" (1921). In *Organnoe Mnogogolos'e*. Moscow: Ogi, 2013.

Neruda, Pablo. *Holzfäller, wach auf! Hymnus auf den Frieden*. Leipzig: Insel, 1955.

———. *Let the Rail Splitter Awaken and Other Poems*. Translated by Waldeen et al. New York: Masses and Mainstream, 1950.

———. *Obras completas*. 5 vols. Barcelona: Galaxia Gutenberg, 1999–2002.

Nissenson, Aaron. *Dos lebn vil mayse hern*. New York: A. Biderman, 1930.

Opitz, Thoren. "World Wide Walt: Making and Marketing Whitman's Global Persona." In *The New Walt Whitman Studies*, edited by Matt Cohen, 68–82. Cambridge: Cambridge University Press, 2019.

Orlitskii, Iurii. *Stikh i proza v kul'ture Serebrianogo veka*. Moscow: Iazyki slavianskikh kul'tur, 2018.

Ostrovsky, Nikolai. *How the Steel Was Tempered*. Translated by R. Prokofieva. Moscow: Foreign Languages Publishing House, 1952.

Otero, Blas de. *Obra completa*. Edited by Sabina de la Cruz. Barcelona: Galaxia Gutenberg, 2013.

Panova, Olga. "African-American Literature in the Soviet Union, 1917–1930s: Contacts, Translations, Criticism and Editorial Policy." In *The Red and the Black: The Russian Revolution and the Black Atlantic*, edited by David Featherstone and Christian Høgsbjerg, 97–120. Manchester: Manchester University Press, 2021.

Papini, Giovanni. *L'esperienza futurista (1913–1914)*. Florence: Vallecchi, 1919.

———. "Walt Whitman." *Nuova Antologia*, 16 June 1908. Repr. in *24 Cervelli, Saggi non critici*, 330–367. Milan: Lombardo, 1917.

Papini, Giovanni, and Ardengo Soffici. *Carteggio I, 1903–1908, dal "Leonardo" a "La Voce."* Edited by Mario Richter. Rome: Edizioni di Storia e Letteratura, 1991.

Parmentier, Mathilde. "Walt Whitman." *Le Moniteur des consulats et du commerce international*, June 30, 1917.

Parry, Albert. "Walt Whitman in Russia." *American Mercury*, September 1934, 107.

Pasternak, Boris. *Doktor Zhivago*. 1957. Moscow: Eksmo, 2003.

Pásztor, Árpád. "Jegyzetek Walt Whitman századik születésnapjára." *Nyugat*, no. 11 (June 1, 1919).

———. *Walt Whitman*. Budapest: Dick Manó kiadása, 1920.

Patchen, Kenneth. *Red Wine & Yellow Hair*. New York: New Directions, 1949.

Pavese, Cesare. "Whitman." *La Cultura*, June–September 1933. Repr. in *La letteratura americana e oltre saggi*. Turin: Einaudi, 1990 [1951].

Pérez i Jorba, Joan. "Whitman." *Catalònia*, no. 6 (February 10, 1900), 52–54.

Perry, Bliss. *Walt Whitman*. Boston: Houghton and Mifflin, 1906.

Pessoa, Fernando. *Poesias de Álvaro de Campos*. Lisboa: Ática, 1944.

Petrovsky-Shtern, Yohanan. *Anti-Imperial Choice: The Making of the Ukrainian Jew*. New Haven: Yale University Press, 2009.

Philippe, Charles-Louis. *Lettres de jeunesse à Henri Vendeputte*. Paris: Gallimard, 1911.

Polonsky, Rachel. "Translating Whitman, Mistranslating Bal'mont." *Slavonic and East European Review* 75, no. 3 (1997): 401–21

Popov, I. "Kamerado, ia daiu tebe ruku." *Inostrannaia Literatura*, 1973 (no. 5), 201–207.

Popov, P. "Uolt Guitman," *Zagranichnyi Vestnik*, March 1883, 567–580.

Pound, Ezra. *The Spirit of Romance*. London: J. M. Dent & sons, 1910.

Prager, Leonard. "Walt Whitman in Yiddish." *Walt Whitman Quarterly Review* 1, no. 3 (1983): 22–35.

Price, Kenneth. "Walt Whitman in Selected Anthologies: The Politics of His Afterlife." *Virginia Quarterly Review* 81, no. 2 (Spring 2005): 147–162.

Pumpianskii, Lev. "Oktiabr'skie torzhestva i khudozhniki Petrograda." *Plamia*, no. 35 (1919), 14.

Ramalho Santos, Irene. *Atlantic Poets: Fernando Pessoa's Turn in Anglo-American Modernism*. Hanover: University of New England Press, 2003.

Rampersad, Arnold. *The Life of Langston Hughes*. Oxford: Oxford University Press, 1986.

Rancière, Jacques. *Aisthesis: Scènes du régime esthétique de l'art*. Paris: Galilée, 2011.

Ravitch, Melech. *Di fir zaytn fun mayn velt*. Wilno: B. Kletskin, 1929.

Reed, John. "America 1918." *New Masses*, October 15, 1935, 1–19.

Reichard, Piroska. *Walt Whitman. 1819–1892*. Budapest: Franklin, 1914.

Reitblat, Abram. *Kak Pushkin vyshël v genii*. Moscow: NLO, 2001.

Ricciardi, Caterina. "Walt Whitman and the Futurist Muse." In *Utopia in the Present Tense: Walt Whitman and the Language of the New World*, edited by Marina Camboni, 265–284. Rome: Il calamo, 1994.

Richepin, Jean. *L'Âme américaine à travers quelques-uns de ses interprètes*. Paris: Flammarion, 1920.

Riethmuller, Richard Henri. *Walt Whitman and the Germans*. Philadelphia: Philadelphia Americana Germanica Press, 1906.

Robertson, Michael. *Worshipping Walt: The Whitman Disciples*. Princeton: Princeton University Press, 2008.

Robbins, Timothy. "Emma Goldman Reading Walt Whitman: Aesthetics, Agitation, and the Anarchist Ideal." *Texas Studies in Literature and Language* 57, no. 1 (2015): 80–105.

Rozanov, Vasilii. "Eshchë o demokratii, Uitmene i Chukovskom." *Novoe vremia*, August 13 [26], 1915.

———. "Poèziia griadushchei demokratii. Uolt Uitmen." *Novoe vremia*, August 10 [23], 1915.

Rosenfeld, Morris. *Gezamelte lieder*. New York: Aroysgegeben fun der Internatsyonaler bibliothek ferlag kompani, 1904.

Rubinstein, Rachel. *Members of the Tribe: Native America and the Jewish Imagination*. Detroit: Wayne State University, 1990.

Rudd, Charles. *Russian Entrepreneur: Publisher Ivan Sytin of Moscow, 1851–1934*. Montreal: McGill-Queen's University Press, 1990.

Rudniański, Stefan (Ruber). "Walt Whitman. Życie i twórczość." *Wiedza: tygodnik społeczno-polityczny, popularno-naukowy i literacki* 1910, no. 31, 157–160; no. 32, 189–192; no. 33, 220–224.

Rumeau, Delphine. *Fortunes de Walt Whitman: Enjeux d'une réception transatlantique*. Paris: Classiques Garnier, 2019.

———. "Primitif américain et primitivisme russe. Deux cas de réception (Longfellow, Whitman)." *Slavica Occitania*, no. 53 (2021): 249–275.

———. "Whitman, antidote à Mallarmé." *Revue des Sciences Humaines*, no. 340 (2021): 85–100.

Saadi, Youssef. *Qasai'd Sadhijah*. Damascus: al-Mada, 1996.

———. *Without an Alphabet, without a Face*. Translated by Khaled Mattawa. Saint Paul: Graywolf Press, 2002.

Sainson, Katia. "'L'ardent mal de contact:' les 'Paroles avec Walt Whitman' de Jean Sénac." *Algérie Littérature / Action*, nos. 133–136 (September–December 2009): 85–100.

Samorodova, Olga. "Poèt na Kavkaze." *Zvezda*, 1972 (no. 6).

Sandburg, Carl. *Chicago Poems*. New York: Henry Holt & Co., 1916.

Santayana, George. *Interpretations of Poetry and Religion*. New York: Scribner's Sons, 1900.

———. "Walt Whitman: A Dialogue." *Harvard Monthly*, May 1890, 85–91.

Santí, Enrico Mario. *Ciphers of History: Latin American Readings for a Cultural Age*. New York: Palgrave Macmillan, 2005.

Sarrazin, Gabriel. *La Renaissance de la poésie anglaise*. Paris: Perrin et Cie, 1889.

Saunders, Henry S., ed. *Parodies on Walt Whitman*. New York: American Library Service, 1923.

Scherr, Barry. "Dalliance with Language: Chukovsky and Bal'mont Translate Whitman." In *Stikh, iazyk, poèziia: pamiati Mikhaila Leonovicha Gasparova*, edited by Khenryk Baran et al., 654–665. Moscow: RGGU, 2006.

Schlaf, Johannes. "Walt Whitman." *Freie Bühne für den Entwicklungskampf der Zeit*, 1892 (no. 3), 977–988.

———. *Walt Whitman*. Berlin and Leipzig: Schuster & Loeffler, 1904.

Schmidgall, Gary. *Conserving Walt Whitman's Fame: Selections from Horace Traubel's Conservator, 1890–1919*. Iowa City: Iowa University Press, 2006.

Sedgwick, Eve Kosofsky. *Between Men: English Literature and Male Homosocial Desire*. New York: Columbia University Press, 1985.

Segal, Jacob Isaac. *Lyrik*. Montreal: 1930.

Seghers, Pierre. *La Résistance et ses poètes: Récit*. Paris: Pierre Seghers, 2022.

Selincourt, Basil de. *Walt Whitman: A Critical Study*. London: M. Secker, 1914.

Sénac, Jean. *Œuvres poétiques*. Arles: Actes Sud, 1999.

Semenko, Mykhail'. *Kobzar'*. Kyiv: Gol'fstrom, 1924.

Severianin, Igor'. *Medal'ony*. Belgrade: Izd. Avtora, 1934.

Schama, Simon. *Landscape and Memory*. New York: Knopf, 1995.

Shevchenko, Aleksandr. *Neo-Primitivizm: Ego teoriia, ego vozmozhnosti, ego dostizheniia*. Moscow: Tipografiia 1-i Moskovskoi Trudovoi Arteli, 1913.

Shostakovich, Dmitri, *Desiat' poèm na slova revoliutsenykh poètov kontsa XIX–nachala XX stoletii: dlia smeshannogo khora bez soprovozhdeniia, soch. 88*. Moscow: Izdatel'stvo DSCH, 2016.

Sillen, Samuel. *Walt Whitman: Poet of Democracy*. 1944. New York: International Publishers, 1974.

———. "Walt Whitman, Poète de la démocratie américaine." *La Pensée, Revue du rationalisme moderne*, no. 69 (September 1956), 77–91; no. 70 (November 1956), 69–82.

Sillen, Samiuèl. "Zametki ob Uitemene." *Literaturnaia Gazeta*, no. 70, June 14, 1955: 4.

Singer, Ben. "Connoisseurs of Chaos: Whitman, Vertov and the 'poetic survey.'" *Literature Film Quarterly* 15, no. 4 (1987): 247–258.

Skwara, Marta. *Polski Whitman: O funkcjonowaniu poety obcego w kulturze narodowej*. Krakow: Towarzystwo Autorów i Wydawców Prac Naukowych Universitas, 2010.

Smith, Gerry. *D. S. Mirsky: A Russian-English Life, 1890–1939*. Oxford: Oxford University Press, 2000.

Smith, Lawrence G. *Cesare Pavese and America: Life, Love and Literature*. Amherst: University of Massachusetts Press, 2008.

Soffici, Ardengo. *Opere*. Vol. 4. Florence: Vallenchi, 1961.

Sokolicz, Antonina. *Walt Whitman*. Warsaw: Wyd. Zw. Robot. Stowarzyszeń Spółdź, 1921.

Sokolov, Gippolit. "O fil'me 'Shestaia chast' mira.'" *Kino-front*, 1927 (no. 2), 9–12. In *Lines of Resistance: Dziga Vertov and the Twenties*, translated by J. Graffy and edited by Yuri Tsivan, 233–239. Pordenone: Le Giornate del cinema muto, 2004.

Spargo, John. *Karl Marx: His Life and Work*. New York: Huebsch, 1910.

Spier, Leonard. "Walt Whitman." *International Literature*, September 1935, 72–89.

Starkina, Sofiia. *Velimir Khlebnikov*. Moscow: Molodaia Gvardiia, 2007.

Steinroetter, Vanessa. "'Pioneers! O Pioneers!' and Whitman's Early German Translators." *Interdisciplinary Studies in the Long Nineteenth Century*, no. 9 (November 2009). https://doi.org/10.16995/ntn.520.

Stella, Joseph. "The New Art." *Trend* 5, June 1913, 393–395.

Stepanchev, Stepan. "Walt Whitman and Russia." In *Walt Whitman and the World*, edited by Gay Wilson Allen and Ed Folsom, 300–338. Iowa City: University of Iowa Press, 1995.

Stremin, Milii (Sergei Proskurnin). "Vecher tovarishcha Uitmena." *Vechernie ogni*, no. 77 (July 22, 1918), 4.

Swinburne, Algernon Charles. *Songs before Sunrise*. 1871. Portland: Thomas B. Mosher, 1901.

———. *Under the Microscope*. 1872. Portland: Thomas B. Mosher, 1899.

———. "Whitmania." *The Fortnightly Review*, August 1, 1887: 170–176.

———. *William Blake: A Critical Essay*. London: John Camden Hotten, 1868.

Symonds, John Addington. *A Problem in Modern Ethics*. London: 1896.

———. *Studies of Greek Poets*. London: Smith, Elder, 1873.

———. *Walt Whitman. A Study*. London: John C. Nimmo, 1893.

Taggard, Genevieve. *Calling Western Union*. New York: Harper and Brothers, 1936.

Tane, Susan Jaffe, and Karen Karbiener. *Poet of the Body: New York's Walt Whitman*. New York: Grolier Club, 2019.

Thomas, M. Wynn. *Transatlantic Connections: Whitman U. S., Whitman U. K.* Iowa City: University of Iowa Press, 2005.

Tihanov, Galin. *The Birth and Death of Literary Theory: Regimes of Relevance in Russia and Beyond*. Stanford: Stanford University Press, 2019.

Tiger, Theobald (Kurt Tucholsky). "Die fünf Sinne." *Die Weltbühne* 21.2, no. 37 (September 15, 1925), 420–422.

Tolstoi, Lev. *Polnoe sobranie sochinenii v 90 tomakh*. Moscow: Khudozhestvennaia Literatura, 1928–1958.

Torre, Guillermo de. *Hélices: Poemas, 1918–1922*. Madrid: Editorial Mundo Latino, 1923.

———. *Literaturas europeas de vanguardia*. Madrid: R. Caro Raggio, 1925.

Traubel, Horace. *Communal Songs*. Boston: Small, Maynard & Co., 1904.

———. *Optimos*. New York: Huebsch, 1910.

———. *Weckrufe: Kommunistische Gesänge*. Translated by O. E. Lessing. Munich, Leipzig: Piper & Co., 1907.

Traverso, Enzo. *Left-Wing Melancholia: Marxism, History and Memory*. New York: Columbia University Press, 2017.

Tychyna, Pavlo. *V kosmichnomu orkestri*. Lviv: Nova kultura, 1921, 1923.

Unamuno, Miguel de. "El canto adámico." *Los Lunes de El Imparcial*, Madrid, August 6, 1906.

Varshe, Moyshe. *A Translator's Diary*. Translated from Yiddish by Corbin Allardice. "Taytshworks: a yiddish translation blog," accessed September 8, 2023. https://www.taytshworks.com/moyshe-varshe-a-translator-s-diary.

Venediktova, Tatiana. *Poèziia Uolta Uitmena*. Moscow: MGU, 1982.

Vincenz, Stanislaw. "Religia Walta Whitmana." *Naród*, no. 23 (1921), 3–4.

Vladeck, Baruch, ed. *Fun der tiefenish fun harts a bukh fun layden un kampf*. New York: Miller & Hillman, 1917.

Von Geldern, James. *Bolshevik Festivals, 1917–1920*. Berkeley: University of California Press, 1993.

Waldinger, Albert. "Stopping by the Woods: Classic American Poems in Yiddish." *TTR*, 16, no. 2 (2003): 155–174.

Waterfield, Robin. *Prophet: The Life and Times of Khalil Gibran*. New York: St Martin's Press, 1998.

Werfel, Franz. *Der Weltfreund*. Leipzig: Kurt Wolff, 1918.

Werth, Barry. *The Scarlet Professor: Newton Arvin: A Literary Life Shattered by Scandal*. New York: Doubleday, 2001.

Wharton, Marian. *Plain English. For the Education of the Workers by the Workers*. Fort Scott: The People's College, 1917.

Wrobel, Ignaz (Kurt Tucholsky). "Salut au Monde!" *Die Schaubühne*, no. 49 (December 4, 1913), 1205.

Wilde, Oscar. "A Talk with Wilde." *Philadelphia Press*, January 17, 1882.

Winwar, Frances. *American Giant Walt Whitman and His Times*. New York: Harpers & Brothers, 1941.

———. *Walt Whitman Builder for America*. New York: Julian Messner, 1941.

Yevtushenko, Yevgeny. *The Poetry of Yevgeny Yevtushenko, 1952–1963*. Translated and edited by George Reavey, bilingual edition. New York: October House, 1965.

Zassoursky, Yassen. "Whitman's Reception and Influence in the Soviet Union." *Mickle Street Review* 9, no. 2 (1988): 42–49.

Zasurskii, Iasen. "Uitmen na stranitsakh *Ordine Nuovo*." *Ogonëk*, June 1955 (no. 27), 23.

Zolotnitskii, David. *Zori teatral'nogo Oktiabria*. Leningrad: Iskusstvo, 1976.

Zweig, Stefan. *Émile Verhaeren, sa vie, son œuvre*. Translated from the manuscript by P. Morisse and H. Cherver.

———. "Das neue Pathos." *Das Literarische Echo*, September 15, 1909, 1701–1707.

Index of Walt Whitman's Poems and Works

A Song for Occupations, 9, 122, 167n57, 235
A Woman Waits for Me, 84–86, 137, 182
Beat! Beat! Drums!, 9n23, 127, 133, 143, 146, 150, 158, 177, 232, 232–33
Calamus, 82, 127, 137
Children of Adam, 26, 84, 128, 137, 143
City Dead-House, The, 160, 174
Crossing Brooklyn Ferry, 53–54, 253
Democratic Vistas, 143, 166, 184, 232, 237, 262, 292
Drum-Taps, 114, 205
Europe. The 72d and 73d Years of These States, 101, 113, 121, 127, 130, 143–44, 146, 150, 158–59, 173, 224, 235, 269, 311
For You O Democracy, 116, 176, 237n20, 246, 250, 269, 306
Great City, The, 116
I Dream'd in a Dream, 101, 146
In Cabin'd Ships at Sea, 147
I Sing the Body Electric, 45, 84–85, 131, 143, 152, 293
Miracles, 106
Mystic Trumpeter, The, 118, 133, 269
No Labor-Saving Machine, 128
O Captain! My Captain!, 54, 104, 127, 145, 152, 217, 232–33, 238
O Star of France, 127, 135, 235, 239,
Out of the Cradle Endlessly Rocking, 249
Pioneers! O Pioneers!, 9, 17, 23, 113–14, 121, 124, 126, 131, 148, 176–77, 205–9, 211–12, 214–17, 222, 232–33, 235, 242n36, 266, 306

Poets to Come, 152
Respondez!, 287
Salut au Monde!, 2, 16, 21–23, 54, 59, 72–73, 86, 104–7, 111, 120–21, 128, 146, 150, 153, 167–68, 174–79, 187–91, 196, 199, 201–5, 222, 225, 242n36, 244–45, 256, 259–61, 265, 305, 307292268, 275
So Long!, 6, 106
Song of the Broad-Axe, 9, 116, 128, 147, 167n57, 169, 235
Song of Myself, 2, 6n20, 26, 29, 54, 56, 64, 67–69, 87, 95, 106, 127, 151, 157n37, 158, 161, 167–68, 174, 176, 190, 216, 220, 223, 225–26, 228, 230–31, 242n36, 262, 277, 296–97
Song of the Banner at Daybreak, 160, 162
Song of the Open Road, 104–5, 145, 183, 238, 279, 294
Spain, 1873–74, 224–25, 235–36, 269
Starting from Paumanok, 6, 106, 151, 289
To a Foil'd European Revolutionaire, 113, 122, 127, 173–74, 218, 235, 237, 269, 313
To Think of Time, 106
We Two Boys Together Clinging, 160
When Lilacs Last in the Dooryard Bloom'd, 148
Years of the Modern (Years of the Unperform'd), 2, 121, 127, 143, 146–48, 150, 152, 158–60, 176, 224, 268, 315
You Felons on Trial in Courts, 142, 150, 182

Index of Names

A
Abbey, The, 121–23, 137–38
Aćamović, Bojana, 177, 217
Adlington, 98
Adonis, 297
Africa, 198–99, 275
Agnone, 115
Aiken, William, 233–35, 239
Akhmatova, Anna, 18n44, 133
Alberti, Rafael, 200–201, 254
Alekseyev, Nikolay, 303
Aleramo, Sibilla, 245
Algeria, 293–94, 296
Alkvit, B. (Eliezer Blum), 55
Allen, Gay Wilson, 4, 245, 272, 275–76, 290
Allende, Salvador, 285, 288
Alpers, Boris, 164–65
Alston, Charlotte, 101
Altman, Nathan, 212
Amaravella, 95
Americas, 5, 16, 200, 222
Andersen, Hans Christian, 267
Apollinaire, Guillaume, 100, 133–34, 136, 272
Aragon, Louis, 283, 291
Arcadia, 62
Arcos, René, 121, 137
Arendt, Hannah, 283–84
Argentina, 16, 190, 243
Arkansas, 193, 205
Arkhangelsk, 238–39
Armenia, 149
Arminius, 36
Arnold, Matthew, 33
Arvin, Newton, 185, 186n46, 235
Asen, Abraham, 89, 104–5, 107
Asia, 15, 154, 168, 254, 275
Asselineau, Roger, 298n59
Athens, 34
Aub Mohrenwitz, Max, 231–32
Auberjonois, Fernand, 225
Augier, Ángel, 252n27
Auschwitz, 240
Austin, Mary, 197
Australia, 103
Austria, 258

B
Bahr, Hermann, 36, 140
Baku, 64–65, 148
Balmont, Konstantin, 9, 11–13, 17–19, 27, 66, 84–85, 91–92, 95, 100, 103, 124–28, 130, 144, 146, 148, 150, 160, 168–69, 214, 269
Baltic States, 71–73, 222, 278
Balzac, Honoré de, 89
Baniulis, Julius, 127
Barabanov, Boris, 165
Barbarossa, operation, 237
Barbusse, Henri, 268
Barcelona, 37
Barnabooth A. O., 48
Barreda, Ernesto, 259
Basterra, Ramón de, 52
Batista, José Manuel, 262n46, 265
Bayev, Nikolay, 303
Bazalgette, Léon, 3, 6, 37, 43–44, 47, 96, 103, 119, 121–23, 135–39, 173, 176, 183, 196, 202–3, 268
Becher, Johannes, 172, 241
Beecher Stowe, Harriet, 131
Beersheba, 108
Beijing, 292
Belinsky, Vissarion, 235
Belomorsk, 162
Belorussia, 108, 277
Belukha, Evgeny, 145
Benét, Stephen Vincent, 191–92, 194, 218
Bentzon, Thérèse, 3n10
Berceo, Gonzalo de, 261
Berkeley, 275
Berlin, 85, 102, 179
Bernabe, Rafael, 262n46
Bernardini, Caterina, 5, 12, 58n21, 114–15, 121, 173, 245
Bertz, Dr., 84

Bevir, Marc, 98
Bidney, Martin, 27
Bidwell, George, 269
Binns, Henry Bryan, 6, 82
Blake, William, 45, 89, 144n6, 183, 198
Bloch, Jean-Richard, 122–23
Blok, Alexander, 18, 41, 55, 75, 174
Bloom, Harold, 82
Bloomsbury group, 153
Bloor, Ella Reeve, 118
Boas, George, 30
Bogdanov, Alexander, 164
Bogoraz, Vladimir Germanovich (Tan), 124–25, 209, 211
Bokanowski, Hélène, 246
Bolton, 97–98, 208
Bonetti Paro, Maria Clara, 250
Borges, Jorge Luis, 63n38, 229, 265
Borodin, A., 65, 148
Bovshover, Joseph, 20, 105–7, 187
Bradley, Sculley, 236
Brazil, 13, 16, 201, 250
Brest (Brest-Litovsk), 105, 128
Brezhnev, Leonid, 298
Brik, Lili, 146
Britain, 12–13, 28, 32–35, 45, 81–82, 96, 100–101, 113–15, 119, 123, 152–53, 171, 206, 208, 249
Brodsky, Joseph, 18
Brooklyn, 3, 53–54, 99, 253
Brown, John, 189, 191
Bryusov, Valery, 12, 41
Buber, Martin, 119
Bucke, Richard Maurice, 3n10, 65, 89–91, 98, 152, 272
Budapest, 174–75, 268
Buddha, 75, 106
Buell, Lawrence, 2
Buenos Aires, 105
Bulyga, Oleksii, 280
Bund, 22, 104, 106, 190, 217
Bureau of Indian Affairs, 246–47, 268
Burganov, Alexander, 300–301, 303
Burliuk brothers, 64
Burroughs, John, 97
Buzzi, Paolo, 58

C

Caeiro, Alberto. *See* Pessoa, Fernando
California, 189, 272, 275, 291
Camden, 4, 95, 116, 118, 277
Campos, Álvaro de. *See* Pessoa, Fernando
Canedo, Enrique Díez, 58, 232
Capek, Abe, 269, 271, 287
Carducci, Giosuè, 39

Caribbean Sea, 201, 244, 262
Carlyle, Thomas, 101, 152
Carnevali, Emanuel, 54
Carpenter, Edward, 6, 28, 32–33, 36–37, 82–83, 85, 89, 97, 99, 101–3, 112, 115–16, 124, 182–83, 206, 208n9
Casanova, Pascale, 3
Cascudo, Luís da Câmara, 250
Casseres, Benjamin de, 58
Castro, Fidel, 289
Catalonia, 37
Cather, Willa, 206
Caucasus, 65
Cavanagh, Clare, 66n50
Cervantes, Miguel de, 59, 267–68
Césaire, Aimé, 199
Chadourne, Marc, 245
Chagall, Marc, 218
Chamberlain, Neville, 225, 227
Chapman, Abraham, 269
Charents, Yeghishe, 150, 152
Chatham, 98
Chekan, Victoria, 157, 160–61
Chekhov, Anton, 133
Chennevière, Georges, 172, 237n20
Chernobyl, 145
Chesterton, G. K., 99–100
Chicago, 62, 70, 96, 109–110
Chile, 242–43, 251, 260, 273, 285–86, 288
China, 15, 22, 171, 232, 244, 249, 271, 275, 292, 298
Chocano, José Santos, 16, 196
Chu, Tunan (Gao Han), 232n9, 271
Chukovskaya, Lydia, 18n44
Chukovsky, Korney, 9–14, 16–19, 40–41, 51, 56–57, 61–69, 83–85, 90–91, 93, 95, 100, 102–3, 112, 114–15, 124–32, 142–43, 145–48, 150, 152–55, 158, 161, 164–66, 177, 209, 211–16, 225, 236–39, 266–67, 269, 276, 278, 287, 299, 303
Churchill, Winston, 227
Chuzhyi, Andrii (Andrii Storozhuk), 74–76, 150n20, 280–81
CIA, 292
Clark, Katerina, 14
Clarke, William, 115
Claudel, Paul, 32, 136
Cleveland, 198
Clinton, Hilary, 302–3
Cohen, Matt, 2, 4, 263
Cold War, 22, 170, 230, 243, 252, 256, 285
Coleridge, Samuel Taylor, 144n6, 285
Colombia, 284
Colorado, river, 252
Comintern, 14, 178, 204, 237

Confucius, 75, 100
Conway, Christopher, 265n50
Coodley, Broche, 107
Corso, Gregory, 290n44
Corvin, Ada, 160, 162
Cot, Pierre, 248
Cracow, 72
Crane, Stephen, 192
Cravan, Arthur, 53
Créteil, Abbey of. *See* Abbey, The
Croatia, 245n3
Crosby, Ernst, 102
Cuba, 16, 252, 261, 265, 253n27, 289, 291
Cunard, Nancy, 243
Curth, Hermann, 177
Czechoslovakia, 269

D

D'Annunzio, Gabriele, 39
Damas, Léon-Gontran, 199
Dandeles, Gregory, 291
Dante Alighieri, 56, 89, 153, 236, 268, 286
Danton, Georges, 106
Darío, Rubén, 15–16, 49, 63n38, 196, 269
Davidson, Jo, 238
Debs, Eugene, 118, 180
Decour, Jacques, 239
Deitch, Mattes, 109
Dell, Floyd, 184
Denmark, 4
Depestre, René, 265n53
Deutsch, Babette, 235
Di Yunge, 21, 104, 187
Diederich, Franz, 133
Diederichs, Eugen, 36
Dionysus, 40–41
Djagalov, Rossen, 15, 244
Dnieper, river, 72
Doctor Zhivago, 55
Dostoevsky, Fyodor, 142, 302
Doyle, Peter, 272
Drey, Arthur, 27
Dubnov, Simon, 212
Dubnova, Sofia, 212
Duhamel, Georges, 43n70, 85, 121
Duncan, Isadora, 87
Dürer, Albrecht, 95

E

Eastman, Max, 184–85, 200, 236
Eckart, Gabriele, 282
Eckel, Leslie, 2
Ecuador, 257
Edelstadt, David, 105
Edwards, Michael, 32n29

Egle, Rūdolfs, 72
Ehrenburg, Ilya, 258
Einboden, Jeffrey, 110–111
Eisenstein, Sergei, 28, 42, 167–69
Eisner, Pavel, 242
Eliot, Thomas Stearn, 191–92, 218, 257n33
Éluard, Paul, 240–41
Emerson, Ralph Waldo, 28, 38, 105, 152
Engels, Friedrich, 288
England, 97–98, 103, 114, 116, 182–83, 206
Eraliev, Suyunbai, 277
Ercilla, Alonso de, 286
Erkkilä, Betsy, 37n46, 121n36
Ermolaeva, Vera, 212–13
Espagne, Michel, 13
Estonia, 126, 277
Etherington, Ben, 26n6
Etkind, Efim, 18
Europe, 1, 3, 5, 12, 15, 20, 22, 27, 31, 37, 40, 43, 52, 58, 61, 71, 79, 81, 91, 106, 108, 135–36, 144, 151, 154, 163, 169, 177, 180, 182, 199, 217, 222, 232, 241–42, 244–45
Evich, Elena, 19n47

F

Fabian society, 115
Fabulet, Louis, 137
Faccioli, Carlo Giovanni, 156
Fadeyev, Alexander, 257n33
Falkenstein, Waldeen. *See* Waldeen
Faludy, György, 270, 278
Farforovsky, Sergei, 147
Fateev, Pyotr (Fateyev, Peter), 95, 96n41
Faust, 131
FDT (Federal Dance Theatre), 203–4
Federn, Karl, 36
Feinsod, Harris, 256
Felipe, León, 223, 225–32, 258–59, 264–65, 275, 287
Ferlinghetti, Lawrence, 289–90, 292
Fininberg, Ezra, 74
Fletcher, Alfred, 101
Folsom, Ed, 199
Fondane, Benjamin (Laquedem, Isaac), 240–41
Ford, Alexander, 190
France, 3, 12, 15, 28–29, 32, 36–37, 85, 91, 96, 113, 119, 122–123, 133, 136, 171–73, 175–76, 182, 190, 199, 232, 240, 244–47, 249, 268–69, 283, 285
Franco, Francisco, 225, 291
Freiligrath, Ferdinand, 114, 119, 182
Freyre, Gilberto, 250
Friche, Vladimir, 146, 148, 152

Frost, Robert, 237
Fyodorov, Nikolay, 91

G
Gaillard, Marcel, 137
Galicia, 86
Galkin, Schmuel, 110n82
Gamberale, Luigi, 115, 196
Gao, Han. *See* Chu, Tunan
García Lorca, Federico, 200, 246, 264, 272, 275, 289, 291, 296–98
Gasman, Gregorio, 259–60
Gáspár, Endre, 174
Gasquet, Joachim, 32
Gastev, Aleksey, 157, 181
Gatchina, 161
Gaucheron, Jacques, 247–48
Gauguin, Paul, 95
GDR (German Democratic Republic), 258, 284
Geiser, Matvei, 212n16
Geneva, 137
Genghis Khan, 63
Genoa, 199
Gerasimov, Mikhail, 163, 164n49
Germany, 12, 22, 35, 96, 113, 118–19, 123, 133, 135–36, 140, 171–72, 177, 182, 202, 224, 232, 237, 249, 269, 282
Ghéon, Henri, 121
Giachino, Enzo, 245
Gibran, Khalil, 82
Gide, André, 85, 136–137, 140, 295
Ginsberg, Allen, 245, 272, 275–76, 290–93, 296
Goethe, Johann Wolfgang von, 14, 131, 144n6, 153, 236
Gogoberidze, Lana, 277
Gold, Mike (Michael) (Irwin Granich), 184–85, 187, 195n61, 219–220
Goldman, Emma, 117, 181–82, 191
Goll, Ivan, 136
Gombrich, Ernst, 25
Gómez de la Serna, Javier, 58
González Tuñón, Raúl, 225, 242–43
González Videla, Gabriel, 251–52, 259, 260n40
Gorbov, Dmitri, 237
Gorelik, Shemarye, 102
Gorky, Maxim, 13, 91, 103, 125, 127, 143, 153
Gosse, Edmund, 26, 45
Graham, Marcus, 183
Gramsci, Antonio, 173
Granich, Itzok Isaak (Irwin). *See* Gold, Mike
Grant, Ulysses S., 135

Greece, 34, 61
Greenberg, Uri Zvi, 86, 110
Griffes, Charles T., 202
Grigoriev, Boris, 93, 95, 155, 303–5
Grinshpan, Dovid, 86
Grünzweig, Walter, 2n5, 3, 5, 96, 114, 119, 123, 172, 269–70, 282–83
Guatemala, 261, 264n48
Guilbeaux, Henri, 123, 137
Guillén, Nicolás, 200, 252
Gumilev, Nikolay, 62
Guo, Moruo, 172n1, 271
Guthrie, Woody, 288

H
Haldeman-Julius, Emanuel, 183
Halévy, Daniel, 121n36, 122
Halkin, Simon, 110–111
Hamsun, Knut, 13, 56
Hardie, Keir, 208
Harlan, James, 246, 268
Harlem, 197–98
Harned, Thomas B., 152
Harris, Kirsten, 97, 112, 115n13, 206, 208, 256
Hartmann, Sadakichi, 3
Hayek, Max, 133, 177
Hayes, Will, 98
Haykuni, Gurgen, 149, 152
He, Qifang, 271
Heine, Heinrich, 21, 105, 144n6, 150, 266
Heinrich, Helmut, 284n26
Helsztyński, Stanisław, 222n31
Hemingway, Ernest, 266
Herasymchuk, Les, 277
Hernández, Miguel, 225, 284, 296
Herra, Maurice, 268–69
Hicks, Granville, 185
Hikmet, Nâzım, 297n58
Hindemith, Paul, 172, 241
Hirshbein, Peretz, 21
Ho Chi Minh, 267, 297
Hobsbawn, Eric, 98
Hobson, Sam, 208
Holloway, Emory, 185
Homer, 26–27, 35, 40–42
Hoover, J. Edgar, 118n28
Horthy, Nicholas, 174–75
Houston, Cisco, 288
Huang, Guiyou, 271
Hughes, Langston, 177, 198–201, 221–22, 233, 246, 254, 287
Hugo, Victor, 150, 236, 240, 277
Hungary, 174, 270

I

Ibsen, Henrik, 41
Ignatov, David, 21
Illinois, 193
India, 258
Indochina, 245
Ionia, 61
Iowa, 193
Iran, 13, 249
Isaacson, Isaac, 105, 190
Isaiah, 103, 226
Israel, 108, 110
Italy, 12, 31, 39, 113, 121, 224
Ivanov, Vyacheslav, 41, 213
Ivens, Joris, 249

J

Jabotinsky, Vladimir, 9n24, 11
Jamati, Paul, 246–47, 252n26, 266, 268
James, William, 13, 59, 90–92, 101
Jammes, Francis, 32n29
Jannacone, Pasquale, 31
Japan, 172n1
Jaurès, Jean, 122, 133
Jēkabsons, Kārlis, 72
Jékely, Zoltán, 270
Jensen, Johannes V., 35–36
Jerusalem, 61, 108, 110
Jesus Christ, 65, 75, 83, 89–90, 92, 97–99, 213
Jewel, Andrew, 233
Joliot-Curie, Pierre, 249
Jouve, Pierre Jean, 32
Jouvenel, Renaud de, 268
Juin, Hubert, 297n58

K

Kabur, Boris, 277–78
Kahn, Gustave, 58
Kalniņš, Jēkabs (Makonis), 127
Kansas, 183, 193
Karsner, David and Rose, 180
Kashkin, Ivan, 195, 266
Kateb, Yacine, 293
Kaufman, Mikhail, 167n56
Kaufman, Naum, 167
Kaunas, 85
Kautsky, Karl, 305
Kazakhstan, 277–78
Keller, Helen, 180
Ķempe, Mirdza, 277–78
Kent, Rockwell, 223–24, 287
Kerouac, Jack, 289
KGB, 292
Khadda, Mohammed, 294
Kharkiv, 85, 105, 151–52
Khashchevatski, Moyshe, 74
Khlebnikov, Velimir, 19, 42, 52, 62–66, 90, 148, 269
Kirillov, Vladimir, 157, 162–163
Kisin, I., 106
Klyuev, Nikolai, 133
Knortz, Karl, 96, 119
Kolář, Jiří, 270
Koptiaeva, Antonina, 125
Korchagin, Kirill, 303n11
Korotich, Vitaly, 277
Korsakas, Kostas, 177
Kostroma, 166
Kozlov, D., 64
Krasnoe Selo, 161
Krasnoshchyokov, Alexander, 145
Kravchenko, Victor, 248
Kreymborg, Alfred, 197
Kronstadt, 161
Kropotkin, Peter, 83, 119
Kubilius, Vytautas, 177n21
Kugel, Alexander, 157, 163
Kulbin, Nikolay, 66
Kuleshov, Lev, 141
Kulyk, Ivan, 73n57, 150–52, 195
Kun, Béla, 174
Kuokkala, 66
Kurbas, Les, 75
Kurtz, Aaron, 267
Kutzinski, Vera, 200
Kuzmin, Mikhail, 18
Kvitko, Leib, 74
Kyiv, 20, 102, 105
Kyrgyzstan, 277

L

Laforgue, Jules, 29, 45–48, 239
Landau, Zishe, 89
Landauer, Gustav, 35–36, 119, 136, 178
Lange, Antoni, 100n58
Lange, Dorothea, 222
Lanivtsi, 20
Lao-Tzu, 103
Lapshin, Nikolai, 212
Laquedem, Isaac. *See* Benjamin Fondane
Larbaud, Valery, 3, 45, 47–48, 122, 136
Larionov, Mikhail, 63, 269
Las Casas, Bartolomé de, 89
Lator, László, 270
Latvia, 72, 160, 177, 277
Lavrov, Sergei, 301–2
Lawrence, David Herbert, 32, 34, 50, 57, 82–83
Le Sueur, Meridel, 118, 181, 183

Lebesgue, Philéas, 44, 123
LeBlond, Maurice, 28
Lecomte, Joseph, 123n45
Leftwich, Joseph, 89
Leipzig, 128, 270
Leivick, Israel, 108
Lemberg. *See* Lviv
Lenin, Vladimir, 71, 146, 167, 174, 185, 215, 220–21, 224, 269, 279, 288, 305
Leningrad, 299
León, Fray Luis de, 297n58
Lermontov, Mikhail, 150
Levik, Vilgem, 266
Levinson, Julian, 21, 105, 107
Lévis Mano, Guy, 246
Lewisohn, Irene, 202–3
Li, Po, 236, 271
Li, Xilao, 271
Libman, Valentina, 17n38
Liessin, Abraham, 217–18
Lima, Jorge de, 196–97, 250
Limanovskaia, V., 266
Lincoln, Abraham, 29, 65, 108–9, 148, 181, 183, 187–91, 199, 241, 246–47, 251, 252n27, 256–57, 266, 285, 289, 292, 301
Lindsay, Vachel, 186, 197
Lithuania, 20, 85, 177, 191, 277
Liverpool, 101
Locke, Alain, 198
London, 10, 113, 270
London, Jack, 277, 279
Longfellow, Henry Wadsworth, 40, 131, 152, 278
Los Angeles, 107
Lowenfels, Walter, 118n28, 287–88
Lucini, Gian Pietro, 35
Ludwig, Ruben, 20, 187, 189, 194
Luga, 161
Lugones, Leopoldo, 16, 196
Lukash, Ivan, 63
Lukianova, Irina, 9n24
Lunacharsky, Anatoly, 44, 142, 144–46, 148, 152, 157, 164, 177
Lundkvist, Artur, 30
Lurçat, Jean, 137
Luzhkov, Yuri, 301, 303
Lviv, 86
Lyubavichi, 20, 105

M

Machado, Antonio, 297n58
MacLeish, Archibald, 222
Madrid, 200
Maeterlinck, Maurice, 27
Magadan, 154

Maizels, Dmitri, 147, 154, 216
Makonis. *See* Kalniņš, Jēkabs
Maliuchenko, G. S., 156
Malková, Ivá, 270
Mallarmé, Stéphane, 29, 43
Mally, Lynn, 160n41
Manchester, 98
Mandelstam, Osip, 40
Manhattan, 53–55, 109, 194, 219–220, 253, 261–62, 297
Mann, Thomas, 140
Mao, Zedong, 249, 267
Maples Arce, Manuel, 59–60
Marcinkevičius, Justinas, 279–80
Marinetti, Filippo Tommaso, 45, 58, 77
Marinello, Juan, 252n27
Markham, Edwin, 105
Markish, Peretz, 86
Marques, Oswaldino, 250
Marseille, 239
Marshak, Samuil, 212, 266
Martí, José, 15, 196
Martinet, Marcel, 176
Marx, Karl, 9n23, 14, 114, 206, 277, 288
Marx, Leo, 51
Masanov, Ivan, 212n15
Masereel, Frans, 137–38
Massachusetts, 98
Masson, Elsie, 122
Matthiessen, Francis Otto, 152, 235
Maude, Aylmer, 101
Mayakovsky, Vladimir, 19, 52, 63–71, 73, 77–79, 146, 150, 155, 190, 194, 200, 240, 249, 251, 269, 271, 290–93
McGrath, Thomas, 288
McKay, Claude, 184, 195n61, 200
Mediterranean, 293, 296
Meler, Eliezer, 190
Melville, Herman, 253
Mendelson, Maurice, 238, 266–71, 278–79, 301
Mendoza, Miguel, 250
Meriküla, 126
Merrill, Stuart, 29–30
Mexico, 225, 231, 250, 257–58, 264n48
Meyerhold, Vsevolod, 157, 162
Mgebrov, Alexander, 157–65
Mgebrov-Chekan, Kotia, 157n38
Michaud, Régis, 91
Michelangelo, 113, 202
Mickiewicz, Adam, 267
Miel, Jacques, 295n54
Mieželaitis, Eduardas, 279–80
Miller, Louis, 20, 54, 104, 190, 218, 232
Miłosz, Czesław, 242

Milton, John, 105, 131
Minnesota, 193
Minsk, 217
Mirsky, D. S., 152–54, 181, 186, 266
Miškinis, Antanas, 277–78
Mississippi, 189, 193–94, 199, 222
Missouri, 191, 205
Moldavia, 240
Molotov-Ribbentrop pact, 108, 225, 236
Moncada, Julio, 252
Montana, 193
Montes, Eugenio, 59
Montesquieu, 267
Monticello, 193
Montoliu, Cebrià, 37–38
Montreal, 86, 151, 191
Morris, William, 41, 101, 104–6, 115–16, 174, 183, 206, 208
Moscow, 15, 22, 72, 77, 105, 126, 144–45, 148–149, 152, 161, 169, 242–43, 245, 266–69, 271, 293, 298, 300–303
Moses, 75, 89, 105–6, 109
Mstislavskii, Semion, 212
Mukataev, Mukagali, 277
Murmansk, 279

N
Nascimento, Abdias do, 201
Nebraska, 205
Negri, Ada, 121, 129
Nekrasov, Nikolay, 13, 129, 143
Neldikhen, Sergey, 63
Neman, river, 85
Nencioni, Enrico, 3n10, 39, 114
Neruda, Pablo, 16, 191, 201, 225, 242–243, 245, 248, 250–61, 265, 271–74, 276, 283–92, 297–98
Nerval, Gérard de, 47
Neva, river, 155
Nevedomsky, Mikhail, 130
New Jersey, 4, 187, 288
New Orleans, 189, 199
Niagara, 10, 279
Nicolas, Pierre, 122
Nietzsche, Friedrich, 39–40, 102
Nigeria, 198
Nikiforov, Lev, 101
Nissenson, Aaron, 55, 107

O
O'Connor, William, 97
Odesa, 9, 11, 126, 150, 239
Ohio, 183, 193
Olenets, 304
Ontario, 301

Opitz, Thoren, 2n5
Oredezh, Ivan, 63, 269
Orlitsky, Yuri, 19
Oslo, 72
Ossian, 26
Ostrovsky, Nikolay, 261
Otero, Blas de, 296–297

P
Palenke, 196
Palestine, 108, 110
Pan, 34
Panama, 225
Papini, Giovanni, 56, 58
Paris, 54, 77, 126, 134, 172, 174, 199, 235, 249, 277
Parry, Albert, 181
Pasternak, Boris, 14, 55
Pásztor, Árpád, 174, 270
Patchen, Kenneth, 183
Paulhan, Jean, 239
Pavese, Cesare, 31
Paz, Octavio, 265
Pearsall, G. Frank, 7, 94, 104, 269, 305
Peñiscola, 293
Pennsylvania, 4
Peredelkino, 13
Pérez I Jorba, Joan, 37
Peru, 257
Pessoa, Fernando, 38, 49–50, 52, 293
Petrarch, 56
Petrograd, 93, 95, 105, 133, 142, 148, 155, 157, 161, 164, 212, 303, 305
Petrovsky-Shtern, Yohanan, 150
Pindar, 31, 35
Pittsburgh, 193
Plato, 84
Podolia, 107, 190
Poe, Edgar Allan, 152, 253, 270
Poland, 85, 88, 96, 110, 171–72, 175, 190, 222, 266, 269–70
Polyakov, Sergey, 12–13
Popov, I., 288
Popov, P., 9, 124, 131
Portugal, 37–38
Potemkin mutiny, 126
Pound, Ezra, 3, 272
Prager, Leonard, 21
Prague, 202, 268, 291
Preissig, Vojtěch, 201
Price, Kenneth, 233
Proletkult, 19, 95, 150, 157, 161, 164, 168, 173, 185, 203
Proskurnin, Sergei, 163
Proudhon, 119

Pskov, 162, 303–5
Pumpianskii, Lev, 155n32
Pushkin, Alexander, 62, 73, 100, 106, 150, 224, 236, 278, 300–302

Q
Queens, 297
Quevedo, Francisco de, 286

R
Ramadan, Abdel Muneim, 298n61
Rancière, Jacques, 57, 168n60
Ravitch, Melech, 86–87
Recsk camp, 270
Reed, John, 180, 187, 195
Reichard, Piroska, 174n12
Reisen, Abraham (Reysen, Avrom), 107
Reisinger, Hans, 140, 172, 245
Reitblat, Abram, 17n38
Repin, Ilya, 100, 102–3
Rhys, Ernest, 101, 113–14, 183, 207–8, 215, 218, 222
Richepin, Jean, 37
Rickett, Edmond W., 202
Riel, Louis, 150
Riethmuller, Richard Henri, 3
Riga, 105, 160–62, 175
Rihani, Ameen, 82n6
Rimbaud, Arthur, 47, 240, 251
Rivera, Diego, 191
Roberts, Sam, 183
Robeson, Paul, 271
Roerich, Nicholas, 93, 95, 278
Rolland, Romain, 87n18, 123, 137, 142, 155, 176–77, 183, 267
Romains, Jules, 85, 121
Ronsard, Pierre de, 266
Roosevelt, Franklin Delano, 196, 225, 227, 236, 241n34
Rosenfeld, Morris, 88–89, 104–5, 174
Rossetti, Michael, 12, 45, 113–14, 116, 122, 129n59, 207
Roumain, Jacques, 199
Rousseau, Jean-Jacques, 106
Rozanov, Vasily, 57, 62
Rubinstein, Rachel, 21
Rudniański, Stefan, 127–28, 176n16
Rudzītis, Rihards, 277–78
Runa, 95n40
Ruskin, John, 38, 41, 101–2, 106
Russell, Bertrand, 180

S
Sá-Carneiro, Mário de, 38
Saadi, Youssef, 298
Sainson, Katia, 294n53
Saint Petersburg, 124–26, 131, 213, 292
Samorodova, Olga, 65
San Francisco, 289, 292
Sandburg, Carl, 154, 186, 195, 200
Santayana, George, 30–31
Santí, Enrico Mario, 265
Santiago (Chile), 251
São Paolo, 250
Sardan, Alexander, 95n40
Sarrazin, Gabriel, 37
Sartre, Jean-Paul, 257n33
Schabelitz, Jacob, 114
Scheeler, Charles, 54
Schickele, René, 136
Schigolev, George, 95n40
Schiller, Friedrich, 267
Schlaf, Johannes, 3, 25, 43, 83, 96, 114, 119, 122–23, 128, 172
Schlumberger, Jean, 137
Schmidt, Rudolf, 3n10
Schölermann, Wilhelm, 36, 206n1
Schreker, Franz, 172
Schwartz, I. J., 20–22, 104, 106–7, 189
Sedgwick, Eve, 34
Segal, Jacob, 107
Seghers, Pierre, 246
Sélincourt, Basil de, 58
Semenko, Mykhail, 75–76
Semper, Johannes, 72
Sénac, Jean, 293–297
Severyanin, Igor, 62–63
Shahn, Ben, 191
Shakespeare, William, 66, 84, 105, 236, 266, 268
Shanghai, 258
Shaw, George Bernard, 36, 115, 182n36
Shaw, Robert, 241n34
Shcheglov, Dmitri, 164
Shelley, Percy Bysshe, 99, 116, 144, 157, 183
Shevchenko, Aleksandr, 39
Shevchenko, Taras, 73–76, 151
Shklovsky, Victor, 168, 169n65
Schyberg, Frederik, 4n15
Shostakovich, Dmitri, 125
Siberia, 106, 108, 124, 150, 175, 278, 293
Sijé, Ramón, 296
Sileby, 208
Sillamäe, 126
Sillen, Samuel, 7, 16–17, 234–35, 257, 268, 271
Simpson, Louis, 289
Sipakov, Yanka, 277
Siporin, Mitchell, 191
Skovoroda, Grigori, 281

Skwara, Marta, 5, 128, 266, 270
Slisarenko, Oleksa, 76, 78–79
Slutsky, Boris, 277
Smekhov, Beniamin, 279
Smirnoff-Rusetsky, Boris, 95n40
Smolensk, 127
Socrates, 75, 89
Soffici, Ardengo, 56, 61n34
Sokolicz, Antonina, 175, 176n16, 217
Sokolov, Ippolit, 168
Soviet Union, 14–16, 19, 22, 95, 105, 123, 149, 153, 172, 174, 182, 184, 190, 195, 198, 200–201, 222–24, 232, 236–39, 241–44, 248–49, 253–54, 256, 266, 268–69, 276–77, 279–80, 291, 293, 298–99
Spain, 16, 31, 200–201, 203, 224–25, 235–36, 242, 258, 269, 284, 293, 296
Spargo, John, 206
Spier, Leonard, 181
St. Louis, 191
Stalin, Joseph, 125, 249, 268–69, 278, 280, 293
Stalingrad, 256
Stefanović, Svetislav, 217
Steinroetter, Vanessa, 206n1
Stella, Joseph, 54
Stepanchev, Stephan, 299
Stepanova, Lenochka, 157
Sterian, Margareta, 242
Stieglitz's circle, 54
Stockholm, 72
Sveshnikov, A. V., 125n50
Swinburne, Algernon, 12, 45–46
Swinton, John, 9n23
Switzerland, 102, 107, 136–37
Symonds, John Addington, 13, 27–28, 32–34, 82, 84, 182
Sytin, Ivan, 101n62, 115, 131–32
Szábo, Magda, 270
Szilágyi, Géza, 175n15

T
Tabari, Ehsan, 249
Taggard, Genevieve, 194–95
Tagore, Rabindranath, 21
Tamiris, Helen, 203–4
Tan. *See* Bogoraz, Vladimir Germanovich
Tarnovsky, Mykola, 54
Tbilisi, 149, 277
Tel Aviv, 109
Tenichevsky school, 133
Tepper, Kolya, 106
Texas, 118
Thomas, M. Wynn, 32, 101, 140, 288

Thoreau, Henry David, 27, 114
Thovez, Enrico, 39
Tihanov, Galin, 169n65
Tiersot, Julien, 156
Tiger, Theobald. *See* Tucholsky, Kurt
Tocqueville, Alexis de, 302
Togliatti, Palmiro, 173
Tolstoy, Aleksey, 62
Tolstoy, Leo, 28, 100–102, 114, 305
Torre, Guillermo de, 44, 59
Totma, 148
Trachtenberg, Alexander, 234
Traubel, Horace, 3, 95, 97, 116–19, 124, 151–52, 180, 182, 195, 202
Traverso, Enzo, 289
Trevor, John, 98
Trotsky, Leon, 176–77, 200
Trujillo, Rafael, 261
Truman, Harry, 247, 249
Tsvetaeva, Marina, 278
Tsvetkovskaya, Elena, 17n40
Tucholsky, Kurt, 120, 178–79
Turgenev, Ivan, 9n23
Turner, J. M. W., 59–60
Turner, Lorenzo Dow, 198
Tuwim, Julian, 85–86
Twain, Mark, 266
Tychyna, Pavlo, 74–76

U
Ujević, Tin, 245
Ukraine, 20, 73, 150, 190, 277, 303
Ukrainka, Lesya, 75
Uman, 74–76, 150, 280–81
Unamuno, Miguel de, 31–32, 48
United States, 3, 16, 20–21, 37–38, 82, 97, 107, 127, 163, 181, 188, 196–97, 199, 206, 225, 252, 256–57, 267, 275, 285, 298
Urbánek, Zdeněk, 270
Uruguay, 46, 236
USSR. *See* Soviet Union
Utatlán, 196

V
Vabalas, Raimondas, 279n15
Vabbe, Ado, 73
Valk, 162
Van Gogh, Vincent, 291
Varshe, Moyshe, 104–5
Vasseur, Armando, 16, 195–96, 207, 260
Venclova, Antanas, 177, 200n77
Venediktova, Tatiana, 278, 303n11
Vengerova, Zinaida, 40
Verde, Cesario, 38

Verhaeren, Émile, 29, 43–45, 55, 58, 63n42, 74, 133, 141–42, 150–51, 157, 198
Verlaine, Paul, 47
Vertov, Dziga, 167–68, 256
Victoroff, Tatiana, 95
Vidbergs, Sigismunds, 146
Vielé-Griffin, Francis, 29
Vienna, 86, 174
Vietnam War, 276, 287–88
Vildrac, Charles, 121
Vilnius (Vilna), 102, 110, 127
Virginia, 193
Vitebsk, 213
Vivekananda, 87n18
Vladeck, Baruch, 106–7
Volga, river, 72
Volhynia, 190
Voloshin, Maximilian, 75
Voronezh, 156
Voznesensky, Andrei, 291
Vrchlický, Jaroslav, 63n38
Vroon, Ronald, 42n69

W

Waldeen, 251n21, 256–58, 292
Walkowitz, Abraham, 53–54, 87
Wallace, James William, 98, 115–16, 208
Warsaw, 72, 86, 128, 249, 257, 268
Washington, 272
Waskiewitz, Josef. *See* Aub Mohrenwitz, Max
Weill, Kurt, 232
Weimar, Republic, 140, 172
Werfel, Franz, 29, 88
Wharton, Marian, 118

Wilde, Oscar, 34, 83
Wilson, Woodrow, 70
Winchevsky, Morris, 105
Winwar, Frances, 235
Wisconsin, 178–79, 193
Wordsworth, William, 144n6, 198

Y

Yakutsk, 124–25
Yalta, 249
Yavorskaya, Lydia, 133
Yesenin, Sergey, 65–66, 133, 150, 213, 271, 293
Yevtushenko, Yevgeny, 271–272, 291, 293
Young, Brigham, 153
Youngstown, 183
Yugoslavia, 177, 217
Yuriev, 162

Z

Zamyatin, Evgeny, 143, 166
Zarathustra, 40
Zardoya, Concha, 242
Zassoursky, Yassen, 20, 267, 277
Zenkevich, Mikhail, 195, 237, 266
Zetkin, Clara, 119
Zheleznovodsk, 65
Zhivtsov, Alexander, 238
Zhou, Enlai, 267
Zhou, Yang, 271
Zingman, Kalman, 85
Zolotnitsky, David, 164–65
Zweig, Stefan, 36, 44

www.ingramcontent.com/pod-product-compliance
Lightning Source LLC
Chambersburg PA
CBHW071358300426
44114CB00016B/2103